# Integration and Difference

"An important book for continental philosophy."
**Professor David F. Hoinski**

"One of today's most original thinkers."
**Professor Vernon W. Cisney**

"A tremendously exciting and generative book."
**Professor Roderick Main**

"A deep and poetic rumination."
**Professor Barbara Jenkins**

"Brilliant."
**Peter Salmon**

"A hugely stimulating read."
**Professor Mark Saban**

This groundbreaking work synthesizes concepts from thirteen crucial philosophers and psychologists, relating how the ancient problem of opposites has been opening to an integration which not only conserves differentiation but enacts it, especially through the integration of myth into the dialectic.

Weaving a fascinating narrative that 'thinks with' the complex encounters of theorists from Baruch Spinoza, G. W. F. Hegel, Friedrich Nietzsche, and William James to Alfred North Whitehead, C. G. Jung, Gilles Deleuze, and Isabelle Stengers, this book uniquely performs the convergence of continental philosophy, pragmatism, depth psychology, and constructivist 'postmodern' theory as a complement to the trajectory culminating in Jacques Derrida's deconstruction.

This is an important book for professionals and academics working across the humanities and social sciences, particularly for continental theorists and depth psychologists interested in the construction of a novel epoch after the modern.

**Grant Maxwell** is an editor of the *Archai* journal and he holds a PhD from the City University of New York's Graduate Center. He is the author of multiple books including *The Dynamics of Transformation: Tracing an Emerging World View*, and he has written for *Deleuze and Guattari Studies, the American Philosophical Association blog, American Songwriter magazine, and the Journal of Religion and Popular Culture.*

# Philosophy & Psychoanalysis Book Series
Series Editor: JON MILLS

*Philosophy & Psychoanalysis* is dedicated to current developments and cutting-edge research in the philosophical sciences, phenomenology, hermeneutics, existentialism, logic, semiotics, cultural studies, social criticism, and the humanities that engage and enrich psychoanalytic thought through philosophical rigor. With the philosophical turn in psychoanalysis comes a new era of theoretical research that revisits past paradigms while invigorating new approaches to theoretical, historical, contemporary, and applied psychoanalysis. No subject or discipline is immune from psychoanalytic reflection within a philosophical context including psychology, sociology, anthropology, politics, the arts, religion, science, culture, physics, and the nature of morality. Philosophical approaches to psychoanalysis may stimulate new areas of knowledge that have conceptual and applied value beyond the consulting room reflective of greater society at large. In the spirit of pluralism, *Philosophy & Psychoanalysis* is open to any theoretical school in philosophy and psychoanalysis that offers novel, scholarly, and important insights in the way we come to understand our world.

Titles in this series:

**Psychoanalysis and the Mind-Body Problem**
*Jon Mills*

**Jung's Alchemical Philosophy**
Psyche and the Mercurial Play of Image and Idea
*Stanton Marlan*

**Integration and Difference**
Constructing a Mythical Dialectic
*Grant Maxwell*

# Integration and Difference

## Constructing a Mythical Dialectic

## Grant Maxwell

LONDON AND NEW YORK

Cover image: *Orange* by Christian Kurt Ebert

First published 2022
by Routledge
4 Park Square, Milton Park, Abingdon, Oxon OX14 4RN

and by Routledge
605 Third Avenue, New York, NY 10158

*Routledge is an imprint of the Taylor & Francis Group, an informa business*

© 2022 Grant Maxwell

The right of Grant Maxwell to be identified as author of this work has been asserted in accordance with sections 77 and 78 of the Copyright, Designs and Patents Act 1988.

All rights reserved. No part of this book may be reprinted or reproduced or utilised in any form or by any electronic, mechanical, or other means, now known or hereafter invented, including photocopying and recording, or in any information storage or retrieval system, without permission in writing from the publishers.

*Trademark notice*: Product or corporate names may be trademarks or registered trademarks, and are used only for identification and explanation without intent to infringe.

*British Library Cataloguing-in-Publication Data*
A catalogue record for this book is available from the British Library

*Library of Congress Cataloging-in-Publication Data*
A catalog record for this book has been requested

ISBN: 978-1-032-04987-8 (hbk)
ISBN: 978-1-032-04985-4 (pbk)
ISBN: 978-1-003-19549-8 (ebk)

DOI: 10.4324/9781003195498

Typeset in Times New Roman
by Apex CoVantage, LLC

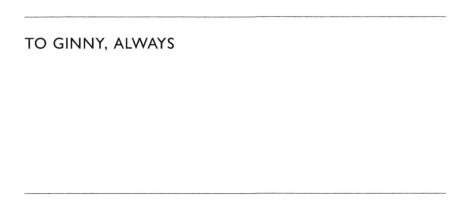

TO GINNY, ALWAYS

# Contents

| | |
|---|---|
| *Acknowledgments* | ix |
| Introduction: Turning Deconstruction on Its Head | 1 |
| 1 The Final Writing of an Epoch: Jacques Derrida's *Of Grammatology* | 11 |
| 2 Freedom of Mind: Baruch Spinoza's *Ethics* | 32 |
| 3 Well-Founded Fictions: Gottfried Wilhelm Leibniz's *Monadology* | 45 |
| 4 The Life of the Whole: G.W.F. Hegel's *On Scientific Cognition* | 52 |
| 5 God-Positing Potencies: F.W.J. Schelling's *Berlin Lectures* | 64 |
| 6 Something Higher Than Any Reconciliation: Friedrich Nietzsche's *The Birth of Tragedy* | 83 |
| 7 An Integrated Affair: William James' *Pragmatism* | 107 |
| 8 A True Work of Integration: Henri Bergson's *Creative Evolution* | 126 |
| 9 The Process of Integration: Alfred North Whitehead's *Process and Reality* | 144 |

| | | |
|---|---|---|
| 10 | A Widening of Consciousness Through Integration: C.G. Jung's *Mysterium Coniunctionis* | 165 |
| 11 | Integrating Myth Into the Dialectic: Gilles Deleuze's *Difference and Repetition* | 197 |
| 12 | Disintegrated Integration: James Hillman's *Re-Visioning Psychology* | 268 |
| 13 | The Question of Integration: Concluding with Isabelle Stengers | 310 |
| | *Works Cited* | 332 |
| | *Index* | 340 |

# Acknowledgments

I would like to express my profound gratitude to the colleagues who have contributed in some way to this book's composition, and to my friends and family whose love and support has helped to make the writing process a highly enjoyable experience despite the collective difficulties we have all been immersed in these last few years. Thank you to Taylor Adkins, Charles Alunni, Rachael Anderson-Watts, Frida Beckman, Eli Bortz, Richard Bright, Kent Bye, John Campbell, Cooper Cherry, Vern Cisney, Don Curren, Mark Dean, Tod Desmond, Jackie DiSalvo, Kevin Drost, Simon Duffy, Russell Duvernoy, Susannah Frearson, Dwight Gaudet, Béa Gonzalez, Will Grissom, David Henderson, David Hoinski, Ken Jedding, Barbara Jenkins, Sean Kelly, Jeremy Liebman, Roderick Main, Tim McKague, Sam Mickey, Jon Mills, Hellmut Monz, Kelly Nezat, Laurent Nottale, Alexis O'Brien, Nathan Oseroff-Spicer, John Protevi, Jason Quetel, Joshua Ramey, Katie Randall, Joan Richardson, Mark Saban, Peter Salmon, Matthew Segall, Ike Sharpless, Matthew Stoulil, Becca Tarnas, Rick Tarnas, Dan Tyler, Stephanie von Behr, and Scott Zimmerle. And, as always, thank you to my family: Ginny Maxwell, Mason Maxwell, Dylan Maxwell, Dan Orsborn, Carol Orsborn, Jody Orsborn, Don Edwards, Susan Edwards, and Kitty Edwards. Thank you, finally, to *Deleuze and Guattari Studies* and *Interalia Magazine* for permission to republish material in modified form, and to Christian Kurt Ebert for permission to use his painting *Orange* on the cover.

*This is the problem of the solidarity of the universe. The classical doctrines of universals and particulars, of subject and predicate, of individual substances not present in other individual substances, of the externality of relations, alike render this problem incapable of solution. The answer given by the organic philosophy is the doctrine of prehensions, involved in concrescent integrations. . . . The process of integration, which lies at the very heart of the concrescence, is the urge imposed on the concrescent unity of that universe.*

Alfred North Whitehead, *Process and Reality*[1]

*Alchemy is the herald of a still-unconscious drive for maximal integration which seems to be reserved for a distant future. . . . The question then arises as to how all these divergent factors, previously kept apart by apparently insuperable incompatibilities, will behave, and what the ego is going to do about it. . . . The sight of its darkness is itself an illumination, a widening of consciousness through integration of the hitherto unconscious components of the personality. . . . Above all, consciousness experiences a widening of its horizon.*

C.G. Jung, *Mysterium Coniunctionis*[2]

*Dialectic discovers its true method in division. Division overcomes this duality and integrates myth into the dialectic; it makes myth an element of the dialectic itself. . . . Each differenciation is a local integration or a local solution which then connects with others in the overall solution or the global integration. . . . The act of individuation consists not in suppressing the problem, but in integrating the elements of the disparateness into a state of coupling which ensures its internal resonance.*

Gilles Deleuze, *Difference and Repetition*[3]

## Notes

1 Whitehead, *Process*, 56, 228.
2 Jung, *Mysterium*, 205, 253, 290.
3 Deleuze, *Difference*, 61, 211, 246.

# Introduction
Turning Deconstruction on Its Head

Since the last few decades of the twentieth century, the deconstruction enacted by Jacques Derrida has been a dominant force in American humanities and social sciences, often explicitly, but more often implicitly defining the directions and limits of research.[1] Even beyond deconstruction's direct influence, the prevailing tendency has been toward critical problematizing, although especially in the years since the turn of the twenty-first century, theorists from various disciplines have sought to move beyond the exclusivity of a primarily negative approach to the production of knowledge to generate more explicitly constructive modes of thought. Nevertheless, deconstruction and the more general mode of thought it exemplifies still reign at the heart of intellectual culture in the West because no subsequent movement under a unified nomination with a comparably potent aesthetic allure has yet captured the attention of the guardians and producers of knowledge en masse, though an urgent collective desire for such a fresh dispensation, however multifarious, is evident.[2]

A novel mode of thought that integrates essential insights of deconstruction but turns them on their head, inverting those insights, and bringing them into intimate relation with other conceptual domains to produce new ways of knowing, is showing the early signs of emerging into broad academic awareness.[3] As has often been suggested, deconstruction was prefigured in essential ways by the Sophists in ancient Greece.[4] But the approach which I am calling integration, a term derived especially from Gottfried Wilhelm Leibniz, William James, Henri Bergson, Alfred North Whitehead, C.G. Jung, Gilles Deleuze, James Hillman, and Isabelle Stengers, an approach always complexly intertwined with differentiation, also has a long history. The two modes, deconstructive and integrative, can be conceived as complementary, and I will propose that deconstruction

DOI: 10.4324/9781003195498-1

can be understood as a necessary element in a more encompassing mode of thought, a moment in a more expansive process of becoming.

The first chapter attempts to distill essential insights of deconstruction as expressed in Derrida's 1967 book *Of Grammatology*, suggesting that Derrida's thought is deeply resonant with the other twentieth century theorists to whom chapters are devoted, though he primarily expresses the negative valences of the positive conceptual complexes traced below. The subsequent chapters are each devoted to one, or in some cases several, foundational works from twelve other theorists ranging from the seventeenth century until the twenty-first century who have expressed various aspects of this mode of thought, which is ripe for emergence into broad discourse as a definitive step beyond the necessary deconstruction of one-sided, hierarchical modern metanarratives, from Baruch Spinoza, Gottfried Wilhelm Leibniz, G.W. F. Hegel, F.W.J. Schelling, Friedrich Nietzsche, and William James to Henri Bergson, Alfred North Whitehead, C.G. Jung, Gilles Deleuze, James Hillman, and Isabelle Stengers. I cannot hope to be even remotely comprehensive, either in the choice of theorists or in reference to each theorist's body of work.[5] But I will offer that there is an underlying coherence of approach among these thinkers, despite many significant – indeed constitutive – differences, that provides a theoretical orientation for moving beyond the still-deconstructive quality of much of contemporary academia, which often serves to enforce a narrowness of concern despite the liberating quality of Derrida's project, while retaining and recontextualizing the undeniably potent, rigorous, and useful deconstructive mode forged during the height of postmodernity, perhaps especially in the United States, over the last few decades.

Although the readings performed below adhere closely to these texts, this work is not primarily a history of philosophy, but rather a "thinking with"[6] inspired by Stengers' *Thinking With Whitehead* and Deleuze's books on individual philosophers (Spinoza, Leibniz, Nietzsche, Bergson). In fact, Deleuze has said that he sees "no difference between writing a book on the history of philosophy and a book of philosophy,"[7] a provocation to which I have sought to do justice. More than a history, this book can be conceived as a kind of staging in a philosophical theater, in which the theorists under consideration are playing out their problematic and variable relational dramas, each enacting a distinct role in an often obscure and enigmatic narrative.[8] The problem whose history this book stages, a problem coextensive with the trajectory initiated at the dawn of Western philosophy in Heraclitus, is what to do about opposed, conflicting, incompatible, paradoxical, or otherwise incommensurable truths, modes of thought, values, judgments, inclinations, and affects. This is a recurring question that the texts explicated in this work have sought to address in increasingly subtle and profound ways, from Spinozan parallelism, Leibnizian *mathesis universalis*, Hegelian dialectic, Schelling's positive philosophy, Nietzsche's evocation of "something higher than any reconciliation,"[9] and Jamesian pragmatism to Bergson's intuitive method, Whitehead's concrescent integration, Jungian and Hillmanian psychological integration, and the constructivist and integrative expressions of Deleuze and Stengers.

The framing of this project as "turning deconstruction on its head" can be conceived as an appropriation of the way in which Hegel's dialectic was appropriated by Karl Marx with rather different intentions to those which animated Hegelian logic, Marx claiming to have turned the dialectic back on its feet (having previously been "standing on its head"[10]). And much like the idealism of Hegel and his German contemporaries Kant, Fichte, and Schelling, pragmatism, despite the protestations of James' many devotees, has taken on a different, and much simpler meaning than James and Peirce originally intended, so that political debates are often framed in terms of facile and reductive versions of these two terms. Although I agree with James on most subjects, I am pushing against him in my somewhat heterodox suggestion that the core mode of thought characteristic of pragmatism is ultimately a different inflection of the dialectic as, like most of the post-Hegelian philosophers discussed in these pages, James was very critical of Hegel, finding precious little common ground with the man who had been the most influential philosopher in the century in which James began his work.[11] However, as John Dewey observed in a letter to James after reading *The Principles of Psychology*, "parts of it were perhaps more Hegelian than James might wish to admit."[12]

These are the kinds of theoretical and terminological concerns that have rendered attempts to assert an underlying coherence in the work of these theorists and others problematic. However, I will suggest that the difficulty in discerning a mode that potentially subsumes and surpasses deconstruction is itself largely a result of the often implicit dominance of deconstruction. In contrast, I will seek to demonstrate that the work of all of these theorists has contributed to a stream of thought, still often subterranean and difficult to locate, which discerns that every positive concept, every claim that does not explicitly or implicitly deny or negate some other opposing conception, is necessary for the production of an increasingly expansive, and finely differentiated, mode of relation for constructively negotiating the potentialities and constraints of process. And while this suggestion may appear fairly straightforward, determining which claims made by any mode of thought are positive and which are negative can be troublesome to disentangle, as ideas and their opposites must evolve in tension, and through many compromise formations of difference, for novel concepts to emerge. Nevertheless, this mode of relation, when pursued with assiduous care and rigorous discernment, can lead to some startling conclusions about the world and our place in it. Each of the theorists whose work is examined in the following pages has contributed essential insights to this multivalent mode of integrating apparently incommensurable entities, an integration which not only conserves differentiation but enacts it. In a recursive operation, the integration of these disparate, and sometimes even opposed, theorists directly puts into practice the very integrative mode that they have articulated in its different inflections.

Although this mode itself is more significant than the name by which it is called, the naming of a concept nevertheless plays a large role in determining its fate, as there are many historical and contextual factors that can enable or inhibit the passage of a word into various interconnected discursive streams. I am emphasizing the word integration, not only because it directly answers the lexical force and appeal of the deconstructive denomination, but because other, more established contenders, including the Hegelian dialectic and Jamesian pragmatism, though still eminently useful, have become ossified with time, and are inextricably associated with the historically bound complexities of their origins. Following James, who called pragmatism "a new name for some old ways of thinking"[13] (though he claims not to have liked the term chosen by his elder colleague Peirce), I am suggesting an even newer name for this mode of thought (though variations of the word "integrate" are employed more or less copiously by most of the theorists below, as well as many other theorists) and, in the process, attempting to integrate pragmatism with other, apparently disparate streams of thought, including Hegelian ones.

Constructivism is another good word for describing the mode traced in these pages, whose virtue is directly to contrast with the deconstructive designation, though, like idealism and pragmatism, it has generally come to be understood in a greatly reduced form relative to the full complexity in which Deleuze and Stengers have employed the term; the most pervasive caricature of "postmodernism" is that reality is purely a social construct, which is a drastic oversimplification of what these constructivist theorists actually think, and which Stengers recognizes as a polemical "curse that weighs upon constructivism."[14] This word is now often erroneously associated with a complete solipsistic relativism, so that rather than attempting belatedly to disentangle the technical use of this term from its popular caricatures, it may be more efficacious to emphasize a novel term, at least in this context, that may finally serve to carry us past the fixed oppositions characteristic of the culture and science wars of the nineties, in which we often still seem to be embroiled. Furthermore, it might be suggested that any lexical modifications of modernism, such as postmodernism (even a constructive variety[15]) or metamodernism,[16] or of materialism, namely new materialism[17] (though excellent work has certainly been produced under these designations), are analogous to the epicyclic corrections that hoped to maintain the Earth's centrality in the cosmos by adding ever-more-elaborate refinements to this primary premise, and which Copernicus, Kepler, and Galileo swept away over the course of the sixteenth and early seventeenth centuries.

The derivation of the term integration from Whitehead in particular provides a satisfying parallel to Derrida's derivation of deconstruction from Heidegger (as a translation of *Destruktion*, which is not merely "destruction"[18]), echoing Steven Shaviro's speculative reimagining of twentieth-century philosophy, in which he provocatively describes an alternate scenario for which Whitehead has been the dominant influence on continental philosophy rather than Heidegger.[19] By contrast, difference is perhaps the most representative term of postmodernism, a putative movement whose defining characteristic is that it paradoxically resists definition, as this term perhaps more accurately describes a condition or an era rather than a movement.[20] As Stengers observes, "French-speaking onlookers" to American conversations about postmodernism are often "perplexed" in relation to "the very possibility of bringing together Gilles Deleuze and Jacques Derrida, Michel Foucault and Jacques Lacan under the same label,"[21] as these theorists are all very different, despite certain similarities of style and concern, which perhaps have more to do with their nationality than with some dubious devotion to a coherent school of thought. Nevertheless, the two primary representatives of what is generally referred to, in English, as postmodern thought discussed in these pages, Derrida and Deleuze, both extensively employ the term difference, both philosophers using the word in titles of major works. However, as

Vernon Cisney offers, although both philosophers propound a differential ontology, Derrida's is primarily negative while Deleuze's is primarily positive.[22] For both Deleuze and Derrida, difference is the relationality from which the world is constructed, but for Derrida, the différance which constitutes thought is imprisoned within the autoerotic enclosure of textuality whose outside is unthinkable, and thus he enacts a refusal or effacement of metaphysics, while for Deleuze, difference is the groundless ground of becoming, a metaphysical constructivism which liberates thought into vast and open domains of novel creation.

Far from the "reactive integration"[23] characteristic of Catholic integralism and other totalizing regimes, though perhaps not as far from the active integrations of biology, sociology, and engineering, the term integration, like difference, is partially derived, in all of the theorists discussed in these pages who employ these words, from the integral and differential calculus independently invented by Leibniz and Newton in different forms, though it is significant that Newton began his discovery with the differential calculus and Leibniz with the integral calculus (both of which he named), given that Newtonian physics, while undeniably efficacious, has come to epitomize atomistic reductionism, whereas Leibniz's philosophical thought is a clear precursor to the conceptual form of integration traced in these pages. While the calculus, in both its integral and differential forms, is generally considered purely quantitative, breaking a curve or an area up into miniscule parts and then summing them together to produce a discontinuous description of continuous, nondifferentiable phenomena, Leibniz's version of the calculus, distinguished from Newton's particularly by the concept of the infinitesimal, which Newton initially affirmed but subsequently discarded in favor of limits, is intimately bound up with his metaphysics; for the stream of thought of which Leibniz is a primary initiator, mathematical and conceptual integration can be understood as more than merely analogous.

Although Derrida, "the Great Deconstructor"[24] as Stengers quips (without explicitly mentioning Derrida), is chronologically situated after Hegel, and he positions himself as something like a deepening of Hegel through the intermediary of Heidegger,[25] it seems that Derrida carried the impulse mediated by Hegel into the vortex of a rationality against exclusive rationalism, though this carrying has served a necessary and important historical function, whereas Hegel is affectively beyond Derrida. While acknowledging the legitimate criticisms of Hegel leveled by most of the post-Hegelian theorists below, it can perhaps be recognized that Hegel's expansive openness to transformation and becoming is much closer to all of the other thinkers discussed in these pages, including Deleuze, than to Derrida. Derrida carries the traditional metaphysics to their extreme logical conclusion in a self-deconstruction, but what he rejects, which is perhaps Hegel's greatest contribution, is the presentiment of a way beyond not only his own philosophical system, but beyond his epoch, through the dialectical reconciliation of opposites, which it may now be possible to resituate in broader terms, thanks in part to Derrida, as the integration of difference, or as differentiating integration. And although Deleuze convincingly demonstrates, partially through his readings of Spinoza, Nietzsche, and Bergson, that the Hegelian dialectic alone is insufficient for this epochal task, it can be understood as an essential moment in this self-overcoming of process.

Like all of the other theorists discussed below who thought after Hegel, Deleuze has served significantly to deepen and complicate the concept of integration, providing a definitive opening from binarity, even binarity reconciled by a third entity, to a more expansive relationality conceivable in numerical, geometrical, and topological terms.[26] Derrida and Deleuze, whom Lyotard aptly designated "the two geniuses"[27] of the generation that rose to philosophical dominance in the sixties in France, can be understood as writing at a liminal border between two epochs, "suspended between two histories,"[28] as Stengers writes, though whereas Derrida sees no viable way beyond the logocentric epoch's closure, Deleuze provides an opening, a rift in the modern horizon, through which we can glimpse the exponentially wider world beyond that enclosure. Deleuze thus performs a central role in this narrative, enacting the forward-looking face of Janus, the two-faced Roman god, to Derrida's backward-looking face. For integration, what is important in both Derrida and Deleuze, as in Hegel and Schelling, or numerous other dyads, is not what they deny, but what they affirm, which in Derrida's case is the importance of the negative itself, a negativity beyond the negative,[29] and in Deleuze's case, among many other things, is the affirmation of difference, and thus the incompleteness and openness to transformation of any mode of thought, including the dialectic.

Although I am positioning Deleuze as a constructive complement to Derrida's primarily negative deconstruction, as Deleuze (along with Félix Guattari, and followed by Stengers) explicitly positions philosophy as "a constructivism" which creates novel concepts,[30] I will suggest that Derrida also has something essential to offer Deleuze. In my reading, Deleuze's only major "blind spot,"[31] to employ Derrida's term, is his reading of

Hegel, which, although it contains an important critique and extension of Hegel, goes too far in a sustained argument which can be shown to deconstruct itself. And, without going into the details of this complex operation at this stage, the deconstruction of this one aspect of Deleuze's work may serve to liberate the vast multiplicity of concepts he creates from this extraordinarily complex weight, this weighty complex, which in turn may allow Deleuze's thought fully to inhabit a novel mode after the "postmodern" rather than remaining with one foot in this liminal border and one in an emerging mode, necessarily carrying the deconstructive mode as a constitutive element in this novel mode's emergence.

In turn, I will suggest that, although Derrida is affectively prohibited from entering this promised novel domain, he sacrifices this possibility in order ultimately to serve as the "conceptual persona"[32] who provides the element missing from Deleuze's thought, offering the gift of a potential integration of Deleuze with that which he denies, namely the Hegelian negative, which may constitute a necessary step in allowing us collectively to make the transition into this novel domain, this "new earth,"[33] rather than ambivalently lingering at the threshold. And I will further suggest that Whitehead, Jung, Hillman, and Stengers particularly provide essential insights for moving beyond the duality epochally engaged by both Deleuze and Derrida, their modes of thought resonant with Deleuze, and especially with a Deleuze liberated by deconstruction from his most subtle fetters to enter fully into the novel mode that he did so much to render thinkable. Derrida writes in his moving eulogy for Deleuze in 1995 that "Deleuze remains no doubt, despite so many dissimilarities, the one to whom I have always considered myself closest among all of this 'generation'" and that, after Deleuze's death, "I will have to wander all alone in this long conversation we should have had together." Perhaps the project undertaken in these pages can assist in carrying this conversation forward, in integrating the deeply complementary modes of thought expressed so brilliantly by these two philosophers, an integration constituted in an affirmation of their differential relations.[34]

In a lecture in 1987, Deleuze tells his audience of filmmakers, with a vaguely amused shrug, that, like cinema, "philosophy also tells stories"[35] (a "fiction-philosophy," "story-repetition," "legending," or "story-telling of the people to come," as he writes elsewhere[36]). Similarly, Stengers writes that "the Whiteheadian adventure" is "a storytelling."[37] In fact, Logos, a term which resides at the heart of the Western philosophical tradition, is derived from the verb *legein*, one of whose meanings is to recount, as in the telling of a legendary tale. Even Descartes, the supreme rationalist, described his *Discourse on Method*, arguably the founding text of modern philosophy, as a "story" or "fable" in which the core of his method is to "pretend."[38] The "convoluted story"[39] I will recount in the following pages, with as little pretense as possible, is about the development of a conceptual complex which, over the course of millennia, has been expressed again and again in increasingly subtle fabulations, refined and deepened by generation after generation of theorists until, in our time, we find this complex poised to emerge from its long gestation into the light of day.

After narrating the Hegelian peak of the primarily oppositional form of the dialectic, which began with Heraclitus and Plato, as well as differentiating two other essential threads complexly interwoven in the later chapters – the "freedom of mind" characteristic of Spinozan immanence and Leibnizian *mathesis universalis* – the majority of the pages below compose the story of how the oppositional dialectic has been opening to a pluralist multiplicity of dynamisms. This opening began in earnest with Schelling's theory of mythological potencies and Nietzsche's will to potency in the eternal return, passing through Jamesian, Bergsonian, and Whiteheadian speculatively empirical pluralist constructions beyond exclusivist rationalism and materialism, and culminating with Deleuze's conception of a more profound dialectic differentially integrated with an obscure and enigmatic expression of the gods of Hellenic polytheism. This mythical dialectic is deeply, and perhaps unexpectedly, resonant with the work of Jung, whose sustained influence on Deleuze (as well as on other French philosophers like Gaston Bachelard and Gilbert Simondon, who both also influenced Deleuze) has been under-acknowledged. Deleuze's novel dialectical conception, both with and without Guattari, is also strongly resonant with Hillman's archetypal polytheism which dissolves the totalitarian monocentric ego in a deeper integration, and with Stengers' Leibnizian, Whiteheadian, and Deleuzean evocations of a cosmopolitical peace which enables not only a reclaiming of animism, but perhaps also of polytheism.

## Notes

1 Keller, *Process*, 56; Cusset, *Theory*, 77.
2 Salmon, *Event*, 272.
3 Deleuze, *Negotiations*, 165.
4 Badiou, *Conditions*, 20.

5 Hegel, *Logic*, 21.
6 Stengers, *Thinking*, 185, 242.
7 Deleuze and Parnet, *L'Abécédaire*, 94; Cf. Deleuze, *Difference*, xv.
8 Deleuze, *Desert*, 144.
9 Nietzsche, *Zarathustra*, 112.
10 Marx, *Capital I*, 103.
11 Cusset, *Theory*, 97.
12 Menand, *Metaphysical*, 359.
13 James, *Pragmatism*.
14 Stengers, *Thinking*, 19; Stengers, *Catastrophic*, 112.
15 See Griffin et al., *Founders*; Keller, *Process*, 2–3.
16 See Van Den Akker, *Metamodernism*.
17 See MacLure, "New Materialisms."
18 Salmon, *Event*, 129; Peeters, *Derrida*, 160.
19 Shaviro, *Without*, ix. There are many resonances between Heidegger and the theorists discussed in this book, but although I recognize his importance, I have decided not to give my primary time and attention to a Nazi, however brilliant (Salmon, *Event*, 56; Blattner, *Heidegger's*, 7).
20 Lyotard, *Condition*.
21 Stengers, "Beyond," 235.
22 Cisney, *Deleuze*, 143.
23 Deleuze, *Two*, 28.
24 Stengers, *Thinking*, 2.
25 Inwood, *Heidegger*, 114.
26 Deleuze and Guattari, *Anti-Oedipus*, 17.
27 Dosse, *Intersecting*, 354.
28 Stengers, *Catastrophic*, 17.
29 Derrida, *Writing*, 390n4.
30 Deleuze and Guattari, *Philosophy?* 35; Deleuze, *Negotiations*, 25; Deleuze, *Cinema 2*, 146, 280.
31 Derrida, *Grammatology*, 164.
32 Deleuze and Guattari, *Philosophy?* 10.
33 Deleuze and Guattari, *Philosophy?* 101.
34 Derrida, "Wander."
35 Deleuze, *Two*, 314.
36 Deleuze, *Desert*, 157; Deleuze, *Difference*, 62; Deleuze, *Negotiations*, 125–6; Deleuze, *Cinema 2*, 223.
37 Stengers, *Thinking*, 516. See Stengers, *Another*, 156.
38 Descartes, *Discourse*, 3, 18.
39 Deleuze, *Logic*, xiv.

Chapter 1

# The Final Writing of an Epoch
Jacques Derrida's *Of Grammatology*

Derrida refuses to call deconstruction a method in 1967's *Of Grammatology*, preferring to nominate the mode of thought he offers as "a theoretical matrix"[1] which performs the self-deconstruction of texts. And this denial of methodology from the outset is characteristic of Derridean deconstruction: It declines to be defined, resists simple meanings, and problematizes the implicit dominance of logocentrism, the privileging of phonetic writing with its system of logical relations, inscribing the particular modes of analyzing, explicating, reading, and interpreting characteristic of the "West" and its most fundamental metaphysical presuppositions. This problematizing of the implicit privileging of these logocentric modes of thought has been a crucially important project for the Western mind to undertake in its development (if we understand this figure of the Western mind, like all identities, as a real, but limited, fiction), though the deconstructive mode problematizes a coherent movement of cultural development, bringing into question the traditional metaphysical progression from nonlife to animality to consciousness, which allows for the deepening of this figural movement by other theorists, Bergson for instance (though he wrote before Derrida) describing a multiplicity of radiating trajectories rather than a single developmental line. However, now that the deconstructive project has outgrown its initial allure, one might notice that deconstruction, while playing a vitally necessary role in clearing away the often unexamined, implicit, and pervasive biases culminating in modernity, has taught intellectual culture to take a suspicious and problematizing stance toward any larger coherence, toward any Lyotardian metanarrative for fear that it might be used to exclude, dominate, or marginalize.[2]

But ironically, the very urge to seek a more expansively generative narrative has effectively been excluded and marginalized by deconstruction,

DOI: 10.4324/9781003195498-2

so that Derrida summarizes his "final intention in this book" as "to make enigmatic what one thinks one understands" about the traditional metaphysics of presence, attempting "to produce, often embarrassing myself in the process, the problems of critical reading."[3] While there is certainly value in this kind of enigmatic and embarrassed problematizing, and although Derrida gestures toward an opening to "'positive' discovery"[4] intimately intertwined with his deconstruction of texts, which is not a mere doubling reproduction, the activity undertaken in this work is nevertheless almost purely negative, delineating a problematic field, admittedly a pervasive and ancient one, without offering a way to move beyond that problematic situation toward deeper questions. It seeks to break the bonds of the dominance of written words, untying archaic constraints built into the semiotic systems through which we construct our identities and the world, leaving an open field of loose threads. However, deconstruction does nothing to populate this void, to weave those disparate threads into a novel tapestry of symbolic coherence through which a dynamic and generative story can be unfurled, though its virtue is that it avoids filling this lack with a static plenum.[5] It is a metanarrative against metanarratives, and Derrida is the messiah of the end of monocentric messianic consciousness, an impossibly paradoxical and problematic stance.[6]

The story Derrida tells is about the closure of a logocentric epoch, which he describes as defined by a metaphysical tendency stretching from the pre-Socratics through Plato, Leibniz, Hegel, and even Heidegger, who performs a cancelation of the traditional conceptions of being and truth that Derrida conceives as "the final writing of an epoch," which he evokes as "also the first writing," though of what he does not tell us. This conception applies perhaps even more completely to Derrida himself, as he generally eschews gesturing toward a novel mode that might emerge phoenix-like from the ashes of the old mode, almost exclusively dwelling with the risk of "falling back within what is being deconstructed," even as he exposes the workings of the textual machine while precariously clinging to the inside of its still-enclosing outer shell, squinting intently, lips pursed, into its ultimately complex machinations. Deconstruction dismantles the logocentric structures from the inside,[7] Derrida positioning himself liminally within the machinic border, facing into the depths of the assemblage while the shell begins to crack, like an egg, behind his back, just past the edge of his vision. Derrida describes this deconstructive moment, which he associates especially with Nietzsche and Heidegger, as "a trembling proper to all post-Hegelian attempts and to this passage between two epochs," though we can discern a half-century later that Derrida himself is the peak expression of this subtly embarrassed and eloquently terrified trembling. The problematizing reading produced by Derrida is, as he suggests, an extremely difficult, but necessary, liberation from the overwhelming gravity of the past, and the widespread embrace of this exhortation toward freedom from the existing categories of thought in the last half-century should be celebrated as a triumph of truly critical thinking in the academy, an affirmation of the obligation for theorists to question every assumption, to take nothing for granted.[8] However, as I will suggest in the chapters that follow, there is one fundamental assumption, or perhaps a deeply intertwined set of assumptions, of which deconstruction cannot quite bring itself to let go, which does not allow Derrida to turn around and peer through the cracks in the "world egg"[9] into a more expansive domain, as do the other twentieth-century theorists discussed below. Derrida acknowledges that "deconstruction always in a certain way falls prey to its own work" because it operates from within the existing structure, employing the conceptual instruments characteristic of the logocentric epoch to subvert and destabilize the structural assumptions that have generally resided below conscious awareness in an enactment of pure reason devouring itself, locked in a fixed circulation like a snake eating its own tail, until the snake eats its own head.[10]

It is undoubtedly true that Derrida's thought developed significantly over the course of his long, extremely prolific career, and that his tone and approach had shifted somewhat by the late eighties and nineties. Derrida is almost positive at certain moments in texts like 1987's "A Number of Yes" and 1993's *The Gift of Death*, despite the latter's subject matter, writing of "an incorporation of an earlier mystery that blurs the limits of every epoch," perhaps creating an opening to characteristically nonmodern modes of thought, an insight resonant with Derrida's recognition in *Of Grammatology* that traces of an "ultra-transcendental text" beyond the logocentric metaphysics remain in the texts of the logocentric epoch, so that a novel expression exceeding logocentrism is not merely a regression to a naïve mode which cannot be distinguished from texts written prior to the advent of critical thought, but must retain the whole course of its movement within its emergent actuality.[11] Similarly, in *The Gift of Death*, Derrida suggests that "every revolution, whether atheistic or religious, bears witness to a return of the sacred in the form of enthusiasm or fervor, otherwise known as the presence of the gods within us,"[12] an ambiguous suggestion perhaps resonant with the evocations of gods by Schelling, Nietzsche, Jung, Deleuze, Hillman, and Stengers discussed below. Derrida also deeply and sympathetically explores the intertwining of spirit and animality in his concept of "divinanimality" in *The Animal That Therefore I Am*, a 1997 lecture published in 2008.

However, as evident in this late text, he never manages to move past the dwelling with embarrassment that marks his earlier readings, telling his audience that "I have trouble, yes, a bad time overcoming my embarrassment," in this case standing naked in front of his cat, an affect he identifies as a malaise in which he is "ashamed of being ashamed," similarly expressing shame in 1993's *Specters of Marx* for not having recently read *The Communist Manifesto*.[13] In a 1996 interview, Derrida asserts "I think about nothing but death,"[14] tarrying perpetually within the self-enclosed vortex of negative affect intimately entwined with the critical rationality of a negative philosophy devouring itself, a vicious affective-theoretical circle from which he cannot seem to escape, as such an escape requires a leap beyond rationality, a positive trust variously evoked by James, Bergson, Whitehead, and Stengers.[15] As John Protevi writes, "we must not exaggerate the import of this shift," as Derrida's development from the fifties to the nineties "maintains a continuity of concerns with his earlier work,"[16] Peter Salmon observing that "the coherence of Derrida's thinking, from his earliest works through to his last is remarkable,"[17] and Derrida himself definitively stating: "I don't think I have ever repudiated anything."[18] Deconstruction is a profoundly useful and necessary tool for problematizing and destabilizing binary sites of existing oppression based on race, sex, gender, sexual orientation, class, geography, disability, and many other hierarchical privilegings, including epistemology, for which "the writing of reason" has been privileged over "the writing of the heart" (resonant with Deleuze's capital "organ of exchange" and "amorous organ of repetition"[19]), and the privileging of "man" over that which defines this figure by its exclusion: woman, nature, animality, primitivism, childhood, madness, divinity.[20] However, I agree with Cisney's assessment that deconstruction is primarily a negative differential ontology[21] less useful for the creation of novel positive concepts than the work of the other theorists discussed in these pages. It remains the fact, then, that *Of Grammatology* serves as the primary exemplification of the deconstructive mode of thought, "the founding text of deconstruction,"[22] as Salmon writes, which Derrida's later texts further elaborated, but never supplanted.

The difficulty in interpreting Derrida is similar in some ways to the difficulty in reading Plato: It is often uncertain if these philosophers are speaking for themselves or as others, as Plato's characters in the dialogues or as the texts Derrida amplifies and deconstructs, but does not exactly critique. In a section of *The Gift of Death* in which he is discussing the Biblical story of Abraham's interrupted sacrifice of Isaac, Derrida might as well be describing his own approach, so that deconstruction can be understood as "the exposure of conceptual thinking to its limit, to its death and finitude," as Derrida's writing can be conceived as a sustained metarhetorical gambit whose purpose is to "intrigue, disconcert, question." He primarily "speaks without saying anything either true or false, says nothing determinate that would be equivalent to a statement, a promise, or a lie," and he "utters nothing fixed, determinable, positive or negative," so that Derrida's expression of this disconcerting questioning perhaps became more subtle over the decades of his work, but it was never abandoned.[23] One does not come away from Derrida's texts with a clear sense of what he believes or asserts, but only with a sense of disorienting dislocation which nevertheless impels one to think carefully and to interrogate every assumption, an activity which Derrida obliquely associates with Socratic irony, but which tends to produce an affect of hollowness and exhaustion very different from the invigorating plenitude of Plato's dialogues, or the other theorists discussed below.[24]

However, this is not a book against deconstruction, but rather a work that appreciates the profound novelty of Derrida's thought, but that also recognizes its affective sense of being enclosed, even imprisoned, despite its explicit orientation toward liberation. It is a liberation without an outside into which one might escape, an ultimately complex instrument for untying oppositional bonds and unlocking hierarchical doors, which nevertheless is unable (at least without the help of the allies discussed in the chapters below) to provide a means for crossing the threshold to a vast openness beneath a star-strewn sky, a more expansive domain beyond the horizon that deconstruction allows one to see so clearly, but does not engender the means to pursue; a way of seeing through, but not a means of movement. So rather than denounce deconstruction, which is extraordinarily efficacious and valid as far as it goes, and whose terms and moves are imbricated with other, complementary verbal modes throughout the present text, I instead want to assist in deconstruction's liberation from itself as gratitude for its having provided essential instruments for its own overcoming.[25] I want to participate in the collective embracing of deconstruction's epochal concepts and forms of language, which we can never unlearn once they have been established, within a mode of thought that may serve to carry deconstruction into a continually created paradoxical promised land just beyond an ever-receding horizon, though its author must remain forever outside this novel domain.[26]

In fact, Derrida's thought is deeply resonant with concepts expressed by the other theorists to whom this book devotes chapters, and he was even influenced by some of them, but whereas all of the other theorists employ the negative mode to generate openings for their positive conceptual creations, Derrida dwells primarily with the negative inflections of these concepts. While deconstruction is very close to integration, it is the most complete and profound expression of that mode's shadow, the negative space which partially constitutes its structure, and thus all of the other texts discussed below enable a Whiteheadian "slightest change of tone which yet makes all the difference"[27] from deconstruction into a novel mode of relation. My intention is not primarily to critique Derrida, though critique inevitably plays a role when attempting to go beyond a mode of thought, but to demonstrate how Derrida has cleared the space that was filled by exclusivist rationality, allowing the expression of novel modes of thought, though he generally articulates the negative inflections of these conceptual modes which are nevertheless profoundly resonant with the positive concepts created and refined by the other theorists. Deconstruction is a nearly pure negative philosophy, in Schelling's sense, in that it does not posit metaphysical concepts or potencies, denying metaphysics altogether, dwelling almost entirely with absence, negative affect, and the negative inflections of the vast and multifarious conceptual complexes explored in their positive inflections by the others. It might even be said that this chapter's aim is to demonstrate how deconstruction deconstructs itself, to assist in its self-deconstruction.

From *Of Grammatology*'s outset, Derrida circulates around the recognition that the past is only represented to us in semiotic traces. As he notoriously and ambiguously expresses it, "there is nothing outside of the text" (or, more accurately, "there is no outside-text"), by which he seems to connote that everything we know, our largest field of lived reality, is constructed from the relations of sign systems, that the fabric of our most basic experience is ultimately con-textual.[28] For Derrida, this constructed quality of reality has been almost impossible to perceive, has been obscured by the fact that the very verbal, conceptual, and perceptual relations through which we know reality condition the reality we can know. These semiotic networks, in fact, constitute our reality, as "we think only in signs,"[29] though our signifying systems are culturally bound, and can take radically different forms in different times and different places. But for him, this mutability of language and signs, and thus of the world they largely constitute, indicates that a profound violence has been done, that an invisibly pervasive trick has been played on us, and that we should be skeptical of any meanings assumed as given, a mode which has been nominated as a "hermeneutics of suspicion,"[30] genealogically related to Nietzsche's "schooling in suspicion,"[31] though Derrida even judges "the Nietzschean demolition" as "a captive of that metaphysical edifice which it professes to overthrow."[32] Derrida does not quite seem to see that this judgment applies perhaps even more to his own demolition than to Nietzsche's, as although Nietzsche certainly engages in a Schellingian negative philosophy of critique and denouncement, this destruction is oriented toward the creation of important positive concepts like the Apollonian and Dionysian, the will to power, the eternal return, and the Overman, while Derrida's conceptual creations are almost exclusively tools, however useful and profound, for a negative and disconcerting problematizing.

Derrida is suspicious of the very concepts of history and time, suggesting that the values of logocentrism have constituted the predominant mode of thought in modernity, though this mode has its roots in the pre-Socratic Greek philosophers and the ancient Hebrews. He recognizes that our understanding of history and temporality itself is predicated upon the privileging of the Logos of written language and, if we are to see through this privileging, we are left without an adequate frame for our self-understanding, a narrative for rendering our relationship to our past intelligible. If we have not been progressively extricating ourselves from irrational and naïve superstitions and beliefs in the ascent of science and intellect, which are complicit with writing, how can we understand our current situation? Derrida defines the problem again and again, attacking the implicit privileging of logocentrism from every conceivable angle until the metaphysical presuppositions of the last several millennia of primarily Western culture have been demolished, or at least rendered extremely unstable. And at the root of this pervasive logocentrism, Derrida finds an internal speech which brings forth opposition, suggesting that conceptual thought is constituted in a speaking to oneself in silent words,[33] that conceptual thought can only occur through words, and that this internal speech is intimately bound up with opposition, as thought first must discriminate, must divide the world, as in Plato's dialectical "method of division,"[34] from its undifferentiated prerationality into verbal duality, monocentrically circulating within "the system of oppositions of metaphysics."[35] We differentiate between different kinds of entities through pervasive binarity, and this oppositional structure of language emerged coextensively with the interior monologue of conceptual mentality – or perhaps dialogue, assuming a generally silent other as implicit witness to the internal monologic utterance – and in order to liberate ourselves from this oppositional metaphysics, he suggests, we must attain a mode of thought which enacts a deconstruction of the oppositional system of verbal differentiation at the heart of written language.

For Derrida, the deconstruction of the logocentric metaphysics dominant for the last several thousand years is a brave descent into the abyss, shedding a conception of the world that is generally conflated with reality itself without the promise of anything to replace it, as "one does not leave the epoch whose closure one can outline."[36] This deconstructive activity is not primarily a movement toward a future – or if it is future-oriented, it constructs this future to come as an eternally deferred haunting absence, as in *Specters of Marx* – not the positive transition to a novel epoch, but rather a closure without a commensurate opening in sight, as Derrida generally does not evoke any new mode that might emerge from the closure of this epoch, foreclosing the positing of such a further development in anything other than the most enigmatic intimations.[37] The possible exits from this enclosure are blocked because any words one might employ to describe such an emergence are circumscribed by the implicit assumptions that reside in language itself, so that Derrida is brilliant, profound, and almost utterly desolate, because the very verbally constructed concepts through which we might generate a novel mode of thought keep us confined.[38] Derrida's conception of liberation through deconstruction is of mind devouring itself, the inevitably futile attempt to think one's way beyond thought, to push rationality to its limits in order to go beyond rationality rather than taking the leap, as James, Bergson, Whitehead, and Stengers all especially conceive it, into a radically novel domain beyond the exclusive privileging of the rational. Derrida maintains that the metaphysics of difference at the root of writing, with fundamental constraints built into its relational structure, cannot be employed to go outside that semiotic system, as conceptual thought is thinkable only by means of language, and anything beyond that domain is not capable of being thought.[39]

Although I will argue against this mode, often implicitly, in the pages and chapters that follow (the kind of argument one might have with an old friend with whom one has far more in common than not), I would like to take a moment to give this position its due, to acknowledge that all of us, at one time or another, have felt completely constrained, have dwelled with the profound bodily sense that there is no way out of our predicament. During these times, no matter how we look at things, our usually inspired and incisive rational capacities can see no logical conclusion other than that everything we have known, including logic itself, has been a lie, a kind of metaphysical dirty trick, and there is no escaping this complex self-enclosed situation, which is both affective and theoretical. Although Derrida briefly gestures toward a possible overcoming of this state in "the ineluctable world of the future which proclaims itself at present, beyond the closure of knowledge,"[40] a domain that can only barely be discerned in "the crevice through which the yet unnamable glimmer beyond the closure can be glimpsed,"[41] twitching back the curtain for the briefest of moments, he denies the possibility of a contemporary knowledge about such a self-overcoming. Others, however, perhaps especially Deleuze (of those in Derrida's milieu), were doing much more than merely glimpsing this future in 1967. But Derrida sees no possibility of catching more than this glimpse of any potential future opening, not only because it is "an absolute danger" and "a monstrosity"[42] (a different kind of relation to monstrosity than the one Deleuze embraces), indicating a legitimate terror of venturing into indiscernible domains, of the absence of normative certainty, but also because there is no exergue, the motto on the back of a coin, for a future emergence, no precedent for what is to come.

I will spend the rest of this book pushing against Derrida's claim, offering an exergual plenitude for an emerging dispensation, as Derrida's terror of the dangerous and the monstrous forms a significant element of the affective tone constituting the pre-philosophical background of the deconstructive mode of thought. I will suggest that the theorists referred to in the chapters that follow who preceded Derrida were often articulating a mode developmentally subsequent to the one Derrida so completely and brilliantly exemplifies, an insight especially derived from Whitehead, as it might be suggested that the conceptual constructions expressed by Derrida, or any of these other theorists, are not fundamentally new. These two modes, the deconstructive and the integrative, can be conceived as having been enacting a relational drama circulating through polarity since at least the controversy between Plato and the Sophists. Derrida and the movement of thought he exemplifies have perhaps coincided with the apex of the sophistic end of the polarity in the contemporary cultural sphere (though this is not merely an insult as it has often been intended), the deconstructive mode having often dominated the central nodes of discursive power of the Anglophone humanities in the last few decades of the twentieth century, and perhaps even the first decade of the twenty-first, serving as the decentering theoretical center of the more expansive critique and disavowal of modernity in many domains. The other twentieth-century theorists discussed in the chapters below are primary representatives of a complementary mode of thought that has begun to surge into collective awareness over the last few decades, a mode for which deconstruction has cleared a space and prepared the way.[43]

The majority of *Of Grammatology* is involved in a sympathetic deconstructive reading of several texts by Rousseau, with the anthropologist Claude Lévi-Strauss, who felt himself to be Rousseau's heir, serving as an entrée to this reading, his texts providing "somewhat more than an exergue"[44] for the central concerns of Derrida's text, which, like the work of Ferdinand de Saussure, inhabit a liminal border between the logocentric metaphysics and their deconstruction, though we may further discern that Derrida's work is similarly situated on another liminal border, which can be recognized as deconstruction itself, between two epochs. It is striking that this work of scholarship on primarily a single figure from the eighteenth century should be accorded a status as *magnum opus* similar to other great works in the history of philosophy by figures like Kant, Hegel, and Heidegger. This text seems to have been elevated over others because its deconstructive mode of reading is so novel, and its style so startling and subtle, but also because it exemplifies the primary spirit of what would come to be called "poststructuralism," a peak expression of Schellingian negative philosophy, which does not posit anything, but brilliantly expresses the problems and questions of the epoch coming to a close by performing the deconstruction of Rousseau's texts.

Rousseau plays a unique role in the progression from Plato to Hegel, enacting perhaps the most decisive and revealing defensive reaction in the eighteenth century against attacks on the logocentric metaphysics, mediating the enigmatic and paradoxical threshold between the Enlightenment and Romanticism.[45] A reading of Derrida resembling, in another register, the close reading Derrida gives to Rousseau may discern that deconstruction enacts the peak expression of a negative philosophy while paradoxically presiding over the threshold to a novel positive mode. Derrida's orientation is almost exclusively toward interrogating and destabilizing the logocentric epoch, but the constructive threads of Derrida's text, relatively rare and ambiguous in comparison to its primary deconstructive project, can be brought into resonance with the other theorists to show how their concepts, many of which are already complexly interwoven, can be further integrated, while maintaining their contrasting differentiation, to create novel conceptual domains beyond deconstruction that we can collectively inhabit.

For Derrida, these proper names – Plato, Rousseau, Hegel – nominate problems or symptoms more than the "the authors of movements"[46] embodying "the original myth of a transparent legibility,"[47] a negative inflection of the mythical as a naïve self-identity to whose violent obliteration Derrida bears eloquent witness. For Deleuze and Guattari, however, the names of philosophers are conceptual personae in the long, complex, and periodically revised philosophical narrative internally resonant with mythical potencies precisely because they are constituted in a problematic and pathological multiplicity beyond the mere identity of egoic monocentrism, carried along a series of nonlocal and nonlinear differential repetitions, through the affirmation and selection of the eternal return, to the higher expressions of the faculties, a conceptual complex partially derived from Spinoza, Leibniz, Schelling, and Nietzsche.

Derrida is not precisely critical of Rousseau. Rather, he tarries with Rousseau's negative relation to writing and essential presence, dwelling sustainedly with him as an exemplar of the logocentric epoch over whose closure Derrida presides so that "a text always has several epochs,"[48] the epochs to which it responds, the epoch of its writing, and the epochs of its later reception, all complexly imbricated in the text and the various appropriations, extensions, critiques, and rejections it has afforded in its readers (or its non-readers, as is often the case with Derrida himself[49]). Through his close reading, Derrida allows the aporias and inconsistencies, the lacunae and margins of the rhizomatic "root system"[50] of logocentric metaphysics subtending Rousseau's texts to reveal themselves, uncovering a genealogy that greatly exceeds the explicit textual system which represents its presence within the limits of a single epoch. He does not denounce Rousseau or offer an alternative as do the other theorists, but circulates within the self-enclosed auto-affection of rationalist consciousness in the wake of

Descartes, a biunivocal self-presence divided into solitary mind and one true God that circumscribes the logocentric epoch.

As Derrida recognizes in relation to the nonrational which Rousseau violently excluded precisely because this domain "fascinated and tormented him more than it did others,"[51] it is often those domains which most trouble us, which are most affectively problematic for us, that lure us toward our greatest achievements, an insight discussed below especially in relation to Nietzsche's concept of ressentiment and Deleuze's conception, with Guattari, of the anti-Oedipal. This formulation is reminiscent of Derrida's observation during a 1990 interview at his home in Paris, which has just been interrupted by a phone call from Emmanuel Lévinas, that his friend "always thinks I am going to hang up before the conversation is over, and constantly interrupts with anxious exclamations," which Derrida recognizes as a deeply ironic anxiety for the philosopher "who talks about faith in the other," an endearing moment which reveals that, like Nietzsche's personal and conceptual struggle with ressentiment, Lévinas' undeniably brilliant work was nevertheless at least partially motivated by a fear of abandonment, perhaps related to his experience in a Nazi prison camp.[52] And without being "biographically reductive," as Salmon cautions, one might posit a similar recognition in which Derrida's dwelling primarily with the negative in order heroically to liberate his epoch from a negative logocentrism is partially motivated by his sustained and problematic experience with the negative affects to which he so often returns – terror, shame, mourning. These affects are partially traceable to the death of his older brother only ten months before Derrida's birth, which "haunted Jackie throughout his life," and to the political upheavals that occurred during his childhood "in the margins" in Algeria, where his family's place as Jews in a majority Muslim country under French colonial rule was complex and problematic, a liminal "quasi-subgroup" between French and Arab suffering from a "disorder of identity."[53] In fact, Derrida explicitly recognizes the significance of his biography for understanding the origins of his philosophy, writing: "A Judeo-Franco-Maghrebian genealogy does not clarify everything, far from it. But could I explain anything without it, ever? No, nothing."[54]

Although he subtly distances his authorial voice from Rousseau's negativity toward those domains that exceed rationality, Derrida's text amplifies the affectively negative currents of Rousseau's thought, inhabiting a moment of closure which mourns the terrifying loss of that negativity as at least a kind of solid grounding, a dwelling with the loss of grounding in an affective and conceptual "negativity so negative that it could not even be called such any longer."[55] Derrida invokes a negativity that exceeds mere critical negation as well as positive affirmation, not erasing, but defining a negative space, as in visual art, which serves as a blank, groundless background for concepts that complementary theorists, culminating with Deleuze, Hillman, and Stengers, will express in their positive valences, though always entwined with negative differentiation, by carrying the concepts from the earlier theorists discussed in these pages into ever more subtly differentiated and integrated formulations. No one is more subtle than Derrida, but perhaps it is easier to be subtle when one's field of vision is limited almost entirely to discerning shades and gradations within the shadows of an enclosed space, while the others are peering into the heavens, some, perhaps culminating with Hegel, toward the unifying centrality of the Sun, and some toward the multiplicity of centers figured by the labyrinthine nighttime sky.

Through the medium of writing, Derrida tarries sustainedly with Rousseau's ironic exposure and denouncement of the evil and enslavement of writing, also expressed in writing, so that this text doubly imprisons the reader in a cage of writing which Derrida dismantles, but for which there is nothing outside, perhaps only a faint glimmer. For Derrida "the outside is the inside,"[56] a phrase written with the "is" crossed out, ambiguously evoking an affectively and theoretically enclosed space which cannot be escaped even by going outside, as this escape leads inexorably back into the labyrinth, an insight which only requires the affective inversion characteristic of a joyful and creative liberation to take on its constructive valence, to which Derrida gestures for the briefest of moments as "radically empiricist," evoking James, entwined with an experimental "errancy"[57] especially resonant with Deleuze and Hillman. For the constructivist theorists, however, the constructed quality of language, and the semiotic relation to experience in general, is not imprisoning or enslaving, but a liberation from the givenness of the traditional metaphysics into a radically "free and wild creation of concepts," a phrase from Deleuze and Guattari that Stengers employs as the subtitle to *Thinking With Whitehead*. Although Deleuze overturns the Platonic escape from the cave to resituate this exit as an infinite labyrinth of caves that we reciprocally construct as we explore, these caverns, far from inducing claustrophobia as they seem to do for Derrida, can also be conceived as the vast cosmos opened through our liberated creation.[58] This paradoxical inversion is thus an affective-theoretical shift that enables an overturning and reappropriation of deconstruction, allowing the positive construction of novel worlds through a radical, metaphysical, speculative, transcendental empiricism expressed through writing.

Derrida's conception of "différance" as an ungrounded but originary domain of infinite reflections, the paradoxically nonoriginary "trace" which figures the differential "origin of the origin,"[59] and the terrifying, dangerous, and maddening "supplement" between presence and absence, whose "strange essence" is "not to have essentiality,"[60] is, like Deleuze's ungrounding ground of difference, a recognition that our experience of the world is constructed from an ultimate relationality, which does not rest on a fixed, transcendent grounding, the thing itself which Derrida nominates the "transcendental signified,"[61] whether of Platonic Forms, monotheistic divinity, physical materiality, or the Hegelian absolute. However, whereas Derrida almost exclusively dwells with this ungrounding "middle term"[62] as a dire and frustrating loss of certainty to be lamented, Deleuze expresses this ungrounding relationality in "the middle" where "one begins again"[63] as a deeper kind of paradoxical grounding which, like Derrida's conception, liberates from the old metaphysical conceptions of a monocentric "ontotheology"[64] (a Kantian and Heideggerian term combining the ontology of God and the theology of Being), but which serves for Deleuze as an immensely expanded domain for the joyful creation of novel concepts.

Like Deleuze, Derrida discerns Hegel as the peak expression of a logocentric metaphysics, though he also evinces an appreciation for Hegel as "the thinker of irreducible difference,"[65] an appreciation not as present in Deleuze, but which will inform the reading of *Difference and Repetition* below. Derrida evokes Hegel as delimiting "the horizon of absolute knowledge"[66] beyond which Derrida cannot see, an unthinkable domain "outside of the horizon"[67] circumscribed by writing, only accessible to the "limitlessness of play," which sounds joyful and creative of positive conceptions until Derrida immediately equates this play with the decidedly negative "destruction of ontotheology and the metaphysics of presence."[68] In contrast, Deleuze, despite his valorization of creative destruction,[69] evokes a "transcendental horizon"[70] infinitely pursued by means of conceptual creation from all kinds of topologically figured differences beyond the dominance of dialectical opposition. The horizon can only be constructed as a fixed, constraining boundary, "the widest horizon of the questions"[71] of the closure of logocentric metaphysics, if one does not trace a line of flight casting the dice beyond this fenced grounding where play occurs, this

Heraclitan-Aeonic playground for "the game of the world,"[72] and the horizon only expands or recedes with our creative movements through spatiotemporal dimensions. For Derrida, it is the image of play in Saussurean linguistics, a "reassuring closing of play"[73] imagined as the game of chess and its virtually infinite variations within the perfectly delimited space of the board mirroring its fixed rules and relations in a "total system,"[74] that must be overcome through deconstruction, though it is Deleuze who especially expresses play as a "divine game"[75] of affirmative creation beyond the enclosure with which Derrida lingers.[76]

Leibnizian *mathesis universalis* is a mode of apprehension both mathematical and metaphysical, which Derrida judges as still constrained within logocentrism, whereas, although Deleuze offers some similar criticisms of Leibniz, he does this in order to differentiate the Leibnizian infinitesimal form of the integral and differential calculus to serve as a primary element in his conception of a deeper kind of dialectic beyond opposition. Stengers takes up this conception in her discussions of Leibniz's concept of *Calculemus* as a primary method for forging a peace, however risky and provisional, from discordant modes of relation with their various constraints and obligations, rather than merely asserting reasoning in the mode of reductive calculation as Derrida seems to suggest. Stengers implicitly recognizes Derrida as ironically reducing Leibniz's concepts, defining them too narrowly in order to shoehorn them into a purely logocentric metaphysics, while for Deleuze and Stengers, Leibniz cannot be so easily categorized as a mere logocentric rationalist.

Derrida is especially dismissive of final causation, asserting that it has generally constituted a naïve and illusory Western "ethnocentric metaphysics,"[77] a rejection that has been fairly pervasive in both modern and "postmodern" thought. However, the "onto-theo-teleology"[78] Derrida rejects, like the finalism rejected by Spinoza, is ironically the most naïve conception of teleology constructed as moving toward a fixed, given end, an oversimplification (one of only a very few to which both Derrida and Spinoza succumb) that most of the theorists below will complicate and deepen as an inclinational finalism receding toward the dissolution of the binary of finalism and its rejection, a decentered conception of teleology beyond the exclusively privileged Logos as central telos more evocative of the strange attractor of fractal geometry. Derrida recognizes that the deconstructive moment constitutes "a crisis of the logos," though he deconstructs the "concept of crisis" itself, rendering it "suspect" as enacting "a dialectical and teleological" mode of thought, problematizing the concept of epochal catastrophic rupture through his reading of Rousseau,[79] whereas most of the others will recognize crisis as the precondition for transformative renascence in more profound dialectical and teleological conceptions. In a text written in the 1950s but only published in 2002, Deleuze writes that "it is not that there is a second birth because there has been a catastrophe, but the reverse, there is a catastrophe after the origin because there must be, from the beginning, a second birth,"[80] expressing a more subtle valence of teleological death-and-rebirth than the one Derrida ambiguously refuses, ultimately resonant with *amor fati*, the love of fate traceable back through Nietzsche to Spinoza and the Stoics, as much as with the subtle conceptions of final causation expressed by most of the other theorists below. In fact, Derrida recognizes that it is "essentially impossible"[81] to avoid teleological modes of discourse, and although his valiant attempt to enact this avoidance has produced a liberating differentiation, it may be recognized that this liberation can never exceed teleology as such, but can only overcome the naïve form of teleology grounded in a transcendent domain, liberated into a more subtle expression of inclinational teleology grounded in ungrounding differential relationality.

Similarly, Derrida obliquely expresses différance as that which exceeds formal causation and its rejection, as "the formation of form,"[82] an insight resonant with Deleuze's infinite regress which recedes beyond the opposition of formality and formlessness, Derrida, like Deleuze, evoking Bergson's concept of the virtual as a way potentially to dissolve this opposition. However, whereas Derrida almost exclusively eschews the essentialism of the Platonic Forms, problematizing an "infinitist metaphysics,"[83] which he also associates with the monocentrism of Christian theology and the Hegelian absolute, only gesturing toward a "plurivocity,"[84] Deleuze copiously expresses a heterogenous pluralism of infinite multiplicity, appropriating the *eidos* in his Platonic overturning of Platonism to express them in a more profound and subtle valence as virtual Ideas, simulacra, phantasms, multiplicities, problems, questions, and gods, a reframing of formal causes resonant with most of the other theorists below. Whereas Derrida inherits the denouncement of metaphysics from Heidegger, so that the differential trace cannot be described by any metaphysics,[85] Deleuze affirms metaphysics so completely that his conception exceeds even a Schellingian metaphysical empiricism in the form of a transcendental empiricism, or even pataphysics, a novel mode of thought which, as Deleuze quotes

Alfred Jarry in 1964, is a conception "extending as far beyond metaphysics as metaphysics extends beyond physics,"[86] though in 1980, Deleuze states that "I see myself as a pure metaphysician."[87] Like Deleuze and Hillman, Derrida recognizes that the trace beyond formality and formlessness "exceeds the question What is? and contingently makes it possible,"[88] though he does not risk the leap explicitly undertaken by both Deleuze and Hillman (and implicitly by Schelling, Nietzsche, Jung, and Stengers) of asking "Who?", addressing their questions about the deepest becomings of process to transcendental persons variously imagined as ontologically ambiguous potencies, archetypes, ancestors, or gods.

Expressing a conception whose negative valence is a resonant inversion of the more positive valences of Spinoza, Nietzsche, Bergson, Whitehead, Jung, and Deleuze, Derrida recognizes that differential relationality does not occur in time, but rather that linear temporality itself (whether straight or cyclical in a monocentric circulation) is violently extracted by means of language, and especially phonetic writing, from a deeper domain of difference. Derrida generally does not positively describe the suppressed temporal constructions exceeding the successive and homogenous linearity of historical temporality, a Heideggerian "vulgar concept of time"[89] that emerged in "an extraordinary leap"[90] coextensive with linear writing about four thousand years ago, which finds its peak expression in the reductive absolute time of Newtonian physics (despite Newton's interest in alchemy), and which has been the almost exclusively dominant philosophical conception of time from Aristotle to Hegel. This temporal conception has provided a sense of secure order in "a dangerous and anguishing world" through its enabling of technology, economy, ideology, and hierarchy, but it has suppressed other legitimate modes of temporal construction with their concomitant faculties. Derrida only briefly gestures toward the concept of the symbolically situated mythogram derived from André Leroi-Gourhan, which Derrida describes as "a writing that spells its symbols pluri-dimensionally," and which "corresponds to another level of historical experience,"[91] and the theorists below will have much more to say about heterodox modes of temporal construction intertwined with nonlinear linguistic forms, symbolic mythography, and plural dimensionalities, from the Nietzschean-Deleuzean eternal return to Bergsonian duration, the Whiteheadian epochal theory of time, and Jungian synchronicity.

For Derrida, "the end of linear writing," and the accompanying closure of the dominance of an exclusively linear temporal construction, is not primarily to be enacted by "confiding new writings to the envelope of the book," but rather by "finally reading what wrote itself between the lines in the volumes"[92] that have formed the central canon of the logocentric metaphysics, so that while his deconstructions of the texts of Lévi-Strauss or Rousseau certainly problematize the linear constructions of writing and temporality, these close readings exhibit a parasitical character, which Derrida recognized.[93] However, this deconstruction, which Derrida understands as a culmination of the destruction of linearity that has been occurring since the mid-nineteenth century, constituting a caesura partially initiated by Schelling and Nietzsche from which we are perhaps only now beginning to emerge, has cleared space for the decidedly novel compositions of the post-Hegelian theorists below, who nevertheless remain deeply involved with earlier theorists, whose writing was no less novel in their moments. Derrida and Deleuze can be conceived as together enacting the apex of a "suspense between two ages of writing," though Derrida is primarily concerned with the closure of the first age, while Deleuze offers a multiplicity of openings to the second. Like most of the other theorists, however, Derrida understands that the emergence of a nonlinear and pluridimensional mode of thought after the closure of logocentrism is not merely constituted in a regression to nonmodern mythography, but is rather a recognition that linear rationality itself is one kind of mythography among others, enacting the emergence from the exclusive privileging of a rational mythography into a "meta-rationality"[94] which acknowledges the partial validity of all modes of mythographical construction, integrating them into a more deeply differentiated mode of relation. This recognition is resonant not only with broadly constructivist theorists like Nietzsche, James, Bergson, Whitehead, Deleuze, and Stengers, but also, perhaps surprisingly, with archetypal thinkers like Jung and Hillman. In fact, the chapters below partially excavate an unexpected, almost secret, Jungian lineage at the heart of the major stream of French philosophy running from Bachelard and Simondon through Deleuze and Guattari.

In a conception especially congruent with Hillman, Derrida recognizes that metaphorical and figurative language are more profound than a literal nominalism reductively extracted from a deeper domain of differential relations. Derrida expresses logocentrism as a "heliocentric concept,"[95] referring not only to the Copernican revolution which, perhaps more than any other discovery, served as a symbolic enactment of the ascendance of egoic reason in modernity, but also to the Platonic association of the

Logos with the sun, the good, the intelligible, the king, and the father. This is an assemblage of correlations which evokes the mythologically derived Apollonian potency described by Nietzsche in concert with the figure of Kronos as explicated by Schelling, Jung, Hillman, and Deleuze and Guattari, serving to decenter this totalitarian expression of the solar potency in a novel polycentric mythical dialectic especially articulated by Deleuze, to which Derrida only briefly gestures as a mode beyond the dominance of rationalist philosophy and science, a logocentric dominance which organizes domains as varied as politics and the family, economics and diplomacy, agriculture and penal law. This mythically integrated dialectic is not a mere regression to a prescientific discursive mode prior to the emergence of philosophy with the pre-Socratics and Plato, but a novel approach, characteristic of both constructivist continental theory and depth psychology, which integrates the philosophical and scientific with the literary, poetic, and mythographic, a new mode of writing composing "a future epoch of différance"[96] variously expressed by all of the twentieth-century theorists below in its fully differentiated and nuanced complexity beyond the closure over which Derrida primarily presides.

## Notes

1. Derrida, *Grammatology*, lxxxix.
2. Derrida, *Grammatology*, 43, 46–7.
3. Derrida, *Grammatology*, lxxxix, 70, 246.
4. Derrida, *Grammatology*, 83, 158.
5. Deleuze, *Desert*, 190.
6. Derrida, *Grammatology*, 7.
7. Derrida, *Grammatology*, 14, 23–4.
8. Derrida, *Grammatology*, 24, 88.
9. Deleuze, *Difference*, 216, 251.
10. Derrida, *Grammatology*, lxxxix, 24.
11. Derrida, *Grammatology*, 61.
12. Derrida, *Gift*, 23.
13. Derrida, *Specters*, 2.
14. Derrida and Ferraris, *Taste*, 88.
15. Derrida, *Animal*, 4, 132.
16. Patton and Protevi, *Between*, 184.
17. Salmon, *Event*, 6.
18. Derrida, *Ear*, 142.
19. Deleuze, *Difference*, 2.
20. Derrida, *Grammatology*, 174.
21. Cisney, *Deleuze*, 13.
22. Salmon, *Event*, 127.

23 See Derrida, *Writing*, 193–4.
24 Derrida, *Gift*, 77; Derrida, *Grammatology*, 212, 215; Stengers, *Another*, 145.
25 Nietzsche, *Gay*, 99.
26 Deleuze and Guattari, *Anti-Oedipus*, 322.
27 Whitehead, *Science*, 2; Cf. Derrida, *Grammatology*, 257.
28 Derrida, *Grammatology*, 158.
29 Derrida, *Grammatology*, 50.
30 See Ricoeur, *Freud*.
31 Nietzsche, *Human*, 5.
32 Derrida, *Grammatology*, 19.
33 See Hippolyte, *Logic*, 8.
34 Plato, *Works*, 294.
35 Derrida, *Grammatology*, 9.
36 Derrida, *Grammatology*, 12.
37 Derrida, *Grammatology*, 4.
38 Derrida, *Grammatology*, 24.
39 Derrida, *Grammatology*, 60.
40 Derrida, *Grammatology*, 4.
41 Derrida, *Grammatology*, 14.
42 Derrida, *Grammatology*, 5.
43 Patton and Protevi, *Between*, 9.
44 Derrida, *Grammatology*, 100.
45 See Marshall, "Rousseau."
46 Derrida, *Grammatology*, 99.
47 Derrida, *Grammatology*, 109.
48 Derrida, *Grammatology*, 102.
49 Salmon, *Event*, 184.
50 Derrida, *Grammatology*, 102.
51 Derrida, *Grammatology*, 98.
52 Derrida, "Interview."
53 Salmon, *Event*, 19, 22, 24, 165.
54 Derrida, *Monolingualism*, 71–2.
55 Derrida, *Writing*, 390n4.
56 Derrida, *Grammatology*, 44.
57 Derrida, *Grammatology*, 162.
58 Deleuze, *Foucault*, 89; Deleuze, *Bacon*, 134.
59 Derrida, *Grammatology*, 61.
60 Derrida, *Grammatology*, 314.
61 Derrida, *Grammatology*, 20.
62 Derrida, *Grammatology*, 157.
63 Deleuze and Parnet, *Dialogues*, viii, 39.
64 Derrida, *Grammatology*, 10.
65 Derrida, *Grammatology*, 26.
66 Derrida, *Grammatology*, 26.
67 Derrida, *Grammatology*, 44.
68 Derrida, *Grammatology*, 50.
69 Deleuze, *Desert*, 136, 139.

70 Deleuze, *Difference*, 195.
71 Derrida, *Grammatology*, 102.
72 Derrida, *Grammatology*, 50.
73 Derrida, *Grammatology*, 57.
74 Derrida, *Grammatology*, 45.
75 Deleuze, *Difference*, 116.
76 Deleuze, *Desert*, 36.
77 Derrida, *Grammatology*, 79.
78 Derrida, *Grammatology*, 73.
79 Derrida, *Grammatology*, 40.
80 Deleuze, *Desert*, 13.
81 Derrida, *Grammatology*, 85.
82 Derrida, *Grammatology*, 63.
83 Derrida, *Grammatology*, 71.
84 Derrida, *Grammatology*, 74.
85 Derrida, *Grammatology*, 65.
86 Deleuze, *Desert*, 75; Deleuze, *Negotiations*, 137.
87 Deleuze, *Letters*, 78.
88 Derrida, *Grammatology*, 75.
89 Derrida, *Grammatology*, 72.
90 Derrida, *Grammatology*, 131.
91 Derrida, *Grammatology*, 85.
92 Derrida, *Grammatology*, 86.
93 Salmon, *Event*, 186–7.
94 Derrida, *Grammatology*, 87.
95 Derrida, *Grammatology*, 91.
96 Derrida, *Grammatology*, 93.

Chapter 2

# Freedom of Mind

Baruch Spinoza's *Ethics*

Bergson quipped that "every philosopher has two philosophies: his own and Spinoza's,"[1] implying that although the Dutch philosopher's thought is deceptively simple to a surface reading, his work "is not what it seems at first glance,"[2] as Deleuze writes, containing a mysterious depth, especially his concepts of freedom of mind and of immanence, which Deleuze calls "the vertigo of philosophy,"[3] a paradoxical disorientation that eludes conceptual purchase, and which impelled not only Bergson and Deleuze, but Leibniz, Hegel, Nietzsche, Schelling, James, Whitehead, and Stengers to engage with his concepts, even when they disagreed with them. Leibniz wrote of Spinoza's metaphysics that it is "strange and full of paradoxes," though he deeply respected Spinoza, with whom he spent several days in 1676, the year before Spinoza's death and the publication of the *Ethics*.[4] And although Hegel was profoundly influenced by Spinoza, proclaiming that "you are either a Spinozist or not a philosopher at all,"[5] he was dissatisfied with the concept of univocity which lacks the negative, judging that Leibniz's work "outwardly integrates Spinoza's system"[6] through the differentiation of monadic individuality, an integration paving the way toward the Hegelian dialectic as well as its overcoming in the integration of the central concepts of both Spinoza and Leibniz, especially in Deleuze. This overcoming of Hegel, which required Hegel's dialectic as an opening to a novel mode of thought, was largely initiated by Nietzsche who, upon first reading Spinoza in 1881, wrote to a friend: "I am really amazed, really delighted! I have a precursor!"[7] – although he acknowledges their significant differences.

James writes that there is a "healthy-mindedness woven into the heart of"[8] Spinoza's thought, which partially accounts for its enigmatic allure, and Whitehead offers that although the direct philosophical successors to Descartes are Locke, Berkeley, Hume, and Kant, "two great names lie outside this list, Spinoza and Leibniz," as although they were two immediate successors to Descartes, they both "strayed to extremes which lie outside the boundaries of safe philosophy," creating concepts that have allowed subsequent philosophers to think beyond the conventional rationalism of modern thought. Even as brilliant and enigmatic a figure as Derrida does not know what to make of the assertion of pure immanence by Deleuze, adopted from Spinoza, writing of an imagined conversation with his contemporary, who had just passed, that his primary question for Deleuze would concern "the word 'immanence' on which he always insisted, in order to make him or let him say something that no doubt still remains secret to us."[9] Deleuze and Guattari explicitly equate Spinozan immanence with Artaud's notoriously elusive concept of the body without organs,[10] and also with the Tao whose ultimate reality eludes verbal expression, and thus we may temporarily take comfort in the recognition that even Derrida did not quite understand what Spinoza and Deleuze meant in their assertion of this concept, though it may become clearer over the course of this narrative.

Spinoza, followed by Deleuze, overturns the oppositional privileging of transcendent over immanent characteristic of both the philosophical tradition derived from Plato and of Christianity in order to assert that "God is the immanent," as opposed to the transcendent, "cause of all things," though the monotheistic divinity is deemphasized by Deleuze's expression of immanence.[11] This is perhaps a necessary but transitional reversal for, as with most concepts expressed through language, immanence is unintelligible without its opposite in relation to which it must be defined, a concept of the transcendent to which it can be immanent. However, the essential innovation somewhat obscurely proffered by Spinoza, and brought to its most subtle and complex formulation by Deleuze, which Deleuze nominates a "transcendental empiricism," is that the transcendent has been a necessary concept which is nevertheless unknowable and unthinkable, a placeholder for that which subsists at an "always receding cosmological horizon."[12] An experience of what seems to be a transcendent domain always occurs within immanence, as any experience that can be had is had immanently, a fold in a univocal manifold operative in dimensions beyond the four familiar axes of spacetime so that, like a Möbius strip,[13] the inside is always continuous with the outside, thereby dissolving the duality,[14] and thus, as Deleuze writes in his first book, "the question is no longer about transcendence but rather about integration."[15] As soon as an experience or a concept passes from an indiscernible zone into discernibility, it is already immanent, with the putatively transcendent located just past an eternally pursued horizon of knowability.[16]

Like all of the verbal concepts discussed in these pages, it is necessary to tease apart the positive affirmation of the immanent as the world's univocity from the negative denial of the transcendent, a denial which has been contextually necessary for the differentiation of immanence from the hegemony of transcendence, but which perhaps can now be seen, despite Deleuze's implicit objections discussed at length and rendered explicit below, as the dialectical negative that allowed this further step to be taken. The negation of the transcendent forms the negative space within the differentiated structure that can carry us beyond the fixed duality of immanent and transcendent, integrating them in what can be described as a transcendental immanence. In fact, this is what Deleuze generally contends, explicitly stating that "immanence is constructivism,"[17] and the duality of immanent and transcendent itself is constructed from a more profound univocity, though this aspect of his work is often misunderstood, in part because he was in the process of formulating this novel conceptual mode and thus, like all true pioneers, was sometimes inconsistent, and often obscure.[18]

The concept of pure immanence may be considered a kind of sleight-of-hand, an erasure of the transcendent which leaves a smudged blank space, as the concept of immanence, by its very definition, is only thinkable in relation to a concept of transcendence, though the attempt to think pure immanence has not merely been an error that could have been avoided, but is rather a dialectical tarrying with the negative deeply resonant with the unmistakably dialectical attempt to reject the Hegelian dialectic itself, hence its vertiginous quality. The word immanence requires opposition to a transcendent conceptuality for its very definition, so asserting pure immanence can only be a transitional reversal that always implicitly refers to a hidden, crossed-out transcendent,[19] a problematic dualism which the lineage running through Spinoza and Deleuze dissolves with the assistance of the Kantian concept of the transcendental.[20] Whereas the transcendent posits a higher, static, eternal domain beyond a horizon of conception, as in the Platonic world of Forms or the Christian Heaven, the transcendental concept constitutes the recognition that any conception of the transcendent is always already immanent because that conception is occurring in mind and language which are immanent in the world – there can be no other "world" than the open totality described by this word – and thus the domain beyond a horizon of conception can only be envisaged as a virtual potentiality not yet expressed in actuality, though its actualization is the means by which the horizon recedes.

The problem of immanence derived from Spinoza is intimately related to the metaphysical correlate of the Leibnizian calculus based on the concept of the infinitesimal, as the transcendental is the always-receding horizon of conception, which our novel modes of thought and language continue to push back or pursue, two spatial descriptions for a phenomenon that exceeds either activity, but which we can never cross. This horizon itself is our consciousness and its constructive elicitation of the world, so although consciousness can transcend its current horizon, and thus can potentially be expanded and involuted into infinite folds of infinite dimension, consciousness can never cross the always-receding horizon to a given transcendent domain, as transcendence is an activity, not a location. The problem of immanence may find its culmination in the integration of Leibnizian metaphysical integration with the conception of virtual dynamic potencies expressed especially by Schelling, Nietzsche, Jung, and Hillman, an integration most closely approached by Deleuze in a mythical dialectic, although this mode of thought has required the intervening centuries and their increasingly complex controversies to begin to come to fruition, for as Spinoza concludes the *Ethics*: "All things excellent are as difficult as they are rare."[21]

Spinoza circulates around oppositions, not only of transcendent and immanent, but of joyful and sad affects, of efficient and final causation, and of determinism and freedom, spiraling in upon a mode of thought which overcomes these differentiating binaries in an always-already integrated univocity of being, so that "this union of bodies,"[22] both organismic and otherwise, is conceived as composing an infinite multiplicity of variations enacted through complexly intertwining trajectories and speeds.[23] For Spinoza, contra Cartesian dualism, the human mind and body are two envisagements of the same unified individuality, for which the mind is the intensive aspect and the body is the extensive aspect, and the mind is itself the "idea of the mind,"[24] the recursive, involuted awareness of itself as an embodied mentality, so that it might be said that consciousness is always already self-consciousness. And it follows from this intertwined unity of mind and body that the more versatile and capable the body is in its affective motivity, the more the mind can perceive and conceive. Spinoza suggests that all of the ideas which occur in the mind-body complex are ultimately true "insofar as they are related to God,"[25] because like the unity of mind and body, God is the world itself rather than a being transcendent to the world – Spinoza's most controversial doctrine of pantheism, for which he was unjustly accused of atheism, and which is the primary reason he did not publish the *Ethics* during his lifetime.

For those of us in the twenty-first century who are accustomed to such a generally secular conception, which Spinoza played a large role in creating, the most striking and enigmatic result of this unity of God and world is that every idea is ultimately an affirmation, and that falsity is the affirmation of an idea which contradicts another idea that was previously affirmed. In this conception, falsity and error are not things which positively exist, but are rather the result of the inadequate expression of ideas through language. Controversies between apparently opposed or incommensurable modes of thought are generally the result of misunderstanding and confusion, of one or both of the parties to the disagreement not attending closely enough to the subtle nuances of the words employed in articulating the concepts, to the conceptual complexes which the words can only asymptotically approach. It may even be the case that language does not yet exist which is complexly differentiated enough to discern the interstices where the binary conflict dissolves, leading ultimately to a deeper coherence constituted from the contrasting elements, a conceptual language which it is the collective project of all of the theorists discussed in these pages to create. For Spinoza, this movement toward greater understanding is not merely an abstract philosophical exercise, but the way in which a society composed of individuals can mitigate discord, which Spinoza associates with evil, and harmoniously coexist, which is his definition of the good. Even in cases for which opposition and incommensurability appear insurmountable, they remain contrasting entities in the totality of relations, sometimes as dualities reconciled in a transformative third element, as in the Hegelian dialectic, but more often opening out into a pluralistic multiplicity of relations in more expansive topological manifolds.[26]

Spinoza delineates this process of coming to greater understanding as progressing through three kinds of knowledge: the first is imagination and opinion, the second is the common notions and adequate ideas of reason, and the third is intuition, which discerns the formal essences of the things that constitute the world. Imagination is the affective precondition for knowledge, though it is not yet differentiated into the dualistic light of truth and the accompanying shadow of falsity characteristic of reason, which itself is the precondition for an intuitive knowledge higher than imagination and reason, which most of the theorists below will conceive as subsuming the first two modes of relation in its emergent efficacy. One of Spinoza's greatest contributions is to have integrated mind and body, thoughts and affects, reason and imagination, as different attributes of a single, univocal substance accessible to intuition, which Descartes had sundered as his opening, differentiating gambit.[27]

But Spinoza's theory of the affects remains primarily dualistic even in its assertion of univocity, though there are many complex permutations of this dualism, either an affirmative joy which composes variously expressed as love, wonder, hope, and confidence, or a negative sadness which decomposes expressed as hate, anger, fear, and envy – a binarity of good pleasure leading to a greater perfection or evil pain leading to a lesser perfection, though he also posits desire as a third primary affect which lures us toward becoming in the form of striving, impulse, appetite, and volition, a positing especially relevant to his causal theory. There is much truth in this primarily dualistic construction of the bodily affections, which allowed the modern mind to think philosophically about affect for the first time in any depth, though for a twenty-first century sensibility informed by depth psychology and modernist literature, the *Ethics* can often seem like an artificial intelligence attempting to comprehend human emotions, and only partially succeeding, though all of the post-Hegelian philosophers discussed in the chapters below have contributed to the development of a more geometrically complex and pluralist theory of affect for which Spinoza's theory created a primary precondition.

Spinoza recognizes that affects are subjective modes, so that different human bodies are affected in different ways by encounters with the same things, and when these encountered objects are external to us, they are constructed as images accessible to imagination. Memory is constituted in the relational interconnection of these external images as ideas that correlate with internal affections which, unlike Cartesian reason, are confused as long as they are discerned only in the mind, so that attention to internal affect, "the duration of our body," is required to render ideas "clear and distinct"[28] as they are constructed for that particular body and its network of relations to other bodies. Deleuze writes that Spinoza's "entire philosophy is a philosophy of 'potentia,'"[29] as the affects are real potencies, singular forces or necessities which we encounter in ourselves and with which we must contend, choosing how to relate to them through the moderating power of the mind, liberating the body into free activity through adequate ideas of the affects, or otherwise allowing them to rule us in passive bondage as mere passions because of inadequate ideas. Affects are undeniable bodily and imaginal realities which cannot be merely repressed or eliminated, but which can be counteracted by opposite affects, so that if a sad affect predominates, a joyful affect may be intellectually (i.e., consciously) cultivated in order to render our bodies and minds active. The more we become conscious of the affects in their complex differentiation, the more active we become in their expression, which is practically unlimited, as "no one has yet determined what the body can do,"[30] Spinoza recognizing a radical openness to novel domains of experience and activity that Nietzsche would later embody in the figure of the Overman, a recognition, variously evoked by all of the theorists below, that humanity is undergoing a process of transformation into more profoundly individuated modes of existence that have not yet been actualized.

Substance is that which exists in itself, while intellect perceives the essential forms of substances, affections express the modes of substances, and God is the infinite substance with infinite attributes expressing an infinite essence. While two substances can have completely different attributes, and thus have no point of connection in experience, the substances and attributes are always already integrated in the essential unity of the world, and thus of God, for whom the apparently irreconcilable differences of incommensurable attributes and discordant affects compose the contrasting internal elements. All substances, all of the things which constitute the world, are infinite in that the cause of their being recedes infinitely toward a transcendental divinity which is never finally attainable, but which is the cause of everything. Efficient and formal causation are two immanent modalities of a single essential substance, two finite descriptions of an infinite God as a self-causing cause, and thus the finite expressions of God are affirmations of the infinite essence, but they are negative in what they exclude or deny in service to their differentiation, while the transcendental divine which they eternally approach is pure affirmation. And the more perfectly beings approach the infinite, essential substance, the more of reality they express, and therefore the more attributes and potency they evince. God is both the efficient and formal cause of everything that exists, two finite modes of thought, two parallel ways of expressing the singular divine potency, so that "the order and connection of ideas is the same as the order and connection of things."[31] Deleuze, both with and without Guattari, designates this as a radical approach, for which formal and efficient causation, intensive idea and extensive substance, are two immanent modes of expression for a unified "species of eternity"[32] which exceeds them, and temporality itself, and thus the formal idea of the circle, for one example especially relevant to the calculus invented by Leibniz with its accompanying metaphysics, always recedes toward infinity as it is approached. And it is the same with the multiplicity of ideas which compose the human mind, which eternally recede toward the infinite, univocal substance at an always-unattainable transcendental horizon, and thus the mind is constituted in the self-knowing of the infinite formal ideas, corresponding acausally to the infinite essential substance in an absolute parallelism, which can be known by the third, intuitive kind of knowledge.[33]

While affirming material, efficient, and formal causation, Spinoza dismissively rejects final causes, though the final causation he rejects is the most naïve kind of teleology, more simplistic than the subtle, complex finality that finds its nascent expression in Leibniz, and that is refined by all of the theorists below. Spinoza's rejection of "radical finalism,"[34] Bergson's term for the more naïve form of teleology which assumes a fixed, pregiven end, may at first seem incompatible with his rejection of free will, as if the entire history of the universe is perfectly and mechanistically determined in advance by efficient causes, it is just as susceptible to explanation by radical finalism, for which the end must be just as static and eternal as the origin. For pure determinism, efficient and final causation are essentially equivalent, two modes of description for a fixed, eternal block universe which precludes real becoming, though Spinoza intimates a dissolution of the duality of these two kinds of causation even as he rejects teleology, a recognition which may provide the key to overcoming the often too-hasty objections to his rejection of free will in a novel mode of thought developed by most of the theorists below.

In fact, Spinoza rejects radical finalism in favor of something that looks remarkably like the inclinational form of teleology variously evoked by Leibniz and the others, for which the affects that constitute the will are determined, but the mind is free to choose at which register to express these affective potencies – a determinism of the will, but a "freedom of mind" – so that, for instance, one cannot choose whether or not to feel anger, but one can choose whether to express this affect destructively through violence or creatively through energetically directed physical or intellectual activity. This suggestion, that the disparate kinds of finalism conflated by Spinoza must be differentiated, is a precondition for integrating Spinoza's causal theory with all of the other theorists discussed below, even Nietzsche, despite his notorious inconsistency, who warns in *Beyond Good and Evil* against "*superfluous* teleological principles" like "the drive for self-preservation," a bemusing superfluity which he ironically traces back to "Spinoza's inconsistency" about final causation, while implicitly affirming the will to power as properly teleological, not primarily as a will to dominate, but as a will to potencies which demand to be expressed one way or another.[35] Deleuze writes, in an essay on Spinoza, that affects "make us conceive of suprasensible beings who would be their final cause,"[36] though as early as 1953 he writes, in his distinctly Bergsonian reading of Hume, that this "purposiveness is more an elan vital, and less the project or the design of an infinite intelligence."[37] Spinoza's heirs have thus refined and extended his causal theory, though Spinoza might reciprocally offer Bergson a more subtle kind of formal causation than the naïve, Platonic formal theory that Bergson rejects, so that one can discern Spinoza and Bergson as particularly complementing one another's limitations, constituted in what they deny, to allow the affirmation of more subtle theories of both formal and final causation than those they respectively reject.

The common conception of Spinoza as a pure determinist who simply denies freedom of choice is a reductive misinterpretation, though an understandable one given Spinoza's somewhat confusing inconsistency on this subject. Much of the *Ethics* is devoted to meditations on how one can choose to relate to the affects and, in fact, although Spinoza explicitly denies final causation and affirms efficient and formal causation, much of the book implicitly affirms a more subtle form of teleology as affective inclination, appetition, desire, temperament, and striving for self-preservation and understanding, which Spinoza defines as the essence of virtue, blessedness, and freedom of mind. Despite Spinoza's explicit rejection of teleology, this conception is resonant with the more profound reimagining of final causation affirmed by the other theorists, including Deleuze, perhaps Spinoza's most influential twentieth-century devotee, in his affirmation of a "destiny" which must be enacted in a lower or higher register, as opposed to a static and pregiven fate. If Spinoza's philosophy asserted the mechanistic determination of particular actualities, it would render all of his ideas about how one can choose to relate to affects moot, as these relations themselves would be predetermined in their particularity. Rather, it seems that Spinoza is rejecting the radical finalism characteristic of much ancient and medieval thought, which is practically indistinguishable from a determinism based solely on efficient causation for which all movements down to the smallest particle are predetermined for all time, in which case explanations based on efficient causation and radical finalism would be effectively equivalent.[38] Both kinds of causation would just be inverse modes of cognizing a universe whose moments always already exist as a fixed block for which there is no real becoming, and thus whether these moments are pushed from the past or pulled toward the future would ultimately be irrelevant, different ways of explaining the same static reality that would render these two causal modes practically identical.

Spinoza is evidently after something more profound and paradoxical than a mere mechanistic or fatalistic determinism, as he describes freedom as a being acting "from the necessity of its nature,"[39] from its formal essence, rather than from an external cause, which he defines as bondage. As Deleuze will render more explicit, the affects and the infinite formal potencies of which they are modes of expression are necessary and determined, but determining the ways in which those potencies and affects are expressed is the ultimate task of the individual, so that liberating oneself from the bondage of external causes through reason and knowledge of the affects in order to express one's essential nature is the primary activity of human life. The potent affects that constitute our being are determined, but the degree of consciousness that we bring to their moderate expression by means of adequate ideas, our more-or-less profound conceptual constructions, determines how they are expressed, whether through reactive hatred, envy, and resentment or active justice, fairness, and love.

For Spinoza, this freedom of mind to choose the particular expressions of affects is caused by God, who is the world in its totality and who himself lacks free will, but who is nevertheless not subject to fate,[40] so that it is the world as a whole which acts through us and which constitutes our being in a reciprocal relation between God and human, dissolving the usual opposition between freedom and determinism. This binary is merely a partial verbal construction of a reality which exceeds it, an insight brilliantly, if obscurely, proffered by Spinoza, as it would require several more centuries for others to create the language and concepts to bring this mode of thought into fuller actuality. In fact, although Spinoza writes that "all final causes are nothing but human fictions,"[41] some of his primary transtemporal peers, particularly Leibniz, Deleuze, and Stengers, have affirmed that reality in the specific forms in which we encounter it, like the calculus, is itself "a convenient and well-founded fiction,"[42] a constructivist mode of thought which Spinoza did a great deal to render thinkable, obliquely acknowledging that his conception is a "construction."[43] Deleuze suggests that "constructivist logic" specifically "finds its model in mathematics,"[44] and like the infinitesimal calculus which is central to both Leibnizian and Deleuzean metaphysics, Spinoza discerns that the divine immanent potency which causes the will to act is a transcendental domain of singular "metaphysical beings"[45] which can never be finally attained.

This divine cause infinitely recedes as we approach it and, as with the infinitesimal, which is greater than zero but less than any positive number, the mind inhabits a paradoxical interstice between determinism and freedom, Spinoza employing the word "choose" to describe his composition of this text, implicitly recognizing that we possess decisional freedom in regard to the particular expressions of the affectively determined will.[46] Like the syncategorematic quality of the infinitesimal calculus, which is potentially infinite rather than absolutely infinite, the potentially infinite mind effectively has freedom of choice, and is only determined in its abstract ontological definition located at an always-receding horizon with an "absolutely infinite"[47] God. Thus, the duality of determinism and freedom, like the dualities of finite and infinite or of continuity and discontinuity, is dissolved in this more profound conception, Spinoza presciently presaging the infinitesimal calculus several decades before its discovery by Leibniz. The freedom to choose how one relates to the affects operates in a recursive relationship with the affects that are acting on one's mind, as we can actively decide to attend to good things, for instance, in order to cultivate joy so that we may be reciprocally determined by that affect. In this paradoxical way, we are choosing, by means of attention, how the affects determine us.[48]

According to Spinoza, "all things have been determined from the necessity of the divine nature, not only to exist, but to exist in a certain way, and to produce effects in a certain way,"[49] but the particular expressions of this certain way – the word "way" evidently indicating a manner or mode of efficacy rather than a minutely specific given configuration – are variable and susceptible to the freedom of mind, though this freedom itself is paradoxically determined by the divine nature. The certain way in which everything occurs is determined, as "there is nothing contingent,"[50] though elsewhere Spinoza writes that "all particular things are contingent,"[51] a paradoxical contradiction which leads to the more profound conception that the particular actualities determined by certain ways of existing can be chosen through lower or higher registers of understanding, a Whiteheadian "slightest change of tone" intimating a dissolution of the oppositional duality of determinism and freedom that will find a more fully elaborated expression in Deleuze's conception of differential repetition. Each being is determined by its nature to act in a certain way, but the order of expression of this certain way is determined by the degree of that being's understanding, so that a person with a lesser understanding is acted upon by the affective modes of potencies that determine the will and demand to be brought into expression, while a person who strives to achieve a more elevated understanding has power over the particular expressions of the affectively determined will.[52]

The crux of the vexing question of Spinozan determinism is that determinate necessity is not primarily discerned through efficient causation, but especially in formal causation, as determination by formal necessity is open to free expression as long as the essential nature is expressed in some way, while efficient causation constitutes the more conventional kind of determinism in which each minutely particular act is caused by the actions of the previous moment, though these two causal modes are parallel, constituting two different constructions of temporality.[53] Spinoza emphasizes that duration is not determined by efficient causation, a mode of causal construction which itself presupposes a linear conception of temporality, but rather that "an indefinite duration" is transversally determined through formal causation.[54] A determination can be restrained by a recollected image or by the idea of freedom, for instance, so this is evidently not a mechanistic efficient determinism, but a formal determination in which an essential nature can be variously expressed through different particular acts,[55] formal causation constraining choice to an infinite variety of expressions within a thematic unity whose causal efficacy is transversal rather than linear. Efficient causation is a parallel surface effect of the deeper essential determination of the infinite divine potency demanding expression, and thus the affective will is determined, but the mind is free to choose the order and specificity of the actual expressions of its formal nature.[56]

## Notes

1 Quoted in Yovel, *Spinoza*, 5.
2 Deleuze, *Essays*, 138.
3 Deleuze, *Expressionism*, 180.
4 Antognazza, *Leibniz*, 168, 178; Jolley, *Leibniz*, 18.
5 Westphal, "Hegel," 144.
6 Hegel, *History* (Brown), 155.
7 Sue Prideaux, *Dynamite!* 185.
8 James, *Writings*, 121.
9 Derrida, "Wander."
10 Deleuze and Guattari, *Anti-Oedipus*, 327.

11 Spinoza, *Works*, 428.
12 Deleuze, *Cinema 2*, 17.
13 Deleuze, *Essays*, 21.
14 Deleuze, *Foucault*, 97.
15 Deleuze, *Empiricism*, 36.
16 Kerslake, *Unconscious*, 4–5.
17 Deleuze, *Negotiations*, 146.
18 Kerslake, *Unconscious*, 4–5.
19 Latour, *Fragments*, 33.
20 Deleuze, *Letters*, 88.
21 Kerslake, *Immanence*, 2; Spinoza, *Works*, 617.
22 Spinoza, *Works*, 460.
23 Deleuze, *Expressionism*, 236–7.
24 Spinoza, *Works*, 467.
25 Spinoza, *Works*, 472.
26 Deleuze, *Expressionism*, 248, 275, 335.
27 Deleuze, *Expressionism*, 223; Deleuze, *Desert*, 150, 153.
28 Spinoza, *Works*, 470–1.
29 Deleuze, *Two*, 191.
30 Spinoza, *Works*, 495.
31 Spinoza, *Works*, 597.
32 Spinoza, *Works*, 607.
33 Deleuze, *Spinoza*, 53–4; Deleuze and Guattari, *Thousand*, 253–4.
34 Bergson, *Evolution*, 45–50.
35 Nietzsche, *Beyond*, 15; Deleuze, *Two*, 205.
36 Deleuze, *Essays*, 139.
37 Deleuze, *Empiricism*, 77.
38 Spinoza, *Works*, 544.
39 Spinoza, *Works*, 409.
40 Spinoza, *Works*, 439.
41 Spinoza, *Works*, 442.
42 Deleuze, *Fold*, 110; Deleuze, *Empiricism*, 80; Antognazza, *Leibniz*, 430.
43 Spinoza, *Works*, 441.
44 Deleuze, *Empiricism*, 87.
45 Spinoza, *Works*, 483.
46 Spinoza, *Works*, 543, 615.
47 Spinoza, *Works*, 409.
48 Spinoza, *Works*, 601–2.
49 Spinoza, *Works*, 434.
50 Spinoza, *Works*, 434.
51 Spinoza, *Works*, 472.
52 Spinoza, *Works*, 558.
53 Spinoza, *Works*, 436.
54 Spinoza, *Works*, 447, 499.
55 Spinoza, *Works*, 520.
56 Spinoza, *Works*, 439.

# Chapter 3

# Well-Founded Fictions
## Gottfried Wilhelm Leibniz's *Monadology*

Academic journals were a new invention in Leibniz's time, and although he wrote several longer books, Leibniz preferred more concise formats, publishing some of his most profound ideas, including the calculus, in journals, and even in letters, maintaining a prolific correspondence. The *Monadology*, written in 1714, was composed in just such a novel manner, not in the form of a book, but in a brief series of highly concentrated notes meant to serve as the basis for a poem by one of his regular correspondents. And it is partially the fact that he did not intend it for publication that makes this text so fascinating, allowing him to express his vast vision of the world in condensed form, without the usual rhetorical concessions, copiously fulfilling his formulation of twenty-eight years earlier that "an intelligent author encloses the most of reality in the least possible compass."[1] The *Monadology* was startlingly novel when it was first published four years after Leibniz's death at the beginning of the Enlightenment, but we can now see in it a mode of thought that would come to be expressed in great depth, not in all its details, but in different valences of its general trajectory by Hegel, Schelling, Bergson, Whitehead, Deleuze, and Stengers, all of whom would explicitly engage with Leibniz's concepts. Schelling proclaims that, after what he portrays as the hollow and contemptible quality of scholastic theology, "it required nothing less than the entire stature of a Leibniz to partially restore philosophy's honor,"[2] Whitehead that Leibniz "really did inherit more of the varied thoughts of his predecessors than any man before or since,"[3] Stengers that Leibniz was "the philosopher who harmonized apparently contradictory points of view,"[4] and Deleuze that "perhaps no other philosopher created so much," that "one has to follow in Leibniz's footsteps," and thus "we all remain Leibnizian."[5]

DOI: 10.4324/9781003195498-4

Although Leibniz does not extensively discuss mathematics in the *Monadology*, the metaphysical system he outlines in this brief work is intimately coextensive with his conception of the calculus, a mathematical and conceptual narrative construction which Deleuze describes as "adequate to psychic mechanics where Newton's is operative for physical mechanics," so that "the difference between the two is as much metaphysical as it is mathematical."[6] The integral calculus, whose roots in the thought of Archimedes go much further back in history than the differential calculus, is thus deeply intertwined with the conceptual integration for which Leibniz was a primary modern initiator.[7] This philosophical integration is embodied in the Leibnizian *Calculemus* ("Let us calculate"), which Stengers recognizes as the singular Leibnizian slogan, not as an exhortation to measuring, adding, or comparing, but to "creating commensurability," to negotiating peaceful solutions to philosophical and practical controversies.[8]

This approach constitutes a mode of speculative philosophy that discerns a fundamental correlation of conceptual and mathematical domains, as Leibniz created his form of the calculus, distinguished from Newton's calculus particularly by the concept of the infinitesimal, during the same years he was developing his metaphysical system, and the two endeavors were part of what he conceived as a *scientia generalis* in which all domains of human knowledge could be integrated through analysis into fundamental concepts and their combinatorial synthesis, formally mirroring the structure of mathematical differentiation and integration. And this differentiating integration is intimately bound up with Leibniz's renewed conception of the substantial forms derived from Aristotle and the scholastics after their rejection by the Cartesians, but which Leibniz, like Spinoza, came to associate with the immanent active power of the *conatus*, the inclinational striving for which each physical body is constituted in an "aggregate of points" both containing and flowing from a metaphysical formal cause. Leibniz likened this epiphany to one who, "having wandered for a long time in a forest, suddenly emerges into an open field and against all hope finds himself back in the same place from which he had first strayed,"[9] an entrance into an interior labyrinth, and a dialectical return to discover the traditional conception of formal causes transformed through its resonance with the calculus.[10]

Furthermore, as Simon Duffy explains, the two forms of integration initiated by Newton and Leibniz, and developed by numerous others over the succeeding centuries, contain a fundamental difference which is essential for the conceptual form of integration propounded by Leibniz, who conceived of the integral calculus "as a method of summation in the form of series, rather than the canonical approach that treats integration as the inverse transformation of differentiation."[11] This canonical approach derived from Newton, which Deleuze and Guattari nominate "royal science,"[12] renders differentiation primary and integration merely a formal transformation of the procedure which divides a curve into ever-smaller linear segments to approximate the length of that curve. But whereas Newton ultimately settled into a conception of these segments as finite, Leibniz affirmed the concept of infinitesimals, the "well-founded fictions"[13] of intensive, potential magnitudes which are paradoxically less than any positive number but greater than zero. Although the increasingly divided linear segments can never become identical with the curve, they always approach it so that, in Leibniz's conception, infinitesimals are syncategorematic – potentially infinite rather than absolutely infinite in that they are always sufficiently miniscule to provide the solution to any given problem, always receding as they are approached. And thus, for all practical purposes, the integration of these infinitesimal segments is precisely equivalent to the curve, and their only difference from the curve itself is in their abstract definition, which can never be encountered in actuality, but is a horizon which always recedes as one approaches it. In fact, this form of the calculus, which was long denigrated in the primacy of the standard Newtonian formulation employing limits, but which reemerged as a deeper approach developed by Abraham Robinson in the twentieth century, would find perhaps its primary locus of efficacy in relation to nondifferentiable fractal geometry. Although standard analysis has been extraordinarily productive in the creation of the modern world, the nonstandard analysis which extends and makes rigorous the Leibnizian infinitesimal approach renders visible a richer cosmos saturated by a more expansive multiplicity of entities.[14] And this conception serves to integrate continuity and discontinuity, as the differentiation between the continuous curve and the differential analysis of that curve into discontinuous segments is maintained on one plane of description, but on another plane, they are effectively indistinguishable, and thus these two planes of conceptual description are themselves both differentiated and integrated by means of the metaphysical correlate of the mathematical method for the summation of series.[15]

In the *Theodicy*, Leibniz asserts that "ultimately one should not doubt for the sake of doubting: doubts should serve us as a gangway to get to the truth,"[16] a dictum that seems directly to answer the hermeneutics of suspicion which Derrida generally exemplified in its most subtle form.[17] Leibniz was largely unconstrained by doubt in the texts written in his sixties, including the *Monadology*, offering expansive and sweeping concepts about the nature of being resonant with the infinitesimal calculus, at the heart of which resides his theory of monads, a term employed by the Pythagoreans, derived from the Greek word for "unit," "atom," or "singularity," which embody the differentiated integration of efficient and final modes of causation. "The true atoms of nature," monads are simple, indivisible, imperishable, unalterable, unique substances created by God, which make up the world in all its profusion by aggregating into compound entities, though monads possess qualities, and relate to one another through their internal qualitative differences, which allow for change.[18] As Duffy observes, monads are the metaphysical correlate to the infinitesimals of the calculus, "indivisible unities whose reality provides a metaphysical foundation for matter while residing outside of the indefinite regress of parts within parts."[19]

Although monads cannot be affected by other monads, they are teleological entelechies which contain an active force of appetition luring continuous internal change, and thus within each infinitesimal monadic unity resides an affective and relational plurality that can nevertheless not be divided into component parts, which Leibniz terms perception, a non-mechanical mode of becoming. All monads mirror all other monads in the universe, and are thus pervasively interconnected,[20] which Hegel describes as the "great thought" of monadic perception, "the intellectuality of all things,"[21] though he seems to have meant something closer to what we would understand as the potential for mind in felt relationality, which would find perhaps its most direct descendent in Whitehead's concept of prehension. Composites of monads, constituted in their affective, differential relationality, are organic or divine machines, each of the parts of which are also organic machines, unmistakably fractal gardens within gardens, fishponds within fishponds, receding through series of infinitely minute compound entities, with all of reality vital and organismic at all levels, and all bodies in constant flux. Leibniz goes so far as to assert that no organic entity is ever really generated or annihilated, but rather that death is merely an enfolding back into the organic, affective relationality that constitutes the world, and that birth is a transformation into a higher order in a continuation of perpetual development. Out of the pre-mental affective perceptions of these compound organic, divine machines can potentially emerge apperception, the consciousness of rational human souls or minds, from the deep sleep of unconscious monadic perception, and from the unconsciousness of animal composites. These minds are characterized by memory and reflexive self-awareness, and they are uniquely capable of discerning eternal truths, which are formal ideas in the mind of God, as our minds mirror the infinite divinity by virtue of universal monadic interconnection.

Implicit in this description of monads and their relations is the duality of efficient and final causation, which forms a site of integration. Efficient causes are constituted in the infinite motions of material objects and their physical relations, while final causes are the infinite inclinations of all entities toward particular directions of temporal becoming, though the ends are not predetermined, but are rather tendencies for ingression, a subtle reframing of teleology that allows Leibniz, much like Spinoza despite his apparently opposed view on this subject, to reconcile final causation and freedom of choice, though not of the will. The soul follows the laws of final causes, while the body follows the laws of efficient causes, and although these two causal domains are apparently independent, they are perfectly correlated with one another through a preestablished harmony, an accord which renders final and efficient causation as two equally efficacious explanatory modes for the intensive and extensive aspects of a single reality. Most of the theorists below extend and refine this multicausal theory in relation to a more subtle conception of final causes as inclinational tendencies rather than as pregiven ends, as well as of formal causes as dynamic relational potentialities and constraints rather than static transcendent forms.

Leibniz asserts that there are infinite worlds, and he was perhaps justifiably satirized by Voltaire for his extreme optimism that God has chosen "the best of all possible worlds,"[22] an assertion which Hegel calls "lame and wearisome,"[23] Whitehead designates "an audacious fudge produced in order to save the face of a Creator,"[24] and Deleuze finds "really strange,"[25] despite the deep admiration all three philosophers express for their mutual precursor in other respects. This optimization hypothesis is an overgeneralization of the principle of least action, so it is understandable that Leibniz might have gotten carried away in his extrapolation of this limited optimization of refracted trajectories to the world in general given the primary role he played in explaining this phenomenon through the calculus, and Whitehead, the mathematician-turned-philosopher, would explicitly reframe the principle of preestablished harmony in a deeper register beyond universal optimization.[26] Leibniz differentiated between absolute and contingent necessity by means of the concept of the infinitesimal central to the calculus: the absolute necessity of reality is the infinity knowable only to God, while humans can only approach this absolute through integration. However, as with the syncategorematic quality of the Leibnizian calculus, this is apparently a distinction without a difference because the infinitesimally differentiated elements can always be further subdivided so that their discreteness becomes irrelevant at the scale of any given process, and the two kinds of necessity can always be rendered effectively equivalent, and only abstractly differentiated by virtue of their respective continuity and discreteness, though their domain of difference is an always-receding horizon. In this way, the very opposition between the infinite and the finite is integrated in the emergent actuality of a metaphysical operation which precisely mirrors the calculus, but which nevertheless maintains the differentiation of mathematics and metaphysics.[27]

For Leibniz, much like Spinoza, humans act with freedom according to their nature, but their nature is determined in an ultimately unreachable infinite domain by God, a paradox which is resolved through conceptual integration, but which also does not require the overgeneralized optimization hypothesis. Monads each inhabit a different perspective on the world, and the infinite multiplicity of worlds is really constituted in different, incompossible points of view of one universe, like views of a town from every possible location. And thus the infinite differential relations of affective monadic multiplicity find integration in this radically perspectival theory of reality, which contains both the pluralism of infinite possible worlds and the monism for which each world is a different view of a single plenum, in which everything is alive and constantly changing, and in which everything relates to everything else through pervasive interconnection, though each soul only distinctly enfolds certain relations, while others are indistinct, fading off into a shadowy penumbra, and the higher the soul, the more of reality it enfolds.[28]

## Notes

1 Leibniz, *Discourse*, 5.
2 Schelling, *Grounding*, 97.
3 Whitehead, *Modes*, 3.
4 Stengers, *Cosmopolitics I*, 99.
5 Deleuze, *Negotiations*, 154–5; Deleuze, *Fold*, 158.
6 Deleuze, *Fold*, 112.

7 Strogatz, *Infinite*, 89.
8 Stengers, *Cosmopolitics II*, 399–401.
9 Antognazza, *Leibniz*, 251–2.
10 Duffy, *Mathematics*, 3.
11 Duffy, *Mathematics*, 162.
12 Deleuze and Guattari, *Thousand*, 363.
13 Antognazza, *Leibniz*, 430.
14 Duffy, *Mathematics*, 15.
15 See Stanford Encyclopedia of Philosophy, "Continuity"; Duffy, *Mathematics*, 12, 15, 32, 35, 38.
16 Leibniz, *Monadology*, 245.
17 Derrida, *Memoires*, 259.
18 Leibniz, *Monadology*, 14–15.
19 Duffy, *Mathematics*, 39.
20 Leibniz, *Monadology*, 25.
21 Hegel, *History* (Haldane), 335.
22 Voltaire, *Candide*.
23 Hegel, *History* (Haldane), 340.
24 Whitehead, *Process*, 47.
25 Deleuze, *Fold*, 77.
26 Strogatz, *Infinite*, 118; Whitehead, *Process*, 27; Stengers, *Thinking*, 279.
27 Antognazza, *Leibniz*, 254–5; Duffy, *Mathematics*, 33.
28 Leibniz, *Monadology*, 24–6; Duffy, *Mathematics*, 33.

Chapter 4

# The Life of the Whole

## G.W.F. Hegel's *On Scientific Cognition*

Hegel published *The Phenomenology of Spirit*, to which "On Scientific Cognition" is the Preface, in 1807, three years after Kant's death, definitively taking up the mantle of German idealism through the intermediaries of Fichte and Schelling. His complex relationship with his friend and rival Schelling is discussed in the chapter on the slightly younger philosopher below, and Hegel was deeply influenced by both Spinoza and Leibniz, Schelling writing that Hegel's "entire system is Spinoza's translated into idealism."[1] Hegel's expression, in 1812's *The Science of Logic*, of affects "as independent forces and powers" constituting the essential character of the will, while thought constitutes the domain of freedom,[2] is indeed remarkably resonant with Spinoza given the Dutch philosopher's primary influence on Nietzsche and Deleuze, especially considering Deleuze's notoriously scathing critiques of Hegel. Hegel's ambition throughout his twenties was to be a "popular philosopher," and it was only in his thirties, largely under the influence of his friend Friedrich Hölderlin, that Hegel developed his more complex and difficult style, which he thought was necessary to push the concepts expressible by the current language to their limit,[3] ultimately becoming the "towering Master,"[4] as Slavoj Žižek writes, Marx's "mighty thinker"[5] in relation to whom much subsequent philosophy has defined itself. Hegel's thought was so dominant in the nineteenth century that it can seem almost commonsensical, despite the extreme complexity of Hegel's writing, to a sensibility informed by twentieth-century continental philosophy, though this dialectical conception was radically novel two centuries ago. The sense of self-evidence which the Hegelian dialectic may elicit in some readers is a testament to its extraordinary success and ubiquity, though Hegel's texts are amenable to infinite interpretation, so although Hegel's work constitutes a profoundly influential and indispensable opening to an integrative mode of thought, it is certainly not the final expression of such a mode, which must perhaps always be reserved for some future theorist.

While it is not necessary to enter fully into the legitimate critiques of Hegel in this chapter, as he will receive copious criticism below, especially from Schelling, James, and Deleuze, it does seem opportune to mention Hegel's relation to the calculus, which he discusses in *The Science of Logic*. Hegel, like Leibniz, conceived of his metaphysical system as intimately related to the calculus, though he employs the more conventional version of the integral calculus derived from Newton, which constructs integration as merely the inverse transformation of differentiation rather than as a method for the summation of series, an approach which resides at the heart of Deleuze's differential philosophy.[6] However, this employment by Hegel of the more standard version of the calculus does not render the dialectic invalid, but allows for a different, and perhaps complementary, metaphysical construction. Although the Deleuzean metaphysics based upon the Leibnizian infinitesimal calculus may be more profound than the Hegelian metaphysics based on the conventional Newtonian construction, despite Leibniz's considerable influence on Hegel, the dialectic remains a profoundly useful mode of thought, echoing the limited and approximate character of Newtonian dynamics in the twenty-first century, a mode surprisingly resonant even with the theorists who are most critical of Hegel, so that the reconciliation of opposites can eventually be resituated as a special case of the integration of all kinds of difference, including opposition.[7]

Hegel spends the nearly six-hundred pages of the *Phenomenology*, of which the Preface was the last section composed – forty-five pages that Jean Hippolyte, the French translator of this text, nominates as "perhaps the best statement of Hegelian philosophy"[8] – elucidating a dialectical logic closer to the multivalent concept of Logos than to the formal logic of analytic philosophy, an organismic logic of growth, becoming, and transformation that evokes domains of process across scale that exceed the Aristotelian *tertium non datur*, the law of excluded middle demanding either-or answers to problematic questions. And in fact, the smooth infinitesimal analysis developed in the 1960s would ultimately demonstrate the limits of this law mathematically, though Hegel is ironically critical of the concept of the infinitesimal.[9] In the *Logic*, Hegel critiques the classic formulation of the dialectic as thesis, antithesis, and synthesis articulated by

Fichte, writing that "the name of synthesis, of synthetic unity, has rightly gone out of use."[10] Nevertheless, he describes a movement in which an initial entity – for which consciousness is the primary order of attention in the *Phenomenology*, but also chemical reactions, organisms, philosophies, or social movements – produces its own opposite, like a male child born from the mother's body, and then the opposition, through long, complex tension, eventually generates a reconciliation, out of which a novel emergent entity is born. Hegel warns that this triune structure must not be "reduced to a lifeless schema, a mere shadow," but must be conceived in its multifarious vitality instead of as a Procrustean formula into which one can cram the concrete details of experience.[11]

In Hegel's time as in ours, the conventional orthodoxy of philosophical thought often stakes out oppositional positions, schools defined against other schools, becoming "fixated on the antithesis of truth and falsity," attempting logically and rationally to determine if one definite claim or its opposite is true, whether manifested in the opposition of materialism and idealism, or monism and pluralism. The assumption underlying this still-predominant mode of philosophical activity is that if one's argument is strong enough, the critique of one's opponent sufficiently devastating, then one can hope to defeat one's adversary, so that a system of philosophy can either be proven as true or rejected as merely false through logical combat.[12] However, Hegel understood that whenever one school of thought seems finally to have demolished its opposing school, to have salted its fields and left no one standing, a small bud inevitably blooms forth that eventually, often cultivated in some obscure corner, comes raging back to life, rising up to challenge its hoary adversary once again in a new form. It may even be claimed that every controversy in philosophical thought finds its origin, at least in germ, in the work of ancient philosophers, leading back to a Deleuzean "dark precursor,"[13] so that these conflicts between opposed conceptual systems never seem completely to be resolved, eternally returning in increasingly subtle and vexing ways.[14]

Hegel sought a larger coherence for which the full array of philosophical systems is not categorized and prepackaged as mere oppositional disagreement, but rather traces "the progressive unfolding of truth,"[15] a vital, organismic process figured in the bud that "disappears in the bursting-forth of the blossom," for which the fixed entity that we call "bud" no longer exists, and in its place is a different entity known by the word "blossom." For the conventional logical mode, "one might say that the former is refuted by the latter," that the blossom negates the bud's existence and that the two forms are simply incompatible, though this way of thinking is obviously absurd, as we know that the bud becomes the blossom, is the precondition for the blossom's emergence, and that they are both the same plant in different guises, at different stages of their becoming. But for traditional modes of logic based on the *tertium non datur*, how could one explain that where there was a bud, now there is a blossom?[16] Hegel recognized that conventional logic is inadequate for describing the living reality in which we are immersed, and provided an alternative to this logical mode that had become so characteristic of philosophical thought by the early nineteenth century, and which is in fact still largely dominant in analytic philosophy, though this dominance may be waning, for one primary instance in Robert Brandom's work on Hegel.[17] For Hegel, it is partially true that blossom negates bud, but it is also true that one flows into the other as a continuous unity for which they are not opposed but mutually necessary, so that the moments of an organismic process can be in real opposition on one level of description while also containing, and being contained within, a deeper complementarity in which they are essential moments in a process of becoming, and in which "this mutual necessity alone constitutes the life of the whole." This process of transformation and becoming occurs in domains across scale, from the conception, birth, and development of an organism, to the psychological development of an individual, to the philosophical development of a concept, to the complex becomings of social, political, scientific, and religious movements.[18]

Even the development of the concept of dialectic itself is mediated through a dialectical process as, for Hegel, it is naïve and inexperienced philosophers who think primarily through oppositions, who seek to define themselves against some alternate philosophical school.[19] But this opposition is also characteristic of a certain stage of culture, which reiterates (in a way that Hegel might have called "fractal" if that geometry had existed in his time) the development of individuals, who necessarily progress along the same successively organized "formative stages"[20] through which the developmental process of history has already passed. Not only must each philosopher begin their career by defining themself against an opposed philosophy, but Hegel also discerns this oppositional mode, characteristic of what we might recognize as an exclusivist modern rationality defined by its disqualification of nonrational modes, as a stage in a process of becoming. Hegel can thus be understood, along with Spinoza and Leibniz, as a primary initiator of the mode of thought that would inevitably come after the modern: not "postmodernism" as exemplified by Derridean deconstruction, which may be understood as a clearing of the stage (or perhaps a dismantling of the stage itself), but a novel mode that does not name itself as coming after what it supplants, rather absorbing the modern into a more expansive mode with its own original nomination, enabled by the transitional postmodern dissolution, as Newtonian mechanics would become a special case of relativity. Each individual must pass through a microcosm of the trajectory undertaken by human culture, rediscovering the stages through which culture has already passed on a path "made level with toil,"[21] so that the many philosophers, perhaps still the majority, who engage primarily in the oppositional, exclusively rationalist mode of thought, are enacting the refinement of a necessary stage of process that Hegel indicates the way beyond, distilling this mode down to its essence in preparation for integration with more characteristically nonmodern modes of thought.

Dialectical logic describes the movements of vital processes across scale, so that organisms, individual consciousnesses, social movements, and philosophies begin with an undifferentiated unity, a potential subject that becomes actual through a self-positing, through the movement of exceeding its originary simple unity, itself the result of a previous dialectical process, and relating to itself in a self-othering which mediates a relational becoming.[22] For example, an infant's consciousness, initially containing no self-awareness, an undivided unity of pure sensation, is teleologically impelled to become aware of itself as an entity separate from the world it encounters. This self becoming conscious of itself is constituted in a negation of the original unity of consciousness which, like the bud, is lost in the blooming awareness of the child, constituting an oppositional doubling so that as we age, we relate to the initial, pure self in various ways, at first simply becoming conscious that we are a being with various sensations and impulses, and then learning to relate to that originary self as an other.[23] Through this self-relational reflection, the initial, undifferentiated self is transformed in reciprocal negotiation with self-consciousness of its own internal otherness, as the truth of this process is not found in the originary unity, but in the process of reconciling the self that observes with the self that simply is prior to observation, mediating its becoming through a "circle that presupposes its end as its goal, having its end also as its beginning; and only by being worked out to its end, is it actual."[24] This dialectical process is the movement of pure potentiality becoming actual, the relational tension of the original self with its own self-consciousness, or of the philosophical movement with its antithetical movement, which transforms the entity emerging from this relation, whether the individual person or the philosophical milieu.

Applying Hegelian terms to a movement that came long after him, but which he seems to have intimated in its broad outlines, deconstruction is an almost pure expression of the negative, a negativity beyond even the Hegelian negative, the moment in the dialectic when the original unity, the modern, rationalist, logocentric mode of thought, itself the product of an earlier dialectical process, becomes other than itself and rejects its original being, going deeply into the domains of reality that the initial positing had repressed. Hegel describes this stage of the dialectic as "tarrying with the negative," and we can recognize deconstruction as the "utter dismemberment" of privileging oppositions, including the opposition of unity and oppositionality itself. Deconstruction has carried the oppositional mode characteristic of modern rationality to its logical conclusion, employing this mode against itself, enacting the Hegelian negative in the death of the modern for which deconstruction is both the completion and the dissolution.[25]

However, Hegel understands that this death is not a closure whose complementary opening into a novel epoch cannot be written, as it seems to Derrida, as only the death of one stage of a process can lead to a rebirth, and renascence is always the product of an integration of moments which were previously incommensurable, so that Hegel can write that "this tarrying with the negative is the magical power that converts it into being."[26] It is the encounter with the negative other that mediates the originary positing's ingression from potentiality into actuality, a spiral circulation that, for instance, impels children to differentiate from their parents, the familiar adolescent rebellion that allows the child to become an individual in their own right rather than merely an extension of the family. And though there are those who never exceed this stage of differentiation, of the rejection and critique of the family from which they emerged, the individual can only become a mature adult by reconciling with their parents, or at least their *imago* (to smuggle in a Jungian term), after having rebelled against them, for as long as they define themselves against their parents, they are still in their thrall, still being psychologically dominated by what they reject, still clinging to a partial view of reality against its opposite conception.

This circular reconciliation or sublation is paradoxically a liberation from the original familial matrix through an embrace of the partial validity of that originary mode by an individuated self, "the whole which, having traversed its content in time and space, has returned into itself,"[27] transformed by this process of differentiation and reintegration, attaining an emergent wholeness that contains the partiality of both the original simplicity and its antithetical negation, both theism and atheism to frame the dialectic in religious terms. The result of this long process of differentiation and reconciliation is a mature truth more profound than the initial simplicity, though the final form of the sublation is not the "real" form of the initial potentiality any more than is the original positing.[28] The truth of an entity is not to be found only in the origin or end of its process of becoming, but in the entire complex trajectory that leads to the emergent entity through the reconciliation of its opposed moments, as the concrete details of each moment, which were emphasized at their peak of efficacy, sink into the background as integral parts of the entity, losing something of their vivid urgency, but still forming essential elements of the whole.[29] For Hegel, the moment of sublation has the character of a liberated self-conscious peace which rejects nothing,[30] and which has become other than what it was in the beginning, so that by dwelling with this tension endemic to its own self-relation, it has produced a harmonious and veracious integration of its seemingly incommensurable and contradictory moments, a process which Hegel sums up in the uncharacteristically pithy adage: "Truth is its own self-movement."[31]

Even the emergent result is not a fixed end, but is immediately drawn back into the stream of becoming as a novel positing in a more expansive domain of opposition, and thus does the teleological impulse toward polarity issuing into reconciliation drive the successive self-overcomings through the graduated stages of development that constitute disparate processes across scale. The dialectic can be discerned in the consummation of sexual reproduction, in which the opposite sexes are drawn to one another in relations that are by turns harmonious and discordant to produce a third entity, the child that embodies a seamless integration of the two parents, and which itself is capable of eventually producing a further emergence from opposition by producing a child through such consummation.[32] And like a newborn child, a bare philosophical principle is only an incitement to activity, is only a potentiality until it goes through decades, generations, or even centuries of expression in relation to concrete experience, receives critiques and refutations that provoke its refinement and expansion, until the initial conception is developed into a mature, nuanced system of thought. Even when philosophies seem starkly opposed with no common ground, they are really participating in one stage of a larger dialectical becoming,[33] as whether they know it or not, the fiercely antagonistic debaters are, through their tension, contributing to the production of a mode of thought which transcends them both, perhaps bending one another's beliefs slightly, imperceptibly toward the other, forcing them to discern the lacunae and margins of their theory, often creating the precondition for an integration that only takes place long after the two interlocutors are dust. But lest one think this failure to produce a final reconciliation is a tragedy, Hegel acknowledges that even the greatest philosophers can at best exemplify and enact one moment in the grand dialectic that encompasses the vast sweep of history.[34]

Holding the negative pole of the opposition in intimate relation with the initial one-sidedness of any positing, rather than repressing the negative as other, is a necessary moment of the dialectic, struggling not only with external foes, but with the internal conflict externalized through projective enactments.[35] Maintaining the opposites in tense relation clarifies and refines the positions, a discordant containment which often, of its own accord, reveals that the two positions are not actually opposed, but are both partial aspects of a larger reality, which Hegel describes as a novel identity that emerges from the process. The resolution of a persistent controversy in philosophy is almost always found in the recognition that the two sides were too shallow in their formulations, their encounter producing a mutual deepening that discovers, usually surprisingly, agreement in this more profound domain of discourse, an insight perhaps even relevant to the controversy between Hegelians and Schellingians, or Hegelians and Deleuzeans. Truth is generally partial, and the opposite of a truth is almost never a mere falsehood if the two positions are, over time, brought into greater nuance and complexity of expression through their mutual engagement.[36] The deeper one enters into the nuances of an opposition by engaging with the negative of one's own conscious position, the more one's thinking is transformed until the opposition is no longer relevant, is a relic of an earlier stage that one now sees through, but which nevertheless had to be lived through moment by moment, year by year, in order for it to be sublated and overcome.[37] The conflicts that seemed burningly important to us in our youth often appear trivial or reductive in retrospect, and the same is often true of earlier stages of culture, as the controversies that engaged our ancestors can seem inconsequential and easily resolved, though we also certainly have much to learn from nonmodern modes that have been disqualified in the differentiation of the modern. This dialectic traces a movement toward self-consciousness, as each reconciled opposition expands one's conscious view of the world by absorbing that which was previously experienced as other in the formation of a differentiated unitary structure, thereby deepening and complicating both elements in the opposition through their sublation in a novel entity, a chemical reaction that produces a new substance with unforeseen properties.[38]

But this knowledge only comes from living through the tension, as one cannot rush an emergence through the dialectical movement any more than one can rush the growth of a child, though one can inhibit such an emergence by refusing to bend, dogmatically refusing to take in the partially valid perspective that one encounters in the other.[39] Such a totalitarian rejection of a novel element, constituted in the suppression of the other, whether in the form of a novel concept or a minority group, is generally motivated by the fear that one's freedom and power will be eclipsed by that external opponent, and this fear is justified in a limited way, as the bud must, in one sense, die for the blossom to be born, and the doxa in any domain must pass away in order for a heterodox mode to arise out of its ashes, even the orthodoxies defended by Hegelians, Schellingians, or Deleuzeans.[40] But even if an individual or a collective organization rigidly refuses to be transformed, this rigidity often generates a compensatory drive toward transformation in those that this entity encounters, so that an authoritarian father often produces children who rebel in more extreme ways than the children of more moderate parents, for instance, driving a child raised in a conservative religious family into an atheistic, scientific mode of thought. And then the child of that rebellious child, now the parent, may seek a reconciling middle position between the atheistic mode and the theistic mode that the parents rejected. Or similarly, a particularly repressive and authoritarian regime, like that found by Jesus of Nazareth in the Romans, or by Nicolaus Copernicus in the medieval Church, often produces a revolutionary reaction that does not only reject the oppressive regime, but ultimately transforms that regime, so that over the course of centuries, the teachings of the provincial rabbi become the dominant religion of the empire, with the capital city of that empire becoming the world center of the previously upstart religious movement that rebelled against it. And once that religion has become a vast empire in its own right, not primarily political (though the Church has certainly been political), but an empire of the spirit and mind, we again find an upstart, marginal movement initiated by Copernicus, and carried on nearly a century later by Kepler and Galileo, that eventually comes to supplant the Christian religion as the dominant mode of thought in the West, serving not only as a political force or a system of belief (though science is certainly both of these things), but also as a method for understanding and shaping the world. Each of these empires was utterly transformed by what it repressed, the other ultimately returning to rest at the heart of these systems, with both the initial system and its negative integrated in the process.

Like empires, religions, or sciences, conceptual thought is open to being transformed by the other when consciousness understands that this encounter with otherness, this becoming-other, is an essential moment in a process of individuation.[41] But this openness to the other can be painful, as the upheaval and uncertainty of transformation are often more difficult than the static certainty of adhering to a fixed, supposedly complete system, whether political, religious, scientific, or philosophical. Eventually, however, those elements that are repressed, whether in an individual consciousness or in a culture, rise up against that fixed structure, and the more rigid and oppressive it has become, the more destructive the revolution will be before a novel integration can occur. Of course, as seen in many revolutions, perhaps most notoriously in the French Revolution and in the Communist revolutions in China and Russia, the revolutionaries can be just as rigid in their ideologies, so a radical openness to the other is required not only by the ones in power, but also by those who seek to upset the balance of power if they hope to achieve a novel mode of relation rather than merely a reversal of the privileging opposition in which what was repressed now itself becomes the agent of repression.

But then again, this reversal can also act as a transitional step in a dialectic luring process ever onward toward reconciliation, as it is only through experience, even the experience of self-alienation, which seems so empty, hopeless, and devoid of meaning in the throes of its despairing moment, that our modes of thought, on both individual and collective scales, are deepened and expanded. It is the tension between self and other that impels becoming, as this encounter with the alien, the other, death, the negative, the shadow, and the void, all various nominations for the unconscious elements repressed in the positing of the original entity, drives the teleological movement toward more encompassing modes through the integration of that which is unconscious or experienced as external to the conscious, subjective identity. The individual or collective seeks out, draws toward it, or otherwise elicits from external experience that which is repressed, rejected, or disqualified in the formation of its own self-conception.[42] For Hegel, this pervasive urge to go through the dialectic in all its multifariousness is the essence of what it means to be human, a being whose nature is "to press onward to agreement with others" in order to generate "an achieved community of minds," an integration of all modes of thought serving as the teleological purpose toward which philosophy is inexorably lured.[43] And with the moment of sublation and emergent reconciliation, "the Phenomenology of Spirit is concluded,"[44] for rather than experiencing the opposed moments of its development as separate, as subject and object, self and other, the emergent entity, whether in the guise of an individual or a cultural consciousness, viscerally understands that each of these moments is a part of itself because it has lived through these moments, it has been them and seen them pass away like the leaves which fall from the tree only to become part of the soil that feeds further arborescent growth and development. True knowledge is not the self knowing the world as something external and other, but knowing the world as an intimate aspect of its own interiority, incorporated through the fraught encounter with otherness, a conception which forms a primary precondition for much subsequent philosophy.[45]

## Notes

1 Schelling, *Grundlegung*, 235.
2 Hegel, *Logic*, 15.
3 Pinkard, *Hegel*, 46–7.
4 Žižek, *Organs*, 51.
5 Marx, *Capital I*, 103.
6 Hegel, *Logic*, 234–59.
7 Duffy, *Mathematics*, 166–7, 172; Duffy, *Expression*, 58–63, 73–5.
8 Hippolyte, *Logic*, 4.
9 Stanford Encyclopedia of Philosophy, "Continuity"; Hegel, *Logic*, 79, 252–3.
10 Hegel, *Phenomenology*, 72.
11 Hegel, *Phenomenology*, 29.
12 Hegel, *Phenomenology*, 2.
13 Deleuze, *Difference*, 119.
14 Hegel, *Phenomenology*, 36.
15 Hegel, *Phenomenology*, 2.
16 Hegel, *Phenomenology*, 2.
17 Brandom, *Spirit*.
18 Hegel, *Phenomenology*, 2.
19 Hegel, *Phenomenology*, 2.

20 Hegel, *Phenomenology*, 16.
21 Hegel, *Phenomenology*, 16.
22 Hegel, *Phenomenology*, 10, 14.
23 Hegel, *Phenomenology*, 10.
24 Hegel, *Phenomenology*, 10.
25 Hegel, *Phenomenology*, 19.
26 Hegel, *Phenomenology*, 19, 36.
27 Hegel, *Phenomenology*, 7.
28 Hegel, *Phenomenology*, 43.
29 Hegel, *Phenomenology*, 7.
30 Hegel, *Phenomenology*, 12.
31 Hegel, *Phenomenology*, 28.
32 Hegel, *Phenomenology*, 11.
33 Hegel, *Phenomenology*, 13.
34 Hegel, *Phenomenology*, 45.
35 Hegel, *Phenomenology*, 13; Kelly, *Individuation*.
36 Hegel, *Phenomenology*, 23.
37 Hegel, *Phenomenology*, 16.
38 Hegel, *Phenomenology*, 17.
39 Hegel, *Phenomenology*, 17, 23.
40 Hegel, *Phenomenology*, 35.
41 Hegel, *Phenomenology*, 20.
42 Hegel, *Phenomenology*, 21.
43 Hegel, *Phenomenology*, 43.
44 Hegel, *Phenomenology*, 21.
45 Hegel, *Phenomenology*, 22.

Chapter 5

# God-Positing Potencies
F.W.J. Schelling's *Berlin Lectures*

The two series of lectures discussed in this chapter, *The Grounding of Positive Philosophy* and *Historical-Critical Introduction to the Philosophy of Mythology*, were given in Berlin starting in 1842 when Schelling was sixty-seven, published in the years following his death in 1854, and only translated into English in 2007. Schelling's late work can be conceived as providing a way beyond the Hegelian dialectic, which nevertheless is deeply indebted to that mode of thought, so that while Hegel's first book initially positioned him as Schelling's follower, despite the fact that he was five years older than his university roommate, posterity has generally judged that it is with the *Phenomenology* that Hegel definitively surpassed his friend as the leading figure in German philosophy. However, after being almost forgotten in the long shadow cast into the twentieth century by Hegel, Schelling's later work was reexamined as a way potentially to go beyond Hegel, first by Heidegger in a series of 1936 lectures (though it was only published in the 1970s), and then by Karl Jaspers, Jürgen Habermas, Maurice Merleau-Ponty, and Walter Schulz in the 1950s, and by Deleuze and Žižek in later decades. Both of the primary narratives about the relation between Schelling and Hegel contain partial truth, and can be integrated to compose a more expansive narrative in which Schelling was surpassed by Hegel in certain ways in the early nineteenth century, but in which Schelling also offers an essential critique of his friend's work, as well as his own novel conceptual contributions, that have enabled philosophy ultimately to go beyond Hegel while retaining and recontextualizing his epochal mode of thought.

There is no doubt that Schelling is brilliant, though in 1809's *Of Human Freedom*, the last work he published during his lifetime, considered his masterpiece by some,[1] one suspects that he is trying to prove that he is as brilliant

DOI: 10.4324/9781003195498-6

as his friend and former supporter Hegel, whose *Phenomenology* was published two years earlier, initiating the rift between them. Schelling evidently wants to demonstrate that he is an equal to his old lieutenant, who would become the most influential philosopher in the nineteenth century, but he is apparently driven by this willful desire to begin to articulate a critique of the Hegelian dialectic, a way beyond the dialectic's eventual near-hegemony, though he could only evoke it, gesture toward it.[2] A fully articulated critique of Hegel would only be possible after significantly more time had passed, and the dialectic had been integrated and rendered almost commonsensical among many philosophers, so that the ultimate self-immolating critique of the dialectic could only emerge a century-and-a-half later in Deleuze's *Difference and Repetition*. Although *Of Human Freedom* is perhaps an implicit response to Hegel, Schelling waited until 1834, three years after Hegel's death, explicitly to criticize his former friend,[3] at least in public, which is a bit pusillanimous given Hegel's inability to answer these criticisms, as there were twenty-four years between the publication of the *Phenomenology* and his passing when Schelling could have engaged in critical dialogue with his friend's work. Hegel has usually been judged by posterity to be the more overwhelmingly potent thinker, or at least more successful in propagating his undoubtedly more consistent and coherent theory as the greatest monument of his philosophical era, while Schelling evinces a gloriously inconsistent and profligate creativity not as evident in Hegel.[4]

Although Schelling makes some important refinements and extensions to the Hegelian dialectic, one is frankly hard-pressed to recognize the full scope, depth, and complexity of Hegel's work in Schelling's critique, and Schelling's characterization of Hegel's philosophy as primarily negative in the *Grounding*, an evaluation later taken up by Deleuze, is misleading. Although the negative is certainly an essential moment of the dialectic, it constitutes the struggle, opposition, labor, and ordeal necessary for overcoming a particular phase of process, the death and dismemberment required for a positive rebirth into a novel emergent domain. Negative and positive are intimately entwined in the dialectic, and the primary content which Hegel posits, his primary contribution to a positive philosophy, is the dialectical movement itself.[5] As James writes, describing his experiments with nitrous oxide intoxication: "What reader of Hegel can doubt that that sense of a perfected Being with all its otherness soaked up into itself, which dominates his whole philosophy, must have come from the prominence in his consciousness of mystical moods," positive intimations of "potential forms of consciousness entirely different" from "our normal waking consciousness," which contain a "metaphysical significance" whose primary feature is the "reconciliation" of "the opposites of the world."[6] Contrary to Schelling's often dismissive evaluation of Hegel as a mere logical rationalist, as expressing "a pathetic reason" only concerned "with a chimera,"[7] there is indeed an organismic quality to Hegel's thought which sometimes verges on mysticism, though of a more monistic kind than that of Schelling.[8]

It might be suggested that what is important in Hegel is not primarily the concept of the absolute, which is yoked to a monocentric mode of consciousness characteristic of monotheism, or the assertion that Hegel's system is complete and final, which it clearly is not[9] (despite Hegel's insistence in the *Logic* that the dialectic "is the one and only true method"[10]), but his positive articulation of the dialectical movement itself, which contains a powerful, though limited, explanatory efficacy for processes across scales and orders, not only in human consciousness, but in the domains accessible to biology, chemistry, sociology, and history. And because of its explanatory power, which still partially accounts for even the current movements and countermovements in philosophy, politics, and culture, it required about a century for the recognition to emerge broadly among philosophers (though certainly presaged by Schelling and Nietzsche) that there are other modes of relation not susceptible to an oppositional mode of dialectical explanation.[11]

One can certainly understand why Schelling avoided engaging in direct conflict with his friendly rival given the overwhelming potency of Hegel's thought, despite its limitations, and it is especially in Schelling's philosophy of mythology that he provides a profound complement to Hegel's dialectical conception, ultimately acknowledging the partial validity of that conception, while expressing a novel mode of thought which is essential to the developments traced in the chapters below. As with the other complementary dyads discussed in the present text (Spinoza-Leibniz, Spinoza-Bergson, Hegel-James, Freud-Jung, Hegel-Deleuze, Derrida-Deleuze), Schelling and Hegel can be understood as expressing correlative aspects for their era of a still more expansive mode that would only begin to find an integral expression in the twentieth century, a project that continues to be carried forward in the twenty-first century. In a lecture on Schelling's philosophy in 1826, Hegel writes that, although Schelling "never managed to achieve a popular appeal," his philosophy begins with "intellectual intuition" and "the power of imagination"[12] in order speculatively to resolve antitheses in a transcendental idealism concerned especially with formal potencies discerned in nature and mythology. Hegel was critical of this conceptual complex, despite his affirmation of affective powers which constitute the will, though Schelling's conception of agential potencies forms the primary complement to the Hegelian dialectic for our narrative, especially in the extensive employment of the figures of mythology by Nietzsche, Jung, Deleuze, and Hillman, all of whom were influenced by Schelling. Deleuze contends that "the most important aspect of Schelling's philosophy" is "his consideration of powers," the mythological potencies, a mode of thought through which Schelling, in contrast with Hegel, "brings difference out of the night of the Identical" by means of "a differential calculus adequate to the dialectic" derived especially from Leibniz.[13]

In the *Grounding*, Schelling explicates the dualistic historical relation of what he terms negative and positive philosophy, which, despite his harsh critiques of Hegel, looks remarkably like a dialectical process, though when differentiated from Schelling's more excessive denouncements, these critiques serve as refinements and extensions of Hegel's approach, which opens into Schelling's theory of potencies, abstractly explicated in this text, and delineated in a more specific mode in relation to polytheism in the *Introduction*. In fact, the Hegelian dialectic is partially derived from the early work of Schelling himself,[14] which in turn is partially derived from Fichte, so it is no surprise that Schelling employs a mode of thought that looks strikingly Hegelian to posterity, and it is also unsurprising that he transparently resents Hegel for appropriating one of his most profound concepts, itself partially appropriated from Fichte, and elaborating it in a more fully realized, and popularly successful, way. Despite his resentment of Hegel, Schelling affirms that the development of the mode of thought he traces from Heraclitus, Plato, and Aristotle through Spinoza, Leibniz, Kant, and Fichte "cannot be the work of one person, of one individual, and, for that matter, not even of one epoch," and the chapters below trace the continuation of this collective endeavor into the twenty-first century.[15]

Ultimately, it must be recognized that the dialectic which came to be called Hegelian is the collective creation of this lineage of philosophers culminating in the late eighteenth and early nineteenth centuries in the wake of Kant in Germany. They all expressed different and complementary aspects of the dialectic, and Schelling's critique and extension of the dialectic into the series of polytheistic potencies of mythology is itself partially explicable in dialectical terms, while also making possible the deeper form of the dialectic expressed most completely over a century later by Deleuze, so that the young Fichteans Schelling and Hegel produced a novel expression of this mode of thought after its initial positing by Fichte, which itself was the result of a dialectical process. And then from the new positing of Schellingian philosophy, Hegel became other than this identity, differentiating himself from Schelling, a dialectical self-othering of this collective movement which allowed Schelling, over thirty years later, to produce a further differentiation, taken up and further refined and differentiated more than a century later by Deleuze, so that it is only in our time another half-century after Deleuze that it may be possible to enact a differentiated dialectical integration of Hegel and Schelling through the Deleuzean intermediary.[16] Although Schelling presents his positive philosophy as a rejection of Hegel, he expresses a dialectical conception very close to Hegel in certain respects, so that Schelling's real innovations on Hegel's system are more shifts of emphasis away from logic and toward nature and experience, though these are certainly present in Hegel as well. Schelling's primary innovation, which is more radical than these other shifts of emphasis, is the theory of potencies, which serves the same role as the absolute in Hegel, and in Schelling's early work, opening the dialectical mode of thought from a monocentric consciousness to a polycentric mode which will be greatly elaborated by Nietzsche, Jung, Deleuze, and Hillman.[17]

The passage in the *Phenomenology* that initiated the decades-long controversy between Hegel and Schelling concerns Hegel's critique of a simplistic conception of the absolute as "the night in which, as the saying goes, all cows are black," which he describes as "cognition naïvely reduced to vacuity."[18] Schelling interpreted this passage as a veiled attack on his work, but when he asked his friend about this critique, Hegel claimed it was a response to reductive interpretations by some of Schelling's followers, "the abusers and the chatterers," as Schelling puts it, though as Schelling notes, "this distinction is not made in the text." Nevertheless, as John Laughland observes, "although he was very hurt by Hegel's perceived attack," which is a relatively mild and subtle conceptual disagreement compared to the sustained vitriol Schelling would hurl at Hegel after his friend's death, "it jolted him into making further changes to his philosophical system," which is "doubtless because Hegel had hit his mark,"[19] though Heidegger disagrees.[20] In fact, the controversy continues between the often fixed camps of Hegelians and Schellingians, enacting a differentiating opposition which it was a primary project of both philosophers to overcome, at least in its more abstract valences.

Nevertheless, over thirty years later in the *Grounding*, Schelling, still evidently incensed over Hegel's indirect critique, and apparently reacting not only to Hegel's superior philosophical eminence, but also to aggressive attacks by some of Hegel's most vociferous followers – whom he describes as thoroughly "deplorable" and "childishly delighted" with their "platitudes and slogans"[21] – suggests that although he has been accused of merely rejecting the negative philosophy, and thus Hegel, in favor of a positive philosophy, in fact Hegel "wants to be positive,"[22] but does not even achieve a negative philosophy, let alone a positive one. Rather, Hegel ignobly seeks to carry the negative beyond its limits of efficacy in his "false system"[23] which is "totally devoid of intuition,"[24] giving in to the "temptation to break into the territory of the positive,"[25] indulgently wallowing in a "misguided"[26] and "miserly" logical dogmatism which "is the most repugnant form of any dogmatism,"[27] and which is "hostile to all that is meaningful and inspired."[28] However, this ironically immoderate dismissal of Hegel as immoderate, ignoble, misguided, miserly, repugnant, pathetic, unintuitive, uninspired, meaningless, and generally wrongheaded is not supported by a careful reading of Hegel's actual work, which continues to be profoundly influential. It seems, rather, to be the result of a resentful and inconsistent Schelling (despite his dubious claims of consistency), still embroiled in the personal controversies permeating his relationship with his old friend even a decade after Hegel's death, evidently projecting onto Hegel qualities that could perhaps more accurately be attributed to Schelling himself, or perhaps to his unconscious fears about himself after having spent half his life in his early supporter's shadow, and not having published any major works for over three decades, recalling Jung's insight that we tend to be most troubled in others by the things that most trouble us about ourselves. Although Schelling aptly affirms that attention to felt experience can guard against the "unnatural" and "artificial" quality that he unfairly attributes to Hegel's work, this attribution is ironic given that Schelling's writing is at least as "laborious and unclear"[29] as Hegel's, as Schelling describes his friend's compositions. A few pages later, however, Schelling, apparently in a more conciliatory mood, describes Hegel as a "powerful thinker," instead blaming Hegel's students for misunderstanding and insulting Hegel, even as they praise him with "melodramatic phrases,"[30] which is again ironic given the manic melodrama exclusively directed toward Hegel that pervades Schelling's otherwise brilliant lectures.

In a definitive evaluation, Stephen Houlgate writes that although "Schelling's interpretation of the *Logic* has been hugely influential"[31] on continental philosophers from Kierkegaard, Nietzsche, and Heidegger to Lévinas, Derrida, and Deleuze, this "interpretation is, to say the least, cavalier,"[32] as Schelling "passes judgment on Hegel's system on the basis of certain assumptions about thought and existence that Hegel does not share," and "those very assumptions lead him seriously to misrepresent what Hegel is saying,"[33] an observation that also applies to the *Phenomenology*, of which the *Logic* is a continuous development.[34] Ultimately, Houlgate writes, "Hegel's concept of pure being comes much closer to what Schelling has in mind than Schelling allows,"[35] a determination which seems irrefutable from close readings of these texts, though there are certainly significant differences between them having to do with the scope and limits of conceptual thought and the role of potencies, which may nevertheless be integrated two centuries later in a more expansive mode of thought to which both philosophers made pivotal contributions. In fact, Hegel's suggestion that the equation of thought and judgment by the metaphysical tradition culminating in Kant should be brought into question is remarkably, surprisingly resonant with Deleuze's primary philosophical impulse "to do away with the system of judgment"[36] given Deleuze's equally extensive critiques of Hegel.

But far from dismissing Schelling's thought, an affirmation of the central role of personal relationality in philosophy – refusing the prohibition against "psychologizing" pervasive in the analytic tradition – enables the recognition that the conceptual persona of Schelling provides a creative, generative chaos as complement to the lucid, systematizing order of Hegel, a complementarity which embodies and enacts the Dionysian and Apollonian principles expressed thirty years after these Berlin Lectures by Nietzsche. And in fact, it is Schelling himself, through his elucidation of the divine personal potencies, who plants the seeds that will come to fruition in Nietzsche, Jung, Deleuze, and especially in Hillman's conception of personifying. Schelling presciently recognizes that it is the task of reason to trace the "successive potencies" in order to discern the "inner organism" which provides "the key to all being," an obscure formulation which will find a more complete expression in Schelling's explication of the lineal series of gods dominant in Greek mythology (Uranus, Kronos,

Zeus) traced below, and especially in Deleuze's integration of this polytheistic mode of thought with the Leibnizian calculus, which integrates successive series like the potencies discussed by Schelling.[37]

The term "potency" is largely derived from Aristotle's Greek term δύναμη ("dynamis," the root of dynamic and dynamism), translated into Latin as *potentia*, for which power and potential are closely related terms, as opposed to the actual, so that the seed is the potential and the plant is the actual form of the organism. Schelling makes an important distinction between *potentia passiva*, merely passive possibility, and *potentia activa*, an active, universal, infinite potency of being, which for Schelling is the immediate *prius*, the primary, objective being, essence, and cause prior to conceptual thought that contains the potentiality for infinite expression by passing over into difference, which renders it thinkable by reason, and which is motivated by the will, the expression of an infinitely open potency in the human freely to choose the modes of pure potentiality's expression.[38]

For Schelling, reason is the negative, that which logically critiques, divides, differentiates, and eliminates error and contingency, and which cannot go beyond the monocentric circular self-confirmation of rational thought to cognize being in its immediate actuality, but only in its indeterminate possibility. The negative philosophy has formed the necessary complement and correction to the ancient and medieval assertions of pre-critical dogmatic belief in various potencies, especially revealed divinity, and this rational negative philosophy has served to differentiate and liberate conceptual thought from that which is affirmed in the transitional attempt of the traditional metaphysics rationally to prove the dogmatic existence of God. Schelling locates the culmination of the negative movement with Kant's critical philosophy, which rendered the older metaphysics obsolete, though for Schelling, this negative philosophy is not the end of philosophy, but the preparation and precondition demanding the emergence of a novel, differentiated positive philosophy, which Schelling describes Kant as having incipiently reintroduced "through the back door of the practical."[39]

However, Schelling recognizes that both the negative and positive philosophies have existed in only partially differentiated forms since at least the beginnings of Western philosophy in Heraclitus, Plato, and Aristotle, who discusses a class of philosophers primarily concerned with the positive reality of mythology and the Orphic mysteries existing alongside the more rationally oriented philosophers of antiquity, perhaps especially Socrates with his dialectical method of critical destruction, which nevertheless requires a positive knowledge as the implicit precondition for his learned ignorance. Schelling writes that Socrates' "spirit lingered precisely on the boundary of the merely logical and the positive,"[40] an insight which Nietzsche will express in a complementary valence. Both modes of thought, the negative dialectical philosophy and the positive mythological philosophy, can be found complexly intermixed in Socrates and Plato, for instance in the cosmological speculations of the *Timaeus*, so that Schelling designates these two philosophers as prophetic of a more differentiated future positive philosophy, while their mutual student Aristotle began to differentiate a positive philosophy in the domain of a broadly empirical engagement with the relatively limited actual reality he encountered beyond mere logic. In turn, this nascent empiricism allowed him to begin to express the logical negative philosophy within its proper sphere of efficacy, largely initiating the differentiation of rationalism and empiricism that would pass through scholasticism and the Enlightenment into the Kantian culmination of the negative philosophy, which prepared the way for the sublation of the opposition of rational and empirical in the positive philosophy.

In Schelling's conception, a more completely differentiated positive philosophy affirms potencies beyond the grasp of reason, emerging not from a hierarchical privileging of positive over negative, but from an integration, whose form is remarkably resonant with the Hegelian dialectic, of the nonmodern dogmatic affirmations of potencies which exceed logical rationality with the modern critical differentiation of these potencies, a "third element"[41] which sublates and reconciles the opposition of objective and subjective being in a new identity, a novel philosophy which integrates both the negative and the positive philosophies in their differentiated articulations. For Schelling, as for Hegel, being does not reside in any one of the three moments of this process, in subject, object, or their integration, but in the movement through this unmistakably dialectical sublation, a movement which occurs through the infinite potency becoming *for itself* rather than *in itself*, and thus unequal and differentiated from itself as a subject relating to an object. However, whereas Hegel does not see the value in the concept of personified potencies, Schelling conceives potencies, multiplicitous expressions of a singular infinite potency, as the content luring thought to leap beyond the merely rational toward actual being in itself, a conception in which potency is itself this "leaping toward being," producing an "empirical knowledge" beyond what can be merely thought. Thought asymptotically approaches a "correspondence with what is present in experience,"[42] and rationality asymptotically approaches, but never becomes identical with, empiricism, a mode of relation which James, influenced by Schelling a half-century later, would nominate a "radical empiricism," and which Deleuze would refine and reframe as a "transcendental empiricism." Infinite potency liberates thought from its self-enclosed monocentric circular necessity into a transcendental movement toward a reality beyond, and prior to, rational thought.

Schelling describes the positive as the existence "above being,"[43] providing a transrational and extralogical foundation and origin for rationally discernible being, an unknowable grounding prior to consciousness, ultimately unattainable by the pure reason of negative philosophy, a positive being which is radically free and open. The positive philosophy, which Schelling designates as metaphysical, finds that actuality is prior to thought and its discernment of potencies, including both monotheistic and polytheistic divinities. Actuality is a "potency that is no longer potency," an inversion which he designates as "the existing potency,"[44] "*potentia universalis*," "universal essence,"[45] "absolute spirit," or "the One,"[46] and which, contra Descartes who begins with doubt, "indubitably exists"[47] prior to differentiation. For Schelling, being descends from an ultimately unattainable transcendent actuality toward immanent potentiality, so that actual existence is that which is prior to any possible conceptualization, including the concepts of a God or gods which can only be encountered empirically and historically, and this existence beyond reason is only accessible to an "absolutely ecstatic"[48] mode of relation, an experience of that which exceeds the possibility of being thought, an unknowable actuality prior to potency, and to any concept of divinity.

Schelling describes the Neoplatonists as reviving this mode of thought from the positive, though largely undifferentiated, elements in Plato, especially in relation to mythology, after the culmination for antiquity of the negative philosophy in Aristotle, who rejected mythology as a legitimate means of acquiring knowledge. The Neoplatonists associated these two philosophers with the major and minor forms of the Eleusinian mysteries, the renowned initiatory rites of ancient Greek religion, possibly involving the ingestion of a psychedelic compound like ergot, or even psilocybin, enacting the mythical ordeal of Persephone's descent into, and subsequent emergence from, Hades. The Neoplatonists discerned the major mysteries of the positive philosophy in Plato, who participated in the initiation, and the minor mysteries of the negative philosophy in Aristotle, who only wrote about the rites. In turn, the Christian scholastics became the primary inheritors of the Aristotelian negative philosophy, despite the positive dogmas of Christianity, in a compromise formation which Schelling describes as "a rational dogmatism or positive rationalism,"[49] a containment of the positive within the negative orthodoxies of scholastic rationalism held relatively static by the institution of the Church, which nevertheless formed the enclosing womb for the long development and refinement of rationality. Scholasticism was the precondition for the dominance of reason in the Enlightenment, with its complementary differentiation of a purely materialist, sensible empiricism, ultimately leading to their integration in a positive philosophy. However, with hindsight it becomes clear that Schelling did not express the final form of this positive philosophy but rather formed, along with Hegel in a conflicting and complementary dyad, the precondition for the further developments of this positive mode of thought, which would pass through Nietzsche into the twentieth century, and into the increasingly differentiated integrations of the last half-century since the emergence of Deleuze and Derrida, primary conceptual personae complexly embodying the positive and negative philosophies, respectively. Deleuze created a precondition for their more expansive integration, especially in relation to the theory of mythological potencies largely derived from Schelling, which may serve to integrate rationalism and empiricism in a transcendental empiricism for which the reasons of thought and the experience of actuality, both physical and metaphysical, intimately converge and interrelate in a pervasive internal resonance.[50]

Like the character of an individual, the fundamental character of the world, both the sensible character to which the usual conception of empiricism is limited, and the supersensible character that the more expansive form of "metaphysical empiricism"[51] advocated by Schelling recognizes, can only be discerned a posteriori through its actual expressions in experience, not rationally derived from a priori premises. These metaphysical actualities were elucidated by the stream of thought which Schelling designates as a mystical or speculative empiricism, whose modes of discernment are describable as intuition or revelation, running parallel to dogmatic medieval scholastic rationalism, a mode of thought especially evident in the alchemical texts discussed below in relation to Jung, which acted as a potent complement to rationalism, demanding the integration of these two differentiated streams, which have always coexisted, in a positive philosophy that exceeds both metaphysical empiricism and logical rationalism. For Schelling, the primary positive contribution of metaphysical empiricism is that it seeks to understand emergent actualities by tracing them through a series of actual events, a tracing more fully integrated with differentiating critical rationality undertaken in the *Introduction*.

Positive philosophy is not only an a posteriori empirical tracing of this actual series any more than it is only an a priori rational conception of being but an emergent integration of these two differentiated modes of relation, which discerns a "transcendent being"[52] that is also a "pure actuality"[53] exceeding both experience and thought, the unknowable ground and truth of the actual in which rationalism and empiricism are always already integrated. The potencies traced through series asymptotically lure transcendental thought toward an unattainable, always-receding horizon of knowledge and experience beyond the existing potency, never finally attained in its complete actuality. However, as with the concepts of God and the absolute, the transcendent quality of this unthinkable actuality posited by Schelling has tended to be deemphasized over subsequent developments spanning nearly two centuries, serving as a bridge to the pure immanence of Deleuze by paradoxically equating the actual and the transcendent, inverting the traditional metaphysics for which the transcendent is pure potentiality which becomes immanently actual in a compromise formation that provocatively locates actuality in a transcendent domain forever inaccessible to thought.

While it is undoubtedly true that actuality is inaccessible to pure rationality divorced from broadly empirical knowledge, most of the theorists below will discern that actuality is accessible to the immanent apprehension which results from the integration of conceptual thought and bodily intuition, and thus the further step will be taken, building upon Schelling's work through subsequent developments in the twentieth century by broadly constructivist theorists, of leaving behind the conception of a transcendent domain altogether in favor of a transcendental immanence which is ultimately relational. In fact, Schelling ambiguously presages this conception in the final pages of the *Grounding* despite his insistence on the word "transcendent."[54] Perhaps more than this strange, and historically necessary, transitional inversion in the concept of transcendent actuality, Schelling's greatest contribution is the integration of logical, critical rationality and intuitive, metaphysical empiricism lured by empirically encountered and revealed potencies, often in the form of monotheistic or polytheistic divinities, through actual series of historical events toward radically free and open constructive becomings.

The *Introduction* consists of ten lectures which take the origin and meaning of mythology as their primary subject, and Schelling spends much of these lectures describing, carefully and in great detail, the theories which had previously been proposed over several millennia to explain mythology, though some of these earlier theories are perhaps more plausible to a nineteenth century sensibility than to a twenty-first century one. In an approach resonant with the ancient "method of exhaustion" which formed a precursor to the integral calculus, he carefully traces all of the previous theories about mythology in order fully to differentiate them in what he calls a "dialectic."[55] The majority of these lectures are engaged in an application of the negative philosophy by sublating the aspects of all previous theories of mythology which obstruct the passage of the positive affirmation of the mythological, metaphysical empiricism that Schelling ultimately offers in a differentiated integration of these previous theories, leading to what Jason M. Wirth aptly designates as "one of the boldest claims of the nineteenth century, a claim whose strangeness no doubt still abides,"[56] that the gods of mythology are historical and empirical actualities which must be affirmed by a fully realized positive philosophy. These lectures thus fulfill the ambition expressed by Schelling more than four decades earlier in a letter to Hegel: "Monotheism of reason and the heart, polytheism of the imagination and art, that is what we need!"[57]

Although mythology is involved in the poetic, symbolic, and allegorical expression of ethical and religious doctrine, and of conceptual thought; although the gods correspond with natural cycles and forces, their origin and history corresponding with the origin and history of nature; and although various figures like Heracles or Asclepius have been elevated to divine status for their deeds, Schelling contends that the gods must nevertheless have been encountered, through a metaphysical empiricism, as "actually existing essences"[58] prior to these various explanations in order for mythology to exist in its full scope. The gods cannot be reduced to any of these explanations, but rather all of these explanations express partial aspects of a more expansive reality, a mode of thought that Schelling discerns as incipiently reemerging with the Neoplatonists. However, as Schelling acknowledges from the outset, although philosophy and mythology were intimately intertwined in antiquity, in the wake of rationalism and materialist empiricism in the eighteenth century, these two domains were starkly opposed, though it is this very disparateness that demands their reintegration in a novel mode of thought. Schelling suggests that such a positive philosophy of mythology, even more than the philosophy of nature he propounded in earlier decades to which the philosophy of mythology is closely related, may require time before it is fully integrated into academic discourse. However, perhaps enough time has now passed, and enough eminent philosophers and psychologists have complexly affirmed this mode of thought, including Nietzsche, Jung, Deleuze, and Hillman, that we may be nearing a time when justifications in the face of the rationalist doubts of negative philosophy can be deemphasized, and we can proceed with philosophically exploring this archaic domain of human experience in novel registers, an integration which would profoundly affect many other areas of study.

The primary object of inquiry for these lectures is "the world of the gods,"[59] a domain of reality that has been conceived by the mythological mode of thought in a "system of the gods"[60] stretching back into an obscure pre-antiquity as a radically "different order of things"[61] from the human world, though the events of these two domains are understood by this mode as existing in complex relationality. This mythological consciousness recognizes the divine personalities as relating to one another historically, in a temporality as profoundly different from the modern conception of time as that of childhood is from the temporality of modern adulthood, with which it is nevertheless continuous, and only rendered "pre-historical"[62] by the lack of written documentation, a conception for which neither of these temporalities is privileged. In fact, the absence of written language is characteristic of this relative prehistory, which itself evidently emerged from a pretemporal, timeless, cyclical domain prior to conception, a succession of distinctly enfolded temporalities traced below especially in relation to Deleuze. The castration and overthrowing of Uranus by his son Kronos is understood as an actual, though ontologically ambiguous, historical event, forming a theogony, a "history of the gods"[63] traced from their actual, though ultimately unknowable, prehistoric genesis, the groundless ground and universal potency of the positive philosophy, a temporal domain for which mythology provides one of the very few points of entry.

The theories considered by Schelling which posit monotheism as prior to polytheism, a view dominant in the West for roughly a millennium from the beginning of the Middle Ages until the Enlightenment, are perhaps especially implausible to a twenty-first century sensibility. More plausible is the suggestion, now generally accepted, that monotheism emerged out of a prior polytheism, which in turn emerged out of animism, though the earlier modes were never completely abandoned, and this trajectory certainly does not imply that a monotheistic conception of divinity as the one true God is the final telos of a process of ascension through successive conceptions of divinity, but only the stage in this process, teleologically lured by a potent "destiny" toward more individuated modes of consciousness, that has been dominant since the rise of Christianity in the West. However, although the earliest human consciousness undoubtedly contained the potential for monotheism, and even for a specifically Christian monotheism (as well as its other forms), the current consensus that polytheism, practiced in a wide diversity of human groups, existed in a multiplicity of gods emerging from a multifold animism prior to the exclusivist unification of monotheism beginning in the first or second millennium BCE is evident not only from the archaeological and historical records, but from the very names for God employed in the Hebrew Bible.

In this ancient text, the angels are called Elohim, which means "gods" or, more literally, "children of El," the Phoenician or Canaanite god associated with Kronos by the Greeks, but it is also the Elohim among whom God includes himself when he says that "man has become like one of us," both God and man as members in a multiplicity possessing a divine knowledge of good and evil, perhaps indicating a universal potency containing the multiplicity. However, the assertion of a primordial monotheism does not undermine Schelling's profound recognition that the primary difference between the monotheistic and polytheistic conceptions of divinity is that whereas Hellenic mythology is generated by a "successive polytheism"[64] in which the highest gods, Uranus, Kronos, and Zeus, succeed one another in an actual historical series, the multiplicity of gods in the Hebrew Bible are simultaneous and subservient to the singular, eternal God, Yahweh, whose names are nevertheless differentiated through the genealogical series leading from Adam, through Seth, to Enosh, who is the first to call God Yahweh instead of the more generic Elohim.

In contrast with the monotheistic conception, which the actual text of the Bible complicates, the succession of gods in Greek mythology contains the lived history of a succession of peoples leading to Hellenic culture, in which each of the three primary deities was successively dominant, each potency embodying a real historical stage or moment through which that culture has passed, and with which its collective consciousness has tarried. Each deity was forced out of its one-sided dominance through an all-consuming crisis and controversy which required that the earlier highest gods be dialectically retained and sublated in the subsequent mythical narratives. That there subsisted a profound "awe and reverence" for Kronos-Saturn in antiquity after the emergence of Zeus-Jupiter as the primary power indicates that the earlier deity still retained his numinosity from "an unthinkable prior time" in which he had still been dominant. Although Schelling recognizes that "mythology has no reality outside of consciousness,"[65] it can be reciprocally maintained that consciousness could not have come into existence without mythology, as the gods are not merely products of poetic imagination, but are rather objectively real "God-positing potencies"[66] that have successively possessed the consciousness of humanity. The gods are ideal persons, whom Nietzsche, Jung, Hillman, and even Deleuze will call archetypes, to whom humans have related in a sustained historical engagement spanning millennia, metaphysical beings who empirically exist in actuality, though their ontological status is elusive and paradoxical, and thus they cannot be reduced either to a mere physicality or to a mere poetic or conceptual invention. Rather, they complexly interpenetrate the physical and the metaphysical in the form of potencies, which can be variously encountered as real historical humans elevated to divinity, as forces of nature, as modes of consciousness, and as metaphysical beings, though they are prior to and exceed these categories.

For Schelling, the emergence of a people coextensive with its language, mythology, laws, and general mode of consciousness is always mediated by a profound crisis, often in the form of a sickness of body and soul, just as an illness can mediate a conversion or liberation in an individual, so that a novel mode of consciousness cannot emerge without the overcoming of such a crisis, a transformative initiatory ordeal on a collective scale. This observation inevitably brings to mind the pervasive crisis of our own time, a crisis of consciousness profoundly intertwined with climate change, global pandemic, political corruption, and social polarization, apparently creating the necessary precondition for the emergence of a novel mode of relation presaged by Schelling as a positive philosophy. However, in a conception greatly elaborated by Deleuze, Schelling recognizes that the overcoming of such a transformative crisis is not primarily found in complete solutions to the problems of which this crisis consists, but in the formulation of more profound questions that mark the emergent inception of a novel epoch as an opening to more expansive domains of thought and experience. It is the collective task of such a novel epoch to create new concepts and modes of thought to answer these deeper questions, a task which can only be vaguely presaged or intimated in its nascence. Whereas, according to Schelling, the peoples that emerged coextensively with mythology in pre-antiquity were generally defined by unified languages and cultures, a primary question that we now face is how to integrate the inextricably intertwined dissonance of our multicultural and multilingual nations into an emergent entity that satisfies the urgent requirement for global solutions to global problems while avoiding the totalitarian erasure of heterogenous difference, thus maintaining an open and pluralist society.

We are perhaps undergoing a Deleuzean differential repetition, on a more expansive scale, of the successive critical emergences of mythological deities that each mediated a transformative renascence into a more liberated order of consciousness, an emergence prophetically prefigured in Abrahamic monotheism as a future-oriented salvation, the translation of the biblical word which literally means "to lead from the narrows and into the expanse,"[67] an expansion of our horizons of conception. However, this promised future state in which "all presently dispersed and separated nations shall again be united"[68] may take place not through a totalizing monotheistic unification, but through a more expansively differentiated integration characteristic of polytheistic consciousness, a "philosophical religion"[69] subsisting in "relation to the great powers and forces,"[70] realized in art as much as in philosophy. Perhaps this positive philosophy will emerge as a pluralist mode of relation in which even the monotheistic submission to legislation and negative judgment, as well as the more positive aspects of monotheism, can find an appropriate place as a non-exclusive moment, expressing partial truth, in a deeper dialectical process which affirms a multiplicitous series of potencies, the progressive unfolding of a univocal potency whose integral truth is discerned in the movement through the series of successive systems of philosophy as a differential repetition, in another domain, of the movement through the mythological series of gods.

## Notes

1 Heidegger, *Schelling*, 2.
2 Heidegger, *Schelling*, 97; Schelling, *Freedom*, 146n27.
3 Rush, "Critique," 216.
4 Heidegger, *Schelling*, 6.
5 Hegel, *Logic*, 10.
6 James, *Writings*, 349–50.

7 Schelling, *Grounding*, 130.
8 Houlgate, "Critique," 120–1.
9 Houlgate, "Critique," 127.
10 Hegel, *Logic*, 33.
11 Schelling, *Mythology*, 121.
12 Hegel, *History* (Brown), 262, 265.
13 Deleuze, *Difference*, 190–1.
14 Heidegger, *Schelling*, 471; Althaus, *Hegel*, 88.
15 Schelling, *Grounding*, 152.
16 Schelling, *Idealism*, xii–xiv, xxxiv.
17 Schelling, *Grounding*, 149.
18 Hegel, *Phenomenology*, 9.
19 Laughlin, *Schelling*, 59.
20 Heidegger, *Schelling*, 13.
21 Schelling, *Grounding*, 150.
22 Schelling, *Grounding*, 145.
23 Schelling, *Grounding*, 150.
24 Schelling, *Grounding*, 176.
25 Schelling, *Grounding*, 145.
26 Schelling, *Grounding*, 151.
27 Schelling, *Grounding*, 146.
28 Schelling, *Grounding*, 150.
29 Schelling, *Grounding*, 150.
30 Schelling, *Grounding*, 153.
31 Houlgate, "Critique," 115.
32 Houlgate, *Opening*, 295.
33 Houlgate, "Critique," 100.
34 Hegel, *Logic*, 11.
35 Houlgate, "Critique," 104n16.
36 Deleuze and Parnet, *L'Abécédaire*, 59.
37 Schelling, *Grounding*, 142, 162.
38 Schelling, *Grounding*, 132–5.
39 Schelling, *Grounding*, 148.
40 Schelling, *Grounding*, 159.
41 Schelling, *Grounding*, 143.
42 Schelling, *Grounding*, 160.
43 Schelling, *Grounding*, 202.
44 Schelling, *Grounding*, 198.
45 Schelling, *Grounding*, 211.
46 Schelling, *Grounding*, 212.
47 Schelling, *Grounding*, 203.
48 Schelling, *Grounding*, 203.
49 Schelling, *Grounding*, 165.
50 See Hippolyte, *Logic*, 4.
51 Schelling, *Grounding*, 169.
52 Schelling, *Grounding*, 179.
53 Schelling, *Grounding*, 194.

54 Schelling, *Grounding*, 208–9.
55 Schelling, *Grounding*, 11, 153.
56 Schelling, *Grounding*, xii.
57 Schelling, *Grounding*, x.
58 Schelling, *Grounding*, 136.
59 Schelling, *Grounding*, 18.
60 Schelling, *Grounding*, 21.
61 Schelling, *Grounding*, 9.
62 Schelling, *Grounding*, 9.
63 Schelling, *Grounding*, 10.
64 Schelling, *Grounding*, 134.
65 Schelling, *Grounding*, 88–9.
66 Schelling, *Grounding*, 145.
67 Schelling, *Grounding*, 125.
68 Schelling, *Grounding*, 120.
69 Schelling, *Grounding*, 170.
70 Schelling, *Grounding*, 167.

# Chapter 6

# Something Higher Than Any Reconciliation

Friedrich Nietzsche's *The Birth of Tragedy*

Nietzsche was deeply influenced by Spinoza and Schelling, and by Hegel, whom he strongly critiqued, but also admired. As Jean Wahl, who played a large role in reintroducing Nietzsche to France after World War II, in part through his student Deleuze, observed, "which author has, more than Nietzsche, declared that others, so many others, are in error?"[1] Nevertheless, it might not be too much to say that Nietzsche has been the most influential philosopher in the twentieth century, not only notoriously influencing the Nazis through their overly simplistic misinterpretations of his work, encouraged by his sister after his descent into madness in 1889 and his death in 1900,[2] but also deeply influencing the depth psychologies of Freud and Jung, the sociology of Max Weber, the existentialisms of Heidegger, Sartre, and Camus, and the poststructuralisms of Derrida, Foucault, and Deleuze. Nietzsche's intermittent misanthropy, misogyny, and flirtation with anti-Semitism and authoritarianism cannot be denied, and they must be kept in mind when reading his harsher denouncements of modernity or Socrates or Christianity.[3] We have no choice but to take Nietzsche with a large grain of salt if we hope to avoid succumbing to these pitfalls intertwined with the positive "revaluation of all values,"[4] pitfalls partially connected to his descent into madness, which in turn may have been caused by a hereditary condition. But Nietzsche was also extraordinarily profound, and his concepts cannot be ignored if we hope to understand how to move beyond the deconstructive "postmodern," as there is a large strain of thought in his work, perhaps especially in *The Birth of Tragedy*, that can be designated as integrative.

After this first work, which struck a balance between diagnosis and cure, specifically through the reconciliation of opposites, Nietzsche became the critical diagnostician par excellence, which is why almost exclusively

DOI: 10.4324/9781003195498-7

diagnostic theorists like Freud and Derrida could be so deeply influenced by his work. There are certainly many brilliant positive insights in Nietzsche's subsequent books, but the overarching tone of his work is primarily critical. While he brilliantly prophesied and influenced the trajectory of culture and thought over the century-and-a-half following his writing, it is this first book which perhaps provides us with the clearest envisagement of how the deep historical problems he diagnoses can be overcome in a constructive moment after deconstruction, still far in the future in 1872. Certainly, the concepts of the eternal return, the will to power, and the Overman are also positive gestures in this direction, and they are more profound in some ways than this early work, but they are also more obscure and ambiguous. Nevertheless, those later concepts can be understood as developments, forged during Nietzsche's darker days, of the mode of thought he expressed during his happiest and most conventionally successful years. We can recognize the profundity of the work he wrested from his great suffering without diminishing the importance of his first work, which may be understood as the most hopeful expression of the mode that Nietzsche would articulate in his later works, not fundamentally different – more naïve, but also more constructive, the lightest color in Nietzsche's palette.[5]

The revaluation of all values he undertook in his later books is not an activity that most of us would be willing, or even able, fully to undertake in our lived experience, "to live what is unlivable, or to think what is unthinkable," as Stengers writes, which would in some cases entail violations of the most basic progressive principles of equality and compassion, but a primary contribution of these later works is "to refer to the unlivable and the unthinkable, to criticize or deconstruct that in which others still 'believe.'"[6] We may be willing to part with the affects of ressentiment and guilt, but we may also want to preserve the positive progressive ideals of compassion, tolerance, and forgiveness, often derived from Christianity, as ethical principles rather than moral laws.[7] In fact, Nietzsche was by all accounts generally polite and mild-mannered in his personal relations, so rather than take seriously Nietzsche's extreme rhetoric, sometimes bordering on reactionary, that we can cast aside morality, as the Nazis did, we should rather understand Nietzsche as liberating us from the unquestioning obedience to moral laws and their affective bondage. As Nietzsche exhorts us: "Let us remain faithful to Wagner in what is true and original in him – and especially, as his disciples, by remaining faithful to ourselves in what is true and original in us."[8] This exhortation can be extended to

Nietzsche himself, and to any of the theorists discussed in these pages, so that we can affirm both the truth and originality we find in others and the truth and originality we find in ourselves, though these truths may appear incommensurable with what is less true and original in the other, perhaps primarily constituted in what they deny.

Nietzsche presaged the descent of the world into madness, culminating in the death and rebirth of the mid-twentieth century, from the abyssal horrors of the World Wars to the ecstatic heights of the counterculture and the ultimate complexities of poststructuralism in the sixties and seventies. But his initiatory text, before he was battered by disappointment, seems most consistently to suggest a way forward, though some of the concepts he introduced later were indispensable additions to this initial vision, not in its specifics in relation to Nietzsche's time, which rely far too heavily on Schopenhauer and Wagner – Nietzsche later acknowledging that one could simply replace Wagner's name with Zarathustra, or even with Nietzsche himself[9] – but in its impulse toward the integration of the Apollonian and the Dionysian, of ordered, moderate consciousness and the chaotic, transformative unconscious, two of a multiplicity of "the gods which are in *us*," as he would write a decade later.[10]

Nietzsche is perhaps the most autobiographical of all philosophers, so his fascinating and tragic biography must be taken into account when discussing his work. He was in chronic pain, which he understood as deeply affecting, and even impelling his philosophy.[11] Far from nullifying his ideas – and equally far from glorifying his pain – this recognition demonstrates how different kinds of truths, different valid narrative constructions of reality, are at least partially motivated by different bodily feelings. Nietzsche is more affectively negative than most of the other thinkers discussed in these pages, perhaps because he experienced more physical pain, but his great triumph is to have transmuted these affects into epochally creative and inspired concepts. Among many more positive concepts, Nietzsche teaches us that we cannot hope to integrate the disparate multiplicity of affective and conceptual experience if we do not acknowledge, and even tarry with, the negative, the apparently incommensurable and irreconcilable. Hegel understood this, but Nietzsche explicitly rejected the negative, while implicitly giving it voice, because he lived it in his body, but sought to transmute this negativity into pure affirmation, an extraordinarily admirable goal that he achieved with only partial success. As he wrote just two months before his final break with sanity: "The psychological problem about the type of Zarathustra is how one who to an unprecedented degree says 'no,' does 'no' to everything people previously said 'yes' to, can nevertheless be the opposite of a no-saying spirit."[12] This problematic paradox also applies to Nietzsche himself, and it is not possible to achieve a differentiated theory of integration without taking Nietzsche's paradoxical transgressivity into account, without dwelling deeply with him in his pain as well as in his sublime genius.

It may be surmised that what Nietzsche found objectionable in Hegel is that he made the negative a formula, despite Hegel's protestations, something to be reconciled in a return to unity rather than an irreducible bodily experience, perhaps in part because Hegel did not dwell with constant pain. Although we can recognize Hegel as immensely profound, he was perhaps prevented from achieving the particular kind of depth that Nietzsche explored by his lack of persistent, extraordinary physical affliction. He simply did not suffer enough to attain those particular insights, though he attained his own more consistently positive affectively impelled insights, despite his emphasis of the negative. The specific circumstances of philosophers' lives, as well as their intrinsic temperaments, deeply condition the particular contours of their work, which in turn condition the way their ideas are received, forming both the limitations and the essential textures of their historical development in actuality, rather than as abstract, disembodied conceptual systems. Philosophers are not less because of the particular contingencies of their lives, but more. As Spinoza and James especially recognize, affect is destiny, and the contingencies of birth and circumstance that determine the particular affective complexes of each individual are the constraining and impelling forces that forge philosophers in all their glorious humanity, allowing them to create their conceptual personae as works of art expressing different kinds of truth.

Nietzsche understood that illness and health, pain or its lack, inevitably inform the work of a philosopher, so that while we can be grateful to him for having endured immense pain for the two decades of his great productivity, which impelled him to explore the profoundest depths and darknesses of human experience, and thereby render these realms legitimate areas of inquiry for depth psychology and continental philosophy in the twentieth century, we can also find great value for our current era in his first book. Written in the wake of the happiest time in Nietzsche's life, despite the terrible horrors he had witnessed and the grievous wounds he had suffered as an ambulance driver in the Franco-Prussian war, he was carried through this book's composition by the wave of good fortune that began with him becoming a professor of philology at the University of Basel at the extremely young age of twenty-four, and then becoming very close with Richard and Cosima Wagner, when Wagner was one of the most revered composers of his generation. A high-spirited optimism permeates this book, though inevitably tempered by Nietzsche's incipient suffering, so that it is not merely a work of naïve youthful folly, as it is sometimes judged, but Nietzsche's most sustained positive expression of a "philosophy of the future,"[13] along with much of *Thus Spoke Zarathustra* and parts of other works, not yet filled with the ressentiment that would ironically come to permeate much of his later work, even, and perhaps especially, in the undeniably brilliant denouncement of ressentiment.

For one instance of many, Nietzsche's first piece of published writing after *The Birth of Tragedy* was the "untimely meditation" on David Strauss, whom Nietzsche viciously, gleefully denounces as a conventionally Christian-humanist philistine.[14] Although there is surely much truth in Nietzsche's critique, one might also notice that Strauss' book, published the same year as Nietzsche's first book, sold many copies and received wide acclaim, while Nietzsche's was, at first, largely rejected and neglected. It only adds to the awareness of Nietzsche's apparent jealousy, expressed in a joyously scornful fugue of hate-reading, that he denounces the philistines exemplified by Strauss' readers for having resisted, and not having recognized, previous great German writers in their own time, a grievance which transparently displays Nietzsche's resentment over his own genius not having been immediately recognized upon the publication of his first book. Perhaps Nietzsche even envied Strauss' moderate courage in critiquing a literalist Christian faith in the miraculous, while still upholding Christian morality, as Nietzsche later expressed regret for not having extended his critique of Socrates in his first book to Christianity, which would become a primary object of his wrath for the rest of his career.[15] But far from discounting Nietzsche, this transparent irony is a large element in his paradoxical charm, through which he expressed some of the darkest and most dangerous thoughts in a way that allows the discerning reader to recognize his woundedness and insecurity, and thus to love him as an endearingly pathetic and brilliant figure despite his many harsh and transgressive pronouncements.

In all honesty, we generally become experts in subjects that are urgently, intimately important to us, a situation that Nietzsche himself recognizes, writing: "Does not everything that we take to be important betray us?"[16]

Nietzsche's constant suffering and his relative lack of worldly success impelled him to effect a reversal in which the suffering philosopher-artist is superior to the physically healthy, bourgeois member of society. While this great driving force of his work is ironic given his denouncement of the Christian notion that "the meek shall inherit the earth,"[17] as he was the epitome of a physically meek person incapable of a normative life, despite his vigorous hiking schedule, this fundamental, inescapable contradiction in his thought allowed him to illuminate the complexities of ressentiment with a penetrating insight that would have been impossible had he not experienced this affect so completely himself. As James observes in relation to Nietzsche's denouncement of Christian saints: "Poor Nietzsche's antipathy is itself sickly enough, but we all know what he means."[18] Nietzsche is most closely associated with the negative critical philosophy that is the phenomenological correlate of suffering, but his first book is where he perhaps most fully expresses a way beyond the suffering characteristic of the death of the modern, which had to be gone through, with the current political regressions in the United States and Europe perhaps marking one of the last gasps of modernity and patriarchy, a torturous contraction in an epochal renascence. Nietzsche's vision of the reconciliation of the Apollonian and Dionysian opposites in the imminent work of Wagner was doomed to failure, as the whole descent, which he so strikingly presaged, into the horrors of the World Wars had to be gone through before the reascent could begin with the counterculture. This rebirth from the egoic death of Western culture, which found one culmination in 1945, was a new Hellenic renaissance inspired to a large degree by Nietzsche himself, one in a series of transformative deaths and rebirths in which we are evidently still embroiled, like the shamanic initiate who dies and is reborn multiple times over the course of the initiatory ordeal.[19]

If Deleuze can claim in *Nietzsche and Philosophy* that "the final truth of the dialectic"[20] is found in Hegel's early, more explicitly Christian writings, why then can we not recognize the truth of Nietzsche, or at least an essential part of that truth, in his first book? Michael Inwood has posed a similar question about Heidegger, extrapolating from Heidegger's own concepts: "A genuine beginning, he said, is not simple or primitive. It leaps over what is to come. Might this be true of his own early work?"[21] I would suggest that Nietzsche's first book in some ways leaps over what was to come, containing the purest expression of the creative impulse that animated all of his thought, before rejection, disappointment, illness, and isolation deepened him, but also turned him against the world, against himself, and possibly contributed to his descent into madness.[22] Just as Nietzsche suggests that we in the modern era have been living the ages of Ancient Greece backwards, perhaps in the century-and-a-half since this startling insight was expressed, we have been living the development of Nietzsche's thought backwards, following Ariadne's thread through the labyrinth of the unconscious, back to the unprimitive primal imaginary that marked Nietzsche's origin as a philosopher.[23]

Nietzsche writes in *Ecce Homo* that *The Birth of Tragedy* "smells offensively Hegelian,"[24] but this rejection of his dialectical origins cannot be separated from the tragic trajectory Nietzsche traced in his own life. As with many writers, he was a bit embarrassed by his early work, though he also still found value in it at the very end of his career, writing that this book is "utterly remarkable" and "anticipatory," that it was his "first revaluation of all values," and it is illuminating to realize that this is the only book he wrote before being ostracized from the academy.[25] In fact, it is the overwhelmingly negative reception of this book by the philological community that ruined his academic reputation and largely rendered him an outsider, so that before the book was published, hundreds of students were attending his public lectures, while after the book's publication, his courses were being canceled due to lack of enrollment. This work can thus be considered the only relatively mature expression of Nietzsche's thought before he was battered by critical attacks and embittered by the suffering of academic rejection, accompanied by the degeneration of his physical health, which nevertheless allowed him to resign his professorship with a yearly pension to focus on writing.

Although it is true, as Deleuze suggests, that Nietzsche in *The Birth of Tragedy* reifies the opposition of the Dionysian groundless abyss and Apollonian individuation, this oppositional relation is implicitly situated within a more complex multiplicity of agential potencies. In this book, Nietzsche tends to portray these opposed archetypes, as he calls them (*Urbilder*), in a totalizing schema still constrained by the tradition of dualistic western metaphysics ultimately embodied in the Hegelian dialectic, which nevertheless provides an opening to its own self-overcoming. However, Nietzsche's later conception, a primary precursor to Deleuze's expression of a mythical dialectic, does not require the complete abandonment of opposition as an efficacious conceptual construction. Rather, it allows binarity's resituation as one axis in a more expansive topological manifold of singular potencies in constantly shifting complexes of relationality conceivable in geometrical terms, not only as opposed, but also as conjunctive, confluent, perpendicular, parallel, intertwining in tortuous curves, or even missing one another altogether, trajectories sailing on entirely disjointed and eccentric planes of immanence. For Deleuze, the later Nietzsche discovered "a new way of exploring the depth, of bringing a distinct eye to bear upon it, of discerning in it a thousand voices, of making all of these voices speak,"[26] a novel mode embodied in Hillman's Jungian archetypal psychology as much as in Deleuze's "method of dramatization"[27] and Deleuzoguattarian schizoanalysis.

It is not until after his first work that Nietzsche began really to think of himself as untimely, as out of step with his age. He enacted the descent into the Dionysian domain of the irrational unconscious, which he deeply affirms in his work, though the negative inflection of this mythological figure became a dominant fact in the World Wars and the rise of the Nazis in their orgies of mass destruction and the will to power expressed in its most facile and simplistic form as mere dominance.[28] And it is not surprising that the Nazis found some justification for their atrocities in Nietzsche, though this was never his intention, and they misread him badly, for as one Nazi intellectual wryly observed, "apart from the fact that Nietzsche was not a socialist, not a nationalist and opposed to racial thinking, he could have been a leading National Socialist thinker."[29] Nietzsche envisioned an artistic and cultural awakening, not a military or political one.

Although his early depiction of the Dionysian is perhaps somewhat one-sided and overly laudatory, Nietzsche expresses a profound conception of what has been lost in the privileging of theoretical order that he associates with the Apollonian, and eventually with Socrates, and which found its culmination in modern science. He offers a powerful presentiment of how the Socratic-Apollonian order can be integrated with the Dionysian in a novel mode of relation, though it seems to have required the mediation of the twentieth century for this prescience to begin to become a viable actuality, the descent which necessarily preceded any real hope of ascent. Nietzsche's thought is unmistakably dialectical in this text, and there is no denying that Hegel remained the dominant philosophical figure of Nietzsche's era, Deleuze and Guattari going so far as to nominate the period encompassing Nietzsche's life as "his Hegelian epoch."[30] But by incorporating these two gods into an oppositional dialectical conception, Nietzsche began to create the precondition for a more expansively pluralist mythical dialectic beyond binarity, though he came to understand that a descent into the unconscious had to be gone through before this theory of eternal return could be fully expressed, that the sun had to go down in order to rise again in a new dawn, and the rising could not be rushed, but proceeded inexorably at its own steady pace.[31] This work conveys Nietzsche's youthful desire to leap ahead past the tragic descent by affirming tragedy, to master suffering by affirming it, a suffering which he had already experienced in the war, and perhaps hoped quickly to move beyond, though he came to understand that suffering cannot ultimately be mastered, that it demands submission, and that his role was to preside over the descent, to embody, express, and even transmute it in all of its sustained complexity and ambiguity.

Nietzsche primarily portrays the development from the ancient Dionysian chorus to the later Platonic-Socratic philosophy as a loss, but it is a necessary loss, a differentiating separation that could only begin to be overcome in Nietzsche's time after the Enlightenment and Idealism, though he later came to understand that his timeline was far too optimistic. A century later, Derrida is almost completely immersed in this sense of loss and closure, but Nietzsche, like Jung and Deleuze after him, is ambivalent, feeling acutely the loss of nonrational modes of relation, but also envisaging a mode beyond pure reason, to which the dialectic creates an opening, though still enclosed by the Apollonian-Socratic in its privileging of rational intelligibility over other modes characteristic of the Dionysian. While Nietzsche's later works would offer deeper articulations of some of the concepts expressed here, as well as novel, indispensable concepts, and although the critique often dominant in those later works was necessary for the final writing of deconstruction, *The Birth of Tragedy* provides a glimpse of what might come after that deconstruction. In order completely to embody the critical mode and become a primary prophet of modernity's demise, Nietzsche had to choose to leave behind the more affectively positive and hopeful mode of this work, and we can be grateful for his martyrdom, a martyrdom so complete that he would later deny the validity of philosophical martyrdom itself.[32] But for the purpose of moving beyond the critical mode, Nietzsche's primal, youthful expression provides a positive impulsion, enigmatically sustained in the primarily negative trajectory of his later work, which may serve to carry later positive concepts, extracted like precious jewels from their profoundly tortured embedding, into novel affective and conceptual domains.

As Nietzsche understood, he was able to enact the descent into the Dionysian chaos not in spite of his illness, but in part because of it. Similarly, he was able vividly to envision the ascent after a descent in his first book because this was the happiest time of his life, the time when he himself was in the ascent in both his career as a professor and in his personal life with the Wagners. Although his expression of the ascent would become deeper, it would also become profoundly ambiguous, as Zarathustra is only "a shadow of that which must come," the negative space defined by the absence of an anticipated positive illumination, and thus "that will which is will to power must will something higher than any reconciliation – but how shall this happen?"[33] Nietzsche never provides a straightforward answer to this question, and neither Zarathustra nor Nietzsche can tell us what exactly the Overman and the eternal return are except in evocative parables, though these evocations enabled Deleuze's more fully elaborated theory of the eternal return.[34] Nietzsche is reaching for something he can feel but not quite grasp, something like reconciliation but beyond it, a higher register of reconciliation, a will to potencies which can only be alluded to, eternally circled in upon, but never quite attained, at least in his direct expression, through the figures of Zarathustra, Dionysus, Ariadne, and Overman. He recognizes that before he can reach his highest ascent, his fate is that he must "descend deeper into suffering than I ever climbed before," as "from the deepest the highest must come into its height,"[35] and although he was never able to accomplish this ascent that he foresaw, we may carry forward the ascent initiated in the twentieth century in large part because Nietzsche descended so deeply.

In his "Attempt at Self-Criticism" of *The Birth of Tragedy*, written fourteen years after the book's publication, Nietzsche acknowledges that he had been overly optimistic about the possibility of an imminent reconciliation of the Apollonian and the Dionysian embodied in the music of Wagner. This reconciliation not having occurred, and his relationship with Wagner having progressively deteriorated, we find Nietzsche darker, more pessimistic, perhaps because, within the course of his individual life, he could sense Germany marching inexorably toward the horrors of the World Wars, which are after all the extreme expression of the shadow of the Dionysian irrational, the lowest form of the will to power, even as the twentieth century also witnessed a dramatic awakening of the more positive aspects of the Dionysian impulse, not only in philosophy, but in art, literature, cinema, and perhaps most significant for the current context, in music. As he writes with astonishing prescience in *Ecce Homo*: "Some day my name will be linked to the memory of something monstrous, of a crisis as yet unprecedented on earth, the most profound collision of consciences,"[36] the collision of fascist destruction on one hand and the creative trajectory of twentieth century thought and art on the other. He did not create this titanic collision, but only foresaw its inevitability.[37] Within the decades of his life, Nietzsche's growing darkness was perhaps necessary, mirroring the encroaching darkness of the world. But nearly a century-and-a-half after its publication, the hopefulness of his first book may finally be timely, as we may now be witnessing, and collectively creating, the incipient emergence of a novel mode of thought after deconstruction that integrates the Apollonian-Socratic rationality privileged in modernity with older mythical modes that correspond with the figure of Dionysus, situating both Apollo and Dionysus in a more expansive multiplicity of potencies. Although Nietzsche's life and thought enacted a tragic descent into the underworld as much as any other modern figure, we can discern in his first book, this "impossible book,"[38] as he called it, the opening to a more profoundly differentiated positive integration.

Nietzsche's revaluation of all values does not primarily offer a way beyond this diagnosis and descent, but a clearing of the stage, with only subtle clues and intimations that were taken up by the Nazis (however mistakenly) as well as depth psychology and continental philosophy. The Hegelian dialectic, partially conceivable as a rational expression of the ancient dynamics of death and rebirth, is a pivotal step toward the creation of a future mode of ascent and rebirth after the death of the modern, but the dialectic cannot accomplish this task alone. It requires its metadialectical complement in the trajectory that has led from Nietzsche to poststructuralism and yet further, a differentiating integration beyond opposition and reconciliation. Only in this way can a dialectical conception become subtle enough to allow for the emergence of the Overman through the eternal return, though it is Nietzsche's first book which begins to express a novel inflection of the dialectic for which his later work provides a deepening complement, a critique that may ultimately allow that initial dialectical impulse to emerge triumphant, transformed through its integration with differentiating potencies. Nietzsche's work thus contains both the dialectic and the seeds of its overcoming in the twentieth century, especially with Deleuze, who would carry the critique of the dialectic to its final self-immolation, and thus provide a way for philosophy to overcome the Hegelian oppositional dialectic, which had offered a profoundly liberating and novel mode of thought in the early decades of its reception, but which had inevitably come to be felt as a constraining orthodoxy due to its nearly hegemonic dominance in nineteenth-century philosophy.

The mythological and historical figures around whom Nietzsche builds his conception in his first book do not always accurately depict the way these figures were conceived by the Greeks themselves, which is one of the primary critiques that this text received from philologists. But Nietzsche is after a more symbolic, psychological truth, and he employs these figures to begin to express his theory of powers. Nietzsche asserts that for a poetic, artistic mode of thought, which he is employing in his evocation of the development of ancient Greek dramatic art, metaphor plays the role that concepts play for a more rationalist mode. These figures are not merely allegorical characters employed to represent particular abstract qualities, but living, imaginal persons, archetypes as Nietzsche describes them, a term which Jung, Hillman, and others would later take up in great depth.[39] The deities Nietzsche evokes, Apollo and Dionysus, rule their respective domains in a more-than-metaphorical way, and he identifies the height of Greek art, located with Attic tragedy in the fifth century BCE, as the synthesis of these two potencies, reflecting the forces at work in biological evolution as mediated through the often conflictual relation, and occasional reconciliation, of male and female in sexual reproduction.

Nietzsche describes Apollo as exemplified by the placid, ordered visual art of sculpture, correlated with dream and illusion, with prophecy and fantasy, with the higher world of Mount Olympus, with truth and perfection, moderation and self-knowledge, and with the intelligible daylight consciousness of the differentiated self, embodied in the sublime art of Homer. By contrast, Dionysus is exemplified in the discordant, instinctive, affective art of music, correlated with intoxication and revelry, with sexual urges and the profusion of spring, with the descent into the underworld of the unconscious, with excess and hubris, and with the nighttime dissolution of the ego in communion with nature and the collective. The two archetypes eternally clash as an opposition between countervalent impulses, a tension which impels these dynamisms to produce ever-higher and more potent offspring, culminating in rare moments of miraculous metaphysical reconciliation exemplified in the era of Attic tragedy, beginning in 499 BCE with the first performance of a dramatic work by Aeschylus.

The correlation of dreams with daylight consciousness may seem jarring, even paradoxical, as one would tend to think of dreams as correlated with unconscious nighttime slumber, but the Apollonian is not yet the rational, theoretical mode that Nietzsche will associate in later chapters with Socrates, and Nietzsche may have conflated the figure of Apollo with other divine potencies, requiring further differentiations in his wake. For Nietzsche, the Apollonian is the illusion of the Vedic goddess Maya, recalling the Platonic image of the phenomena of existence as shadows on the wall of the cave, the world as a mere echo of transcendent, eternal Forms which it has been the traditional task of philosophers to discern, to see beyond the immanent world to this transcendent domain behind conscious experience. The Apollonian is a relatively undifferentiated precursor to the theoretical consciousness of Socrates, who will eventually take the place of Apollo in Nietzsche's narrative, shifting the opposition from the two gods in tragic art leading up to the fifth century, to that between the god Dionysus and the man Socrates, who lived during the height of tragedy, but who was opposed to this dramatic art in its earlier, higher forms.

Nietzsche is clearly on the side of Dionysus, who would remain a primary figure in his later work, to the point that Nietzsche signed some of his last letters before his break with sanity as Dionysus, while the figure of Apollo quickly fades into the background partway through *The Birth of Tragedy*. But in this work, we see the Dionysian rending the Apollonian veil of illusion to reveal an occulted originary unity behind the many, to which the collective gains access through ecstatic music and dance, in which individuals forget themselves and the conventional modes of relation, the mere walking of daily life, and instead learn to "fly dancing into the heavens."[40] The opposition between Apollonian and Dionysian provides explanatory efficacy at some discursive levels, but it seems to break down into incoherence if one tries, as Nietzsche initially does, to generalize it too far, which seems to be why he shifts the opposition with the Dionysian from Apollo to Socrates. However, within the specific domain of the relation between these two divinities, Nietzsche's evocation is profound, though there are other domains, other orthogonal, diagonal, or eccentric relations with other forces that complicate this too-neat oppositional distinction. Nevertheless, this binary issuing into reconciliation expresses something essential not only to the era of Greek tragedy, but to the historical epoch more generally, a persistent problematic opposition which can also manifest in more confluent ways, among other oppositions, and still other geometrical relations that exceed the figure of binarity, one relational axis among a multiplicity, one degree of freedom and constraint within a more multifarious and expansive topological manifold.

After describing the two potencies in this evocative way, which contains elements of both illumination and obfuscation, Nietzsche offers a complex narrative that traces an unmistakably dialectical movement, from the ancient cult of Dionysus to its negation and complement in the rise of the dominance of Apollo in the Doric art of the eighth through the middle of the fifth century BCE. This period's end is generally located around the decades of Socrates' birth in 470 BCE, serving temporarily to suppress the ecstatic and unitive, but also grotesque and bestial, impulses of the Dionysian, embodied in the earlier forms of Greek art and religion. However, this temporary reactionary oppression of the Dionysian by the Apollonian was disrupted by a spontaneous return of the repressed, which impelled "a timely reconciliation"[41] – a striking phrase given Nietzsche's subsequent embrace of the untimely – which he describes as the central period in ancient Greek religious history, a transformative emergence of something fundamentally novel from this oppositional relation, precisely the type of transformative historical moment which Nietzsche foresaw, but never experienced in his lifetime.

Before this ancient reconciliation, even Greek music was Apollonian, characterized by regular and placid rhythms, recalling the "simple rhythm"[42] of the Hegelian dialectic, which the reemergence of the Dionysian, in the form of the dithyramb, transformed through the production of potent affect, both the glorious heights and the abyssal depths of experience flattened and suppressed in the ordered cultural era dominated by the Apollonian, a critique echoed by the mid-twentieth century counterculture's dim view of the relatively conservative postwar order in the West. This Dionysian impulse is the creative and destructive will of nature, which rends the comforting Apollonian illusion, penetrating through to the primal source behind the veil of Maya, a potency searching for symbolic expression to carry ancient Greek culture beyond the bounds of what it had thus far achieved, a dynamism embodied in liberating ecstatic dance suppressing the individual ego, allowing the transformative power of the Dionysian to manifest through the collective, which could easily be a contemporary description of the music and counterculture of the mid-twentieth century.

Nietzsche finds himself powerfully drawn, apparently by something that exceeds his conscious volition, to assert that the Dionysian drive toward transformation through the depths of suffering requires the transcendent Apollonian dream-order to be redeemed from mere destruction, for its ascent from the underworld, where the hero may be transformed by the Apollonian mirroring of the Dionysian from which the phenomenal world emerges. And, in the opposite trajectory, just as the Apollonian is necessary to redeem the Dionysian, so was the Dionysian necessary to jolt the ancient Greeks out of their restraining, inhibiting moderation to confront the raging torrents of titanic will and desire, of suffering and ecstasy, behind the civilized illusion they had erected against the "barbarian"[43] invasion of the Dionysian. This invasion served as the destructive negative of the Apollonian, paradoxically impelling the Apollonian to its redemptive ascendance, which it would never generate the force to achieve alone, without the penetrating creative chaos of the Dionysian, a death of the ego which allows a more profound truth to be reborn through a by-turns torturous and ecstatic labor. The Dionysian is the force of creative destruction that inexorably arises to transform the periods when the Apollonian is dominant, which have settled into a static, rigid orthodoxy. But the moments when Dionysus is dominant cannot last for long, as their destructive excess becomes too much for a culture to bear, so that a new order is born out of the ashes of the old, and the peak of this order occurs at the moment of reconciliation between the two archetypes, which prepares the way for a novel confrontation, consummation, and emergence. Nietzsche describes this historical process enacted in Greek culture, which can be extrapolated to other cultures and other times – including Nietzsche's and our own – as being teleologically lured toward the highest moment of synthesis exemplified in the Dionysian dithyramb, the song form characteristic of Attic tragedy, the child who emerges from the sustained discord issuing into a union of the two gods.

Having primarily lionized the Dionysian, Nietzsche also acknowledges that the descent into the unconscious can, as with Hamlet's terrible understanding, inhibit action in the world, suppressing the will to act in the egoic death that can only issue into rebirth in concert with the Apollonian, whose illusions constrain and give form to the undifferentiated chaos experienced in the agonies and ecstasies of the Dionysian state, which renders the concerns of the daylight world absurd and irrelevant. Dionysus allows one to see past these conventional orthodoxies, these constructed cultural forms of Apollo, which in turn serve to differentiate the ego from the world so that one can find a reason to act as an individuated self rather than merely watching the world pass by without fear or desire. Although the Dionysian is the will itself, this will can only find a domain of effectuation in relation with the Apollonian veil of the phenomenal world, the mind freely choosing its form of expression, though Nietzsche would not read Spinoza for another nine years when he would joyfully discern a resonance with what he had already intimated. The Apollonian without the Dionysian becomes rigid and static, but the Dionysian without the Apollonian is meaningless and undifferentiated.

The Dionysian chorus is the artistic expression of the tragic and ecstatic depths of reality, mediated through the sublime Apollonian artifice, which provides the structure of dramatic art in order to channel the Dionysian force of creative destruction into a cultural form that allows the collective to participate in the Dionysian self-overcoming, dissolving the binary of audience and chorus while maintaining the constraints necessary for civilized existence, a balance of nature and culture which marries the deepest things with the highest things to generate an emergent mode of relation. The Apollonian artistic form allowed the Dionysian spirit in the audience to witness itself in the mirror of the chorus, and thus to become conscious of itself, and finally to pass through that mirror to become one with its other in the total event of the tragic drama, discontinuously producing a more expansive consciousness, a mythical evocation of the dialectic which describes the process of an entity becoming other than itself in order to become conscious of itself, out of which emerges a reconciliation of opposites on two perpendicular axes, of both the audience and the chorus, and of the Apollonian and the Dionysian.

It is almost precisely halfway through the book that Nietzsche shifts the opposition with Dionysus from Apollo to Socrates, the mask of a radically novel divine force, the embodiment of "theoretical man."[44] Ever since the authorities of Athens had condemned Socrates, making him the founding martyr of a new kind of religion, one that transcended religion as it is generally understood called philosophy, the image of Socrates in Western culture has been almost entirely positive. Nietzsche's philosophical denunciation of Socrates is profoundly transgressive, inverting the general character of the last two millennia of philosophy, which has overwhelmingly conceived of Socrates as initiating a higher stage of culture than the mystery cults of ancient Greek religion. Nietzsche portrays the emergence of theoretical rationality in the figure of Socrates as a loss of primal unity and enchantment, a critique that has been taken up in numerous forms in the twentieth century, and which has found its way in varying degrees into the works discussed in all of the chapters below, which generally express a more balanced view of modernity than either advocating an exclusivist privileging of rationality or the countervalent denouncement complexly embodied in Nietzsche, conceiving modernity as constituting both a loss and a gain, a fall and an ascent.

For Nietzsche, Socrates represents the degeneration of Greek tragedy, as Socrates explicitly preferred the more rationally intelligible aesthetic employed by Euripides to the more mysterious and ecstatic Dionysian mode of Aeschylus. The Apollonian divorced almost entirely from the Dionysian loses its vitality and grandeur, becoming all too human in its more theoretical and naturalist mode, in which the characters on the stage merely reflect the surface, egoic conventionality of the audience back to itself, amplifying this daylight consciousness in the recursive loop of a debased form of art and life. Euripides employs the Apollonian illusion in service to the belief, which would become dominant in modernity, that rationality, especially in the discernment of causality, can single-handedly render the world intelligible. Nietzsche, who would come to be recognized as the preeminent critical voice of his era, critiques Euripidean tragedy for its rationalist criticality and facile intelligibility, which for him flatten the affective and artistic heights and depths that rendered Attic tragedy so elevated, profound, and transformative. Whereas one might usually think of increased consciousness as progress, Nietzsche primarily expresses the loss of the primal unity of the earlier cultural form, though he employs the very verbal and conceptual tools of philosophy to critique the cultural moment exemplified by Euripides and Socrates in the fifth century BCE that is a foundational moment of these critical instruments. This is the self-enclosed quality that would come to characterize Derridean deconstruction in an even more extreme way, employing logocentric rationality to think beyond the rational, an undertaking which Derrida generally deems impossible, but for which Nietzsche variously discerns an opening, first in the reconciliation of opposites in *The Birth of Tragedy*, and then in the mode that goes beyond reconciliation, which he can only express in the obscurely profound figures of the eternal return, the will to power, and the Overman.

Later, Nietzsche would push the potency opposed to the Dionysian even further than the movement from the Apollonian to the Socratic, rendering Christ as Dionysus' opposite, but also identifying himself, in his late letters, not only as Dionysus, but also as The Crucified, suggesting a complex integration which it would not be Nietzsche's destiny to complete, but only to evoke, to create the conditions for the overcoming of this multivalent opposition of Apollo-Socrates-Christ with Dionysus in the work of later theorists. Whereas before Socrates, the instinctual was the primary creative and affirmative force, Socrates inverts this relation to render critical consciousness as the creative dynamism, a mode that was almost exclusively privileged in Nietzsche's time, so that even his critique of this critical consciousness employs that very mode for its self-immolation. Whereas Attic tragedy is the peak artistic expression of the mystical primal unity of being, Socrates is the agent of rationality against mysticism, which has often been understood as progress in the ascent of science in modernity, but the loss of which has been felt acutely at least since the Romantic reaction to the Enlightenment. Nietzsche may be understood as embodying this countervalent tendency carried to an extreme, which would enable the reaction against rationality of the mid-twentieth century counterculture, but also of the mind devouring itself in the figure of Derrida, as well as the emergence of a novel mode of philosophy beyond Cartesian clarity and Hegelian opposition with Deleuze.

For Nietzsche, dialectic, particularly the Platonic variety, is too optimistic, taking as its a priori premise that rational argumentation can produce agreement among the interlocutors, leading to ever-higher domains of truth and understanding. And though we may recognize the great value in rational discourse, we can also see that Nietzsche is right that something profound must be repressed, that a whole domain of human experience, embodied in the figure of Dionysus, must be denied in order to give attention to the rational daylight consciousness of dialectical intelligibility. Although the rise of Socratic-Platonic rationality was generally experienced as a liberating force, and it has ultimately resulted in the modern world in all its profusion, this rational mode has passed through many complex permutations, becoming rigid and ossified in the Roman Empire, and then being dismantled and dissolved by the twin forces of Christianity and "barbarian" invasion, roughly correlating with the Apollonian and Dionysian impulses respectively reawakening in more vital form, not in a mere opposition, but as epochal shifts of emphasis. And then again, the radically novel Christian religion steadily settled into the orthodoxy of late medieval scholasticism, which was again dissolved in the largely Apollonian Reformation and the primarily Dionysian Renaissance. Through these successive ossifications into orthodoxy and periodic dissolutions driven by the Dionysian, inciting novel Apollonian forms, the rational scientific order had reached a new peak in the late nineteenth century, which called forth the Dionysian from the most unlikely of sources, a young professor from a devout family in the staid discipline of philology who came to embody Dionysus in all of his destructive and transformative creative madness.

The Dionysian potency is especially embodied in music, which exceeds rational thought, speaking directly to the affective heights and depths of embodied experience. Nietzsche discerned the peak of Dionysian musical achievement in the work of Wagner, specifically *Tristan and Isolde*, though his expectation that Wagner's later work would transcend even this height to produce an ecstatic reconciliation of German culture in the near future was not realized, as he was especially disappointed with the Christian tone of *Parsifal*, and Nietzsche became increasingly disdainful toward Wagner and the country of his birth, instead taking inspiration from French thinkers and culture in the ensuing years. However, setting aside his extraordinarily overoptimistic expectation, Nietzsche discerns in the narrative of Socrates himself a more profound, though more obscure, register of the reconciliation that Nietzsche intimated somewhere in the future, perhaps just over a temporal horizon. He grudgingly acknowledges that Socrates was the most powerful embodiment of a trajectory that preceded him toward Schopenhauerian individuation, the differentiation of the rational, autonomous human self from the less conscious, but more deeply embedded self exemplified in the ancient mystery religions and Attic tragedy. Nietzsche discerns the necessity of this repression of the Dionysian in the figure of Socrates for the further development of culture, not only enacting a negation of the Dionysian, but also embodying a different kind of creative force, initiating the mode of rational thought in which Nietzsche was deeply immersed, and in which he greatly excelled, but which he found oppressive and limiting.

The episode in the life of Socrates that holds the key to the integration toward which we are lured along with Nietzsche is the moment when Socrates, at the very end of his life, has been imprisoned for supposedly corrupting the youth of Athens with his deeply transgressive free-thinking. In Plato's *Apology*, Socrates describes his *daimonion*, a divine voice which literally speaks to him to warn him against errors in action, though this voice is not described as being received from the gods, but from something closer to Socrates' soul, a personal guiding spirit. This is the specific innovation that the Athenian authorities found so objectionable, and for which Socrates refused to repent, becoming a martyr to rational individualism and, ultimately, the patron saint of science in his assertion that salvation and justification can be found in rational intelligibility, initiating in earnest the millennia-long trajectory of philosophy and natural science that eventually spread throughout the world, so that "we cannot help but see Socrates as the turning-point, the vortex of world history."[45]

Socrates recounts to his fellow prisoners a dream in which something that Nietzsche describes as similar to his *daimonion* instructs Socrates to "make music!" even though he had always been disdainful of "vulgar, popular music,"[46] which he had derided as a lower form of expression than philosophy. Unexpectedly reversing his previous dismissal in a striking *enantiodromia*, he obeys the voice and composes a hymn to Apollo, embracing the nonrational artistic form in praise of Apollonian intelligibility, which Nietzsche recognizes as the one time in Socrates' life, as far as we know, that he implicitly acknowledged that the rational, logical capacity which privileges intelligibility is limited, and that there are domains of reality which exceed intelligibility, which can only be accessed through a nonrational kind of wisdom characteristic of the Dionysian. Nietzsche portrays Socrates as mediating, throughout his life, the eternal opposition between the theoretical and tragic modes, which reiterate in the cultural domain the more ancient and primordial opposition between the Apollonian and the Dionysian. However, at the very end of his life, Socrates mediates the reconciliation of these genetically related oppositions, becoming "the music-making Socrates,"[47] an emergent figure who might remind one of Bob Dylan singing "how does it feel?" in the chorus of 1965's "Like a Rolling Stone." Deleuze observes that American popular music "has a mythical role to play,"[48] and Dylan perhaps enacted one fulfillment of the "rebirth of tragedy" that Nietzsche hoped was imminent in his own time, but which he would never witness, though even in *Ecce Homo*, his last complete work, he writes of his first work: "Ultimately I have no reason to retract my hope in a Dionysian future for music."[49]

Roughly the last third of *The Birth of Tragedy* dwells with this projected rebirth in Nietzsche's own time, though we can further extrapolate his vision to our time, not as a final reconciliation, but perhaps a moment of emergence into a qualitatively more expansive and intensive mode of relation, an emergence inextricably entwined with crisis and tragedy. Nietzsche confidently declared that the era of Socratic rationalism and scientism, which he portrays as having dominated Western culture for the last two-and-a-half millennia, was at an end at that moment in 1872, though it would require another century for this claim to begin to seem plausible leading up to our own time. Nietzsche discerned that science seemed to be reaching the end of its vitality at that moment in the late nineteenth century, though in reality, science would reach its highest peaks only a few decades later in the quantum and relativistic revolutions of the early twentieth century, but often at the expense of the naïve reductive rationalism which Nietzsche associates, perhaps unfairly, with the figure of Socrates. In fact, Socrates, as portrayed especially by Plato, certainly held a far broader and more profound view of the world than the nineteenth century scientism that Nietzsche sees as the ultimate orthodoxy into which the initial Socratic-Platonic philosophical revolution inevitably degenerated, though it is also true that the great heights which science would attain just a few short years after Nietzsche's death were driven by the acceptance into science of domains of reality previously assumed to be beyond the bounds of scientific inquiry. These domains notably include the consciousness of the observer and the probabilistic irrationality of quantum mechanics, which disrupted the neat determinism of classical mechanics, driven by an almost religious belief in the world's intelligibility, and in the healing ability of understanding, which Nietzsche describes as first having emerged in a robust way with Socrates.

Nietzsche contrasts this scientific knowledge with tragic knowledge, which recognizes that, no matter how far scientific intelligibility is pushed, and it has certainly been pushed much further in our own time than in Nietzsche's, there is an always-receding horizon beyond comprehension, an infinite frontier where our most sophisticated and complex logical formulations break down, becoming paradoxical, confronting us with our finitude. The profound hunger that resides in us cannot be satisfied by knowledge alone, which can never reach a final satisfaction, but also requires art, particularly music, which Nietzsche employs as a symbol for Dionysian modes of relation that exceed the Apollonian-Socratic-scientific pursuit of ordered intelligibility, rather appealing to our affective, intuitive, and aesthetic faculties, satisfying the hunger which solitary intellect can never fulfill, providing a joyful affirmation of life in the face of inevitable suffering, which exceeds knowledge and embraces a higher kind of truth.

Returning finally to Apollo and Dionysus, Nietzsche describes their synthesis in the rebirth of tragedy, which overcomes the operatic form of art in his own time, similarly contemptible to the New Attic Comedy of the ancient Greeks, in that it privileges Apollonian sense over Dionysian affect, rendering music the mere servant of words rather than producing an emergent integration of sound and text in which these two elements mutually support and complement one another. Nietzsche discerned this emergent quality in Wagner, a more dynamic mode visible in the twentieth century in the expansive efflorescence not only of music, but of visual art, cinema, literature, philosophy, and many other domains. In concert with the tragic suffering of the World Wars, the twentieth century seems to have copiously fulfilled Nietzsche's vision of a rebirth of tragic art, a process whose extended culmination we may now be witnessing several decades into the twenty-first century. Like Hegel in 1807, Nietzsche recognized in 1872 that "we stand at the boundary between two different modes of existence,"[50] an epochal transition stretching across several centuries, from the era characterized by the scientific rationality that found its nascent expression in Socrates, but became dominant in the Enlightenment in the West, and that may end with the reintegration of the affective and intuitive empiricisms associated with the Dionysian, variously repressed in this long ascendance of the rational.

The modern individual can only find satisfaction by becoming utterly fragmented and destroyed in the tragic Dionysian ecstasy of art, reminiscent of the Eleusinian mysteries and their rebirth in the psychedelic, musical counterculture that emerged in the mid-twentieth century, and then carried back into consciousness by the theoretical knowledge and psychological differentiation of the Apollonian-Socratic. This fracturing ordeal further reminds one of the shamanic initiates who, through some combination of wilderness solitude, fasting, ecstatic dance, vocalization, and the ingestion of psychoactive plants, experience a psychological death and dismemberment, a suffering through which they are transformed, and from which they emerge to bring the esoteric knowledge they have received back to their cultures, a nearly universal process in animism on a global scale, though under disparate designations with many local differences.[51] The Dionysian hero of Attic tragedy, like the shaman, expresses paradoxical knowledge through the medium of comforting Apollonian illusion, the mythical narrative intimately entwined with music to transform the collective in an echo of the initiatory experience of the artist, who carries the deeper burdensome knowledge of the culture so that the majority of that culture can benefit from this esoteric wisdom, going about the many activities that make culture possible with a deep sense of purpose, but safely contained within the dream of individual egoic selfhood necessary to act in the world. This Apollonian illusion deceives the individual group members into believing that the world is only what it conventionally appears to be in that cultural moment, while providing a persistent awareness, acquired during the ecstatic ritual or the tragic Dionysian drama, of deeper forces at play.

It is this synthesis of the two archetypes that defines the peaks of a culture, both for the ancient Greeks and for our own era, in which the two divine figures are understood to be brothers, to be intimately and inextricably related, so that Apollo and Dionysus finally learn to speak each other's languages, the Apollonian giving form and consciousness to the mysterious Dionysian wisdom of the unconscious depths. From the integration of these two archetypal forces emerges the miraculous and the magical, a robust enchantment not only appropriate for children or the less discerning, but necessary to the vitality of a culture, which requires foundational myths that satisfy a collective need for complexity and profundity, myths that are credible to the critical faculty, but that generate expansive affect with the capacity to impel a culture to overcome itself, to create novel forms of relation that can carry it further toward an ever-receding horizon just beyond which the mythical domain perpetually resides.

When a culture's vitality ebbs, when its myths are no longer satisfying, which seems to be the case in our time perhaps even more than it was in Nietzsche's, one must look to ancient precedents for ways to revive one's culture, to move, in our case, beyond the double-bind of exclusivist rationality and its shadow in the reactionary rejection of reason. As especially discerned by Jung, Deleuze, and Hillman, such an ancient precedent can be found in the archetypal mode of thought that Nietzsche employs throughout his work to create a novel narrative, building upon ancient ideas, but adequate to the sophistication and complexity of modern consciousness, awakening from the slumber of an exclusive privileging of reductive materialism and logical rationalism against mere superstition into a more profound domain in which these privileged modes are maintained, but resituated within a more expansive mode of relation. Through the sustained development of a mythical dialectic, the oppositional discord that still agonizes our culture may be discerned not as mere irreconcilable difference, but as the eternally returning conflict of potencies demanding differentiating integration.

## Notes

1 Wahl, "Review," 20.
2 Deleuze, *Desert*, 128.
3 See, for instance, Nietzsche, *Birth*, 112; Deleuze, *Desert*, 256.
4 Nietzsche, *Anti-Christ*, 11.
5 Nietzsche, *Ecce*, 48.
6 Stengers, *Thinking*, 7.
7 Deleuze, *Grounding?* 59.
8 Nietzsche, *Gay*, 98.
9 Nietzsche, *Ecce*, 48; Deleuze, *Cinema 2*, 239.

10 Nietzsche, *Daybreak*, 36. The translation of *The Birth of Tragedy* employed in this chapter renders the two adjectives derived from the two deities as "Apolline" and "Dionysiac," but I use and, where applicable, replace these terms in quoted passages with the more familiar "Apollonian" and "Dionysian."
11 Nietzsche, *Human*, 293.
12 Nietzsche, *Ecce*, 73.
13 Nietzsche, *Beyond*.
14 Nietzsche, *Untimely*, 1–56.
15 Nietzsche, *Ecce*, 46.
16 Nietzsche, *Gay*, 89.
17 Matthew 5:5.
18 James, *Writings*, 337–8.
19 Jung, *Archetypes*, 19; Tarnas, "Rite," 16.
20 Deleuze, *Nietzsche*, 18.
21 Inwood, *Heidegger*, 128.
22 Salomé, *Nietzsche*, 40.
23 Nietzsche, *Birth*, 95.
24 Nietzsche, *Ecce*, 45.
25 Nietzsche, *Ecce*, 45–9; Nietzsche, *Twilight*, 199.
26 Deleuze, *Logic*, 106–8.
27 Deleuze, *Desert*, 94; Jung, *Archetypes*, 23.
28 Deleuze, *Essays*, 133.
29 Prideaux, *Dynamite!* 337.
30 Deleuze and Guattari, *Anti-Oedipus*, 106.
31 Nietzsche, *Zarathustra*, 59.
32 Nietzsche, *Ecce*, 52.
33 Nietzsche, *Zarathustra*, 112.
34 Nietzsche, *Zarathustra*, 177–8.
35 Nietzsche, *Zarathustra*, 122.
36 Nietzsche, *Ecce*, 88.
37 Deleuze, *Desert*, 256.
38 Nietzsche, *Birth*, 2.
39 Nietzsche, *Ecce*, 42.
40 Nietzsche, *Ecce*, 17.
41 Nietzsche, *Ecce*, 20.
42 Hegel, *Logic*, 33.
43 Nietzsche, *Ecce*, 26.
44 Nietzsche, *Ecce*, 72.
45 Nietzsche, *Ecce*, 73.
46 Nietzsche, *Ecce*, 70–1.
47 Nietzsche, *Ecce*, 82.
48 Deleuze, *Two*, 68; Deleuze, *Dialogues*, 8.
49 Nietzsche, *Ecce*, 48.
50 Nietzsche, *Birth*, 95.
51 Jung, *Archetypes*, 36–7; See Eliade, *Shamanism*.

# Chapter 7

# An Integrated Affair
William James' *Pragmatism*

James was not formally trained as a philosopher, though he is considered by many to be the preeminent American philosopher of the twentieth century, Whitehead referring to him as "that adorable genius,"[1] and Deleuze as "an astounding genius."[2] He earned his degree as a medical doctor, but never practiced, and he wrote extensively about psychology in addition to philosophy. His initial status as an outsider in the philosophical profession may have had something to do with allowing him to see beyond the often fixed debates of his contemporaries, espying a more expansive perspective rather than becoming mired in "minute controversy,"[3] as he puts it in *Pragmatism*, which was originally written as a series of lectures. If Descartes was the primary conceptual persona who initiated modern philosophy, with Spinoza and Leibniz as the primary post-Cartesians, and if Kant embodied the peak of modern philosophy, with Fichte, Schelling, and Hegel as the primary post-Kantians, as Deleuze suggests, then Whitehead's qualified suggestion that James plays an analogous role to Descartes in "the inauguration of a new stage of philosophy" would perhaps render Bergson and Whitehead himself as the primary post-Jamesians.[4] James certainly expressed a novel direction in philosophical thought, along with contemporaries like Charles Sanders Peirce, who coined the term "pragmatism," and Bergson, whose *Creative Evolution* was published in 1907, the same year as *Pragmatism*, a very good year for philosophy.

Although James did not like the name that Peirce had chosen for their mutual mode of thought, James became that movement's most prominent theorist, enacting a general tendency emerging at the turn of the twentieth century, exemplifying the generational emergence of this mode, integrating disparate philosophical streams traceable back to the pre-Socratics, which "have all at once become conscious of themselves collectively, and of their combined mission."⁵ James was extremely critical of Hegel, making significant contributions to the by-then popular sport of Hegel-bashing largely initiated by Schelling (who influenced James⁶), writing in 1909 that Hegel "offers the vividest possible example of this vice of intellectualism" in which "the pulse of dialectic commences to beat and the famous triads begin to grind out the cosmos," a conception in which James discerns an "intolerable ambiguity, verbosity, and unscrupulousness of the master's way of deducing things."⁷ Several generations after James, however, it can perhaps be recognized that although Hegel and James were certainly incompatible in some ways, their work contains a profound underlying coherence. We must inevitably define ourselves in relation to, and often against, previous modes of thought, which James does with Hegelian absolute idealism, and which the present text does in a somewhat more ambiguous register with Derridean deconstruction, even while affirming the epochal importance of Derrida's work.

James would perhaps be surprised to discover that a subterranean resonance is being suggested between pragmatism and the Hegelian dialectic, "a kind of logic of which I am the enemy," James writes in *Pragmatism*, which "entangles me in metaphysical paradoxes that are inacceptable."⁸ However, as Dewey suggested, James and Hegel had much more in common than James supposed. James understood that "the history of philosophy is to a great extent that of a certain clash of human temperaments,"⁹ and James' and Hegel's temperaments, exemplified in their styles of writing and thought, are certainly very different, even opposed. But there is a substantial core of similarity in their concepts, which James seems to have been mostly unable to recognize because Hegel served as a conceptual persona against whom James found it necessary to define himself. But James' rejection of Hegel, a rejection whose excessively harsh tone may be partially derived from Schelling, is perhaps one of his few significant misapprehensions, and we can apply the pragmatic method, brilliantly but imperfectly expressed by James (and which of us is perfect?), to James himself.

However, this imperfection is a sword that cuts both ways, as Hegel, despite the overwhelming potency of his thought, is also certainly susceptible to critique. For instance, it may seem like heresy to some Hegelians to suggest that the absolute is not a particularly essential part of his system. Although Hegel himself holds that the absolute constitutes that system's center, one can take it or leave it and still find great value and depth in the dialectical mode of thought, opposition opening into a decentered and pluralist dialectic which Deleuze especially renders thinkable. One need not necessarily be opposed to the absolute any more than one needs to be specifically against the concept of a monotheistic divinity. Rather, these unifying, totalizing concepts simply may not compel one's attention as much as understanding the dynamics through which process becomes. Applying Jamesian pragmatism to James' own relation to Hegel, it seems that the deepest nature of reality is almost certainly unknowable, residing at an ever-receding horizon of discernibility, so disagreeing about whether the world either is fundamentally grounded in a unitary absolute or in a pluralist multiplicity seems not to be an especially productive line of inquiry, though the question of how we construct this reality beyond a fixed grounding is central to this text. Whatever the deepest nature of reality may be, it will encompass all of the possible categories, oppositions, and differences we can verbally assign to it, so one can choose to affirm all of the above in some register. From this perspective, all great philosophers are right but limited and, as James understood, we do not ultimately choose where to focus our efforts of conceptual creation and refinement for rational reasons, but based on our affective proclivities. However, whereas this insight, that we are not purely rational beings, that our philosophical beliefs are impelled by our affective inclinations, has often been taken by James' detractors as evidence of an empty relativism and irrationalism, reduced by lazy readers "to the sad morality of the businessman,"[10] as Stengers writes, providing no grounding for real knowledge or morality, James' recognition that temperament drives belief is resonant not only with an ethical Spinozan freedom of mind, but with the constructivism, broadly defined, of the theorists below, who were all influenced by him.[11]

James was highly aware that the empiricist temperament was at its apex when he was writing at the turn of the twentieth century, and that this widespread devotion to empiricism was practiced with a distinctly religious fervor, a scientistic religion having mostly replaced the older systems of belief in educated milieus. However, pushing against this dominant mode of thought, James recognized that, although temperament was not considered a legitimate basis for the discernment of truth, even the greatest philosophers are at least as motivated in their theories by their temperament as by objective facts, if such things can even be said to exist, so that thinkers tend to divide into "tender-minded" and "tough-minded" and interpret their experience accordingly.[12] Beneath our most sophisticated rationales, we tend to feel strongly that the thoughts of even the most brilliant theorists whose temperaments oppose ours are incompatible with the reality that we experience, just as James does with Hegel. James associates this opposition of temperaments in philosophy with rationalists, whose attention is inexorably drawn toward abstract principles, and empiricists, whose attention is drawn toward the material facts of the world. However, he admits, we all must partake of both principles and facts, which find different emphases in each of us, though these balances of emphasis are at the root of some of our deepest disagreements.[13] As James describes it, rationalism is synonymous with monism, which takes unifying principles as primary, and applies them to the world's multiplicity, while empiricism is synonymous with pluralism, which takes the multifarious facts of existence as primary, and derives abstract principles from the many. James thus leads us from the opposition of rationalism and empiricism to a perhaps more fundamental opposition of monism and pluralism.[14]

However, I would suggest that, in light of James' lengthy and profound defense of abstract mystical states in *The Varieties of Religious Experience* published five years earlier, James' self-confessed stance in *Pragmatism* perhaps leans more toward the "tough-minded" empiricist as a kind of mild conceit, a good-natured ploy by a thinker who was actually more moderate and balanced in this opposition than he presents himself in order to lure those of an empiricist temperament into a mode of thought more open to the tender-minded abstractions, though empirically encountered, that he paid such great tribute to a few years prior.[15] Although he does not dismiss abstraction outright, he seems to position himself as leaning toward the tough-mindedly empirical mode of thought in order to demonstrate how one might come to find respect for the rationalist mode through a more profound kind of empiricism beyond the privileging of material facts resonant with Schelling's metaphysical empiricism. One could call it a radical empiricism, a phrase James had previously coined, but which he explicitly claims has nothing to do with his project in *Pragmatism*.[16]

However, in *The Meaning of Truth*, published only two years later, James seems to retract his denial of a connection between the two theories, writing: "It seems to me that the establishment of the pragmatist theory of truth is a step of first-rate importance in making radical empiricism prevail."[17] One suspects that James is playing an ingenious trick in *Pragmatism* by claiming the more empiricist role in order to demonstrate how a mind skeptical of any lofty abstractions is able to push that skepticism deeper, to see its one-sidedness and thereby produce a differentiated integration of the polarity. This subtle and trickster-like seducing of empiricists into a deeper, broader kind of empiricism that becomes asymptotically coextensive with rationalism may be what allowed James to become the primary exemplar in American philosophy of pragmatism, and the more general multivalent mode of thought traced in these pages. Having proposed the theory, though, that James is expertly manipulating his audience, not in a nefarious way, but with sympathy and affection, in a narrative and pedagogical mode, it is nevertheless abundantly evident that he harbored a real distaste for Hegel, damning "absolutism" with faint praise, writing that it "has a certain sweep and dash about it, while the usual theism is more insipid, but both are equally remote and vacuous."[18] James' presentation of absolute idealism, though to some extent a caricature, is correct in that Hegel's writing, as the primary exemplar of this school, is undeniably abstract.

However, I would contend that James goes too far when he claims that idealism "substitutes a pallid outline for the real world's richness,"[19] as Hegel's specificity is of a more psychological kind and, in fact, he was practicing a kind of radical empiricism, exploring and defining the structures and dynamics of consciousness which, as James would surely agree, are real facts that are inarguably part of the world from which they emerge and in which they are embedded, the mind's dynamic structure at least partially disclosing the dynamic structure of reality. Pragmatism, though it is empirical in its adherence to facts, does not presuppose the abstract principle of exclusive materialism which haunts the conventional understanding of empiricism, but which is nowhere to be found in the things themselves, so that pragmatism recognizes the demand that one's theories must rigorously negotiate the constraints of actual experience, but it also liberates one from any implicit assumption about what the limits of a theory may entail, which constitutes a broadening of one's horizon by a devotion only to the actual state of affairs with the capacity to "carry you somewhere."[20] James' rejection of absolute idealism seems to have more to do with his distaste for its style and its contemporary adherents than its inability to carry.

In other respects so modestly wise and generous, James, in relation to Hegel, takes on something of the character of a cranky naysayer, refusing to see the validity in his own opposite, which is a great irony given that James, along with Hegel, has been a primary agent for bringing the mode of thought which recognizes opposed views as partial and complementary aspects of a more expansive reality into broad cultural awareness. But perhaps his rejection of absolute idealism was a necessary clearing away of a dominant nineteenth-century mode of thought in order to make room for a novel mode, which with another century of perspective can be understood as complementary to absolute idealism rather than merely antagonistic to it. James seems genuinely to be working through his frustration with absolute idealism, as he admits that this mode of thought at least has value insofar as it serves to provide comfort, which is structurally similar to his defense of religious experience, though this recognition takes a negative inflection in this instance.[21] James, apparently holding his nose, is evidently attempting to apply his own pragmatic method to acknowledge the partial validity of absolute idealism, which certainly does provide a kind of comfort by rendering the vast sweep of history as an intelligible, purposive movement. But James misses what John Stuart Mill – to whom James dedicated *Pragmatism*, and whom his "fancy likes to picture as our leader were he alive to-day"[22] – understood: that absolute idealism partially illuminates the movements of becoming in its discernment of dialectical dynamics.[23] Perhaps James went so far over into the need to prove the logical tough-mindedness of pragmatism to the dominant positivism of his day that he momentarily forgot he was a pragmatist in relation to Hegelian idealism. But just because the primary representative of pragmatism seems to have imperfectly implemented his own theory does not mean that the whole theory should be discarded, because this kind of inconsistency is the hallmark of all genuinely novel modes of thought, as James was clearing an uncharted path that is now well-trodden, and we owe a huge amount to his pioneering efforts.

Speaking to his audience of presumably empirically minded individuals, addressing the general character of his intellectual milieu, James begins to articulate the common desire for a mode of thought that integrates the empiricist and rationalist modes. Although James found in Mill a precursor to the kind of integration that his audience apparently sought, the main lines of philosophical discourse in that moment were divided between what James presents as two primary human needs, irreligious empiricism on the one hand and religious rationalism on the other, a different division than the typical construction of rationality and religious belief as opposed. In light of the pragmatic mode of thought, these two impulses can be recognized as complementary, and even intimately intertwined in the radically empirical discernment of metaphysical potencies encountered, for instance, in the various phenomena of religious experience.[24] James affirms that this mode of thought is being teleologically called forth in numerous thinkers, demanding the integration of various streams expressing the general need to reconcile the opposed empirical and rational modes differentiated over centuries, a necessary differentiation of human capacities integrated in a novel mode yearned for by his milieu, a need felt perhaps even more acutely in our own time more than a century later.[25]

James describes the pragmatic method as "primarily a method of settling metaphysical disputes that otherwise might be interminable,"[26] a practical way of overcoming the apparently fixed debates at the heart of philosophy (monism and pluralism, fate and free will, materialism and idealism) impeding further movement beyond the mutual antipathies and polarizations of modernity. And in expressing this pragmatic method, James is also applying that method in the integration of previous streams of thought, which demand a new name.[27] Like the term "idealism" with its several varieties, "pragmatism" has over the last century entered into broad discourse, though inevitably shedding most of the essential nuance of its original philosophical expression. These terms are often employed in political discourse as defining the opposition between an abstract principled moralism and a concrete practical realism, though many of the people who use these terms would be surprised to learn that their initial expressions contain a great complexity which ultimately allows for, and perhaps even demands, their integration in a more expansive mode of relation.

James contends that Socrates, Aristotle, Locke, Berkeley, and Hume all employed the pragmatic method in various ways, and this mode which discerns opposites as problematically complementary can be traced at least back to Heraclitus in the West. But, according to James, these earlier expressions were relatively undifferentiated, fragmentary foreshadowings of the impulse toward integration emerging into philosophical discourse in its pragmatic form in the early twentieth century.[28] It has been necessary for the opposed modes of thought, the rationalist and empiricist tendencies, to develop through countless confrontations and partial reconciliations, through generational reactions and counterreactions, in order for the demand to arise on a collective scale for the integration of these opposed modes. Until James' pragmatic moment, the opposition between monist and pluralist modes of thought had been highly productive, each side pushing against the other in order more fully to differentiate the finer structures of those respective modes, impelling profound discoveries and inventions on both the external scientific and engineering end of the polarity, as well as on the internal psychological and theological end.

However, this polarity, so productive for centuries, has perhaps reached a point of diminishing returns so that the debate between these two modes has become increasingly mired in a fixed entrenchment requiring a novel mode of thought that can dissolve this rigid dichotomy. It is striking that this mode of thought emerged as a predominant philosophical movement at the same historical moment that a revolution in physics was bringing the observing consciousness of the scientist inexorably into the practice of science in a fundamental way, so that the velocity of the observer in special relativity determines the rate at which time is passing for that observer relative to other observers, and the mode of observation in quantum theory determines whether a photon is a wave or a particle. At this same moment, Freud and his successors in depth psychology, especially Jung, who collaborated extensively with the physicist Wolfgang Pauli, were illuminating the depths of the unconscious psyche that profoundly informs our relation to the world, even our most apparently objective scientific pursuits. Although we may tend to dwell on the spectacularly brilliant multifariousness of this transformative moment in Western thought in the realms of science, psychology, and philosophy, we can perhaps also see that the integration of which James and pragmatism were primary agents is still incomplete, and that it falls to later generations, including our own, to carry this project further by integrating pragmatism with modes against which it has defined itself. Pragmatism was a new dialect, building upon and synthesizing previous ways of using language, and defining itself against others, which led to the construction of new facts and new syntheses. But unlike deconstruction, which can only devour itself as it performs the necessary task of problematizing all privileging oppositions, pragmatism, whether by that name (which James did not particularly like anyway) or by another name which allows more expansive formulations, contains the positive tools for its self-overcoming built into the very structure of its theory,[29] Deleuze describing pragmatism "as an attempt to transform the world, to think a new world or new man insofar as they create themselves."[30]

While the specific form that this impulse toward integrating apparently incommensurable differences took in Jamesian pragmatism largely rejected Hegelian idealism, this historical opposition, though necessary in its contextual moment, is not a positive element of pragmatism, but rather the negation of the other which was temporarily required for forging a distinct philosophy. James' successors, especially Whitehead and Stengers, have incorporated this pragmatic mode into a more expansive expression of the virtual potentiality pragmatism embodies, a broader, deeper, and more finely differentiated totality than even James and his contemporaries were able to construct, though their efforts are a primary precondition for our capacity to differentiate between the gifts of the pragmatic method and its contingent, though inarguably brilliant, expression. Absolute idealism formed a monolithic straw man that James employed to define the pragmatic mode of thought, which recognizes that like organisms, our ideas evolve to meet a panoply of environmental and contextual demands, that this evolution largely occurs through the development of language,[31] and that, like biological evolution, the development of verbally mediated concepts is evidently leading, through an inclinational teleology far more subtle than the blunt instrument of intelligent design with its pregiven ends, toward increasingly expansive and intensive conceptual domains.

Extrapolating from metaphors employed by James, pragmatism was a refinement of previous instruments, a vehicle that carried a significant portion of theorists through the transformative revolutions in all domains of human endeavor in the twentieth century.[32] Rather than the deconstructive mode which carefully, painstakingly, and disconcertingly disassembles the vehicular instrument to reveal its inner workings, problematizing the very process of vehicular motivity, precluding the possibility of forward motion by dismantling that which has been constructed, pragmatism is a kind of perpetual motion machine which can be modified as it carries us onward, becoming ever more organismic and nuanced as it goes, mediating a progressive development through the negotiation between existing concepts and novel experience.[33] Although the vehicle may now be nearly unrecognizable as the original, first manufactured over a century ago, deconstruction has allowed us to peer into the inner workings of the pragmatic machinery enough to rebuild that machine as it continues its complex trajectory, enabling the transformation of what could initially be envisaged as an early automobile but, since the mid-twentieth century, can be refigured as a rocket blasting orthogonally into stratospheric domains, allowing us to attain more expansive perspectives on terrestrial modes.

We are the inheritors of a cultural vehicle whose obscure origins extend back far beyond the modern, as many of our most fundamental beliefs about the world, inseparable from the language that expresses them, were invented in the distant past as negotiations between the current doxa and constantly shifting circumstances. The creative discernment of increasingly profound concepts is accomplished by marrying those elements of experience for which we have language, the medium through which nonverbal intimations can be rendered conscious on a collective scale, with the elements which have not yet been brought into the light of cultural awareness through the construction of novel linguistic forms. By means of semiotic invention, we usher those largely unconscious and potential elements of experience into the relational systems that constitute our collective mentality, the actually achieved constraints and potentialities of our existence, not only in spoken and written language, but also in architecture, apparel, bodily gesture, social mores, economic structures, and mechanical tools which constitute the given textures of our collective modes of relation, embodied in a vast web of differential traces constructed over the course of human history, a distinctly positive inflection of a primary negative insight of deconstruction.[34]

These constructed elements pervasively inform our every thought, movement, interaction, and emotion, which are channeled through our verbal, gestural, and material languages for expressing and framing these felt and thought encounters with the world in the guise of objects, agential beings, and our own interiority. Everything we are, know, and do, from our most basic habits of sleeping, eating, and bathing to our most abstract, complex concepts and inventions, exists as more-or-less persistent creodes within an all-encompassing network of relations, a system which expands and deepens through the introduction of novel significations, creations that must be integrated, however problematically, with the totality of our current modes of relation in order to continue existing. Novel assemblages are often constructed in oppositional difference with some previously existing entity until the two elements, through their mutual tension and desire, find consummation and a new mode emerges from this relation, often through the binary's dissolution, though there is a multiplicity of topologically figured differential relations beyond opposition through which becoming occurs. The engine for the introduction of novelty embodied in Jamesian pragmatism integrates disparate modes, including the empirical and the rational, long differentiated through the scientific and Enlightenment rejection of the rationalist religious compromise formation embodied in medieval Christian scholasticism, then through the Romantic and Idealist reactions. This trajectory issued into a moment when even many of the founders of twentieth century physics, including Planck, Einstein, Heisenberg, Bohr, Schrodinger, and Pauli, sought to reconcile their physical theories with various metaphysical and religious ideas, not only from the modern West, but perhaps especially in relation to Eastern and nonmodern modes.

Pragmatism is open to, and seeks to integrate, every domain of human experience, finding that empiricism and rationalism, science and religion, physics and metaphysics are complementary, are each required to complete the other. Despite his initial protestations, this method is closely related to what James meant by a radical empiricism, an empiricism that not only takes into account quantitatively measurable physical phenomena, but also qualitative, subjective, affective phenomena which are, after all, real facts that must be encountered on their own terms, that cannot be reduced to quantitative exteriority without losing the emergent qualitative properties that constitute these psychological experiences, whether mystical or mundane.[35] The more deeply we delve into the interstices of physical reality, the more the rigid boundaries between physical and psychological domains dissolve, in the reintroduction of the observing consciousness in special relativity and quantum mechanics, and then in the last half-century in string theory, a primary candidate for reconciling the quantum and relativistic pillars of physics, but for which there does not seem to be a possibility of traditional empirical verification on the horizon. In fact, this situation is impelling many theoretical physicists and philosophers of science to rethink the privileging of the narrower form of quantitative, materialist empiricism in favor of a broader empiricism that acknowledges internal coherence, explanatory efficacy, and aesthetic elegance as equally valid criteria to experimental repeatability for the verification of a theory.[36] The development of physics over the last century seems to be leading inexorably toward a pragmatic mode of thought which integrates physics with domains that have often defined physics by their exclusion. We are evidently moving away from the reductive mania characteristic of modernity's height, which consisted precisely in reducing emergent phenomena to their constituent parts, toward an integration of materialist modes with a radical, metaphysical empiricism.

In order to effect this integration, we must recognize that all of our concepts and theories are approximate inventions that can never capture the full heights and depths of reality, domains which always exceed total comprehension, so scientific and theistic explanations for phenomena are both valid in their own contexts because they do not change the specificity of what actually occurred in the past. James' contention that the world's past is immutably what it is, and our explanations are valid only insofar as they allow us to enter back into the stream of experience and engage with the world in an effective way, suggests that the causal efficacy of both divinity, in whatever form, and matter are valid truths applicable in their respective domains, complementary to one another, both legitimate modes of constructing embodied experience. Both materialism and theism are coherent explanations for the same past circumstances based on distinct verbal systems, which both contain partial validity, and which are both useful in different ways for shaping future events. All of our interpretations are ultimately oriented toward determining our actions, and there are many decisions in which the explanatory mode we employ in that moment will lead us in a fundamentally different direction than if we had employed a different mode. This recognition impels us not ultimately to privilege one mode of thought over another, but rather to be able to hold each explanatory system within our worldview so that we can employ whichever mode is more effective in that particular moment, and thus our allegiance may be given not primarily to one or another, but to a mode which integrates and coordinates the narrower modes while maintaining, and even enabling, their differentiation.[37]

Rather than rejecting either materialism or some more idealist mode, whether or not it includes a concept of the divine or rather simply acknowledges the efficacy of formal and final causes in addition to material and efficient ones, it can be recognized that all of these modes of explanation and causation are necessary for a more complete comprehension of reality, which always exceeds any verbal construct. Neither materialism nor idealism should be completely rejected and replaced with its opposite if we hope to remain in contact with the indisputably efficacious discoveries of these modes. What can be rejected is the exclusive privileging of one mode over others, so that the negative content of each mode ultimately constitutes a recognition of a contrasting mode's limits of efficacy, and rather than considering oneself an adherent of materialism or idealism against its opposite, claiming exclusive access to truth by disqualifying an other, one might instead position oneself as recognizing the limited efficacy of both material and ideal modes of thought, employing each in their appropriate domain.[38] Through a discursive process that looks, to James' eternal consternation, remarkably like a dialectical movement, he has led us through the apparent necessity of choosing one mode of thought over an opposed mode to the deeper understanding that both the material and efficient causation privileged by science and the formal and final causation often privileged in nonmodern philosophical and religious modes are necessary for an integral mode of thought, and that they are deeply intertwined in every occasion that we encounter. James' shoe, to employ his prosaic example, admits to explanations in terms of both materialism and finalism, in terms of both the mechanism of its construction and its purpose, but it is ultimately itself, an entity which exceeds this dichotomy, an object that has been made both through a mechanism and for a purpose.[39]

James expresses the ultimate question of pragmatism as "What is this world going to be?" or, what amounts to the same thing as far as we are concerned, "What is life eventually to make of itself?" In order to generate satisfying answers to these questions in our evidently liminal epoch, philosophy's "centre of gravity" will be required to shift from the entrenched opposition of schools of thought attempting to find arguments ingenious enough permanently to vanquish their opponents to a mode of thought that recognizes the partial validity in each mode, which understands that each mode of relation expresses complementary capacities.[40] James describes this gravitational shift as a transformation comparable to the Protestant Reformation, so that as one contemporary mode of thought, which we can perhaps identify as capitalism (including its pervasion of scientific research), seems to have triumphed over the others, becoming staid and corrupt like the Catholic Church by the early sixteenth century, inhibiting further progress, we are witnessing, over the course of generations, the emergence of a mode of thought that takes as its primary principle a radical openness, affirming the positive aspects of largely repressed modes rather than shunning and disqualifying them as other.[41] However, this emergent mode cannot simply be conceived as a placid, confluent unification because, in this integration of disparate modes, there must be room for dissent, for difference, for plurality, which in fact constitute the structure of the totality. We can never hope for a complete unification of all modes of thought so that every individual holds the same beliefs, which would produce a repetitive monotony like that of a beehive, however complex. If we were bees or lobsters, we would relate to the world in fundamentally different ways than we do as humans, but as we are definitively not bees or lobsters (despite spurious claims by a certain contemporary psychologist), such an erasure of all difference in a totalitarian unification would be to destroy the ambiguities and disagreements that make us human.[42]

Rather than such a totalizing unification, James advocates the collective adoption of a mode of thought which affirms the attempt to forge a peace, however fragile and provisional, as a primary principle, recognizing that no mode contains complete, exclusive access to reality, holding all modes in a loose, diverse confederation. As James understands, the wisdom of which philosophers are the putative lovers comes not from the subsumption of variety and difference in a single, undifferentiated mode, but from the collective recognition that all modes elicit some aspects of reality that other modes inevitably neglect. James constructs the world as becoming increasingly unified through our activities, bringing all modes of thought into more intimate relation, a pluralist convergence which allows James to describe the universe as an increasingly "'integrated' affair."[43] This progressive integration inclines toward a dynamic assemblage in which each mode of construction can play its singular role in the larger narrative, though as James insists again and again, pragmatism is not merely a drive toward oneness which erases difference, but rather a simultaneous differentiation and unification within an increasingly voluminous domain of relation. Not every part must communicate with every other part, as a significant aspect of the world's truth is discerned in its disjunctions, but every part is ultimately related in some way to a larger whole, "and wisdom lies in knowing which is which at the appropriate moment."[44] What James calls pragmatism, what Hegel calls dialectic, or what we might call integration in order to have some chance of constructing a peace among these various modes which seek to integrate apparently incommensurable differences, are wisdom by other names, though these alternate nominations are not merely static rephrasings, but dynamic inflections of a multivalent and speculative mode, partially constituted in the recognition that once-novel modes periodically require new containers for their continued growth and development.

Our strivings toward purposes, often at odds with one another, lure us toward differentiating integration, as "everything makes strongly for the view that our world is incompletely unified teleologically and is still trying to get its unification better organized."[45] However, although there does seem to be an inclinational teleology drawing disparate human endeavors toward increasing integration, "whoever claims *absolute* teleological unity, saying that there is one purpose that every detail of the universe subserves, dogmatizes at his own risk,"[46] as such absolutism must ultimately quell all dissent and difference. But even if absolutism is recognized as an expression of a less mature stage of historical development that must be overcome, each stage must continue to subsist as an integral aspect of an emergent mode, emphasized less and less in mature individuals, but still constituting phases that each person must pass through on the way to maturity, and which will enduringly remain as essential background elements of our collective constitution. In a process that looks remarkably like the Hegelian dialectic in another register, James suggests that the first two stages of this nonhierarchical progression, in which each stage embodies a valid aspect of the world's truth, are roughly equivalent to the nonmodern development of what we now consider common sense and the modern development of science, with "at least" a third stage apparently emerging with the pragmatic "new dawn" at the beginning of the twentieth century, constituted in a pluralist integration of the modes of thought developed in the first two stages of human history.[47]

It is true that all of this philosophizing about a teleologically lured emergence through progressive developmental stages via the tension and subsequent integration of difference, which nevertheless maintains differentiation is, in fact, a narrative, but this narrative is also an essential aspect of the world's constitution. The emerging mode of thought that we are in the process of collectively constructing is a story we are always telling ourselves, continuously refining our narrative aesthetic in order to discover more efficacious ways of relating to experience. But this constructivist recognition does not mean that this narrative is any less real than some other, perhaps more tough-minded, reductionist materialist narrative, or a deconstructive narrative which seeks to efface narrativity altogether, as from the pragmatic perspective, narrativity is not something added to reality, but is partially constitutive of reality itself, and consciousness, history, and culture are pervasive narrative constructions that allow us continually to create the world anew, to add unceasingly to the narrative's nuance and depth.[48]

The story that pragmatism tells, the story that integration refines and extends, and upon which it builds, is that the world is both one and many, susceptible to interpretations predicated upon both monism and pluralism, and a radical empiricism may reveal that the world is moving toward a progressively differentiated coherence. This narrative seems to be the most efficacious, to possess the capacity to enfold the greatest volume of human truths without relegating any truth, however limited and partial, to mere error. It is more an ideal to strive toward than an achieved way of life, drawing any exclusivist mode of constructing the world, whether rationalist scientism or dogmatic religion, into the narrative as an essential aspect of our collective constitution, as we must all pass through such absolutism, however briefly, in order to emerge into the more balanced openness characteristic of the pragmatic mode. And modes that reject the teleological inclination toward increasing integration, whether in the form of a bravely realist reductionist materialism or the sophisticated, elusive ennui of deconstruction, can be recognized as members in a society of modes, ways of being that many of us have passed through, that have informed our current reality and are indelibly part of our being.[49]

Pragmatism is ultimately pluralist, but it is also paradoxically necessary to recognize that, if this mode is truly to embrace pluralism, then it must also acknowledge the partial validity of even an absolute monism as a moment in a process of becoming which is an essential aspect of the totality of human existence, a naïve mode of constructing the world appropriate at an earlier stage, but inappropriate, and often destructive, at more mature stages.[50] However much a pragmatic integration may reject such absolutism in the practice of advocating for a radical openness to difference, this openness also entails the understanding, relegated to the background though it may be on most occasions, that pluralism cannot be true pluralism unless it absorbs even monism, an organismic metabolization that renders the emergent mode neither simply pluralism nor monism, but a novel mode that encompasses and dissolves this pervasive duality. And this novel mode does not demand perfect tolerance at all times, an impossible task for even the most enlightened among us, and certainly for any human living in the everyday world, but rather it invites us to hold our beliefs lightly, even the belief that there is no absolute truth, the very belief that we must always hold our beliefs lightly. Integration is an openness to paradox, a recognition that all modes of relation coexist in various concentrations in each of us, that these concentrations shift and fluctuate over time, and that the world always exceeds our capacity for final comprehension. Paradoxes are the anomalies that reveal interstices where we can emerge into more expansive domains, the fissures through which the light shines that may illuminate the darkness beyond a bright nucleus of consciousness, the virtual domains of reality brought into actuality through creative invention.

Peering into these cracks in the characteristically modern mode of thought reveals a far more complex relation to temporality than the commonsense construction mathematically formalized by Newton, James alluding to the "plural times and spaces"[51] toward which the founders of twentieth-century physics were reaching in their explorations of nonmodern and non-Western ontologies for explaining the results of their novel discoveries, driven to these alternative constructions by the inadequacy of the modern conception of absolute, static time and space. They found these alternative constructions of space and time to be more adequate for describing the experience of the most startling results of modern physics, from the spacetime continuum and relativistic time dilation to the complementarity of the wave-particle duality, quantum nonlocality, and the atomic electron transition. String theory mathematically and conceptually reveals realities even more challenging to the modern mind, of strange topologies transforming through additional compactified dimensions expressed in mathematical dualities, constituted in two radically different but complementary descriptions of the same phenomenon, out of which emerges the ten-dimensional reconciliation of quantum theory and relativity, but also the reconciliation of the five distinct string theories in an eleven-dimensional M-theory.[52]

These are the esoteric domains to which empirical observation and mathematical innovation have led the majority of theoretical physicists, yet our collective commonsense understanding of these domains of reality is still largely based upon Newtonian concepts from three centuries ago. And these are the kinds of novel, enigmatic domains which pragmatic integration lures us to contemplate, not only in a mathematically rigorous theoretical physics, but in an equally rigorous attention to affect, for which time is much more complex than the static, linear absolute temporality of Newtonian mechanics.[53] If nothing else, integration demands a radical openness to novelty, to other ways of conceiving experience, however apparently bizarre.[54] For those of us paying close attention to twentieth- and twenty-first century physics, our metaphysical speculations are increasingly hard-pressed to outpace the vanguard of physical theory in terms of strangeness and novelty. The more we learn about the world, the less we can cram that knowledge into the Procrustean bed of a primarily reductionist materialist understanding of reality that has been dominant in modernity.

However, it must be reaffirmed that this radical openness to speculation does not mean that anything goes. To be pragmatic, we must be both radically open and rigorously attentive to the many factors that constrain our speculations, not only the physical constraints accounted for by science, but also the constraints of the vast semiotic system constructed over millennia that we call culture. And the passage between these two monumental facts of given reality, our Scylla and Charybdis, is relatively narrow and treacherous, but it does admit to forward movement, to innovation and novelty through the encounter of our wilder fancies with that which undeniably exists. Our novel concepts must not only work in relation to the physical reality in which we find ourselves, but they must also be expressed and framed in ways that can be heard and adopted by enough individuals to generate a critical mass, at which point the incorporation of these concepts becomes feasible, and even necessary. There are many books that simply assert radical novelty without taking the necessary care not only to fit the new theories to material and social facts, but also to express them in aesthetically efficacious enough ways to convince others provisionally to embrace novel beliefs beyond their current modes of thought, not only based on rational considerations, but affective ones, an undertaking whose extraordinary difficulty James aptly recognizes.[55]

Our current modes of thought, vastly complex and profound though they may be, always provide incomplete conceptions of reality, unfinished vehicles for sailing into uncharted domains. The figure of absolute truth is an asymptotic lure toward becoming that impels our self-overcoming, requiring that we always continue to revise our theories and modes of relation. As James understood, there is something in us, and consequently in the reality of which we are a part, that will not allow us to rest, that drives us ever onward past even the most brilliant constructions, so revelatory in their first emergence. And this overcoming of our current modes of thought may partially result from an emergence into broad awareness of the often esoteric recognition that we are not merely seekers after some external truth that lies waiting, fully-formed somewhere in the depths of matter or in the heights of a transcendent domain, but that by integrating, through our various modes of embodied and enminded experience, the oppositions and differences that constitute our thought, we are increasingly building the immanent truth for which we seek, not as a castle in the air lacking foundation, but as an always-moving vehicle constructed in constant negotiation with the multifarious facts of experience, venturing into ever-new terrain.

## Notes

1 Whitehead, *Science*, 2.
2 Deleuze, "Whitehead."
3 James, *Pragmatism*, vii.
4 Deleuze, *Expressionism*, 325; Whitehead, *Science*, 142–3.
5 James, *Pragmatism*, vii.
6 Wilshire, "Breathtaking," 103, 106.
7 James, *Writings 1902–1910*, 678.
8 James, *Pragmatism*, 31.
9 James, *Pragmatism*, 2.
10 Stengers, *Thinking*, 112.
11 See also Bergson, *Mind*, 177.
12 James, *Pragmatism*, 2–3.

13 James, *Pragmatism*, 3.
14 James, *Pragmatism*, 4.
15 James, *Pragmatism*, 4.
16 James, *Pragmatism*, viii.
17 James, *Writings*, 826; Stengers, *Thinking*, 112.
18 James, *Pragmatism*, 6–8. James specifically critiques "the Anglo-Hegelian school," though he critiques Hegel directly in *The Will to Believe* and *A Pluralistic Universe*.
19 James, *Pragmatism*, 28.
20 James, *Pragmatism*, 29.
21 James, *Pragmatism*, 29.
22 James, *Pragmatism*, v.
23 Mill, *Works*, 139.
24 James, *Pragmatism*, 8, 13.
25 James, *Pragmatism*, 16.
26 James, *Pragmatism*, 18.
27 James, *Pragmatism*, 19.
28 James, *Pragmatism*, 20.
29 James, *Pragmatism*, 22–3.
30 Deleuze, *Essays*, 86.
31 See Richardson, *Natural*.
32 James, *Pragmatism*, 23.
33 James, *Pragmatism*, 64.
34 Deleuze, *Cinema 2*, 25.
35 James, *Pragmatism*, 31.
36 See Dawid, *String*.
37 James, *Pragmatism*, 37–9.
38 James, *Pragmatism*, 41.
39 James, *Pragmatism*, 43, 69.
40 James, *Pragmatism*, 47.
41 James, *Pragmatism*, 48.
42 James, *Pragmatism*, 50, 65.
43 James, *Pragmatism*, 53.
44 James, *Pragmatism*, 53.
45 James, *Pragmatism*, 54.
46 James, *Pragmatism*, 55.
47 James, *Pragmatism*, 72.
48 James, *Pragmatism*, 55.
49 James, *Pragmatism*, 60.
50 James, *Pragmatism*, 62.
51 James, *Pragmatism*, 68.
52 Greene, *Elegant*, 298.
53 James, *Pragmatism*, 70.
54 James, *Pragmatism*, 71–2.
55 James, *Pragmatism*, 83.

# Chapter 8

# A True Work of Integration

Henri Bergson's *Creative Evolution*

Bergson and James both profoundly admired and influenced each other. James was planning to write a preface to the English translation of *Creative Evolution* for its publication in 1911, though he died before he was able to complete it, and Bergson wrote a sympathetic and insightful preface to the French edition of *Pragmatism*, also published in 1911.[1] Bergson thought deeply about Spinoza, Leibniz, and Hegel, and he read Nietzsche, whose subterranean influence seems evident in his work, though he directly addresses him only once in his final monograph.[2] Bergson's career, though not as dramatic as Nietzsche's, is one of academic success at the relatively young age of thirty with his first book, though it is with the publication of *Creative Evolution* that Bergson became a genuine philosophical celebrity, influencing all of the theorists discussed below, and winning a Nobel prize for literature in 1927. However, perhaps in reaction to his extraordinary eminence in French philosophy in the first few decades of the twentieth century, similar to the reaction against Hegel's even greater dominance in the previous century, and partially catalyzed by a debate he had with Einstein,[3] Bergson's influence began to wane in the thirties, and he died in 1941. Then, in an unexpected reversal, his star rose abruptly again in the 1960s largely through his influence on Deleuze, who published *Bergsonism* in 1966, and Bergson has since remained highly regarded within continental philosophy, perhaps especially as a precursor to Deleuze himself.

Bergson's subtle argument begins with the suggestion that intelligence has evolved primarily to act on matter, and thus intellect tends to conform to the contours of the materiality which is its natural sphere of efficacy. The primary characteristic of both matter and intellect, as Bergson defines them, is their differentiability, the susceptibility of matter to being indefinitely split up into its constituent parts, and the intellect's tendency to analyze experience in a similarly discontinuous and reductive way, not only in relation to matter, but to any content, however abstract. The logic which comes so naturally to our minds is modeled on the spatial, geometrical organization of physical matter, as matter and intellect have participated in a mutual adaptation in the production of mind. Bergson contrasts this tendency of intellect to life, which he describes as an inverse movement to materiality, a nondifferentiable trajectory toward increasing order countervalent to the entropic movement of nonliving matter toward disorder, and he suggests that this vital evolutionary movement tends to escape the naturally reductive bent of our intellect, molded as it is on inert matter.

But evolutionary theory, especially in the early twentieth century, has generally sought to reduce organismic vitality to its component mechanisms, a mode of thought which has enjoyed great success in physical science, but which possesses a restricted efficacy in describing organismic processes, though Bergson admits that this reductive tendency has been a necessary stage of biological science, which has been highly productive in these restricted mechanical domains. This reductive quality of the intellect is not merely contingent, but expresses the character of the materiality on which intellect has molded itself in order to act, and which tends to pull our more abstract conceptual thought, mediated through language which has evolved coextensively with the material character of intelligence, toward the static repetition of mechanical automatism. The mechanistic tendency of intellect implicitly assumes that individual parts are external to one another, divisible down to increasingly tiny constituent elements, though as the new physics that were just beginning to be understood in 1907 demonstrate, every point in geometrically defined space is intimately related to every other point, a prescient insight in a book published only two years after Einstein's *annus mirabilis*.

Through almost novelistic prose, Bergson enacts the flowing movement of the vital impulse, which carries us along in its forward thrust, but is also variously diverted into conceptual and imaginal eddies and whirlpools, so that the experience of reading this text performs the complex vital processes described. This philosophical approach, so influential in the continental tradition, can be contrasted with much analytic philosophy, an opposition exemplified in Bergson's disagreements with Bertrand Russell, who led the charge in employing formal logic to reduce experience to its constituent elements in order to analyze complex processes.[4] Contrary to this approach, which categorizes concepts, externally related to one another like the spatial objects they mirror, into an endless confrontation of discrete philosophical positions ending with "–ism," Bergson finds more efficacy in evocatively spiraling in upon the concepts he wishes to convey, which exceed the ability of formal logic to contain, leading to irresolvable incommensurabilities and paradoxes, which only a method beyond the logic developed in relation to matter can hope to conjure.

The inverse capacity to intellect, molded on the vital impulse, is instinct, an expansive field of felt organismic experience of which intellect is a condensed nucleus, a bright spotlight illuminating a restricted domain, around which fades off in all directions domains that exceed the grasp of verbal intellect, but which are accessible to instinctual bodily knowledge, a duality reminiscent of Nietzsche's Apollonian and Dionysian. While intellect has become conscious of itself, instinct is an unconscious adherence to the vital movements of process, a felt tracing of the real contours of lived activity complementary to intelligence. Life is a wave moving through the medium of matter, and while matter tends inexorably toward descent into entropic stasis, the vital impulse is embodied in the oscillations that animate materiality, which flow in a countervalent direction, ascending toward increasing organization and freedom of movement liberated from physical determinacy. The vital wave passes through generations of organisms which it animates, becoming more potent and intense as it advances through countless repetitions with slight differences, rather than diminishing in potency as it branches into novel differentiated species. This process of surging differentiation enacts a developmental dissociation of diverse capacities, so that species tend to privilege certain faculties at the expense of others, and these faculties tend to become increasingly developed while the faculties dominant on other evolutionary lines are deemphasized by this selective differentiation, though these other faculties are flames never completely extinguished.

The evolutionary movement is not a single trajectory executing predetermined biological laws, tracing increasing degrees of consciousness, from plants to animals to humans, as most theories descended from Aristotle have assumed, but rather a vital tendency toward the liberation from physical determinism, a multiplicitous differentiation radiating out in all directions toward all kinds of possible adaptations. This radiating movement begins at the smallest scale, with protozoa, single-celled organisms which establish a toehold for the emergence of life from matter, and then divide and aggregate into assemblages until a crisis is reached in which the society of unicellular organisms finds it necessary to self-organize into multicellular organisms, which diverge in every possible direction. Opposed by the inhibiting character of materiality, the vast majority of these trajectories are drawn back into the entropic tendency of material necessity, canalized by the constraints of physical reality into habitual, circular eddies that inhibit further development. Out of this efflorescent polyvalent surge, only a few trajectories, plants and animals, find salutary paths beyond the various constraining obstacles of materiality – though Bergson recognizes that fungi complicate this binary distinction[5] – a conflict which constitutes the essence of evolution, aggregating increasingly complex assemblages of assemblages, which contain increasing differentiation and division of labor within their organismic unity. After periods of relatively linear growth, these assemblages reach a population crisis so that the aggregate is either faced with extinction or must organize itself in an emergent domain of liberated activity, a dynamic of accumulation and discharge which has never ceased to be operative.

There is thus a fine balance maintained between the differentiation of individuals and their integration in emergent entities, whether organismic, psychological, or societal, as in order for the organismic entity to evolve, to become other than it has already been, it is necessary for it to reproduce, for its individuality to be imperfect and permeable with its environment and other organisms, producing other individuals out of its own body, a becoming-other than itself in order to reunite with itself, which, as above, looks remarkably like the movement described by the Hegelian dialectic, though in a pluralist valence. And the relation of sociality between individual and collective entities, operative across scale in all vital domains, from individual organisms and psyches, to the evolution of species, to the development of societies, only requires a slight impetus at the critical moment to tip the assemblage from an unorganized aggregate to an organismic unity that preserves the differentiated individuality of the component organisms. In the individual human organism, for instance, puberty and menopause are crises that serve to reorganize the individual, reiterating the distinct stages, mediated by critical thresholds, of larval and embryonic modes of development, as well as the brief periods of punctuated saltation that mediate the evolutionary transitions between distinct species.

The nervous system, and eventually the brain, is the primary site of this self-organizing complexity in the trajectory that leads to humanity, which in turn requires greater complexity in the other organic systems to support nervous complexity, the automatism of the rest of the organism structured to provide the nervous system with increasing freedom and choice in its activity. This duality of automatism and freedom constitutes the axis that defines vegetable and animal life, not in complete, perfect opposition, but in a difference of emphasis, so that both kingdoms contain both elements in the polarity, but the automatic is emphasized in plants and the voluntary is emphasized in animals. And this freedom of choice is the trajectory that leads to consciousness, a becoming-aware of manifold potentialities for liberated activity and invention. But even in the most complex forms of consciousness, the often antagonistic emphasis of one end of the polarity over the other results not in an ultimate triumph, a complete destruction of one tendency or the other, but in various modes of integration of the opposing tendencies, different balances of emphasis which maintain the complementary contrasts of fixity and mobility in different kinds of organismic wholes. And as the brain becomes increasingly complex, consciousness becomes increasingly emphasized over the instinctual capacity until it reaches a threshold that marks the discontinuous transition from nonhuman animal consciousness to the human mind.

However, it should not be inferred that mind is reducible to the brain, but rather that consciousness and its physical substrate can only be definitively described as corresponding to one another, both primary realities, neither subservient to the other, and not equivalent to one another, but rather two complementary and interdependent ways of delineating a larger reality that exceeds both systems of symbolic characterization, which respectively operate in terms of external structural complexity and internal cognitive intensity. The transition from nonhuman to human consciousness is a difference in kind which emerges coextensively with a difference in degree of complexity of interconnection, so that while the choice available to animals is circumscribed by relative lack of complexity, the human mind is potentially unlimited in its capacity for liberated activity. The moments when we practice this radical freedom and openness to its full extent are relatively rare, though our conscious activity certainly takes place at the qualitative analogy of a higher order of magnitude than the almost completely instinctual activity of nonhuman animals.

One of the primary defining characteristics of intelligence is invention, the ability to design and manufacture tools and habits which serve as extensions of our biological and mental capacities, not only technological devices and ways of organizing material elements, but also language. As opposed to instinct, which limits the possible avenues of activity, intelligence can discover new degrees of freedom through its inventions, and it is often the case that the transformative effects of novel inventions, forms of language, and habitual modes of activity and relation do not even become visible until they have settled into being unremarkable, having made the transition from a technological, verbal, or behavioral curiosity to a commonplace and integral element in daily life.

In order to differentiate the human intellectual capacity, the instinctual capacity has tended to be deemphasized over the course of our evolutionary and historical development. Our senses are relatively dull compared to those of other mammals, due in part to the radical disembedding from nature undertaken with the invention of clothing, shelter, cooked food, and language, not to mention the modern city in which most natural surfaces are covered by artificial materials, in which the stars in the night sky are barely visible due to the ubiquity of electric lights, and in which many of our interactions with other humans take place through electronic media and text. We have come very far from the relatively pure instinct of nonhuman animals, and although we have gained a huge number of novel, emergent capacities over the course of historical development, not least self-awareness, we have also paid the heavy price of alienation from instinctual modes of relation. As Bergson expresses it, "there are things that intelligence alone is able to seek, but which, by itself, it will never find. These things instinct alone could find; but it will never seek them."[6] Our conscious intellectual capacity perpetually seeks after novelty, but divorced as it has become from instinctual, affective knowledge, and although it has been a necessary differentiation, it often lacks the intimate sense of purpose for which felt instinct is the characteristic faculty. Conversely, instinctual animality does not possess the consciousness required to know that there is something to be sought, emergent novelties that allow organismic processes to overcome themselves in order to attain broader modes of existence. Intellect discerns a variety of external objects and concepts, while instinct feels its way through the internal interconnection of these apparently disparate individualities, the integration of which has generally been precluded by a nearly exclusive focus on rationality, if not always intelligence, by modern industrial society.

Intelligence tends to think in terms of fixed, separate objects and states, so even when it is faced with an emergent self-organizing novelty like biological life, it seeks to understand organismic process by reducing it to its constituent elements, blind to the integral vitality that is the domain accessible to instinct. When predicting the future, or evaluating creative novelty, solitary intellect generally assumes that things will go on as they have before, that nothing fundamentally new can come into being, only reorganizations of existing elements. And while this may be true from a materialist perspective, as energy can neither be created nor destroyed, from the inverse perspective accessible to affective epistemologies, the conventional materialist mode is blind to the animating force of becoming ascending wavelike through descending matter. The complementary modes of relation enacted in intelligence and instinct each tend to adhere to the contours around which they have formed themselves, the mechanical and the organic. However, as Bergson suggests, this polarity is not a mere disjunction, but an invitation to integration, a turning of the conscious attention differentiated in the intellectual faculty to the task of rendering conscious the unconscious affective knowledge accessible to instinct, an integration toward which we seem to have progressed considerably in the century since Bergson wrote, not only in the broad academic interest in affect derived in large part from Spinoza, Bergson, and their mutual influence on Deleuze, but also in the efflorescence of countercultures, which have served as primary loci for the integration of affective and intellectual modes.

This integration of intelligence and instinct is enacted in the emergent capacity of intuition, Deleuze nominating Bergson's approach to this faculty as "one of the most fully developed methods in philosophy,"[7] and Bergson describing intuition in 1903 as "integral experience,"[8] a metaphysical method for integrating the precise geometrical discernment of intellect, which divides actions into constituent elements, with the felt continuity of affective experience. Intuition constitutes an awakening of the intimate bodily knowledge derived from the creative novelty characteristic of vital flux, which has been multivalently emphasized in nonhuman evolutionary trajectories, a broadening of the horizon of felt awareness from immediate sensory experience into the more abstract domains accessible to intellect. Intelligence is a becoming-external and other to itself, an unmistakably dialectical liberation which has allowed human consciousness to see far into the depths of space and matter, but which has also alienated it from itself, so that in order to reunite with itself, to overcome this self-othering, it must turn the extraordinarily potent and intensive attention forged in relation to matter back upon itself, back into the flowing movements of its bodily and psychological embedding by means of an intuitive method, carrying the unconscious felt knowledge of vitality into the light of conscious awareness. And it is this intuitive "supraconsciousness"[9] that is both the origin and purpose of life, which must be constructed in actuality through the process of an integration that maintains the differentiated components.

Bergson suggests that it is our inventions – technological, cultural, linguistic – which form the preconditions for our self-overcoming, enabling new modes of complex feeling, emergent platforms for more elevated activations of bodily knowledge providing the material and conceptual frameworks that we can ascend in order to witness new vistas beyond our previous horizons of experience and conception, constructing those novel domains in reciprocal negotiation with virtual potentiality and constraint. Without the logical, geometrical, mechanical quality of intelligence, we would have lacked the tools necessary to build the structures that allow our increasingly towering perspectives, but it is our intuitive capacity, beyond the duality of intellect and instinct, which feels drawn to build these structures, and to climb the heights that we have constructed to explore the vastness of the world rather than only focusing attention on the technical challenges of engineering more durable joists and struts. These structural elements are necessary for the ascent, but not sufficient for their employment, which requires an aesthetic, affective mode of relation. In this light, intelligence is a means to an end, not an end in itself, so that we must go beyond a focus on solitary intellect, which has been singularly instrumental in paradoxically constructing the means of its own overcoming and subsumption into an emergent mode of relation for which the rigorous analytical capacities are maintained, but are toppled from their privileged hierarchical position to become one valid, but partial, kind of knowing among others, a symbolic construction complementary to other contrasting relational systems within the totality of potential experience.

Despite the potentially radical openness that human consciousness affords, we find it necessary to reduce the infinite expanse to a manageable complex of conceptual premises that constellate our mode of relation, whose development resonates with the same dynamics as biological evolution, so that we can recognize our current mode of existence not as an end but as a stage in a trajectory moving through us and beyond us, an insight deeply reminiscent of Nietzsche's concept of the Overman. Bergson even suggests that a "superman"[10] may emerge from an integration of the disparate trajectories that the vital impulse has traced in order to differentiate and refine these faculties, and which it is the task of an intuitive method to integrate in a novel mode which maintains the long-privileged intellectual capacity of humanity, but reembraces the instinctual capacities characteristic of animality, which have been repressed and rendered as other in the protracted differentiation of the human.

Implicit thus far in this "thinking with" Bergson's theory is his essential concept of duration, the continuous and nondifferentiable lived experience of "time freed from measure,"[11] as Deleuze writes, which Bergson contrasts with the clock and calendar time characteristic of science, logic, intellect, linear writing, and common sense that generally constructs temporality as divided into separate moments on a timeline. The ultimate expression of this cutting up of time is the differential calculus, a geometrical approach traceable back to the paradoxes of Zeno of Elea near the dawn of philosophy, Bergson suggesting that this mathematical reconstruction of continuous change and movement out of fixed and immobile units is a paradox which, although it allows for asymptotic approximations of change, can never truly capture the continuity of duration. Bergson likens this method of reconstituting time to the cinematograph, invented a mere decade-and-a-half before Bergson's book was published, in which the illusion of movement and change is produced by the rapid succession of static images, arguing that this technology is in fact the logical extension of the material-intellectual mode to the construction of temporality. However, like Leibniz, Bergson discerns an intimate correlation between the specifically infinitesimal form of the integral calculus and the conceptual integration characteristic of the intuitive method, so that he can write in 1903 that "one of the objects of metaphysics is to operate differentiations and qualitative integrations"[12] explicitly modeled on the calculus. Bergson rejects the ambition to construct "a universal mathematic,"[13] which he associates with Kant's conception of metaphysical law, just as he rejects the fixed, transcendent Platonic Ideas in favor of a mode of metaphysical thought which, like the infinitesimal calculus, constitutes "a true work of integration,"[14] as he writes in 1896, tracing the contours of immanent becoming rather than merely uncovering preexisting transcendent Forms, the syncategorematic quality of the infinitesimal mediating the phase transition from quantitative discontinuity to qualitative continuity.[15]

In order to apprehend the continuous reality of time, we must not remain external to it, as the "cinematographical mechanism of thought"[16] does, but rather insert ourselves into becoming through the intuitive method which lends attention to affect, the faculty which corresponds with the vital movement. It is this duration that underlies the progressive quality of time, a continual surging that demands novel forms of life and consciousness, accreting small changes which, when critical thresholds are reached, tips the process into emergent durational phases, so that there is both continuity in the slow accretion and discontinuity in the brief periods of condensed experience that mark the transitions to novel durations. Duration is the medium of the vital impulse, the will and desire which exceed conscious choice and impel becoming, more accessible to affective epistemologies than intellectual ones. Whereas science generally requires static, absolute time for experimental repeatability, the concept of duration constitutes the recognition that no moment or state can ever be precisely the same (echoing Heraclitus), and this irreducible forward movement is the aspect of reality which eludes the grasp of science and intellect prior to their subsumption in the radical empiricism of the intuitive method, which, as in Spinoza, allows consciousness freely to choose the modes of expression for unconsciously determined affective will. Although, in retrospect, the events that occur in time can be explained mechanically in terms of matter and physical forces, reduced to the rearrangement of existing elements, events involving organisms are not determined in advance, evincing a creative freedom which becomes increasingly expansive the more conscious an entity becomes. It is this durational continuity to which intuition provides the kind of access that intellect alone never can, integrating verbal conceptuality with the affective reality of bodily experience by means of the sustained attention of intellect to durational fluctuations, which expands one's purview from the entropic monotony of pure intelligence to a recognition that matter is the medium through which the creative impulse of life moves.

The duality of mechanistic and teleological modes of explanation, efficient and final causation, plays an essential role in Bergson's conception of duration, as although he acknowledges the efficacy of both kinds of causation, he does not think that either is privileged, but rather that they are two verbal modes of construction which reality exceeds, and which correspond to partial aspects of that reality. For the intellectual mode of thought that has developed primarily in relation to matter, efficient causation (and implicitly material causation) is the characteristic causal mode, for which everything that occurs is caused by material elements pushing from the past, and for which these elements are merely rearranged. In this radically mechanistic causal mode, nothing really novel can come into being, as every moment, every new state of reality, is merely a reorganization of matter that theoretically could have been known in advance by an intellect sufficiently powerful to calculate the trajectory of every particle in the universe, and thus the world in its entirety is deterministic and eternally given. This is the logical consequence of the mode of thought, privileged in modernity, that asserts the exclusive validity of material and efficient causation. Applied to evolution, this exclusivist materialism leads to the Darwinian theory of natural selection, so that, although it is true in the negative sense that natural selection eliminates the majority of vital trajectories that cannot discover a mode conducive to their survival and propagation, Darwin's theory does not explain the vital impulse itself, the recognition that there is a tendency in the nature of reality continually to move, over billions of years, through periodic saltations, sudden transformative reorganizations of relatively static development, toward increasing novelty, freedom, and consciousness. For Bergson, this pervasive efflorescent surge can only be explained retroactively through efficient causation, but it requires final causation to explain why the radiating trajectories exist at all.

However, Bergson is nearly as critical of more traditional, radical forms of teleology as he is of pure mechanism, because radical finalism generally posits a specific design (and thus usually a designer) aiming toward pregiven ends. In contrast, Bergson recommends a more subtle form of final causation in which the ends that species evidently strive toward are not given in advance in their specificity, but are the results of a teleological inclination toward novelty of all kinds rather than any particular form of novelty, an analogue of magnetism luring life toward its self-overcoming. The vast majority of the radiating trajectories have been obstructed in their flights, drawn into circular eddies by the rugged topology of the durational terrain they traverse, halting the advance into novelty at various degrees of complexity and freedom, settling into disparate static emphases of photosynthetic, motor, perceptual, and cognitive capacities. But the trajectory leading to the human has perhaps uniquely managed to avoid being drawn aside, serving as the primary stream that has continued its ascent to increasing liberation from material determinacy by means of increasing nervous complexity, and thus consciousness, though this consciousness could have taken radically different forms, and in fact may have taken them on other planets orbiting other stars.

Only by employing both modes of causation as partial and complementary can we hope to begin to construct a conceptual understanding of the entire process. And in order to accomplish an integration of these two modes of causation through the intuitive method, the attention of intellect, with its genealogical affinity for mechanism, must be directed toward the instinctual affective knowledge more intimately related to the subtle inclinational teleology of the vital impulse, these modes describing perpendicular planes abstracted from a more expansive topological manifold. Neither mode provides ultimate access to the durational reality of the vital movement, but it is through the integration of these two contrasting causalities that a deeper domain exceeding causation can begin to be discerned, as these modes are verbal constructions of a reality that has bodied us forth along with our linguistic, conceptual, affective, and aesthetic faculties. As with Zarathustra's evocation of something beyond reconciliation, the integration of efficient and final causes, and of the faculties of intellect and instinct in intuition, does not merely posit a mode in which both are partially true (an insight also expressed by Hegel[17]), though this positing itself contains partial truth, but gestures in a direction that exceeds and dissolves the duality, that is always already integrated, but which we are still creating the conceptual language to express in itself rather than as a union of disparate elements. This is the difficult task toward which integration calls us, something beyond the reconciliation of opposites, deeper than the dialectic, more subtle and expansive than the pragmatic method, though all of these modes have carried us very far in the direction of this integration, which does not seek to suppress discord, but rather draws the discordant elements increasingly into relational contrast and complementarity as the constitutive lattice from which a novel mode may emerge. If only we can find the words to express it, the concepts, inventions, and forms of life sufficient to carry it from potentiality into actuality, this novel mode, far from fixing reality in a static logical systematization, will constitute a radical opening to wider horizons driven by discordant profusion as much as by harmonious unification, an integration beyond the many and the one.

As with radical finalism, Bergson critiques the notion of eternal formal causes, the Platonic Ideas. However, whereas with final causes he expends considerable effort articulating a novel, more subtle conception of teleological inclination, his discussion of formal causation is relatively limited and primarily critical, with only a few hints from which might be extrapolated a more subtle conception of formal causation to accompany the teloi to which Ideas have generally been considered the counterpart since antiquity, as origin to end. In such a reimagining, which Deleuze produces partially through his appropriation of Bergson's concept of the virtual in *Matter and Memory*, formal causes would not be understood as given transcendent Forms, but as formal potentialities and constraints in the moving topology of process, a landscape continually transformed by the vital impulse flowing over it, carving channels around immovable obstacles, sweeping accumulating elements along in its flood. In fact, these riverine, geographical images are borrowed from Bergson's multifarious evocation of the vital impulse, which he does not quite seem to have explicitly realized could serve as precisely the way to reimagine formal causes that we require. Jung, for whom Bergson expressed "great respect,"[18] reconceived formal causes as archetypes, describing them as "like riverbeds"[19] rather than as static essences, while Whitehead undertook a similar reimagining in his conception of the (misleadingly named) eternal objects, and Deleuze variously evokes formal causes in his conceptions of the virtual, quasi-causes, Ideas, simulacra, and multiplicities.

Bergson describes Plato's invention of the concept of Ideas as a natural, and even necessary, extension of the character of intellect. Nevertheless, this Platonic mode of thought is inadequate for comprehending the organismic reality in which we are constantly immersed, amounting to a Procrustean cramming of experience into rigid, predetermined categories, which is the appropriate and efficacious way of explaining the dynamics of material elements through physical laws, but which it is the character of durational vitality always to exceed. This radical kind of formal causation constructs disparate entities in separate durations as merely degraded or attenuated copies of a superabundance of transcendent eternal Forms, and this transcendent domain is more real than the phenomenal world of experience. Although Bergson acknowledges that this conception of Forms has been extraordinarily productive in its instrumental capacity, implicit even in the mathematically formulated laws of modern science, he ascertains the same error in the domain of eternal Forms or physical laws as he does in the pregiven teleological ends which he thoroughly revises, so that it requires only the smallest leap to extrapolate the revision exercised on final causation to formal potentialities.

It is intuition, conscious attention to affective experience, that allows us to begin to conceive the shape of formal potentialities of a more subtle and fluid character than the Forms, feeling our way through the infinitely complex potentialities and constraints, the folds and inflections, the obstacles and flows of reality with which life and consciousness find it necessary to negotiate in their progressive urge toward novelty and liberation from physical determinism. These potentialities are not ultimately separate, completely disparate entities, but tendencies resulting from a multiplicity of rills over the contingent features of a topological landscape that exceeds the grasp of solitary intellect, and which we can affectively discern through the intuitive method. This method is figured as a fringe around the bright nucleus of intellectual illumination, the faint light at a liminal horizon of conception, which reminds one of Nietzsche's evocation of the horizon as the endlessly receding locus of mythological archetypes, conceivable in Bergsonian terms as canalizations, trans-spatiotemporal trajectories that have been carved by vital flows through more expansive degrees of freedom over a virtual landscape. This reimaging of formal potentiality would constitute a fundamental rupture with the metaphysics implicitly dominant from the ancient Greeks through most modern philosophy, a novel mode in which new forms are continually being created in relation to the potentialities and constraints of temporal and material necessity. For Bergson, the world itself progressively grows and evolves in an organismic way, so that formal potentialities may be reconceived as persistent waves passing through matter in negotiation with reality's virtual contours rather than eternal Forms given in advance.

Bergson discusses several other dualities intimately related to the oppositions above – order and disorder, genera and laws, and affirmation and negation – all eliciting essential nuances, though the third duality is perhaps the most fundamental for understanding the confusion that has often predominated in the verbal construction of philosophical concepts, so that the ability of consciousness to construct one kind of order as a negation of another is predicated on the binary foundation of language and conceptual thought. Bergson reveals that negation itself is really a secondary reactive affirmation against a primary positive affirmation, an affirmation of denial, which rejects the proposition negated in favor of a different, and apparently incommensurable proposition. However, this differentiation of the reactive affirmation of negation can be conceptually separated from positive affirmation, so that any two affirmative positings can be discerned as complementary aspects of a more expansive whole once the negative, secondary affirmations have been relegated to their instrumental, differentiating roles, the negative space that partially constitutes the positive structures of any given totality.

The traditional metaphysics assumes that the foundation of reality is a simple, eternal identity given in advance, and that the phenomenal world is an attenuated degeneration resulting from a negation of this primordial transcendent unity. However, Bergson argues, if everything is given in advance, this givenness precludes the freedom of choice characteristic of vital becoming. Rather, he describes the world as a virtual potentiality which is continually created, affirmed in both its positive vitality and its negative differentiating capacity, which is really nothing other than the instrumental affirmation of a different positive trajectory, so that all positings are progressive developments of some real aspect of the world's potentiality, carried through increasingly expansive domains by the negotiation between the efficient constraints of the past and the teleologically radiating vectors whose defining quality is the urge toward future freedom. And thus, the inhibition of these vital trajectories in the majority of organisms, the relatively static eddies of all lines apart from the human, constitutes an affirmation of limit, a relaxation into habitual repetition, an active settling into basins of attraction in a trans-spatial terrain, with the denial and negation of the vital trajectory as only secondary and derivative additions to the primary entropic affirmation of matter.

The ideas of exclusion and nonexistence are added to reality rather than there being a nothingness beneath and prior to existence, as anything that can be thought exists in some way, even the lack or negation of a particular entity, which includes the idea of the entity and adds the idea of negation to it. There is thus no real absence which is not in a deeper sense a presence of lack. Every movement of reality is the presence of some affect, some concept, and thus negation, disorder, emptiness, and lack are always reactive, second-order affirmations, necessary for differentiation, but ultimately parasitic upon first-order positive affirmations. Negation itself can be conceived as a formal potentiality, a positing which Hegel defines as "the Spirit of the tragic Fate,"[20] Schelling as Kronos, Nietzsche as the "spirit of gravity,"[21] Whitehead as "negative prehensions," and Jung and Hillman as the Senex archetype or the alchemical nigredo. Negation is an active potency whose essential character is to react against the positive powers of the maximal absolute, the regal expansiveness of Zeus, the Dionysian will to power, the creative advance into novelty, and the individuating archetype of wholeness and the coniunctio. At one level of description, negation is the mere opposite of affirmation, but at a more profound discursive level, negation is a secondary degree of affirmation, a modifier attached to a primary affirmation, the inimical other. This modification does not signify the absence of truth, but two propositions dialectically related, the negative proposition mediating the relation between these differences, and paradoxically tending toward integration. If this formulation is somewhat obscure, it is especially in light of the personifying activity of the archetypal mode of thought that Bergson's abstract formulations become more distinct.

Finally, Bergson suggests that the metaphysical intuition which integrates intelligence and instinct, by bringing conscious attention to affective knowledge, has the capacity to produce a novel kind of philosophy, a philosophy which has become conscious of itself in the process of overcoming solitary intellectual understanding. Whereas the dominant modern epistemology has taken physical and astronomical laws as its primary models in their mathematical, geometrical, and spatial character, this epistemology is inadequate to understanding life, and thus we require a complementary epistemology that takes the fluid, organismic becoming of vitality as its primary model. Even a century ago, this metaphysical mode of thought was beginning to be demanded not only by the inadequacy of our biological and psychological theories, but also by the novel theories of mathematical physics centered around Poincaré, Planck, and Einstein's innovations, which efface and dissolve putatively separate particles into a more fundamental fluid relationality and intermeshing. By acknowledging the validity of various modes for the understanding of a polyvalent reality, these modes reciprocally lift one another in a recursive, spiral movement, onward, upward, and inward, from which may emerge a more expansive mode, a radically novel kind of empiricism that integrates the opposition of intellect and affect in a complexly contrasting differentiation.

Philosophy's primary function is to carry us beyond the fixed habits of any given orthodoxy which, in the case of the modern epoch evidently drawing to a close, is exemplified in scientific reductionism, but also now in deconstruction. And in order to accomplish this overcoming, the practice of philosophy must push the mind in directions that may feel unnatural, and even painful in relation to its currently conventional cognitive habits, as a relatively violent heterodoxy is the only way that novel modes of relation can emerge. However, as Bergson recognizes, such a radical transformation in our collective modes of relation, from the privileging of intellect to the intuitive integration of intellectual and instinctive faculties, is a long and extraordinarily complex process requiring generations of thinkers to critique, correct, refine, expand, and synthesize novel concepts in verbal systems sufficiently efficacious to produce an emergent mode of relation. Bergson describes this emergent mode as "a mechanics of transformation," a transformational dynamics which would lift the entire process into a more expansive manifold rather than merely translating from one mode to another on a restricted plane, though at that moment in 1907, Bergson writes that "such an integration can be no more than dreamed of."[22] However, over a century later, the time may have come when we can do more than dream and, as Bergson suggests, such an integration may eventually even result in the overcoming of the all-too-human to body forth the emergence of a mode of a being which has not yet existed in the history of the Earth.

In a conception that seems to presage the mode of thought enacted in Derridean deconstruction, Bergson recognizes that the exclusive privileging of intellect is not capable of overcoming itself by its own means, of thinking its way beyond thought into the domain of affective intuition. Rather, what is required is a brave leap into dangerously indiscernible realms beyond the enclosing horizon of rational givenness, a revolutionary act that cuts the Gordian knot of exclusive intellect, transgresses the bounds of the vicious circle of solitary mentality, just as the only way to learn to swim is to overcome one's fear of the loss of stability and control in a single, undivided act, to dive into the novel medium and simply begin to swim, an activity for which no amount of theoretical preparation can substitute. In fact, this metaphor strikingly echoes Hegel in the *Encyclopedia Logic*, an ironic resonance given Bergson's almost complete lack of direct engagement with Hegel, and Bergson's central influence on Deleuze, who notoriously critiques Hegel.[23] Nevertheless, Bergson invites us to leave the firm, fixed ground of exclusive rationality and plunge into the vast, fluid ocean of vital movement, which may at first be experienced as a frightening and exhilarating emergence into a radically expanded domain, but which, with persistence, may become familiar and even comfortable, a novel, higher kind of common sense. In retrospect, once one has made the leap into this more expansive metaphysical domain, intellect is still there in all of its complex differentiation, ready to explain the dynamic processes which mediated the discontinuous emergence, but it cannot accomplish this emergence alone, requiring an integration of the previously opposed intellectual and instinctual capacities in a novel mode of relation resonant with an integration of the inverse movements described by cosmology and psychology. This mode of relation would enact a radically empirical prolonging of the brief and relatively unreliable flashes of metaphysical intuition into a sustained, collective intuitive method from which may emerge a more expansive mode that integrates our current, and often discordant, modes.

## Notes

1 Bergson, *Mind*, 177.
2 Bergson, *Two*, 267.
3 See Bergson, *Duration*.
4 Russell, "Bergson."
5 Bergson, *Evolution*, 60.
6 Bergson, *Evolution*, 167.
7 Deleuze, *Bergsonism*, 13.
8 Bergson, *Mind*, 93.
9 Bergson, *Evolution*, 245.
10 Bergson, *Evolution*, 290.
11 Deleuze, *Two*, 157.
12 Bergson, *Mind*, 162.
13 Bergson, *Evolution*, 45.
14 Bergson, *Matter*, 138.
15 Deleuze, *Desert*, 46.
16 Bergson, *Evolution*, 272.
17 Hegel, *Science*, 121.
18 Jenkins, *Eros*, 6; Shamdasani, *Jung*, 230n.107.
19 Jung, *Civilization*, 189.
20 Hegel, *Phenomenology*, 456.
21 Nietzsche, *Zarathustra*, 29.
22 Bergson, *Evolution*, 38.
23 Hegel, *Encyclopedia*, 38, 84.

Chapter 9

# The Process of Integration
Alfred North Whitehead's *Process and Reality*

Whitehead only published his first work of philosophy when he was in his mid-fifties, and by his own account, he had never attended a course on philosophy until he taught one himself.[1] Nevertheless, Stengers speaks for many readers that Whitehead is "the most unique speculative thinker of the twentieth century,"[2] echoed by Bruno Latour that he is "the greatest philosopher of the twentieth century,"[3] and by Deleuze that "Whitehead is a great philosopher, one of genius,"[4] standing "provisionally as the last great Anglo-American philosopher before Wittgenstein's disciples spread their misty confusion, sufficiency, and terror."[5] Whitehead was influenced by Leibniz, Deleuze observing that Whitehead is the primary successor of Leibniz who "renews everything"[6] in this lineage. However, despite this superlative praise, Whitehead has had the largest impact in the United States in the discipline of theology, though his work is now evidently ascendant in philosophy as well. Whitehead was also deeply influenced by both Bergson and James, and there is a quality in his writing of subtle wit and modesty similar to James, though much of his work is extremely difficult, especially *Process and Reality*.[7] In fact, among the theorists discussed in the present book at least, Whitehead's difficulty may only be matched by that of Derrida, Hegel, and Deleuze, though Whitehead does not seem to have liked Hegel much more than James did, writing "I have never been able to read Hegel."[8]

Whitehead employs a large system of novel terms to express a view of reality whose generality had perhaps never before been achieved, though to orient his readers, he provides a passage which allows any student of philosophy to hold the more opaque sections within the frame of the massive project he calls for, which he describes as producing a complex union of the primary premodern cosmology in the West, that of Plato, for whom

DOI: 10.4324/9781003195498-10

the world is an expression of eternal formal potentialities, and in which self and world are inextricably and permeably interconnected, and the Enlightenment cosmology of the seventeenth century, which finds a radical separation between mind and world, a world composed of material particles interacting through impersonal physical forces that eventually came to supplant the transcendent in an exclusively materialist worldview.[9] These two modes seem to be incommensurable opposites, though if we have learned anything from the chapters above, it is that such oppositions often lead toward integration in a more profound conception. And in fact, although the word integration and its variations have not been especially emphasized by Whitehead scholars, he employs these terms extensively in this work, so that integration can be understood as a primary Whiteheadian concept.

For Whitehead, process, the moving totality of everything conceivable, is composed of prehensions, felt relations between entities at every level of organization, down to the scale described by quantum physics, where particles prehend one another, constituting the potentiality for the relational feelings that emerge in organisms and, finally, in the comprehension of consciousness. This prehensive relationality is primary, permeating every scale of process, and both physical reality and conscious experience emerge from this relationality in which everything in the universe is ultimately related to everything else, a further generalization of the relativities of Galileo and Einstein.[10] Prehensions have a tendency to come together in emergent actual occasions, a process which Whitehead refers to as concrescence, the progressive integration of disparate entities into novel subjective forms, newly unified organisms in the broadest sense of self-organized entities. Whitehead describes these emergent entities as "real unities" which are "more than a mere collective disjunction of component elements,"[11] so that something fundamentally novel is created in the integrations that produce the successive stages of any process.

Becoming is driven by a teleological urge toward the integration of disparate elements, lured toward the satisfactions of their subjective aims in the realization of final causes by means of the composition of these separate entities in more encompassing unifications, so that entities, in whatever domain, which were apparently incommensurable, have a tendency to integrate into more ordered wholes. This abstract principle is as applicable to the complexities of philosophical controversy as it is to the emergence of carbon dioxide from the separate elements of carbon and oxygen. The disagreements between different schools of thought in philosophy are not merely two alternative theories about the world, one of which can be proven correct and the other refuted. Rather, once a philosophical system has been thoroughly criticized and differentiated, absorbed into the stable pantheon of philosophical opinions that constitute the habit of orthodoxy, it will inevitably come to be seen as not simply true or false, but too limited, not large enough to encompass the felt reality of process. That which a system denies is what ultimately limits its coherence, ignoring or rejecting elements that are required for a more voluminous holding-together of the encountered facts. Every philosophy is finally abandoned as a self-contained and perfect system, but it is absorbed into what comes after, producing a reaction, as with the reaction of James to Hegel, but then later finding new life in an emergent philosophical system which, through novel concepts expressed in new language, often discovers that the older system and the reaction it impelled are coherent in certain respects at a deeper discursive level. Like the emergence of novel chemical elements out of more basic ones, or the emergence of novel organisms through both reproduction and evolution, philosophy is a process of progressive integration of modes of thought which, when integrated, contribute to a greater scope of coherence.

As a prominent mathematician, Whitehead understood that the analytic urge, dominant in Anglophone philosophy for much of the twentieth century, to reduce the world to a vast system of logically provable propositions, while applicable to some limited domains of process, has tended to preclude a larger coherence that exceeds the possibility of logical proof. Partially because of his deep familiarity with the subject, he was able to discern the limits of the mathematical mode of thought, which his student and collaborator Bertrand Russell and the analytic philosophy that he partially founded often sought to generalize to reality as such, vast domains of which are not susceptible to logical formulation.[12] One may think of Hegel's dialectical logic of becoming, which seems to constitute a movement toward the kind of organismic mode of thought Whitehead is calling for, conceived in correlation with the calculus without being reducible to mathematics. This resonance makes it all the more striking that Whitehead claims not to have "been able to read" Hegel, dismissing him much like his elder contemporary James did, especially given that Whitehead's writing is similar to Hegel's in its monumental, abstract complexity. With James, one can see that, although he was an extremely complex and profound thinker, his writing is more direct and practical, even as it is delightfully poetic and witty, so one can understand why he would have found Hegel's high abstraction unpalatable. But Whitehead is one of a very few theorists who might be considered a Hegel for the constructivist stream of twentieth century philosophy, so it is somewhat puzzling that Whitehead rejected Hegel so summarily. Perhaps Whitehead simply had not read enough of Hegel to appreciate how compatible their systems were in certain respects, having started with Hegel's mathematical ideas, presumably in *The Science of Logic*, which Whitehead found to be "complete nonsense."[13] Perhaps Whitehead was also partially participating in the general reaction against Hegel's dominating influence that occurred in the first two-thirds of the twentieth century, culminating in the general vicinity of Derrida's and Deleuze's sixties texts. Or maybe Whitehead even sensed that, in order to produce his own vast system, he needed to remain free of the immense gravitational force of Hegel's thought. But whatever the reason, it is tempting, in the twenty-first century, to discern profound connections between the two philosophers.[14]

Regarding the correlation between the calculus and the philosophical concepts of differentiation and integration, one might suspect that Whitehead, the mathematician-turned-philosopher, would have led the charge in the discernment of this resonance. However, in 1911's *An Introduction to Mathematics*, written in the midst of the publication of the three volumes of *Principia Mathematica*, and nearly a decade before he began writing philosophy in earnest, Whitehead quips that "the general effect of the success of the differential calculus was to generate a large amount of bad philosophy, centering round the idea of the infinitely small,"[15] Leibniz's infinitesimal, Whitehead affirming Berkeley's dismissal of infinitesimals as "ghosts of departed quantities," though even Berkeley later came to consider them "useful fictions."[16] Whitehead goes so far as to assert about this correlation between mathematics and metaphysics that "it is a safe rule to apply that, when a mathematical or philosophical author writes with a misty profundity, he is talking nonsense."[17] In *Process and Reality*, Whitehead definitively asserts that "there are no infinitesimals,"[18] though as John W. Lango observes: "In light of more recent developments in mathematics – in particular, the new infinitesimals of Nonstandard Analysis – it becomes possible to conceive of actual occasions as infinitesimally small."[19] Whitehead was expressing the almost universal consensus among mathematicians during his lifetime, as Abraham Robinson would not prove the validity of infinitesimals for another half-century in the 1960s. Nevertheless, as early as 1925, Whitehead seems at least amenable to the correlation of the calculus and philosophical concepts, writing that

> mental cognition is seen as the reflective experience of a totality, reporting for itself what it is in itself as one unit of occurrence. This unit is the integration of the sum of its partial happenings, but it is not their numerical aggregate. It has its own unity as an event.[20]

While remaining distinctly unmisty, this passage appears to suggest a profound correlation between the integrating quality of a nondifferentiable cognitive event that emerges from its differentiated parts and the calculus.

By the time of *Process and Reality* in 1929, Whitehead is using the word integration as one of his primary philosophical concepts for the emergent unity of all kinds of differentiated entities across scale, so while there does not appear to be a direct retraction of his 1911 dismissal, it seems highly unlikely that the mathematician-turned-philosopher, extremely rigorous and careful with language, was using the term integration philosophically without awareness of its mathematical resonances, which, in fact, he may have been intentionally evoking. Perhaps some more direct evidence will emerge from Whitehead's *Nachlass*, recovered in 2019, but for now, the evidence seems to indicate that Whitehead came to agree with Leibniz, Hegel, and Bergson about a resonance between mathematical and metaphysical differentiations and integrations, though his rejection of the infinitesimal is ironically closest to Hegel.

Like Hegel, Whitehead understood that the truth or falsity of any logical proposition can only be considered a valid judgment within a certain limited system, and that beyond that constrained structure, the opposition breaks down, becoming only partially true, but false in that which it denies because it excludes other truths from its domain of coherence. In order to become more true, a partial truth must be integrated with other truths, which appear incommensurable within the frame where the propositions have been posited. Explicitly referring to Bergson, Whitehead suggests that it is precisely the role of philosophy to discern the partiality of truths, artificially separated into impermeable categories, and to resituate them within the larger context of increasingly expansive generalities in relation to one another, in which the truths are no longer mutually exclusive, but complementary conditions for one another's specific contours. Propositions are limited by their relations to their context, and so they contain partial validity only within a particular kind of ecological order, but they cannot be complete and comprehensive truths if they do not comprehensively describe and explain every particular in the universe, so that propositions can only absorb increasingly broad swaths of that universe into their linguistic conceptual structures.

When a mode of thought settles into a metaphysical orthodoxy, the specific terms and formulations of that system can seem inevitable, permanent, and complete because they have become something approximating common sense.[21] We have been raised and educated within the verbal systems of established modes of thought, whatever they may be, whether Christian scholasticism, Enlightenment rationality, Hegelian idealism, or even poststructuralism, so that we tend to settle into their verbally constructed assumptions as obvious, given. As Whitehead writes, "it requires a very unusual mind to undertake the analysis of the obvious,"[22] in part because words are always inadequate for the full expression of a proposition, as any utterance inevitably leaves out essential unspoken elements, including those implicit in the structures of language itself, leaving loose ends, fissures in the system that render any verbal formulation within which the binary logic of truth and falsity can be applied permeable with a broader domain, so that binary judgment becomes mostly extraneous in the more expansive context of a greater generality of expression.[23]

This forward movement of philosophical thought can be conceived as a vast process of trial-and-error over the course of generations, expressed in numerous volumes of more-or-less-scintillating prose, and then critiqued and refined until the truth which resides at the heart of any plausible mode of thought is distilled. Then it is rejected, rendered obsolete, old-fashioned, an atavistic remnant, until some new philosopher, a decade, a century, or even a millennium later, takes the system up again. And though it may no longer directly address the problems of this new era, this philosopher or group of philosophers may emphasize some aspect of the system, often precisely the aspect that was ignored in that theorist's or movement's heyday, and bring it into relation with other systems, which the originators of that system may never have thought compatible but which, with the freshness of discovery, can be seen to have something at their cores that answer one another, that complement one another's limitations, rendering them again relevant to the forward thrust of conceptual thought, saving them by discerning how they are always already integrated on a more expansive plane.[24]

This process of "selective emphasis,"[25] critique, rejection, and renewal is characteristic of individual consciousness as well as the movements of collective mentality through the history of philosophy. Just as certain eras privilege certain kinds of philosophy, so different elements of consciousness find different emphases at different moments, and even when one mode of relation is repressed in favor of another in consciousness, collective or individual, the repressed mode is still an essential part of the mind's constitution, and must be taken account of in any coherent conception of consciousness. The selective emphasis of consciousness is a narrowness which allows it to achieve greater depth in whatever domain it is emphasizing, but philosophy's primary function is to excavate the univocal reality which the particular emphases of consciousness adumbrate or conceal. For instance, the total experience of an organism is both conceptual and affective, with the two domains intimately intertwined, but in the context of the modern Cartesian split between mind and world, which includes the body, they must be reconciled in order to produce a more intricately differentiated totality.

There is a tendency in process to move from states of disjunction to states of increasing conjunction, which produce emergent entities that are more than merely the sum of their parts. The driving force of this impulsion toward integration is termed creativity, the creative advance into novelty, a teleological trajectory toward the concrescent synthesis of previously disparate elements, which maintains their differentiation as contrast within unity, and thus produces a categorically novel kind of entity. For Whitehead, the most significant type of contrast is that between affirmation and negation, the binary opposition of truth and falsity, which, through their polarized tension, generate emergent integrations. The felt relationalities that constitute process are teleologically drawn toward successive integrations, which mediate concrescence, the progressive coming together of these prehensions, through distinct phases that trace a trajectory toward the incorporation of increasing swaths of the world into organismic systems.

Concrescence is not merely a placid unification, but is driven by engagement with negative prehensions, the felt relations in all domains which negate, reject, divide, and ultimately serve the purpose of generating articulated contrasts within the integral totality, which maintain their difference within unity. That which is excluded from an entity constitutes the antithesis (a word in which one may be hard-pressed not to hear an echo of the dialectic), the negative prehension in relation to which actual (as opposed to potential) entities define themselves, as actual entities are always in relation not only to what they contain, but to the others that delimit the boundaries of their existence as differentiated individuals. Everything is in relation to everything else, even if a specific relation is negative in its current phase of ingression. Echoing Schelling and Bergson, Whitehead suggests that "the negative judgment is the peak of mentality,"[26] that the very mode of intellectual analysis is an essentially negative operation whose primary function is to differentiate, so that separate entities can find deeper and wider loci of integration as contrasts within emergent entities rather than as external, incommensurable differences related to one another only in the character of negative prehensions.

This issue of the negative brings us to "the problem of the solidarity of the universe"[27] referred to in the epigraph above. The traditional categories of thought are oppositional formulations of subject and object, form and matter, internal and external, which have been instrumental in the differentiation of rational mentality that finds its peak in modernity, but which preclude the resolution of these oppositions on the discursive plane that these binaries constellate, leaving the field of conceptual thought polarized into a self and world which are irresolvably separated based on these oppositional premises. However, the Whiteheadian solution to this apparently insoluble situation is the concept of prehensions, the felt relationality of all entities across scale, whose nature is incessantly to produce concrescent integrations, always to be busily at work effecting the progressive unification of disparate elements.

The relational feelings forming the entangled roots of process can be characterized as vectors, and these vectors are directed in each phase toward the unification of all relevant prehensions in an integral satisfaction, the final differentiated unification of a particular emergent entity in actuality. Once the unification of a given phase is accomplished, whether at the physical, chemical, biological, psychological, or sociological scales, the emergent integration becomes an actually existent fact for further integrations. Whereas before, the novel entity only existed as a formal potentiality, an eternal object, and as a final cause, the subjective aim or lure for feeling, once the integral satisfaction of the allied axis of formal-final causation, potentiality and purpose, has been achieved, the novel entity becomes an object susceptible to material and efficient causation, for which any element not positively contained within the emergent actuality becomes opposed or excluded as other to its integral subjective unity as negative prehensions.

Both physical reality and given orthodoxy, philosophical or otherwise, are the domains of reality susceptible to explanation in terms of efficient causation. But for the aspects of process that exceed physicality or orthodoxy, whether the formal relations from which physical reality emerges described at the limits of twentieth century physics or the transformative ruptures and dynamic, heterodox trajectories that animate cultural development, "we require explanation by 'final cause,'"[28] as efficient causation alone is insufficient to explain the organismic movements of process.

Final causation has often been rejected in modernity, partly because of its extreme overemphasis in the Middle Ages in the Christian West, which impelled a reaction (I am tempted to call it dialectical despite Whitehead's imagined protestations) that produced a compensatory overemphasis of efficient causation in the modern scientific mentality. These successive privilegings of opposed kinds of causation may now enable the discernment of efficient and final causation as deeply intertwined and mutually complementary modes of relation, returned to the balance they enjoyed in ancient thought, but differentiated by means of their sequential historical dominance. All actualities, from the smallest elements of microphysics to the human organism and the cosmos itself, exhibit both physicality and mentality, so that even the atoms and quarks which emerge from yet deeper relations are not only physical objects, as they are generally conceived by modern science, but contain, and are contained within, the duality of interiority and exteriority that has reached its current peak of intensity in the human bipolarity of mind and body. The teleological process that lures the creative trajectory toward novelty is produced by an integration of physicality and mentality that Whitehead describes as self-formation, which is again a remarkably similar conception to the self-positing of the dialectic. Mentality is the pole where this integration of opposed modes of causation takes place by means of attention to both conceptual and bodily experience, an integration resonant with Bergsonian intuition.

The teleological emergence of novelty, which Whitehead describes as "the primary meaning of 'life,'"[29] is mediated through the concrescent integration of the felt prehensions that constitute the world, contrary to Kant's supposition that the subject is prior to the world, the subjectivity from which that world emerges.[30] Each integration is constituted in more expansive contrasts, differences arrayed in positive relation within a unified entity as "the assemblage of a multiplicity of lower contrasts,"[31] a phrase reminiscent of both Bergson and Deleuze. The different bodily elements form a relational multiplicity from which emerges a "harmony of contrasts,"[32] and for Whitehead, this harmony is often constituted in oppositions, whose inhibiting relations to one another in the lower contrasts characteristic of negative prehensions are integrated by their transmutation into oppositional contrast which, instead of merely negating one another, become positive, complementary elements constituting a more comprehensive whole, lured by final causation, in which integral entities form constitutive elements in novel organismic syntheses of felt relations.[33]

Positive contrast, the relation of difference within unity, elicits the depths of experience, constituting the finely differentiated precision which depth requires, as the relatively undifferentiated structures of contrast in less-integrated multiplicities allow only for blunt instruments in which every entity is interpreted as a nail, hammering experience in every domain into the Procrustean bed of a more simplistic (though not necessarily simpler) and less-refined relational mode. So, while the higher contrasts produce a broader integration of difference within unity, this width depends upon a fineness of relational organization, as a grand cathedral, the dome of St. Peter's Basilica for instance, contains a vast negative space within its sacred enclosure constituted by the intricate balance of its architectural structure, while a building supported by a much more basic structure can only grow so large before it collapses under its own weight. The emergence of highly integrated entities thus requires not only an encompassing broadness, but also a concomitant structural refinement which consistently mirrors its magnitude.

Whitehead suggests that this pattern of contrasts is established in the relation not only, or even primarily, of physical elements, but of eternal objects, the formal potentialities and constraints that inform reality's relational texture, of which every actuality is an expression. As he modestly writes in a 1936 letter to Charles Hartshorne,

> there is one point as to which you – and everyone – misconstrue me – obviously my usual faults of exposition are to blame. I mean my doctrine of eternal objects. It is a first endeavor to get beyond the absurd simple-mindedness of the traditional treatment of Universals,

which Whitehead refers to as "the root of all evils." As he explains, the "relational essence" of each eternal object "involves its (potential) interconnections with all other eternal objects."[34] Every realization of an eternal object in actuality is a further expression of that formal potentiality in relation to other eternal objects, and this increasingly intricate web of complementary, contrasting formal relations, embodied in felt prehensions, both produces and is produced by the integration of contraries and differences in the satisfaction of a subjective aim. Eternal objects are teleologically lured toward progressive integration, the enfolding of increasing numbers of eternal objects into a balanced and complex unity constituted in increasingly involuted layers of complementary contrasts, in which each contrast is conserved as the exquisitely defined negative space within a network of partially actualized relational potentialities. And it is only in a late phase of this series of integrations that consciousness emerges, derived from the felt relations that constitute the experiential quality of reality, which, in its enfolding of complexity, is also a simplification, a higher unification from which complexity can be derived.

Consciousness is a late stage in a series of distinct phases of concrescence that emerges through the complexly differentiated integrations of previous epochal durations, which implicitly contain the potential for the later stages of ingression, so that electrons exhibit the relationality which is a precondition for the emergence of life and consciousness, which is the product of an integration of relational modes characteristic of physicality and mentality. And when a novel phase of process emerges from the integration of apparently incommensurable entities, it still contains the differentiated entities as essential and contrasting elements of its constitution. When such an emergent integration occurs, the entities or modes, which were previously only related by virtue of negative prehensions, as external relations of felt difference, begin to participate in a mutual unification within an organismic whole, which contains the differences as contrasts within its affective totality. This teleological lure toward contrasting unification is the purpose of the creative advance which, through successive integrations, produces an increasingly profound affective intensity within the organism, a difference within unity that is characteristic of the higher phases of ingression, namely human consciousness and increasingly expansive cultural forms, which contain wider and more intricate networks of relational contrasts that constitute both their structural stability and their animating motivity.

For the later phases of concrescence, specifically those of consciousness, culture, and philosophy, Whitehead articulates a theory of falsity strikingly similar to the Hegelian negative. False logical propositions must be accepted as necessary for the creative advance, as error, the lack of conformity of a premise with the encountered reality, is the force by which we learn, to the extent that Whitehead designates errancy as a primary characteristic of more complexly differentiated forms of life, not just an incidental mistake that can be cast aside, but a central driving element of the development of process toward higher domains of differentiated integration. For Whitehead, consciousness emerges from a play of affirmation and negation, through the intimate involvement of this contrasting polarity, a formulation which is conceptually resonant with Hegel, though whereas for Hegel, this contrast is primarily conceptual, one of Whitehead's great innovations is to resituate this play of opposites as primarily affective, issuing into both physical and conceptual feelings.

For instance, as a young deer may be injured after misjudging its step on uneven ground due to lack of attention, and thus become more careful and attentive in its future ambulations, so too might a scholar, after having asserted certain claims about some complex issue, come upon new information or a novel perspective which impresses upon them the realization that their earlier assertion was erroneous due to an oversimplification, which allows the scholar, perhaps simultaneously both chagrined and illuminated, to deepen their understanding of their subject. Without these encounters with error, organisms would remain developmentally static, naïve, and undifferentiated, unable to progress to the more attentive posture or the more profound comprehension. These falsities or errors can be understood as the negative pole in affective oppositions, whose primary function is to serve as the motive force of teleological becoming, which is more accurately described as a lure, an affective pull toward self-overcoming rather than a push from behind. These prehended contraries are the spur to consciousness, the negative other from which awareness is forged.[35]

At every stage of process, once a particular integration has been achieved, the careful attentiveness of the deer as much as the nuanced discernment of the scholar, the entity or mode settles into a new orthodoxy, a relatively stable society of unified, interlaced prehensions defining the limits and constraints of its current conception of reality, which even its most radical speculations cannot catch a glimpse beyond.[36] But then we encounter another problem, another incommensurability, another lack of conformity between our conceptions and the world we face as external, whether physical, conceptual, or affective, which demands heterodoxy for continued vitality, forcing us either to retreat into a calcified shell which precludes further development, and possibly even survival, or to engage with the felt contrariety or disjunction, to dwell with it until some solution emerges that expands the horizons of our cosmos, both internal and external, and allows our imaginations to risk further leaps into currently indiscernible zones of affective union.[37]

Each emergent integration in this process of ascendance through wider generalities is magnetically lured by the desire of organismic process to bring more and more of reality into its fold, and this is no less true of philosophy, whose teleological purpose is to enfold every conceptual complex, however apparently incompatible with one another, into "one ultimate generalization around which we must weave our philosophical system."[38] If two modes of thought seem incommensurable, the most generative approach is not to choose one system over the other, but to discern the essential structural contours – often occluded by harsh denouncements and fierce defenses, alliances and rivalries, filiations and animosities – which inevitably resonate with each other in some way, contain some loose ends of partiality and limitation which not only can be, but demand to be brought into connection with the opposed mode. But the task of seeing through the minute controversies, contextual counterreformations, stubborn incommensurabilities, and personal grievances is a difficult one, which can only be accomplished if accompanied by the at-least-hypothetical supposition that all modes are ultimately compatible because they all describe the same world and emerge from that world.[39] No mode of thought contains a comprehensive understanding of reality, but reality is susceptible to every mode of thought that has found some success, however minor or marginal. Even though a novel mode, always the product of an emergent integration, is usually associated with one philosopher or group of philosophers, Deleuze and Guattari's conceptual personae, who serve as the symbolic focus and voice of that mode, the creation of this integral concrescence is ultimately social, the network of critics and allies, supporters and detractors, scholars pursuing parallel or oblique projects forming the relational totality out of which this novel unification emerges. And this sociality is not reserved only for diverse human consciousnesses, but is relevant down to the microphysical domain, so that a novel actual entity is only ever produced by the integration of differences as contrasts within a more encompassing society.[40]

However, this process of integration is not usually a confluent coming together in a larger whole, but a difficult labor to birth a novel entity, which must be gone through, and the success of which is not assured, but which faces real danger. The attempt to force an integration before its time is due can impel a miscarriage of that potential emergent actuality, so that the fiery young radicals, who demand revolution before the time is ripe despite who is harmed in the process, misread the temporal quality of their moment, attempting to force the wave rather than ride it. And these angry revolutionaries are often the privileged ones whose life jackets keep them afloat, while the less fortunate are drowned in their wake. This is not to say that genuine revolutions do not periodically occur, and that anger and radicality are not often justified, just that revolutions are always the product of an active integration, and that such integrations cannot be compelled to emerge before their time any more than a blossom can be obliged to emerge from the bud. They can be cultivated, encouraged, and protected, but not forced to grow. And as with revolutions, blossoms, or infants, the period of gestation, the winter of dormancy, ultimately produces a more robust and durable integration because no entity is purely negative, so the other in every encounter with opposition not only inhibits, delays, and forges the development of the primary entity in question, but this negativity is intimately bound up with the specific contours and limits of that other's subjective positing, its partial expression of some aspect of reality that has been excluded from the actual entity which encounters it, an encounter that serves to broaden and deepen the initial entity.[41]

Whereas the typical modern philosophical conception of propositions is that they are claims that must either be true or false, the eternal objects from which they derive contain *in potentia* both the truth and falsity of every possible proposition derived from them within their relational totality, though they are undifferentiated in themselves, and can only become differentiated through the development of novel propositions.[42] While at one stage of development, two concepts or entities may seem incommensurable with one another, for instance the Cartesian mind-body dualism, the creative advance lures a new and deeper proposition from this apparently irresolvable duality which redefines them as a contrast within a broader unity. This emergent unity itself then becomes an element in an even wider incommensurability that requires integration, which can only be achieved through generations writing countless texts, relentlessly subjecting the opposition to sustained contemplation within the fluctuating vicissitudes of their affective experience, testing the limits of the concepts through expression after expression, one philosopher describing the work of another philosopher, synthesizing some essential insight from that theorist with another theorist's concept, which the conventional doxa, and perhaps even the philosopher themself, deems incompatible. The apparently irreconcilable concepts are rarefied in the alchemical alembic of the philosopher's embodied, durational ruminations, embedded in the encompassing organismic whole of the philosophical community (though organisms at all scales can be healthy or sick), which elevates certain problems and their solutions by selective emphasis, by collective attention given to a particular school of thought exemplified by one or several individual theorists. These conceptual personae become the locus of integration for the novel proposition, which saves the constituent propositions from their "mere multiplicity," and thus mediates the creative advance toward increasing propositional unity "in the transcendent future," though for Whitehead, transcendence is not located with the eternal objects, as they were for the Platonic Forms, but in creative activity lured by an always-receding horizon toward which the teleological concrescence draws those potentialities through periodic self-overcomings mediated through integration.[43]

The widest generality of this process of concrescence, which proceeds through relatively discontinuous emergent integrations of prehensive felt relations, and which is teleologically lured toward integral satisfaction by the urge of being toward the creative advance into novelty, is the progression through distinct historical and cosmological epochs. Each epoch becomes a constitutive element of the subsequent epochs, "which transcend it and include it" as an integral part of the more expansive organismic whole. And in this subsumption, the earlier epoch is never simply rejected, but reframed, decentered, devoured, and reconstituted as one aspect of a new unity with a broader balance and a deeper center of gravity.[44] Even when two theorists, or the modes of thought they exemplify and express at their deepest registers, seem fundamentally incompatible, the affective relations which form the texture of a mode of thought, the attitude, orientation, posture, shading, and emphasis behind or beneath the words employed asymptotically to express that mode, are ultimately "compatible for integration"[45] in a later, higher, wider phase of concrescence, becoming complementary contrasts rather than fixed, static incommensurabilities.

Whitehead emphasizes that the kind of philosophy characteristic of the modern epoch has been "deficient in its neglect of bodily reference,"[46] privileging oppositional rationality over the affective modes in which these oppositions are dissolved and integrated, because they are ingressions of coexisting eternal objects, felt expressions of formal potentialities for which words, and the conceptual thought they mediate, play an analogous role to the integral calculus. The felt continuity of bodily experience is differentiated into discrete units whose summation (in both senses of the term: adding together and summarizing) describes the originary totality, but can never become identical with it. Paradoxically though, the verbal expression of felt experience serves to integrate the pervasive modern duality of mind and world by leading the mind, which generally operates through concepts, to direct its attention toward the body, which is in constant negotiation with physical reality, shifting the emphasis from subject encountering object as a separate, pure externality, to attention to the permeability of interiority and exteriority, which find their primary locus of encounter in the body. The mind-body problem is only a problem if a mode of thought asserts, often unconsciously, the primacy of mind over body as a first principle, motivated ironically not by logical considerations, but by affective ones, which Whitehead calls conceptual feelings, echoing James' pragmatic theory of temperament, characteristic of different philosophical and historical eras as much as different philosophical individuals. Whitehead deems the modern Cartesian dualism a profound and temporarily necessary error, which can be overcome by the attention to felt reality, largely initiated by Spinoza, revealing conceptual thought ultimately to be a kind of bodily feeling, an integration of physical and conceptual prehensions that Whitehead explicitly relates to Bergson's intuitive method.

This reframing of mind and body as primarily two affective modes rather than as two fundamentally incommensurable substances renders it possible to think their individuated reintegration after the instrumental separation characteristic of the Cartesian dualism dominant in the modern epoch, so that final causation lures the integration of physical and conceptual feelings, which are defined by their relations to temporality. The physical feelings are temporal, while the conceptual feelings that constitute mind are transtemporal in the sense that, while physicality is closely connected to the linear temporality of efficient causation in which each moment is determined by the state of the previous moment, mentality is free to roam from the past of memory to the future of anticipation, and is only intermittently required to attend to the present. It is in the consciousness characteristic of conceptual feeling that one can, if one is sufficiently attentive, discern internal resonances among moments separated in external physical time, durations interiorly connected by their mutual expressions of eternal objects, which are themselves the relational potentialities and constraints of process, lured toward their emergent elaboration by the teleological urge toward novelty.

The phases of ingression through which process advances are not contained within the linear succession characteristic of physical temporality. Rather, for Whitehead's "epochal theory of time,"[47] discontinuous phases, at whatever scale of process, from the growth of an organism through distinct developmental stages, to the historical development through distinct cultural modes, and even to the dimensional constructions of space and time in different cosmic epochs, are primary, and the temporality characteristic of efficient causation is reductively extracted from these phases. As witnessed in the various relations among the theorists discussed in these pages, an earlier thinker can express a mode of thought that is developmentally subsequent, containing a wider unity of integrated contrasts than the later thinker, though this later theorist can reciprocally bring finer nuance and subtle contrast to the developmentally earlier mode, which creates the conditions in which the mode of thought expressed by the earlier, but developmentally subsequent, theorist can find a wider locus of effectuation. For instance, although Whitehead is prior to Derrida, it may be suggested that his mode of thought is developmentally more mature, though Derrida's undeniable brilliance lies in expressing the deconstructive mode in such an aesthetically and conceptually sophisticated way that it could become a dominant force in academia, while Whitehead's thought remains relatively marginal, though deeply cherished in certain sectors. It seems that our task is to bring the, in some ways, more profound, but less efficaciously formulated, modes of earlier theorists like Whitehead into intimate relation with later, more narrowly focused, but also more culturally dominant thinkers like Derrida, a task for which Deleuze is especially helpful.

Historical time traces the collective emphasis of different modes of thought which are often expressed nonlinearly, complexly repeating through intertwining cycles at different orders of successive expression. Thus, it may be necessary to refer back to broadly constructivist theorists like Whitehead, James, and Bergson to discover a mode of thought which allows us to go beyond the deconstructive mode so completely and finally expressed by Derrida, a novel mode which has not yet been embraced on the widest scale of intellectual culture, and thus requires a renewed articulation in integration with other complementary modes that may allow this novel mode to find a means of expression through which it may become primary within the academy, perhaps even eventually overcoming the continental-analytic divide. We seem to live in the late stages of deconstruction's primacy (though not in Anglophone philosophy), so that even those participants in Western culture who are not explicitly aware of this mode of thought, as well as the many who reject it or define themselves against it, must nevertheless contend with it in some way, fending it off by means of a mere reassertion of the privileged oppositional rationality it problematizes, or even bizarrely conflating deconstruction with communism or reactionary "post-truth" conservatism, rendering it the sophistic scapegoat which must be vanquished. In this very specific sense, deconstruction has played a role for our era analogous to that of Christianity (or more plausibly, given the scale of influence, Hegelianism) for earlier centuries. And in order to move beyond deconstruction's primacy within academia, as we have largely done with the traditional conception of the Christian God within educated milieus, deconstruction must be resituated as a valid mode of thought which may be employed productively within a more expansive mode, but which no longer (ironically, given the decentering project of deconstruction) holds the discursive center. This resituation is not merely a rejection, an a-deconstruction parallel to atheism, which defines itself in opposition to what it rejects and thus has not yet escaped its gravitational pull, but is rather a novel mode which, like the modern era that has decentered God, or post-Hegelian philosophy which has decentered the absolute, reframes these dominant figures as objects of personal choice rather than as normative groundings for a collective worldview.

The mode of thought which may subsume deconstruction will not emerge out of thin air, but will be constituted in a reappropriation and reframing of previous modes, including deconstruction, in integration with one another to produce a novel mode, which will interweave these disparate threads in novel ways. Perhaps a full emergence of this collectively envisioned mode will occur within our lifetimes, or perhaps the theorists now working in these domains will serve as further threads contributing to the contrasting complexity of a future mode of differentiating integration,[48] which those of us who care to gaze toward the conceptual horizon can discern as "the faint discordant light of the dawn of another age."[49] But all of these moments are necessary, as Whitehead discerns greatness in both those who construct the vast systems of belief, religious in the broadest sense, that constitute our worldview, and those like Derrida, "the rebels who destroy such systems," only to have their successors find that they have constructed a new religion, a new orthodoxy that must in turn be dismantled, devoured, and reconstituted in a novel construction. These are both essential moments in the becoming of process, for which it is equally necessary that "the fairies dance, and Christ is nailed to the cross,"[50] each in its appropriate epoch, that we collectively traverse the trajectory from an immanent animism through a transcendent monotheism – between which generally resides the millennia of polytheism in the West, and after which subsists roughly a half-millennium of rationalism – as preparation for a novel mode that subsumes and overcomes all of these moments. Thus, Whitehead can write on the last page of his final book:

> If you like to phrase it so, philosophy is mystical. For mysticism is direct insight into depths as yet unspoken. But the purpose of philosophy is to rationalize mysticism: not by explaining it away, but by the introduction of novel verbal characterizations,[51]

to integrate the epochally differentiated mystical and rational modes, the animist, polytheist, and monotheist modes, by means of the creation of new conceptual language. These epochal modes are partial expressions of a reality which exceeds them, a reality which Whitehead imagines as God's loving enfoldment of the world in all its integral multiplicity, though he explicitly argues against what he terms the fallacy of the traditional conception of an original, transcendent creator in favor of the aesthetic coherence of the process of becoming itself, the creative advance into novelty, and we may discern that other imaginal modes beyond monotheism are more efficacious for further movement.[52]

Whitehead allows us to see that the world is radically open, that even our most fundamental understanding of reality, from our constructions of mind and body to those of space and time, are local assumptions within a sphere of comprehension corresponding to the contours of the specific contrasts that have been integrated within immanent organismic entities, both human and cultural. These apparently fundamental conceptions of the world are ultimately provincial features of the human epoch, which may seem vast in relation to our individual lives, but which is relatively restricted measured on a cosmic scale, and there are barely conceivable domains of reality, just visible at our horizons of conception, which may be very different from our collective construction of reality, merely one specific construction among an infinite potentiality of worlds. And even beyond those scarcely imaginable horizons, there are undoubtedly domains which exceed our current ability even to dream.[53] As we have begun to see above, time itself is susceptible to such an analysis, as beyond our local conception of space and time, "entities with new relationships, unrealized in our experiences and unforeseen by our imaginations, will make their appearance, introducing into the universe new types of order,"[54] so that, for instance "space might as well have three hundred and thirty-three dimensions, instead of the modest three dimensions of our present epoch." The integration of diverse modes of felt experience within ever-wider contrasts by means of novel conceptual creation is the dynamic which allows us to conceive of domains beyond our contemporary constructions of spacetime and the consciousness that knows it.[55]

## Notes

1 Price, *Dialogues*, 322.
2 Stengers, *Thinking*, 190.
3 Stengers, *Thinking*, x.
4 Deleuze, "Whitehead."
5 Delezue, *Fold*, 76.
6 Deleuze, "Whitehead."
7 Stengers, *Thinking*, 112.
8 Whitehead, *Essays*, 10.
9 Whitehead, *Process*, xiv.
10 Whitehead, *Process*, 22. See Nottale, *Relativity*.
11 Whitehead, *Process*, 229.
12 Whitehead, *Process*, 8.
13 Whitehead, *Essays*, 10.
14 See Lucas, *Hegel*.
15 Whitehead, *Mathematics*, 108.
16 Stanford Encyclopedia of Philosophy, "Continuity."
17 Whitehead, *Mathematics*, 108.
18 Whitehead, *Process*, 328.
19 Lango, "Actual," 29.
20 Whitehead, *Science*, 148–9.
21 Whitehead, *Science*, 12–13.
22 Whitehead, *Science*, 4.
23 Whitehead, *Process*, 11.
24 Whitehead, *Process*, 14.
25 Whitehead, *Process*, 15.
26 Whitehead, *Process*, 5.
27 Whitehead, *Process*, 56.
28 Whitehead, *Process*, 104.
29 Whitehead, *Process*, 102.
30 Whitehead, *Process*, 88.

31 Whitehead, *Process*, 95.
32 Whitehead, *Process*, 109.
33 Whitehead, *Process*, 232.
34 Whitehead, *Alfred*, 199.
35 Whitehead, *Process*, 188.
36 Whitehead, *Process*, 193.
37 Whitehead, *Process*, 211.
38 Whitehead, *Process*, 208.
39 Whitehead, *Process*, 337.
40 Whitehead, *Process*, 223.
41 Whitehead, *Process*, 223.
42 Whitehead, *Process*, 256.
43 Whitehead, *Process*, 261, 263.
44 Whitehead, *Process*, 238.
45 Whitehead, *Process*, 240.
46 Whitehead, *Modes*, 153.
47 Whitehead, *Modes*, 283.
48 Whitehead, *Modes*, 283.
49 Whitehead, *Modes*, 339.
50 Whitehead, *Modes*, 337.
51 Whitehead, *Modes*, 174.
52 Stengers, *Thinking*, 220.
53 Whitehead, *Process*, 342.
54 Whitehead, *Process*, 288.
55 Whitehead, *Process*, 289, 350.

Chapter 10

# A Widening of Consciousness Through Integration

C.G. Jung's *Mysterium Coniunctionis*

It may at first seem incongruous to include Jung in a book full of philosophers (excepting Hillman, and partially James), and Jung himself denied that he was a philosopher,[1] always insisting that he was first and foremost a physician, having begun his career working with patients at a psychiatric hospital, and playing a large role in the early development and promulgation of Freudian psychoanalysis. Nevertheless, as Bergson writes in a 1922 letter: "I have great respect for the work of Jung, which isn't only interesting for the psychologist and psychopathologist, but also for the philosopher! It is here that psychoanalysis has found its philosophy."[2] Jung was perhaps nearly as much a philosopher as a psychologist,[3] becoming increasingly philosophical over the course of his six decades of writing, and thus his final full-length monograph, *Mysterium Coniunctionis*, published in 1956 when he was eighty-one years old, provides our entry into his thought. The book's subtitle is "An Inquiry into the Separation and Synthesis of Psychic Opposites in Alchemy," and this text is a sustained meditation on the concepts of difference and integration, a distillation of Jung's mature psychology and philosophy explicated through an analysis of late medieval and early modern alchemical texts.[4] Jung was generally critical of Hegel,[5] despite some striking similarities,[6] and he was influenced by Schelling, Nietzsche, Bergson, and James. As he writes of a conference in 1909, "I spent two delightful evenings with William James alone and I was tremendously impressed by the clearness of his mind and the complete absence of intellectual prejudices," particularly in relation to parapsychology and the psychology of religion, which were their main topics of discussion.[7]

While Jung was a primary influence for Hillman, it is not clear that Deleuze was simply and unambiguously a Jungian, though he certainly engaged with Jung's work in both affirmative and critical ways, writing in *Difference and Repetition*:

> Was not one of the most important points of Jung's theory already to be found here: the force of "questioning" in the unconscious, the conception of the unconscious as an unconscious of "problems" and "tasks"? Drawing out the consequences of this led Jung to the discovery of a process of differenciation more profound than the resulting oppositions.[8]

The concern with problems and integrative differenciation is central to Deleuze's project in what many consider his magnum opus, and it is striking that Deleuze expresses such a strong affinity between his work and that of Jung, as Jung's influence on Deleuze has not tended to be emphasized by scholars, though as Frida Beckman writes, "Deleuze's discussions of the unconscious in *Différence et répétition* may make more sense when we read Jung into the equation."[9]

There are several passages in which Deleuze takes Jung's side against Freud, who nominated Jung his "successor and crown prince"[10] in 1910, and then excommunicated him around 1913 for his purported psychoanalytic heresies. One of the most revealing of these passages by Deleuze is in *L'Abécédaire*, recorded in 1988 as part of a long television interview that would only air after his death, in which he discusses "a text that I adore by Jung" concerning Jung's dream of descent through successive subterranean strata, at the deepest layer of which Jung finds an ossuary, numerous bones that Freud insists on reducing to the unity of a death wish, as a primary example of the concepts of multiplicity and assemblage, "a kind of constructivism"[11] which "keeps very heterogeneous elements together."[12] Deleuze portrays Jung as understanding these concepts, contrary to Freud's egregious misunderstanding, an instance that also finds brief mention in *A Thousand Plateaus*, where Deleuze and Guattari write that "Jung is in any event profounder than Freud."[13] Although Derrida, in a 2004 lecture, suggests that "Deleuze laughs at psychoanalysis, to me, sometimes, a little too quickly," and he jokes that part of Deleuze's "absolute originality in French" is "admiring Jung more than Freud,"[14] it is Derrida himself who perhaps laughs too quickly in this case given the admiration for Jung expressed by Bergson, Bachelard, and Simondon. Deleuze also makes affirmative references to Jung in "From Sacher-Masoch to Masochism,"[15] *Nietzsche and*

*Philosophy*,[16] and *Dialogues II*,[17] and with Guattari in *Anti-Oedipus*.[18] It even seems possible that Deleuze and Guattari's concept of the rhizome is at least partially derived from Jung's discussion of this concept in several texts,[19] a possibility which Slavoj Žižek states as fact, but for which the evidence is not definitive, though it is highly suggestive. Žižek also writes that "there is a direct lineage from Jung to *Anti-Oedipus*,"[20] an insightful observation which he marshals as a criticism of both Deleuze and Jung in favor of Freud, though those of us who deeply admire all of these theorists may reframe it as an endorsement of what Barbara Jenkins describes as "a nascent 'Jungian turn' in Deleuzean and cultural studies."[21]

In 1956's "Bergson's Concept of Difference," Deleuze writes that "there are no accidents in the life of the psyche,"[22] perhaps implicitly correlating the nuances of Bergsonian duration with Jungian synchronicity, a subtle correlation which finds further elaboration in 1966's *Bergsonism* and 1983's *Cinema 1*. In 1969's *The Logic of Sense*, Deleuze explicitly employs the term "synchronicity," and significant portions of that book seem to be explorations of something very much like Jungian archetypes, a term which Deleuze affirmatively employs in 1964's *Proust and Signs*,[23] as well as the subtle kind of formal causation characteristic of the late Jungian conception of synchronicity in other terms. Deleuze indirectly defines synchronicity as a form of resonant correspondence that is not merely a linear logical series operating in terms of the causes and effects of efficient causation, while Jung, in the subtitle of *Synchronicity*, defines it as "an acausal connecting principle," having two decades earlier explicitly equated synchronicity with transversality,[24] a concept employed by Deleuze and Guattari in both volumes of *Capitalism and Schizophrenia*. Deleuze takes up these definitions later in *The Logic of Sense*, in relation to the Stoics and Leibniz, in his discussion of "alogical incompatibilities and noncausal correspondences," of which he writes that "astrology was perhaps the first important attempt to establish a theory," as this ancient mode of thought posits a persistent formal, as opposed to efficient, causal (or perhaps quasi-causal, or even acausal) correspondence between the movements of the heavens and events in the human domain. And similarly, as he writes in a 1970 essay:

> In a sense, humankind renews its ties with a destiny that can be read in the planets and stars. Planetary thought is not unifying: it implies hidden depths in space, an extension of deep universes, incommensurate

distances and proximities, non-exact numbers, an essential opening of our system, a whole fiction-philosophy.[25]

Deleuze and Guattari's 1975 book, *Kafka*, differs not only with the Jungian conception of archetypes, and with Jung's early method of free association, at least in relation to Kafka's work, but with other concepts Deleuze asserts in both earlier and later texts[26] (the symbolic, mythology, the imagination, phantasms[27]), so that one must recall that Deleuze, perhaps especially with the impish Guattari, eschewed consistency in favor of attempts to think in new ways, Deleuze commenting in 1973 that "neither Guattari nor myself are very attached to the pursuit or even the coherence of what we write."[28] But it is significant that these attempts are enacted in relation to Jung, not in a mere rejection, but in the guise of multiply affirmed admirers of Jung who critique the precursor that they nevertheless deem more profound than Freud. This critique is not a mere denouncement, but rather takes seriously Jung's concepts, even when Deleuze and Guattari seem to portray them too narrowly, seeking to go beyond a classic archetypal conception (a project also undertaken by Hillman, based on Jung's later work) by building upon the differentiations this conception affords, much as Deleuze, in *Difference and Repetition*, enacts an overturning of Plato through the appropriation of certain moments in Plato's own texts. In fact, it might be suggested that Deleuze's primary philosophical allegiance is ultimately to Nietzsche because, more than any other figure before Deleuze, Nietzsche was always forging beyond existing categories of thought to create novel conceptions exceeding any systematizing enclosures, though neither Nietzsche nor Deleuze can be understood as simply rejecting the past, but rather as pushing the concepts and language of the past to their limits, willfully transgressing and dissolving existing boundaries in order to open space for novel conceptions. But this transgressive dissolution does not require us to reject all previous categories in favor of the ones that Deleuze, both with and without Guattari, cavalierly constructs and then often carelessly casts aside in the very next book, but rather allows us to employ existing categories and concepts, including those constructed by Deleuze, with a light, even ironic touch as pragmatic tools for novel creation, tools whose refinement and extension these transgressions afford, enabling their employment in the fabrication of new conceptual tools allowing further creation. The irreverence that Deleuze directs toward his precursors, undoubtedly including Jung, cuts both ways, as this irreverence can be directed toward Deleuze himself, whom one can profoundly admire while cavalierly – though still rigorously – selecting among his sometimes conflicting and even incoherent conceptions to achieve the greatest possible efficacy in further attempted creations.

In *A Thousand Plateaus*, composed over the subsequent decade, the figure of Professor Challenger – who is apparently an embodiment of the assemblage of Deleuze and Guattari based on a character by Arthur Conan Doyle – is giving an obscure and difficult lecture which seems partially designed to prune back the audience (and perhaps those reading about this oddly hallucinatory presentation) to the few steadfast die-hards willing to expend the extraordinary effort required to comprehend these esoteric domains, so that "the only ones left were the mathematicians, accustomed to other follies, along with a few astrologers, archaeologists, and scattered individuals." In the same book, Deleuze and Guattari describe Jung's approach as "integrating" any given animal image found in dream or myth "into its archetypal series," though they express dissatisfaction with this construction, seeking further to deterritorialize Jung's theory, which they clearly find great value in along with the Jungian approach of Bachelard in *Lautréamont* (about which Hillman also wrote), and of Simondon in *Individuation in Light of Notions of Form and Information*. "We sorcerers," they write, can discern that "there is still room for something else, something more secret, more subterranean" constituted in a becoming beyond the "progress or regress along a series," an overcoming which they associate with "the whole structuralist critique of the series." However, later in the same text, they quote H.P. Lovecraft's evocation of an ascendance through n-dimensions "up to the dizzy and reachless heights of archetypal infinity" in their description of the "plane of consistency" (as opposed to the "plane of development"), which is the locus of becomings "written like sorcerers' drawings" on that immanent plane, "the ultimate Door providing a way out" or, alternately, "the gates of the Cosmos."[29]

Deleuze and Guattari critique the archetypes as "processes of spiritual reterritorialization"[30] or "intrinsic qualities," instead advocating a conception in which "cosmic forces" or "expressive qualities" (which are concretely symbolic,[31] and "fictional" like the infinitesimal) are real but nonactual formal causes characterized by their function in specific assemblages of becoming, nomadic paths enacting a vital autonomy for which particular effectuations are derivative points, so that the trajectory is primary and the series derived from it secondary. However, this conception is already prefigured in the later work of Jung, where he tends to express the archetypes as cosmic dynamisms rather than as merely intrinsic psychological categories, as he tended to define them in his earlier work, though he remained ambivalent about their ontological status.[32] Rather than merely rejecting Jung's archetypal theory, Deleuze and Guattari, like many Jungians, can be conceived as having refined that theory, rendering it more subtle and general by suggesting that the locus of becoming is not found primarily in the linear, sedentary series of chronological development, but in temporally nonlinear "transformational series" across orders ascending through increasing degrees of freedom. They suggest that the integration of differentiated n-dimensional archetypal series is the conceptual construction characteristic of the infinitesimal version of the integral calculus, and thus that the differentiating metaphysical integration correlated with the calculus specifically integrates these nonlinear and nonlocal archetypal series of diachronic and synchronic resonances, an expression intimately coextensive with the mode of relation characteristic of Jung's late expression of synchronicity, approaching the always-receding transcendental archetypal potencies in their multiplicitous singularity.[33]

While these discussions of Jung's work are profound, they require a Sherlock Holmesian reading of subtle clues to decipher, a recognition that Deleuze implicitly sanctions, writing that "a book of philosophy should be in part a very particular species of detective novel," with hints leading the reader to revelations of ultimately complex networks of intertwined relations that were formerly occluded.[34] Deleuze, with and without Guattari, often only evokes these realms of thought, teasing the reader with references to Jung and his work in ways that cannot easily be pinned down, that remain elusive. One suspects the reason for this coyness is that, although Deleuze clearly found great value in Jung's work, he also understood that Jungian thought has enjoyed an uneasy relationship with the main streams of academia, as Jung brilliantly and profoundly explored domains that were often "beyond the scientific pale,"[35] as Anthony Stevens writes, for the dominant spheres of the twentieth century academy. Additionally, as Jon Mills observes, the fact that Jung has been studied much less by philosophers than Freud "may be in part due to the fact that while Freud was intent on systematizing his theories, Jung was not," and that "Jung often disparaged philosophy in his writing while exalting religion, despite the fact that much of his corpus involves direct engagement with ancient, Gnostic, medieval, modern, Continental, and Eastern philosophical texts."[36] However, this situation currently bears signs of a rapid shift, and the increased recognition of Deleuze's extended, though complex, engagement with Jung may help to carry the Swiss psychologist from the liminal frontiers of thought, where he remains the undisputed king, into the central nodes of academic discourse where Freud has long presided, at least in the humanities. In fact, Deleuze explores most of the same uncharted domains as Jung, though Deleuze's writing is so obscure, while still extremely distinct, that only those who are paying very close attention, and in many cases who are already familiar with Jungian thought, will discern the deep resonances between these theorists. One suspects that this was a subtle and purposive strategy by Deleuze, which has been extraordinarily efficacious in allowing his work to occupy a central place in continental thought, while also allowing him to engage with relatively marginal Jungian concepts, winking at the Jungian cognoscenti while this aspect of his work generally escapes the notice of those who unquestioningly accept the overly hasty dismissal of Jung largely instigated by Freud. Furthermore, Deleuze seems implicitly to have understood Hillman's admonition that "Freud and Jung are psychological masters, not that we may follow them in becoming Freudian and Jungian, but that we may follow them in becoming psychological,"[37] though of course the same can also be said about following Deleuze and Guattari as philosophical and psychological masters.

Especially when Jung was writing *Mysterium Coniunctionis* in the forties and fifties, relatively little scholarly work had been done on medieval alchemical texts, and Jung's book is partially an excavation of this movement countervalent to the dominant Christian scholasticism of that era, as the alchemists' endeavors were largely motivated by a dissatisfaction with the Christian worldview, though they generally seem to have been sincerely believing Christians, and Christian elements pervade the alchemical texts. Although alchemy has often been dismissed as a benighted, and even insane quest to make gold from baser metals serving, at best, as a precursor to the science of chemistry, the more philosophical alchemical texts strikingly presage the concepts of depth psychology, offering a rich and complex system of symbolic images closer to dream and myth than to the long-predominant rationalist philosophy of the scholastics, and later of the Enlightenment. Alchemy was considered of great value not only by Leibniz and Newton in the seventeenth century, but by scholastics like Albertus Magnus, Roger Bacon, and St. Thomas Aquinas in the thirteenth century, and Jung discerns parallels with the coincidentia oppositorum of

Nicholas of Cusa. The Jewish Kabbalah and Arabic thought deeply influenced European alchemy, and there are profound parallels between Western alchemy and Chinese alchemy, as well as Taoist, Confucian, Hindu, and Buddhist texts. Jung quotes the Chinese alchemist Wei Po-Yang, who writes, "when the mind is integral, it will not go astray,"[38] an evocation of psychological integration resonant with the Western alchemical tradition. Jung particularly explicates three alchemical texts, by Albertus Magnus in the thirteenth century, Gerhard Dorn in the sixteenth century, and an anonymous text from the eighteenth century, all of which deeply engage with the problem of opposites. The alchemists considered themselves philosophers, and like the more explicitly philosophical texts discussed in these pages, they often employed obscure and esoteric words, pushing language to its limits to expand the domain of what could be expressed, to open up space for novel conceptual modes correlated with the chemical processes in the alembic.

*Mysterium Coniunctionis* is not primarily a history of alchemy, but an explication of the profound parallels between the Hermetic tradition and depth psychology. Jung interprets the alchemical texts as he would the dreams or active imaginations of a patient, though alchemy has the advantage of being not only the product of an individual mind, but a sustained and involuted tradition contained in numerous texts written over the course of more than a thousand years that expresses the collective unconscious of the medieval and early modern eras stretching beyond Europe, where alchemy was introduced in the twelfth century via the translation of Arabic texts. It is a deep reservoir of those nonrational modes of thought that require integration with modern rationality, a cornucopia of grotesque and fantastic speculations that would usually be designated as merely pathological, but which serve as salutary and necessary complements to the dominant privileging of reason, even contained within its medieval Christian compromise formation. This repression of nonrational modes has not merely been an error, but a process of differentiation that in some ways exceeds human volition, that possesses us in its historical unfolding as much as we possess it through our verbal concepts, in which the oppositional mode of thought increasingly dominant since the axial era[39] summoned a compensatory welling up of the chaotic complexity of alchemy from the oceanic collective unconscious, dissolving the dominant logical forms through fecund paradox and irrepressible metaphorical profusion across scale. Alchemy expresses an often incoherent confusion experienced variously as vitally liberating and destructively hostile, which the alchemists were never able entirely to overcome, but which their heirs in depth psychology have been able to carry further, recognizing these nonrational speculations as empirical psychological facts as real as the facts of physical science, and with just as real an effect in the world, an insight resonant with Jamesian pragmatism.

The alchemical speculations are a reenactment of a previously dominant mode largely repressed by the increasing dominance of rationality in which the psyche is not yet evacuated into the individual human ego, but is "projectively elicited,"[40] to employ Richard Tarnas' phrase, from the world in the form of the spirits of nature and of ancestors, intimately encountered in sorcerous, animistic rites, subsequently divinized in polytheistic mythologemes, and then rendered conceptual in the Platonic Ideas. The chemical substances that the alchemists distilled and combined in the retort embodied mythically correlated archetypes and their corresponding modes of interaction, which the alchemists did not possess the conceptual apparatus to understand as enactments of psychological processes, a conceptual complex which would only truly begin to emerge in the nineteenth century, an emergence for which the alchemical activities of the previous millennium prepared the way. These alchemical speculations were not merely fanciful delusions, but a sustained projection of unconscious contents into the chemical processes, eliciting genuine resonances between the physical and psychological domains. These domains were largely undifferentiated for the alchemists in a *participation mystique*, a pervasive correspondence across orders for which depth psychology would provide conceptual language further to differentiate these domains, increasingly concretizing the integration for which the alchemists sought, embodied in the *lapis philosophorum*, the philosopher's stone, but which it was not possible for them to achieve given their conceptual and chemical instruments, though they nevertheless provided the *prima materia* for the eventual development of later instruments.

The unconscious emerged coextensively with the ego, as the unified individuality especially characteristic of modern subjectivity requires the repression of the experiential domains in opposition to which the ego defines its identity, embodied in the "lower storeys"[41] of the archaeological descent of Jung's dream. The ego, as "Schopenhauerian mirror,"[42] is the negative reflection of the unconscious just as much as the unconscious is the negative of egoic consciousness, a duality which came into actuality with the dawning ego, along with the domains of reality this differentiation allowed us to perceive, and which it is the task of depth psychology to reintegrate while maintaining differentiated autonomy, but overcoming the exclusive privileging of egoic consciousness. As egoic rationality was being forged in the containing structure of Christianity, the ego becoming increasingly unified in its sustained contemplation of a singular transcendent God and his laws, the alchemists worked in the dirt and darkness of immanence to maintain a conceptual connection to the intuitive multiplicity of the imaginal and affective unconscious, finding rational justification in the speculations of the intellect, always embedded in symbol and metaphor, preparing the way for the twentieth-century encounter, through the repetition of archetypal images, of the monocentric mind with that which has been repressed in modern thought. Jung did not claim that the concepts of his psychology were the final word on the alchemical speculations or their intimated integration with rationality but a largely symbolic and metaphorical foreshadowing of this integration, which Jung knew those who came after him would go beyond, and which his work would make possible, an overcoming evidently embodied below in Deleuze and Hillman in very different, though deeply resonant, ways.

The alchemical activities contained real danger, enacting the confrontation with the unconscious shadow necessary for the process of individuation central to Jung's psychological conception, as becoming conscious of that which has been unconscious can release "an avenging deluge"[43] of chaotic and destructive forces. These forces can manifest in the whole range of psychological disorders and psychoses categorized by modern psychology, and even physical illnesses in the body, expressing potencies which require integration into consciousness if the individual hopes to attain a salubrious and ethical psychological balance rather than engaging in the many varieties of self-destructive behavior that humans have devised. The danger of alchemy is closely related to that associated with the use of drugs that Deleuze and Guattari discuss,[44] not in a mere prohibition, but in an admonition toward caution when engaging with substances that allow the forces and powers that exceed egoic consciousness to manifest by altering the speeds of experience. But simply avoiding becoming conscious of the unconscious in a fearful privileging of rationality and a concomitant repression of other modes is perhaps even more dangerous than an intentional encounter with the unconscious, as the repressed contents tend to emerge in more destructive ways the more vigorously they are repressed. On a collective scale, for instance, the tragedies of the World Wars were at least partially the result of the often exclusivist privileging of rationality in the nineteenth and early twentieth centuries over other indispensable modes of relation. Alchemical work also faces the very real danger of being trivialized and dismissed, one of the primary tactics of exclusivist rationality for disqualifying and marginalizing those experiential and conceptual domains that exceed its narrow scope. And it is true that the alchemists were often confused and incoherent in relation to the dominant Christian and then rationalist and empiricist modes of thought, as their domain of exploration was constituted precisely in all of those elements that had been rejected, "the stone which the builder refused,"[45] in order to construct modern rationalism. This tunnel vision made possible the great discoveries and inventions of modernity, which carried us very far into novel domains, but its primary efficacy perhaps began to wane around the time of the French Revolution, and it has reached a peak of tragedy and exhaustion in the twentieth and early twenty-first centuries, despite the many great scientific and cultural achievements, so that a more expansive and intensive reintegration of those aspects of consciousness which have been instrumentally repressed is required for a novel mode to be born from the ashes of the modern.

Alchemical activity is embodied in a self-heating intimately involved with the heating of chemical substances in the alembic, an internal heat that is produced through sustained intense introspection and concentration, enacting a distillation of symbolic, metaphorical, and conceptual elements corresponding to the distillation of the physical materials. These physical and psychological activities were undifferentiated, as the alchemists lacked the verbal concepts that would make such a differentiation possible, but which the language of depth psychology begins to render thinkable, so that the generations following Jung could refine these conceptual forms, and carry them into more intensive and expansive domains of efficacy, which in turn may allow further generations to carry these conceptual, imaginal, and affective differentiations into even more efficacious integrations. The increasing differentiations of conceptual thought, first in alchemy, then in depth psychology, and then in the emergent mode that increasingly obscures the distinction between psychology and philosophy, constructs deeper problems, more subtle and complex questions that demand to be addressed, by something which exceeds our egoic consciousness, in the alchemical alembic of the persistent intensive struggle to type novel words on the page that may bring the increasingly differentiated elements into increasing resonance and renewal.

Over the course of his long career, Jung said many things about the archetypes and, as he explicitly acknowledged, his articulations of this concept became more subtle and differentiated over the decades. But he generally asserted that, as a physician of the mind, he did not discover the archetypes first as metaphysical entities, but rather extrapolated them from his empirical research on images in dream, myth, fantasy, and imagination. His early expression of the archetypes emerged partially from his disagreements with Freud, who employed the figures of Oedipus and Eros in psychoanalysis, but who always insisted on the privileging of rationality and materialist positivism (despite his interest in telepathy[46]), which precluded a conception of the archetypes as autonomous potencies encountered variously as spirits, gods, and physical forces. The archetypes are tendencies toward all kinds of becoming that can only be expressed adequately through metaphor and symbol, and thus the alchemical work, replete with metaphorical and symbolic speculation, is a rich repository of archetypal articulations. In his refinement of the archetypes, Jung came to see them not only as organizing categories of the mind, but as modes of relation that exceed us, and that are brought into actuality through our constructive participation in the nodal clusters of potentiality and constraint that they embody, dynamisms at an ever-receding horizon of conception that elude the rational categorizations of solitary intellect, and require an imaginal mode for their elicitation from the cosmic processes out of which we emerge as differentiated subjects.[47] We constitute the archetypes as much as they constitute us, and thus coming to consciousness of archetypal complexes, the relations between different archetypes that are constellated within us and through us, enacts a coming to consciousness of Self, the entirety of our individual becomings that exceed solitary egoic consciousness and are permeable with the more expansive processes from which we emerge, like whirlpools in a stream. Through this process of bringing the unconscious archetypes into consciousness, the particular complexes we individually embody are integrated into our conscious conceptions of ourselves, so that rather than possessing us and acting through us as fate, we constantly negotiate with the potentialities and constraints of our particular concrescence to traverse the singular lines of flight, the trajectories of becoming toward which the network of archetypal complexes from which we construct our individuated identities are teleologically inclined.[48]

In the process of individuation, these archetypal complexes are generally encountered first through the projection of the archetypal contents of the unconscious into the external world, eliciting from our encounters those domains of process that hold particular libidinal potency for us, so that one person might constantly be engaged in oppositional, martial conflict, while another is always yearning for erotic love, and these projectively elicited archetypal situations complexly intermix and continually shift over time, passing through relatively continuous durations occasionally punctuated by relatively discontinuous changes of state. Projection is not only characteristic of the work of the alchemists and depth psychology, but is the primary means by which humans have emerged from less differentiated psychosocial modes, eliciting mind and agency from the external world, not in a mere pathetic fallacy, but in a *participation mystique* for which agential potencies are not yet localized. Although the alchemists did not possess the language of depth psychology to describe their work, their manipulations of substances in the alembic constituted a sustained projection of their unconscious archetypal complexes into matter, eliciting profound imaginal evocations of archetypal dynamics, though it required a novel conceptual apparatus to bring these processes more fully into conscious awareness.

Projection is an activity necessary for the process of individuation, externalizing the unconscious elements of the Self as other and then struggling against, identifying with, or desiring the object of projection, whether human or nonhuman, a process which, as Sean M. Kelly demonstrates,[49] is closely related to the Hegelian dialectic (despite Jung's by-now-familiar critiques of Hegel) in which the initial thing posited becomes conscious of itself by becoming other than itself, engaging with itself as other in various modalities, and then reintegrating this differentiated awareness within its emergent unity. The integration of egoic consciousness with the archetypal complexes that are projectively elicited from the other is constituted in a withdrawal of naïve projection, a shedding of veils of illusion which enables the incorporation of the previously unconscious archetypal contents into conscious awareness, both differentiated in relation to the internal milieu and to the other into which they are projected. Individuation is an often dangerous and painful process that must nevertheless be undertaken, allowing the other to subsist as genuinely other rather than as a figure in one's waking dream, a differentiation which is, paradoxically, the precondition for a mature relationality, not only to other humans, but to the nonhuman, and to the archetypes themselves.

The archetypal complexes that require integration through projection and its subsequent withdrawal often take the form of paradoxes, which contain two concepts or principles that seem mutually exclusive but which are both valid, a problematic incommensurability luring us toward deeper and more subtle modes of relation. Paradoxes are a primary locus for the discernment of domains that exceed our current horizons of conception, and the alchemists dwelled with paradoxes as they peered into the retort, the substances being distilled and combined embodying the conceptual and affective interstices expressed by the paradoxical formulations. The oppositions which animate paradox are central to the alchemical process, constituted in analysis and synthesis of the numinous substances and the archetypal figures with which they correspond, performing the differentiation of these forces, often through oppositional conflict issuing from the chaos of the *prima materia*, and then integrating them in a novel emergent figure correlated with the novel substance produced in the alembic. This process is resonant with depth psychology, so that the hierarchical repression of one term in a binary produces neurotic or psychotic symptoms, which must be integrated to resolve these disorders, though complete integration and resolution may be conceived of as an always-receding horizon. The archetypes themselves are describable as polarities expressed in both external nature and internal psyche, with the psyche itself constituting a secondary polarity of conscious and unconscious. These axes of meaning and form can be encountered in direct conflict along their polarized linearity, but they can also erotically attract one another along that axis, and combine and interact with other archetypal polarities in a quaternity consisting of two perpendicular polar axes, like the four elements, directions, or seasons, providing a primary opening from dualistic polarity to more complex topological formulations resonant with solving equations by quadrature in the calculus, expressing solutions in terms of integrals.[50] But it is particularly the tension of opposites which Jung discerns as driving the movement toward these more expansively involuted integrations, the transconscious polarities which provide the energetic charge impelling the process of individuation.

Out of these tensions of opposites emerges the alchemical *coniunctio*, a reconciling third structurally resonant with the Trinity and the dialectic, serving as an intimation of the overcoming of the dominance of the dualistic rationality that first emerged in a significant way in the axial era, embodied in the birth of a son, associated with Christ and the *lapis philosophorum*, from the "chymical marriage" of opposites, the "masculine" egoic consciousness and the "feminine" unconscious. One of the primary criticisms that has been leveled against Jung is that he tended to essentialize gender in his evocation of the archetypes, and this criticism is justified. Although he understood that the qualities traditionally associated with masculine and feminine in a patriarchal culture exist in different concentrations in both men and women, he tends to over-associate the masculine with men and the feminine with women, attributing the male "femininity" often characteristic of queer performativity to "the mother-complex,"[51] though elsewhere he recognizes that the diagnosis of homosexuality as "pathological perversion," almost exclusively dominant when he was writing, "is very dubious."[52] While these problematic tendencies should not be minimized, they have been thoroughly deconstructed and corrected by feminist theorists like Susan Rowland, Demaris S. Wehr, and Barbara Jenkins, all of whom argue for Jung's central importance for twentieth-century thought despite his problematic statements, Jenkins suggesting that the archetypal feminine is "associated with, but not equivalent to, the bodies of women."[53] However, when fully differentiated from the essentializing of gender, Jung's explication of the integration of the alchemical duality of the masculine archetype of the Solar King, correlated with sulfur, and the feminine archetype of the Lunar Queen, correlated with salt, in the hermaphroditic figure of Mercurius, associated with Christ and the *lapis*, provides an opening not only from essentializing gender constructions, but from gender binary and the hegemony of dualistic constructions in general.

Jung draws a parallel between the *summa medicina*, the alchemical union of opposites which heals both body and spirit, and the freedom from opposition of the Hindu concept of *Nirvana*. Alchemical thought is permeated by binary images, and the primary purpose of alchemy is, like the dialectic, to produce an integration of these opposites, which define one another and are thus contained within one another, to constitute the alchemical vessel, "the age-old drama of opposites" which can be traced from its Heraclitan inception in Western philosophy. While there is an opposition between conscious and unconscious, corresponding to the figures of Sol and Luna, the opposites themselves are undifferentiated in the pregnant unconscious, and rational egoic consciousness tears the archetypal polarities into dualities, the "method of division" of the Platonic dialectic, in order to differentiate them, and ultimately to prepare the way for a differentiated integration. This integration is only possible once the hierarchical privileging characteristic of binary has reached a dangerous and painful crisis, like that of birth, which requires the emergence of a novel mode in a death-and-rebirth ordeal if literal death is to be avoided, produced by a violent return of the repressed contents of the unconscious. The more vigorously imaginal fantasies and potent affects are repressed as pathological, the more violent and destructive the return of the repressed will be, as these images and fantasies express autonomous archetypal potencies that demand to be recognized and accepted into the consciousness of an individual or a culture, where these cosmic forces can be engaged with in a salutary rather than a destructive way. Whereas the solitary egoic consciousness characteristic of the exclusivism of the *tertium non datur* is barren and desolate, if sustained attention is given to the unconscious, which allows its contents to emerge from the shadow into the bright light of consciousness in the *albedo* stage of the alchemical process, these unconscious archetypal contents "will fructify the conscious like a fountain of living water,"[54] allowing a novel organismic entity to emerge from their union in a *coincidentia oppositorum*.

We all contain all of the archetypes within us in different emphases and relations, which shift over time and constitute our becoming, so that the majority views of our internal assemblages, whether individually or collectively, tend to repress and vilify the minority views, projecting those repressed contents into the other, producing an oppositional energetic potency that impels us eventually to discover that nothing human is alien to us, and that those things we encounter in the world, even the most disturbing or heinous, are also at least potentially present in ourselves. This transparent discernment of our own internal milieu is paradoxical, as by seeing that the dynamics we encounter are also present, however infinitesimally, in ourselves, we can withdraw the projection from the other to see that they are in fact genuinely other, which does not mean condoning the disturbing and heinous, or even the merely annoying qualities that we find in others, but allowing them to exist as themselves rather than as figures in our dreamworld. This differentiation allows us to draw appropriate boundaries, which in turn allow us to empathize with or denounce the other as other rather than because we identify with or against the other, using the other as a screen for the projection of our own unconscious archetypal complexes.

Differentiation is thus a precondition for integration, as without this differentiation of the other as other, the delusional projection serves as a protective and enclosing barrier that walls us off from actual encounters, which is different from the setting of appropriate, but permeable, boundaries which enable an individuated relationality, and even intimacy. Withdrawing projection is an ethical mandate as much as it is a requirement for psychological health and maturity. In alchemical terms, the repressed content is sublimated, corresponding to the vaporization of liquid in the alembical distillation, the shedding of unconscious projection to render the archetypal complex and its corresponding "arcane substance"[55] visible to conscious awareness, carried from the subterranean darkness into the bright light through the fiery ordeal of the *nigredo*, which melts the disparate, archetypally correlated substances into a novel unified substance, enacting the dangerous and transformative descent into the underworld required for an emergent ascent.

Although the alchemists were working toward a deeper understanding of psychological and cosmic processes, the best alchemists were aware that their work was provisional, a stage in a long endeavor that they would not complete in their lifetimes, a limitation which Jung also recognized in depth psychology, and which we may recognize in our own philosophical speculations resonant with these earlier endeavors. In this light, integration would be constituted not in a utopian or salvific perfection, "an exalted state of spiritualization," but in Whitehead's "slightest change of tone," an asymptotically approached "approximate completeness," as Jung writes, constituted in "a wise self-limitation and modesty."[56] The process of descent and confrontation with the unconscious forges the individual through almost unendurable suffering to produce an esoteric knowledge that one can only attain by going through the kind of ordeal exemplified by the Hermetic tradition, which can only be communicated to other brave adepts by pushing language to its limits. It is only through such sustained, and often painful, engagement with the unconscious that one can bring the contents of the unconscious into consciousness, which presages the emergence of a novel mode of relation on a collective scale, birthing into actuality assemblages which are still largely only potential, but which may someday become a novel kind of common sense.

The anima (or animus), the figure of desire for becoming through projection of the unconscious, lures the adept into these domains of conflict and suffering, the promise of an integral satisfaction, syncategorematically approached, impelling the initiate to undertake the descent, resonant with the ordeal of ecstatic animism, on behalf of their culture. In the depths is encountered a figure that exceeds intellect, the Self which is paradoxically the daimonic potency of something beyond egoic individuality, an embodiment of archetypal forces of transformation that leads through suffering to wisdom. It is only by means of this encounter, this *immensa meditatio*, that the alchemists were able to overcome the one-sided certainty of rational mentality to begin to inhabit a mode of thought that could affirm *sic et non*, a yes and no performing an openness to ambiguity and undecidability which, after sustained pressure in the alchemical vessel, may allow an "incommensurable third"[57] to emerge. This third is conceivable as not only the reconciliation of opposites in a return to identity, but as the integration of a differentiated multiplicity for which the opposites form an extreme case, producing the energetic tension required for self-overcoming and the entrance into more topologically plural and expansive affective and conceptual domains. This integration is the final stage of the alchemical work, which would produce the *lapis* through the union of the individual with the *unus mundus*, enacting the immanent integration of the physical and the psychic expressing transcendental potentiality.

When Deleuze and Guattari write that

> the relation between metallurgy and alchemy reposes not, as Jung believed, on the symbolic value of metal and its correspondence with an organic soul but on the immanent power of corporeality in all matter, and on the *esprit de corps* accompanying it,[58]

they seem to be reading Jung too narrowly. Jung often gestures toward this immanent potency of corporeal spirit in the recognition of an intimate entwining of matter and form, not only as correspondence, but in the discernment of correspondence as a symptom or surface manifestation of deeper forces that find both psychic and physical expression, for instance writing: "The symbols of the self arise in the depths of the body and they express its materiality every bit as much as the structure of the perceiving consciousness. The symbol is thus a living body, *corpus et anima*."[59] Although, over the course of his long career, Jung was not always consistent in the distinction between transcendent and transcendental, he tends in *Mysterium Coniunctionis* to articulate a transcendental immanence resonant with Spinoza and Deleuze.[60] He expresses the concept of the archetypes of the collective unconscious as a transcendental reimagining of the transcendent Platonic Forms, which embody the polar potencies and constraints for becoming that can only be asymptotically approached at a horizon, characterized by "transcendental mystery and paradox,"[61] through the discernment of complex series of diachronic and synchronic archetypal resonances. Immanent entities have a definite actuality, while transcendental archetypes can only be approached by means of paradoxical formulations expressing polar axes of potentiality, a requirement for which Jung, along with Pauli in their collaborations and extensive correspondence, discerns a profound correlation with the concepts of quantum mechanics, such as the wave-particle duality, a paradoxical description for a transcendental potentiality which exceeds the current capability of immanent integral expression. Depth psychology, microphysics, and alchemy all explore novel domains through the sustained contemplation of these paradoxes, which suggest a "transcendental background,"[62] the field of a painting fading toward an always-receding horizon rather than a metaphysical grounding, a *unus mundus* or univocal Tao which is expressible in the polarity of the psychic and the physical.[63] The domains of reality accessible to psychology and physics exhibit pervasive and intimate dynamic correspondences across scale as expressions of cosmic forces that exceed this duality.

Jung cautions that the specific contours of our metaphysical conceptions are contextual human constructions of "transcendental facts,"[64] potencies that cannot be encompassed by the particularity of any actual immanent expression, which can only be known through these constructed expressions, beyond which they reside at a virtual horizon of pure potentiality. The fact that these potentialities have been expressed in actuality in very different ways in different cultures at different times provides evidence for the multifariousness of these infinite transcendental potencies, which require limiting construction in finite actuality to be known at all, but which are nevertheless singular, dynamic, numinous powers that can never be known in their totality. These powers assert themselves in both psychotic and mystical experiences, taking forms negotiated in relation with the contextual particularities of individuals and cultures, though they cannot be reduced to any particular formulation, whether rational or religious. Although Jung is not opposed to the word "divine," he does not find these numinous experiences to be proof of a "transcendent God,"[65] but rather expressions of transcendental archetypes, for which a monotheistic God is one particular construction, an insight that engenders a metaphysical humility reminiscent of Jamesian radical empiricism. In fact, absolutist metaphysical certainty is impelled by an unconscious archetypal possession, and thus becoming conscious of the archetypes that animate any particular event or relation tends to produce a tolerance for metaphysical ambiguity, engendering the understanding that one cannot rest on a transcendent metaphysical ground, but that one has both the privilege and responsibility to decide how one will construct and enact archetypal potentialities. And this constructivist, archetypal, transcendental mode of thought can only emerge as the predominant cultural mode once a critical threshold of individuals who persistently engage in this mode has been attained, Deleuze and Guattari's "new people."[66]

The conception of a transcendent God and the ego are two aspects of the same singular entity, the polar correspondence across scale of the transcendental *imago Dei* and the differentiated individual consciousness forged through the sustained contemplation of a single, central divinity. While for the Western mind, God and ego have generally been understood as embodying the extreme opposites of transcendent and immanent, Jung discerns the Hindu atman as constructing a paradoxical polar identity between the macrocosmic God and the microcosmic ego, thus allowing the recognition that consciousness creates the world as much as the world conditions consciousness, a cocreative constructivism which does not deny divinity, but does not render the divine as hierarchically superior to the individual. Human consciousness is the divine coming to know itself in a transcendental immanence that may become differentiated from simple identity to afford a more complex integration which maintains the contrast between different processual domains in the emergent conception of the Self, the archetype of wholeness. Jung discerns this archetype in the *Chên-yên* (true man) of Chinese alchemy and in the *homo totus* (whole man) of Western alchemy, a figure of integration common in active imagination and dreams, which contains both the conscious ego and the transconscious archetypes that have been instrumentally repressed into the unconscious and the body in service to the differentiation of rational autonomy.[67] The Self is the numinous archetype of vital renewal that lures consciousness to overcome the exclusive dominance of ego by means of paradox into a more expansive and intensive domain of coherence, variously embodied for the alchemists in the balsam, the quintessence, the panacea, and the philosophic wine, which must be experienced to be understood, as the experience of this integral archetype exceeds pure reason.

Sol, the *aurum philosophorum*, the gold of the philosophers which was often actually lead, is a primary substance in the alchemical work, embodying the archetype of the solar King, associated with the arcane substance of sulfur, the active aspect of the hermaphroditic Mercurius-*lapis* correlated with the daylight, rational, differentiating, judging, "masculine" consciousness of the Logos. Sol is Adam, the father and son, God and Christ, "the dragon that begets, reproduces, slays, and devours itself,"[68] the wounded physician who heals themself in order to heal others. The integration of the putatively transcendent divine and the immanent ego is embodied in the correspondence between the opposites of the illuminating solar fire and the foul-smelling earthiness of sulfur, a paradox which lures the adept by means of compulsive will toward the Self distilled in the intense pressure and heat of the psychophysical alembic, acting as both efficient and final cause of this transformative ordeal. Sulphur is an ambivalent, "untrustworthy"[69] substance serving as both poison and remedy, like the *pharmakon*, eliciting the projected shadow so that it can be integrated in the light of egoic consciousness.

Luna, the *Mater Alchimia*, is the Queen, the "feminine" aspect of the *prima materia*, the vessel of the alchemical magnum opus, the encompassing womb of the heavens containing the Sun, associated with silver, salt, Eve, and Mary, mother of Christ. Luna is the nocturnal, chthonic, passive, cold satellite and medium of Sol, the Moon which reflects the Sun's light as well as the star-strewn dome of heaven, and the salty ocean (Sal) whose tides follow the Moon, corresponding to Eros, the unconscious, the body, the *anima mundi*, and the merged relationality of both the lovers and the mother and child. This association with the "feminine" Eros as always passively defined in relation to the "masculine" Logos resides at the root of logocentric patriarchy, which emerged coextensively with rationality, though the feminist endeavors of the last several centuries, which have continued to accelerate over the last half-century or so since Jung wrote *Mysterium Coniunctionis*, have largely deconstructed the essentializing identification of women and the "feminine" and men and the "masculine," at least in the most genuinely progressive cultural sectors. It may now perhaps be more efficacious to think in terms of the solar and lunar archetypes, which have been traditionally associated with the sexes, a binary correlation which we must continue to problematize, rendering possible an overcoming for which the hermaphroditic figure of Mercurius indicates the way, the child that is born from the alchemical marriage of opposites in the *rubedo* stage of the work. The *rotundum*, the roundness of both Sun and Moon, and of the pregnant belly of the mother, corresponds to the archetype of wholeness, though the integration of opposites is not only mediated through a confluent, erotic attraction, a quality associated with the lunar end of the polarity, but also through an intense struggle between the solar conscious and lunar unconscious from which emerges a series of animal archetypes embodying that which has been repressed.[70]

In one text, Mercurius hands the Queen a "golden cup of Babylon" containing all of the "animal substances she has to integrate,"[71] polarized animal appetites first embodied in poisonous, cold-blooded creatures like the dragon, serpent, scorpion, basilisk, and toad, which then become warmer in correspondence with mammals like the lion, bear, wolf, and dog, and finally begin to overcome duality in the flight of the eagle and raven, and then in the pair of doves symbolizing the impending marriage of Sol and Luna. As Bachelard observes in *Lautréamont*, a sorcerous, Jungian work that bears striking resemblances to the alchemical texts, "the air, it seems, is a region of easy metamorphosis,"[72] a more expansive domain mirroring the depths of the ocean, both mediums allowing more degrees of freedom than those afforded to earthbound creatures, correlating with the self-overcoming of topologically constructed binary modes. The solar monarch is the dominant force to which all must submit, the light which produces the shadow, and which thus requires an overthrowing and a descent into the nocturnal depths in the form of the royal marriage embodied in the *rubedo*, the redness of the fiery oppositional conflict, which sublimates the noxious, poisonous, violent, and brutal qualities of the shadow in the progression of animal becomings, in the heated alembic which melts the substances in a novel substance. From this uroboric self-devouring emerges the *lapis philosophorum*, an integration for which the solar lion remains differentiated, through self-knowledge, as King, and the lunar serpent as Queen, enacting the transconscious union of conscious and unconscious. It is the androgynous Adam from whose rib Eve is created, so that Eve can subsequently encounter the serpent which offers her the fruit of the Tree of Knowledge of Good and Evil, mythologically marking the Fall from undifferentiated paradisical unity into the oppositional quality of consciousness, a hierarchical privileging of God, good, and man over Satan, evil, and woman which eventually summons forth the avenging deluge of that which has been repressed, a process of differentiation and confrontation which is necessary for integration. As Jung writes, presciently anticipating the necessity of moving beyond Deleuze's partially valid, but paradoxically oppositional, critique of the oppositional Hegelian dialectic discussed below: "One is not a number; the first number is two, and with it multiplicity and reality begin."[73]

The *lapis*, Mercurius, and Christ embody the archetype of wholeness, "a fabulous entity of cosmic dimensions which surpasses human understanding,"[74] the Self that emerges from this paradoxical union of opposites, and that serves as the formal cause and final lure, the Alpha and Omega, of this movement toward differentiated integrality. Mercurius is "duplex" because this figure is both the undifferentiated unconscious *prima materia* of the chaos and the teleological vital impulse and will to power of the creative advance luring the alchemical process toward integral satisfaction, the Nous to the solar Logos and the lunar Eros. Echoing Plato's original spherical being containing three sexes (male-male, female-female, male-female),[75] the androgynous, hermaphroditic Mercurius contains and fully integrates the qualities of both the solar "masculine" and the lunar "feminine," prefiguring the movement in the vanguards of contemporary culture toward the nonbinary constructions of gender and sexuality.[76] Each generation is becoming more comfortable with this nonbinarity, to the extent that the younger generations born around the turn of the twenty-first century and thereafter often take this nonbinarity for granted, marking a relatively rapid, and highly salutary, shift away from patriarchal and logocentric cultural norms. And this nonbinarity is constituted not only in a constructivism of gender and sexuality, but of the opposition of conscious and unconscious, so that there is evident a massive upsurge among younger academics of interest in psychedelics and the occult in its many forms, which are precisely practices for bringing the complex contents of the collective and personal unconscious into sustained relation and integration with egoic consciousness.

Jung advocates the method of active imagination, closely related to the alchemical method, which directs concentrated attention to the subtle fluctuations of dreams, fantasies, moods, and affects, observing the periodic transformations of consciousness, witnessing and naming the archetypal complexes that these transformations express in all their multivalence, learning to enact these always-changing potencies in positive, constructive ways that do not repress or obstruct their expression, as repression inevitably produces a destructive return of the repressed. Instead, this intuitive method intentionally flows with these imaginally and affectively discerned potentialities, like a skillful surfer riding a wave, or the complex confluence of several waves. This sustained and careful attention to the qualitative contours of bodily and imaginal experience has the capacity to heal the oppositional wound at the heart of a schizophrenic exclusivist rationality, which has culminated in modernity, an "affliction of the soul"[77] that demands its own overcoming through the integration of nonrational modes in "the 'thousand-named' arcane substance,"[78] a pluralist devouring of the peacock's flesh to integrate the *omnes colores* in the *lapis*, which "contains or produces all colours."[79]

Each epoch constructs a novel narrative to express the inexhaustible archetypes, to pursue the horizon where these potencies reside, as in holographic string theory for which the entire cosmos is conserved at a cosmic horizon that always recedes as one approaches it, a correlation explicated by Timothy Desmond in *Psyche and Singularity*. Whereas Christianity was profoundly revolutionary in the early centuries of its inception when it was one mode among others in the waning years of the Roman Empire, it inexorably calcified into a stable and inhibiting orthodoxy over the course of "the long, eventful, and terrible night of the Middle Ages,"[80] as Hegel describes it, perhaps culminating in its efficient phase with Aquinas, and then requiring a discontinuously novel mode of thought to emerge with the dual dominance of scientific empiricism and an increasingly secular rationality in modernity. Science and rationalist philosophy were similarly vital and creative in their inception, though we are now evidently embroiled in a further crisis on a more expansive order requiring the emergence of yet another discontinuous novelty, by whatever name this emerging epochal narrative construction ultimately comes to be known. The peak of alchemy coincided with the period of transition between the medieval Christian and the modern scientific eras, so it is no surprise that there has been a reawakening of interest in alchemy and other Hermetic modes of thought in the last century, especially in relation to Jungian psychology, an interest which seems to be reaching a peak of intensity in our multigenerational moment of apparently critical transition between historical eras.

Like the animist and Christian ordeals of death and rebirth, as well as those of mythological figures like Osiris and Dionysus, the alchemical process enacts a death and dismemberment of Sol, the egoic dragon, embodied in the "physical and moral tortures"[81] of the arcane substance in the retort, the melancholia of the *nigredo*, in order for the *lapis* to be born from the fiery chaos. The adept undergoes a Passion parallel to that undergone by Christ, though differentiated by the immanent materiality of the transcendental alchemical process, a Last Supper in which the adept devours their own flesh and drinks the wine of their own blood, like the uroboros devouring its own tail, enacting a recognition and acceptance of the other within themself. The *katabasis*, the descent into the underworld, is a sacrifice of naïve egoic consciousness by engaging in sustained relation with the compensatory shadow of the unconscious in order to birth a novel entity that integrates the constitutive oppositions of medieval consciousness, which have only become more extreme, intense, and critical in modernity. Exclusive egoic consciousness is necessarily delusional, constituted in simplistic narratives that repress the aspects of the Self that elude and contradict narrow narrative constructions. The "tarrying with the negative" characteristic not only of the Hegelian dialectic, but perhaps especially of deconstruction, prolongs the brave leap into a void, enacting the death and putrefaction of the ego, a frightening descent which constructive modes generally discern as a dissolution and dismemberment necessary for the emergence of qualitatively novel modes affirming a decentered ego permeable with the unconscious and the others which it previously repressed.

The *nigredo* is the suffering and despair of the heroic descent into hell undergone by alchemists and philosophers, both often known for their melancholy dispositions because they persistently engage with that which exceeds the doxa of their cultures, like shamans and artists performing the essential function of pushing their minds and bodies to the margins of acceptable modes of relation to prevent their cultures from settling into static, rigid orthodoxies by intensively dwelling with paradox to concretize the emergence of creatively heterodox modes. This archetypal role of the wounded healer who confronts the oppositional wounding of repression in the unconscious requires real courage, because the psychic death necessary for rebirth can easily become real death literalized in the psychological disorders with which alchemists, philosophers, and artists have notoriously struggled. The fearsome dragon embodying the unconscious shadow projected by the exclusively privileged egoic consciousness into the world must be slain within the alembic of the psyche in order to win the "treasure hard to attain,"[82] the conscious integration of the differentiated archetypal potencies that constitute self and world, which are intimately, permeably entwined.

Jung describes the *nigredo* as a confrontation with evil and sin, embodied in the figure of the thief in one of the texts, an integral and inevitable shadow to the light of transcendent divinity embodied in the dove, the instinctual animality which manifests in destructive and violent ways when it is repressed and projected as other. The knowledge of evil as well as good, figured by Adam and Eve eating the fruit from the garden, is constituted in the recognition that the facile narrative construction in which perfect redemption follows sin obscures the intimate, always-problematic tension of good and evil, as light cannot exist without shadow. The coming to consciousness leading to the expulsion from the naïve paradise of unconscious animality ultimately leads toward an integration of the hierarchically repressed opposites in a more expansive domain of ethical awareness "beyond good and evil."[83] This mode recognizes that one can never rest in a one-sided oppositional grounding, but must continue to make difficult, and often ambiguously deceptive, choices as long as one lives, conceiving of these oppositions not only as the projected external spiritual forces of God and the Devil, but as expressing our internal polar constitutions permeable with archetypal potencies. In alchemy, the *unio mystica*, as with the integration of depth psychology, is not a mere triumph of light over darkness, but a complexly differentiated contrast of light and shadow birthing the *homo totus*, forming a bridge between conscious and unconscious, constructing the lattice to behold a more expansive horizon.

Although Jung appreciates the central importance of the reconciling third of the *coniunctio oppositorum* for alchemy, and for the integration of unconscious archetypes, he also discerns the importance for both alchemy and depth psychology of the more complex topological formulations mediated through the quaternity, depicted as two perpendicular polarities in the form of compass or cross, exemplified in the four seasons, directions, elements, colors, and stages of the alchemical process, providing an opening from the binarity reconciled by a third entity of the Trinity, whose peak philosophical expression is the Hegelian dialectic. The primary visual depiction of the Self is the mandala, found in various cultures and traditions under different names, as well as in dreams and active imaginations, the archetype of differentiated integration, the Mercurius quadratus which contains a quaternary structure within a radiating circular totality embodying the process of attaining self-knowledge. The Christian cross participates in this archetypal potency, with the Trinity of Father, Son, and Holy Spirit repressing a fourth archetypal function, variously associated with the Devil, Mary, the feminine, and the projected shadow of the unconscious other. This fourth function was long contemplated by Christians, but only officially recognized in 1950 by Pope Pius XII, acceding to a crescendo of public sentiment, in the dogma of the *Assumptio Mariae*, evidently marking a positive inflection of the return of the repressed by perhaps the primary institution that had perpetrated the long patriarchal, logocentric repression in the West, just a few years after the peak negative expression of this return of the repressed in the Holocaust and the apocalyptic destruction of Hiroshima and Nagasaki. The cross embodies the torturous suffering that is a necessary phase of the processes of both alchemy and individuation, the death of the *nigredo* required for a rebirth in the novel emergent mode embodied in the *lapis*.

The alchemical triunity of Sulphur-Mercurius-Sal is also a disguised quaternity because of the duplex nature of Mercurius, both male and female, spirit and matter, Christ and the Devil, good and evil, with the second terms in all of these binaries corresponding to the fourth function, the *sine qua non* of the alchemical drama. Based on the work of Jolande Jacobi, Jean Gebser discerns a correlation of the quaternity with the emergence into a fourth degree of freedom, which he describes not merely as a fourth dimension, but as an "amension,"[84] a conception resonant with the Axiom of Maria, for which the Fourth is a differentiated return to the One, though the alchemists generally considered this "maximal integration" as "reserved for a distant future."[85] This form of integration is enacted not in the undifferentiated unconscious, but in the "differentiated totality"[86] for which the horizon of consciousness is not a simple circle, but a circular mandala differentiable into the quaternity, a squaring of the circle, and into the twelve signs and three-hundred sixty degrees of the zodiac, but also contained in the three-dimensional spherical retort where the *lapis* is produced. However, this final *effectus* "means something more than integration of the four natures,"[87] an echo of Nietzsche's "something higher than any reconciliation," an integration that passes through number to a syncategorematically approached nondifferentiable horizon beyond number, an integration toward which alchemy strove, but whose paradoxical threshold it could not cross, though it created the preconditions for further psychological and philosophical integrations.

The metaphysical correlate of the mandala is synchronicity, a more subtle revision of formal causation intimately entwined with the transcendental archetypes, a "connecting principle" that is only "acausal" specifically in relation to the efficient causation often exclusively privileged in modernity, a principle which Jung affirms he developed partially in relation to the statistical experiments of J.B. Rhine, discussed at length in *Synchronicity* (though he admits that statistical analysis may be inadequate for capturing the full complexity of this primarily qualitative mode of thought), and which he associates with the Tao. Synchronicity intimately correlates synchronic and diachronic events that are not directly connected by efficient causation. For instance, an internal, subjective experience can correlate with a material, objective event by virtue of their differential expressions of the same archetypal complex even though there is no linear efficient causal relation, including certain angular relations of the planets relative to the Earth as discerned for millennia in many cultures, as well as "the communication of unconsciouses" discussed by Deleuze and Guattari, a set of parapsychological phenomena including telepathy, clairvoyance, and precognition, which, as they note, has also been of great interest to Spinoza, James, and Bergson.[88] The archetypal cosmological mode of thought[89] is especially entwined with alchemy, recognizing the "universal interrelationship of events"[90] exemplified in the condensed Hermetic axiom "as above, so below," in Plotinus' expression "all things are connected,"[91] and in Whitehead's statement that "every spatio-temporal standpoint mirrors the world."[92]

The coming to consciousness of the archetypal potencies, in part through the discernment of their synchronistic expressions, is not only a mandate for individuals, but for the collective, a task especially urgent in our time of extraordinary crisis, which contains the potential for literal destruction through climate change, the descent into fascism, nuclear war, and global pandemic, but also the potential for a radical transformation in our collective mode of relation to the world. This critical transformation constitutes an expansion of horizons through the integration of both characteristically modern and nonmodern modes of relation, Deleuze resonating with Jung when he writes that "the horizon is inseparable from crisis."[93] It is as true in our time as it was in Jung's that the drama of opposites is being played out, through us, in the pervasive and complex conflict between the ideologies characteristic of left and right, a drama which is apparently not ultimately leading us toward the triumph of one ideology over another – though, like Jung, I certainly have much more sympathy for left than right – but toward a novel integration of what is good in both progressive and conservative ideologies – though current conservatives in the United States and elsewhere have become a caricature of principled conservatism, almost exclusively expressing its negative aspects. As Laurie M. Johnson observes, "in a world where no ideological choice was perfect, Jung was a liberal by default,"[94] though he mostly eschewed politics, advocating an integrating psychological balance and the avoidance of ideological possession, whether on the left or right. Insofar as any of his views can be described as "conservative," it is in the classic sense of this term, rather than the currently prevalent reactionary conservatism, conserving what is good from the past and not pushing toward a rationalized ideal of techno-scientific "progress" at any cost. Jung denounced totalitarianism of all kinds, whether fascist or communist, and his general orientation was toward a more profound kind of progress, that of individuation. While one should certainly affirm the compassion, equity, and social justice emphasized by the left, one might also affirm the ultimately traditional respect for elders, ancestors, and the spirits of nature characteristic of animistic cultures more than modern conservatism, while rejecting one-sided, mean-spirited cruelty, hatred, and bigotry, a mode of relation to which the current right has a special relationship. However, cruelty and hatred can be encountered at all points on the ideological spectrum, often in reaction to the current ideologues on the right, so that one might remind those on the radical left of Nietzsche's admonition that "whoever fights with monsters should see to it that he does not become one himself,"[95] justifying misogyny, racism, homophobia, and ageism in service to an all-consuming class war, for instance.[96]

Political propaganda preys on the mode that forfeits an active and efficacious critical consciousness in favor of a passive and deficient mythical projection of the shadow onto the other, allowing brutal totalitarianism to arise from any ideology that becomes too one-sided, whether the fascism of the Nazis, the communism of the Soviets, or the extreme form of capitalism characteristic of the current Republican party in the United States.[97] As witnessed in the alchemical opus and the individuation of depth psychology, a primary way this oppositional one-sidedness in all its forms can be overcome is by cultivating consciousness within ourselves of the archetypal complexes that we encounter in the other, by being willing to sustain the tension of opposites within our own psyches and bodies rather than succumbing to the easy seduction of projecting our collective shadow into the world. This does not mean that we cannot still recognize the shadow in others, denounce those who promote bigotry and put children in cages, which is an essential aspect of ethical activity, but that we must withdraw projection to encounter the other as genuinely other rather than as a figure in our waking dream, and thus come to understand that projection is a healthy and necessary activity at less differentiated stages of individual or cultural development, but that when carried past the duration of its appropriate efficacy, projection becomes the primary vehicle of destruction and hatred. Our culture must emerge from its adolescence, in which it has necessarily rebelled against the parental modes of nonmodern cultures by means of the exclusivist privileging of rationality, to integrate the potent rational capacity differentiated in modernity with affective, intuitive, and imaginal modes of relation if we hope to overcome the current oppositional divisions which agonize us, which pit left against right, city against country, young against old.

In fact, although Jung was often critical of Freud, who badly mistreated him, Jung nevertheless pays Freud respectful tribute, acknowledging that his old mentor foresaw the darkness and brutality to which the world would descend in the World Wars if the shadow in each of us was not bravely and relentlessly exposed to the light of consciousness, though Jung knew that Freud could not go far enough because he equated reason with consciousness, not recognizing the shadow inherent in the privileging of reason itself. Our individual and collective task is to become conscious of all forms of hierarchical opposition, even the transitional reversal which hierarchically privileges heterogenous multiplicity over opposition itself. All of these relational modes are expressions of archetypal complexes, even conflict and discord, which must be intentionally expressed in positive, constructive ways if their negative, destructive aspects are to be avoided, or rather overcome as the psychological conflagration, descent, and egoic death necessary for an ascendant rebirth into a novel mode on a collective scale, as even the negative itself, the alchemical *nigredo*, is an archetypal potency that demands to be acknowledged and expressed one way or another.[98]

## Notes

1 Cf. Jung, *Speaking*, 98.
2 Jenkins, *Eros*, 6; Shamdasani, *Jung*, 230n.107.
3 See von Franz and Hillman, *Lectures*, 98.
4 Jung, *Mysterium*, xiii.
5 Jung, *Memories*, 69.
6 Kelly, *Individuation*.
7 Jung, *Letters*, 530–2. See also Jung, *Archetypes*, 55.
8 Deleuze, *Difference*, 317n17.
9 Beckman, *Deleuze*, 23; McMillan, "Jung," 185.
10 Freud and Jung, *Letters*, 104.
11 Deleuze and Parnet, *L'Abécédaire*, 21.
12 Deleuze, *Two*, 179.
13 Deleuze and Guattari, *Thousand*, 241.
14 Derrida, "Forgiveness," 2/11.
15 Deleuze, "Sacher-Masoch," 128–30, 132–3.

16 Deleuze, *Nietzsche*, 116, 212n8.
17 Deleuze and Parnet, *Dialogues*, 80.
18 Deleuze and Guattari, *Anti-Oedipus*, 46, 162, 278.
19 Jung, *Symbols*, xxiv; Jung, *Alchemical*, 90, 195; Jung, *Memories*, 4; Main, McMillan, and Henderson, *Jung*, 4.
20 Žižek, "Notes," 662–3.
21 Jenkins, *Eros*, 5.
22 Deleuze, *Desert*, 36.
23 Deleuze, *Proust*, 47, 67.
24 Jung, *Visions*, 340.
25 Deleuze, *Logic*, 120, 170–1; McMillan, "Jung," 190, 193; Deleuze, *Desert*, 157; Deleuze, *Cinema 2*, 202.
26 Deleuze, *Kafka*, 7.
27 See for example Deleuze, *Difference*, 17, 61, 76, 126.
28 Deleuze, *Desert*, 278.
29 Deleuze and Guattari, *Thousand*, 43, 57, 235, 237, 250–1, 333.
30 Deleuze, *Kafka*, 13.
31 Deleuze, *Essays*, 48.
32 Tarnas, *Cosmos*, 57.
33 Deleuze and Guattari, *Thousand*, 306, 322–3, 380, 398, 420, 507.
34 Deleuze, *Difference*, xx.
35 Stevens, *Jung*, 1.
36 Mills, *Jung*, 1.
37 Hillman, *Re-Visioning*, xii.
38 Jung, *Mysterium*, 348.
39 See Jaspers, *Origin*.
40 Tarnas, *Passion*, 432.
41 Jung, *Mysterium*, 212.
42 Jung, *Mysterium*, 107.
43 Jung, *Mysterium*, 272.
44 Deleuze and Guattari, *Thousand*, 282–6.
45 Psalm 118:22.
46 See Josephson-Storm, *Myth*; Evrard, Massicotte, and Rabeyron, "Freud."
47 Tarnas, *Cosmos*, 57.
48 Jung, *Archetypes*, 4, 161.
49 Kelly, *Individuation*.
50 Stanford Encyclopedia of Philosophy, "Continuity."
51 Jung, *Memories*, 264.
52 Jung, *Archetypes*, 71.
53 Jenkins, *Eros*, 5, 7–8; Rowland, *Jung*; Wehr, *Feminism*.
54 Jung, *Mysterium*, 163.
55 Jung, *Mysterium*, 219.
56 Jung, *Mysterium*, 428.
57 Jung, *Mysterium*, 495.
58 Deleuze and Guattari, *Thousand*, 411.
59 Jung, *Archetypes*, 173.
60 Main, McMillan, and Henderson, *Jung, Deleuze*, 10.
61 Jung, *Mysterium*, 213.

62  Jung, *Mysterium*, 538.
63  Deleuze, *Two*, 373.
64  Jung, *Mysterium*, 548.
65  Jung, *Mysterium*, 550.
66  Deleuze and Guattari, *Philosophy?* 101.
67  Jung, *Mysterium*, 128.
68  Jung, *Mysterium*, 119.
69  Jung, *Mysterium*, 126.
70  Deleuze, *Two*, 356–8; Deleuze, *Cinema 2*, 11.
71  Jung, *Mysterium*, 310.
72  Bachelard, *Lautréamont*, 27–8.
73  Jung, *Mysterium*, 462.
74  Jung, *Mysterium*, 63.
75  Described by Aristophanes in the *Symposium*.
76  Deleuze, *Two*, 77.
77  Jung, *Mysterium*, 473.
78  Jung, *Mysterium*, 44.
79  Jung, *Mysterium*, 286.
80  Hegel, *Philosophy*, 430.
81  Jung, *Mysterium*, 349.
82  Jung, *Mysterium*, 531.
83  Jung, *Mysterium*, 196.
84  Gebser, *Origin*, 340.
85  Jung, *Mysterium*, 196.
86  Jung, *Mysterium*, 203.
87  Jung, *Mysterium*, 205.
88  Deleuze and Guattari, *Anti-Oedipus*, 278.
89  See Tarnas, *Cosmos*.
90  Jung, *Mysterium*, 464.
91  Plotinus, *Enneads*, 159.
92  Whitehead, *Science*, 91.
93  Deleuze, *Two*, 190.
94  Johnson, *Ideological*, 165.
95  Nietzsche, *Beyond*, 69.
96  Jung, *Mysterium*, 166; Deleuze, *Two*, 61.
97  Deleuze, *Kafka*, 57.
98  Jung, *Mysterium*, 253, 363.

Chapter 11

# Integrating Myth Into the Dialectic

Gilles Deleuze's *Difference and Repetition*

Deleuze's work was not translated and read as widely in the United States and Great Britain as was the work of Derrida and Foucault in the first few decades of what has come to be called postmodernism, in part because Deleuze traveled very little, whereas Derrida and Foucault both began teaching in the United States in the mid-sixties, though Deleuze was considered as important in France as these other two philosophers. In fact, citations to Deleuze's work surpassed those to Derrida's work in 2009,[1] evidently marking the moment when interest in Deleuze slightly surpassed interest in Derrida among academics, though not in Foucault, who nevertheless commented in 1969 that "perhaps one day this century will be known as Deleuzean,"[2] and thus Žižek could write in 2003, with perhaps somewhat approximate accuracy, that, "in the past decade, Deleuze emerged as the central reference of contemporary philosophy,"[3] at least in the continental tradition. Deleuze has come to inhabit a fairly central place in the American humanities, somewhat ironically given his decentering project, though not generally in philosophy departments, enacting a role in continental philosophy comparable, also ironically, to Hegel in the nineteenth century, so that the ironies and paradoxes seem to proliferate with Deleuze, qualities that he embraced and exemplified, writing that "paradox is the pathos or the passion of philosophy."[4] However, whereas like Hegelian idealism or Jamesian pragmatism, the concept of Derridean deconstruction has entered common parlance on the widest scale, at least in simplified or caricatured form, there is no widely agreed upon term to describe Deleuze's philosophy other than simply Deleuzean,[5] though he variously called it transcendental empiricism or constructivism. So, despite his extraordinary popularity among academics, his work remains less known to the world outside of academia, in part due to his extreme, esoteric difficulty, though Derrida is similarly difficult,

DOI: 10.4324/9781003195498-12

which has nevertheless not prevented the concept of deconstruction from being adopted at the largest scales of culture.

With perhaps excessive modesty, Deleuze would describe *Difference and Repetition*, just a few years after its 1968 publication, as a "heavy going" book of which "I like some passages,"[6] though as he would acknowledge elsewhere, "it is difficult for an author to reflect on a book written several years ago."[7] While this text is extremely complex, it is entirely brilliant, even though he suggests that "it was a beginning" of various intertwined lines of thoughts that would require further development, "an attempt to jolt, set in motion, something inside me."[8] However, as he would recognize in another context, "an artist can think that what has been fully achieved is only a step, forwards or backwards, in relation to a deeper aim."[9] This fully realized work has certainly been profoundly generative, not only in Deleuze's later thought, but in much subsequent theory, Deleuze writing in 1986 that "everything I have done since then seems an extension of this book, even the books Guattari and I wrote together."[10] It is possible that Deleuze's work marks the pinnacle of verbal complexity in philosophical thought, but complexity is not everything, and although Deleuze's sheer intellectual potency is perhaps unparalleled, accompanied by an aura of saint-like gentleness mixed with a mischievous transgressivity, there are certain domains where his concepts become paradoxically problematic, despite his affirmation of paradox and problem, requiring novel conceptual differentiations and integrations in order to be overcome. It seems unlikely, though, that these overcomings will be achieved through a mere increase in complexity (a recognition toward which Deleuze gestures[11]), at least not any time soon, but through a greater integration with concepts from thinkers that Deleuze deeply respected and engaged with, but did not explicate as thoroughly as his Trinity (as Todd May aptly calls it[12]) of Spinoza, Nietzsche, and Bergson, especially Whitehead and Jung.

As Deleuze does with Plato, Spinoza, Leibniz, Hegel, Nietzsche, Bergson, and others, this chapter offers a somewhat heterodox reading of Deleuze himself, as have the chapters above to varying extents with other theorists. And it must be acknowledged from the outset that Deleuze implicitly sanctions this heterodox reading of even his own work, observing: "How else can one write but of those things which one doesn't know, or knows badly? It is precisely there that we imagine having something to say. We write only at the frontiers of our knowledge, at the border which separates our knowledge from our ignorance and transforms the one into the other."[13] Deleuze affirms that philosophy, at least good philosophy, is inherently speculative, the creation of novel concepts "at the edge of language"[14] to express that which has not yet been expressed, to think that which has not yet been thought in a coherence that exceeds any individual, and that any great philosopher inevitably provides the tools for their own eventual overcoming and subsumption in novel modes of relation.

Deleuze was writing *Difference and Repetition*, as one of his two doctoral dissertations, leading up to the revolutionary events of May 1968 in Paris, a time when there was a pervasive international sense that radical rupture between the old mode and a new one was occurring, and actually perhaps did occur in its incipience, though the situation turned out to be far more complex than the student revolutionaries and hippies had imagined as the sixties turned into the seventies. It might even be suggested that Deleuze was a bit carried away (along with everyone else) by the sense that a fundamentally new world was imminent, a sense which we may still affirm a half-century later, though in a perhaps somewhat more reserved valence, so that this work is one of the deepest intellectual expressions of that cultural moment, though like any great work of philosophy, it is also untimely, maintaining its primary relevance a half-century on. While Nietzsche presided over the descent of Western culture into the underworld depths of the unconscious, Deleuze's expression of what might be described as a nascent reascent is often obscure and ambiguous in part because the time was not yet ripe for a full reascent even when Deleuze was writing. The descent had to be gone through, and Deleuze occupies the pivotal moment after this trajectory reached its nadir in 1945, and then began the reascent toward a novel Schellingian positive philosophy in the sixties, a position he shares with Derrida, in his peak expression of the negative philosophy as a complement to Deleuze's positive conceptual creation, in an assemblage as the two faces of Janus, an ascent that may find a somewhat more direct and confluent expression in our time several decades into the twenty-first century, though the path we are collectively constructing as we climb remains fraught and uneven.[15] Similarly to Cisney's contention that Deleuze's philosophy is a positive differential ontology to Derrida's negative differential ontology, May asserts that Deleuze embraced ontology while Derrida and Foucault abandoned it, an abandonment that could perhaps be described as a negative ontology.[16] Despite Deleuze's great admiration for these two close contemporaries, especially Foucault with whom he was friends and about whom he wrote a book after his death, Deleuze's orientation is primarily creative and constructive, as opposed to the primarily critical and deconstructive orientations of Foucault and Derrida, though Deleuze was also often critical, especially in relation to Hegel, and with Guattari in relation to Freud and capitalism. This fundamental difference from his primary contemporaries might allow the conceptual persona of Deleuze to be considered an opening to an emerging mode of thought after the "postmodern," somewhat like Nicholas of Cusa served as a Renaissance opening from medieval scholasticism to the modern.[17]

## Hegel and Deleuze

Various prominent philosophers, including Jean Wahl, Judith Butler, Catherine Malabou, and Žižek, have pushed against Deleuze's critique of Hegel, while remaining great admirers of Deleuze's positive concepts.[18] Wahl's and Malabou's critiques of Deleuze's rejection of the Hegelian dialectic particularly confirm my own reading, and so I will explore these objections before moving on to the positive content of this chapter, Deleuze's many essential and profound contributions to a philosophy of differential integration. Although Hegel's philosophy has often been described as negative because of the importance of the negating moment of the dialectic, as well as its purported privileging of rationality as discussed above in relation to Schelling, Hegel's tone and trajectory, and his positing of the dialectical movement itself, are generally quite affectively positive, Deleuze himself recognizing more than a decade before *Difference and Repetition* that "Hegel never harms a philosopher, he agrees with him in a global sense, by accounting"[19] for him. And while, like Nietzsche, Deleuze is a primary theorist of affirmation, of a positive differential philosophy, he is, also like Nietzsche in relation to many subjects, consistently more affectively negative about Hegel than Hegel generally is about anything, despite his affirmation of the negative. I would suggest that Deleuze is right in what he affirms, which in part is affirmation itself, but limited in what he denies, specifically the Hegelian dialectic and, especially, the negative, about which Deleuze is strikingly and paradoxically negative.[20] While Henry Somers-Hall aptly recognizes certain "affinities" between the work of Hegel and Deleuze, he deems their philosophies ultimately "not compatible,"[21] a determination I will push against in the contention that no philosophy is ultimately incompatible with any other philosophy in what it affirms, but only in what it denies.

Wahl always expressed great admiration for his former student Deleuze, who would later write that "apart from Sartre," during Deleuze's apprenticeship in the forties and fifties, "the most important philosopher in France was Jean Wahl."[22] Nevertheless, Wahl was strongly critical of Deleuze's critique of Hegel in *Nietzsche and Philosophy*, writing in a generally positive, though ambivalent, review of Deleuze's 1962 book that "there is clearly in this author a kind of ressentiment towards Hegelian philosophy which sometimes leads him to penetrating insights, but sometimes it risks leading him astray," adding that, contrary to Deleuze's contention in what is indeed an otherwise brilliant and insightful book, "Nietzsche's thought is so often very close, as has frequently been said, to Hegel's." Wahl recognizes that there are numerous passages in Nietzsche, especially in *The Birth of Tragedy*, but also as late as *The Antichrist* written in the last years of his sanity, that allowed Heidegger to render Nietzsche as a partially critical heir to Hegel rather than merely as Hegel's opponent. Wahl observes that, although Deleuze's assertion that only affirmation, and not negation, returns in the eternal return "is ingenious and profound," Wahl also recognizes that "it runs up against some profoundly Nietzschean affirmations, since to affirm a moment of pleasure is to affirm, at the same time, that totality in which the depths of pain as much as the depths of pleasure are integrated," a recognition that integral affirmation is not possible without the affirmation of negation itself, both affective and conceptual, and thus, Wahl asks, "is there not some dialectic" in both Nietzsche and Deleuze?[23] As Cisney observes, despite his sympathy for Deleuze's critique of Hegel, "even in *Nietzsche and Philosophy*, Deleuze's most ardently anti-Hegelian book, Hegel plays more the role of a foil than an interlocutor, a character against whom Nietzsche's Übermensch emerges, rather than an object of extended critique."[24]

However, the relatively mild criticisms of his respected teacher Wahl did not dissuade Deleuze from extendedly critiquing Hegel six years later in *Difference and Repetition*, so that his deepening of the Hegelian dialectic is sometimes occluded by the scorn Deleuze uncharacteristically, and almost uniquely, directs against the German philosopher. In "Who's Afraid of Hegelian Wolves?" Malabou, a French philosopher who collaborated with Derrida, asks

> whether, in the case of Hegel, Deleuze does not in fact repeat the gesture that he condemns in Freud; whether in Deleuze's work, as in

Freud's, one is not faced with this 'reductive glee' by means of which multiplicity becomes a unity.[25]

As with the interpretation of Jung's dream for which Freud reduces a multiplicity of bones to a single death wish discussed by Deleuze, Malabou recognizes that Deleuze reduces Hegel to a caricature, "the abhorred victim of the pack of the thinkers of difference, their absolute enemy,"[26] whom he can use as a "straw man,"[27] as Žižek writes, to define his radically novel theory. Malabou observes that Hegel plays a singular role in Deleuze's thought, serving as "an absolute heteron,"[28] the ultimate adversary, "the accursed exceptional one," in a way that Deleuze did not approach even with Kant, whom he strongly critiqued. In his oppositional rejection of Hegel, Deleuze creates "a block of becoming called Hegel-Deleuze, as unexpected yet plausible as that of the wasp and orchid"[29] discussed in *A Thousand Plateaus*, so that "Deleuze never recognizes Hegel as his white whale, leaving to the reader the task of recognizing in his relentless opposition to the dialectic the impassioned limping of a Captain Ahab,"[30] evoking Deleuze's particular fondness for Melville's novel. As Malabou suggests, this apparent projection by Deleuze onto Hegel is ripe for psychological analysis, which will be undertaken below, though such an analysis is immensely complicated by Deleuze and Guattari's own critique of the Oedipal complex. Nevertheless, rather than asserting a merely incommensurable opposition between Hegel and Deleuze, a simple binarity that both philosophers played primary roles in exceeding in the abstract conceptual domain, we might recognize in Hegel's extraordinarily complex thought "not an opposition but an astonishing proximity to that of Deleuze,"[31] affirming Hegel's central role in Deleuze's work.

Deleuze overstates his case about Hegel, whose work he nevertheless respects enough to describe it as "the final and most powerful homage rendered to the old principle,"[32] the reconciliation of opposites in a return to identity, ultimately derived from Heraclitus and Plato, which Deleuze overturns. Deleuze's innovation that difference is deeper than opposition, that opposition is a special case of difference, is profound, but his denouncement of the negative is extremely ironic, as this denouncement is precisely an enactment of the negative. Deleuze attempts to escape the negative by inconsistently affirming that "being is full positivity and pure affirmation,"[33] but it is ultimately not possible to escape the negative, as witnessed in Deleuze's negation of Hegel, because in order to escape it, one would have to negate the negative, which undermines its own project, and looks remarkably like the dialectic it seeks to reject. However, Deleuze's suggestion that the Hegelian dialectic and the negative are second-order manifestations, as in an illusory "optical 'effect,'"[34] of a deeper order of pure positive difference can be recognized as a pivotal, even epochal, contribution. Deleuze is right that difference is a more profound domain than the opposition and sublation of the dialectic, but not that this dialectic can be completely overcome any more than Newton can be completely overcome. Newton's and Hegel's theories are also epochal, world-constituting, and even when resituated as special cases within broader or deeper theories, they are still valid within their domains of applicability. As Deleuze recognizes, "the constants of one law are in turn variables of a more general law,"[35] the law of the oppositional dialectic reframed as a variable within a broader domain of difference, a deeper dialectic that Deleuze constructs especially in relation to certain moments in Plato, the Leibnizian calculus, Schellingian potencies, and the Nietzschean eternal return.[36]

Nevertheless, Deleuze apparently wants absolutely to overcome opposition because opposition resides at the heart of modern rationalism, and he wants to create something completely new and free from the old modes and categories of thought, an endeavor in which he succeeds beyond all reasonable expectation, though a complete liberation from binarity is impossible, as binarity is deeply embedded in the structure of language and the conceptual thought it expresses, and any emergent mode must subsume the previous verbal and conceptual modes as essential elements in its constitution in order to surpass them. In *A Thousand Plateaus*, Deleuze and Guattari explicitly address the necessity of opposition in the process of conceptual creation, writing: "We employ a dualism of models only in order to arrive at a process that challenges all models. Each time, mental correctives are necessary to undo the dualisms we had no wish to construct but through which we pass."[37] Similarly, in *Foucault*, Deleuze writes that "multiplicity can be realized and the differential of forces integrated only by taking diverging paths, splitting into dualisms, and following lines of differentiation,"[38] also writing in *Cinema 2* that "it is necessary to make a division or make emptiness in order to find the whole again,"[39] thus variously acknowledging the impossibility of completely overcoming binarity as an integral aspect of process as he seems to want to do in *Difference and Repetition*.

When Deleuze was writing this text, oppositional rationality was still almost completely dominant, and the spirit of the sixties, perhaps especially May 1968, the year of its publication, was characterized by a titanic striving toward the total freedom from all constraints, the complete abandonment of the old modes of relation in favor of new ones, though this dream came to seem naïve just a few years later. Deleuze was very profound and ultimately sophisticated, but he was also apparently caught up in the spirit of his moment, as we all are in our moments, so that one of his most important concepts, the deepening of opposition into difference, is historically intertwined with his negation of the negative, a paradoxical position, as perhaps the best mode of thought to explain Deleuze's relation to Hegel is precisely the Hegelian dialectic itself, though Deleuze goes beyond Hegel. Deleuze is not merely Hegelian because he rejected Hegel as his antithesis, but his relation to Hegel is susceptible to a dialectical mode of thought, which explains some aspects of the relation but not others. Deleuze furiously attempts to think his way beyond the Hegelian dialectic, an endeavor in which he is partially successful, but he gloriously fails in completely leaving the Hegelian dialectic and the negative behind, as his relation to these concepts is best accounted for by means of these concepts, is susceptible to their mode of explanation, though, as he so powerfully demonstrates, this mode is far from exhausting the potential modes of relation. He spectacularly succeeds in showing that this dialectic is one mode of relation among others, a special case of a more profound dialectical conception.

The Hegelian dialectic assumes the most extreme case of difference, though not the greatest, that of opposition, and as Derrida especially understood, the privileging of rationality is predicated upon this oppositionality. But Deleuze suggests that the overcoming of the oppositional metaphysics is not primarily to be found in the reconciling third of dialectical sublation, which may be conceived as an initial opening to a novel mode, so that the dialectic must be placed in the context of a "more profound game"[40] in which oppositions are shown to be one kind of differential relation among others, one topological construction in a more expansive domain of difference which has been subordinated since at least Aristotle to the oppositional mediation which assumes an originary identity.[41] I would suggest that part of the reason why Deleuze's writing is so complex, at least as complex as Hegel, Whitehead, and Derrida, is that he is attempting to express this novel mode beyond the hegemony of opposition through language permeated by opposition. His writing is an emancipatory loosening of the categories of thought, not primarily a deconstruction, but a positive, even poetic expression (though Derrida's writing is also poetic) of a novel philosophy that abandons the old certainties in favor of a future mode that we can scarcely imagine, that it is our task collectively to create. Rather than a fully elaborated closed system, Deleuze provides aesthetically profound evocations of the world and the thought to come, a world which remains at the horizon of a temporal singularity.

Opposition is an abstractive reduction from multiplicity, the construction of a binary figure that suppresses the complexity and pluralistic profusion of the world. Deleuze wants to move beyond opposition, not by reconciling the opposites in an emergent third entity, but by relegating opposition to the status of one kind of relation among others. He is attempting to overcome the traditional categories of philosophical thought grounded in opposition to think his way into a novel mode not dominated by opposition, that does not privilege opposition. However, the meta-opposition Deleuze constructs between opposition and multiplicity can be dissolved and reconstituted in the recognition that the only way out is through the opposites, but it is also necessary to produce an expression of what the movement of thought could look like after the reign of opposition has ended, to make this end possible through such an expression. Whereas most of the theorists in the chapters above recognize that there is no getting around the problem of opposites, that it must be faced, Deleuze, writing at the limits of language, evokes destinations toward which thought can move, virtual domains not yet actualized, lures which we can employ to pull ourselves beyond our current constraints. One would certainly hope that some progress would have been made in philosophy in the century-and-a-half that separates *The Phenomenology of Spirit* and *Difference and Repetition*, and Deleuze undoubtedly produced a profoundly innovative deepening of Hegel. But another half-century after Deleuze's book, we can perhaps recognize that his rejection of Hegel was an instrumental necessity in its historical context, for which, as Deleuze writes, "perhaps the majority of philosophers had subordinated difference to identity" and "to the Opposed,"[42] but that this rejection is not what is so creative and novel in Deleuze. Rather, it can be understood as the paradoxically oppositional tension employed to forge his theory of difference, not the theory itself, though the theory inevitably contains the marks and constraints of the instrument employed in its fabrication.

If we are to follow Deleuze's exhortation to affirm difference, just as we followed James' pragmatism imperfectly practiced in his own relation to

Hegel, we must apply Deleuze's affirmation to his own theory, which is inconsistent in this specific case with what he so brilliantly advocates. If he were consistent, he would affirm the partial, contingent validity of the negative, and acknowledge that he is being pervasively, sustainedly negative in relation to the negative itself, a negation of negation which does not generate the positive, an insight which Deleuze recognizes, though he only intermittently implements this recognition.[43] As Deleuze makes it possible for us to understand, the way to overcome the negative is not merely to reject it, because the negative absorbs that negativity into its infinite void, but to affirm the negative as a secondary order of becoming because, as Hegel writes, "a negative nothing is however something affirmative,"[44] a positive, inescapable aspect of process, so that Deleuze's differential innovation would enfold Hegel into Deleuze's mode of thought without making Deleuze Hegelian. Deleuze can thus be imagined as something like a philosophical Einstein relegating Newton to a special case, a diminished role, though it is as if Einstein spent a great deal of his time denouncing Newton rather than simply creating his theory on the shoulders of Newton who, like Hegel, is indeed a giant. So perhaps it is left to our generations, half-a-century after Deleuze, to complete his project, to render it more consistent by removing the charge from the relation to the negative, bringing the Hegelian dialectic into our mode of thought to serve the integral affirmation of the full scope of multiplicity rather than merely railing against it, like a grown son railing against his father, whose gravity he cannot seem to escape, whom he is more like than he would care to admit, genetically descended from him despite all his efforts to be absolutely different.

In spite of Deleuze and Guattari's hugely influential "deconstruction" of the Oedipal complex, it may be suggested that Deleuze still participates in this complex in relation to Hegel, so that the rejection of the dialectic and the rejection of Oedipus are intimately entwined, a relation that Deleuze and Guattari explicitly acknowledge via Foucault.[45] As René Girard writes, *Anti-Oedipus* is "Oedipal to the core since it is completely structured by a triangular rivalry with the theorists of psychoanalysis."[46] And, as Deleuze himself would observe in an essay written in 1967, but published in 1972, the same year as *Anti-Oedipus*, "no book against anything ever has any importance; all that counts are books for something, and that know how to produce it,"[47] an ironic coincidence given that Deleuze's most popular book is precisely a book against the Oedipal, at least according to its title, though it is also for other profound concepts like the axiomatics and, especially, schizoanalysis, producing a more differentiated integration of philosophy and psychology. However, as Deleuze and Guattari would write three years later about Kafka, in a passage that may be read as a defense against the kind of critique leveled by Girard, their project is not merely to reject Oedipus, but "to augment and expand Oedipus by adding to it and making a paranoid and perverse use of it" in order "to escape from submission."[48]

In a 1973 interview, Deleuze asserts that he is more oriented toward the rejection or overcoming of "Oedipal filth" than Guattari, who prefers an Oedipal accelerationism like the one described in *Kafka*, for which "the more Oedipal you are, the better it will be," though Deleuze acknowledges the mutual truth of their differing conceptions, which remain undifferentiated – or perhaps integrated – in their cowritten texts.[49] And although they recognize in 1987 that "*Anti-Oedipus* was a big success," they also admit that "this success was accompanied by a more fundamental failure," as their "dream was to put Oedipus to rest once and for all. But the job was too big for us," and "Oedipus has become our albatross."[50] In *Kafka*, Deleuze and Guattari recognize that "there is always the danger of the return of Oedipal force," as "the amplifying perverse usage of Oedipus is not sufficient to guard against every new closure,"[51] and thus the strategic acceleration of the Oedipal especially advocated by Guattari, intimately entwined with the accelerations of capitalism and schizophrenia, evinces a limited efficacy, and cannot constitute the final escape of an absolute deterritorialization, an activity which is not always positive, Deleuze for instance describing the Crusades as a deterritorialization.[52] As they write in *What Is Philosophy?*: "Movements of deterritorialization are inseparable from territories that open onto an elsewhere; and the process of reterritorialization is inseparable from the earth, which restores territories,"[53] even the territories of the Oedipal and the dialectic themselves, which Deleuzoguattarian deterritorializations allow to be resituated within more expansive territories.

Like Nietzsche's denouncement of ressentiment, then, rather than being refuted by these complex ironies and paradoxes, the profound novelty of Deleuze and Guattari's work is made possible by Deleuze's evidently Oedipal complex, which is clear from reading his biography. And although Beckman, in her biography of Deleuze, is less sympathetic to an Oedipal reading than Francois Dosse in his comprehensive dual biography of Deleuze and Guattari, Beckman nevertheless cites Derrida's rejection of Heidegger's dismissal of the significance of Aristotle's biography in reading the work of the ancient philosopher, Derrida suggesting that biography should be brought "back into the picture,"[54] a suggestion taken up below. Deleuze himself acknowledges the importance of biography in 1953's *Empiricism and Subjectivity*, writing that "certainly, we know that a philosophical theory involves psychological and, above all, sociological factors,"[55] which motivate philosophical questions, similarly affirming, in 1982, "what Nietzsche says on the importance of 'anecdotes' fitting 'thought, in the life of a thinker.'"[56] In *What Is Grounding?*, Deleuze offers an evidently Oedipal reading of Kierkegaard, whose relationship with his father is "a secret in his life which suffocates him,"[57] and he makes a similarly biographical observation with his wife, Fanny Deleuze, about D. H. Lawrence in 1978.[58]

No matter how strenuously the Promethean radical Deleuze, now steadily becoming a traditional ancestor figure, rejected the older metaphysics, exemplified in the saturnine father-figure of Hegel, he could not ultimately escape the pull of Hegel's gravity because, as a son inescapably resembles his father, even if the son adopts a completely different style of dress and mode of thought, the conceptual persona of Deleuze differentially repeats the conceptual persona of Hegel. In fact, Deleuze is perhaps the single philosopher who possesses the greatest claim to playing a role in the early twenty-first century parallel to Hegel's in the nineteenth century, the conceptual persona fulfilling the function of the Hegelian negative of Hegel, an anti-Hegel carrying Hegel's genetic lineage in filial relation with Deleuze's nurturing "maternal" figures (though information about Deleuze's relationship with his actual mother is sparse), especially Spinoza, whom Lacan positions as "the philosopher of feminine assemblage,"[59] though I would eschew any essentializing of gender, and Hegel was also deeply influenced by the Dutch philosopher.

Dosse tells us that Deleuze "found the mere mention of his childhood unbearable,"[60] and although Deleuze describes his father as "a lovely man, very benevolent, very good, very charming," he was also a right-wing anti-Semite, an ideological complex directly opposed to Deleuze's own views, though as Deleuze and Guattari write, again in relation to Kafka in a passage that might as well be about Deleuze himself: "If the father maintains the love and admiration of his son, that's because in his childhood, the father already confronted some of the diabolical powers even if it meant being beaten by them."[61] Deleuze writes elsewhere that Spinoza's genius was "not unrelated to the fact that he was Jewish,"[62] so that one even wonders if the fact that two of Deleuze's three favorite philosophers,

Spinoza and Bergson, as well as the two novelists about whom he wrote books, Proust and Kafka, were Jewish may partially have had something to do with a reaction against his father, whom he nevertheless loved and admired. And that his other favorite philosopher, Nietzsche, struggled with anti-Semitism and ultimately rejected it may also be related to this complex. Despite his words of praise for his father, Claire Parnet, Deleuze's student and collaborator, says to Deleuze in the *L'Abécédaire* interview that "you repressed your childhood, you rejected it like an enemy and as hostile,"[63] a characterization with which Deleuze appears implicitly to agree, or at least he does not argue with it as he does with so many other things in this same interview. That Deleuze spent so much time and energy denouncing the conception of Oedipus as a privileged category – despite Deleuze and Guattari's affirmation of the Oedipal as a uniquely dominant and efficacious cultural machinery for repression and control – much like Nietzsche's denouncement of ressentiment, seems partially to result from Deleuze's own struggle with the suffocating secret of the Oedipal, though this does not by any means render his work with Guattari invalid. Rather, it recalls the suggestion that philosophers primarily make great contributions in areas with which they personally struggle the most, as otherwise the motivation to engage in a sufficiently deep and sustained way to push through to novel domains would be lacking.[64]

Deleuze seems implicitly to sanction this reading elsewhere in *L'Abécédaire*, asking

> why does someone, someone in particular, you or me, get connected to or identify especially with one kind of problem and not another? What is someone's affinity for a particular kind of problem? That seems to me to be one of the greatest mysteries of thought. A person might be fated for one problem since we don't take on just any problem.

As Deleuze concludes, "I feel rather connected to problems that aim at seeking the means to do away with the system of judgment, and to replace it with something else,"[65] and one can discern that he is expressing a multivalent potency, variously described by Schelling, Jung, and Hillman as correlated to the negative, the father, and judgment. Deleuze wants to replace the system of judgment, which "prevents the emergence of any new mode of existence" by reductively transforming differential "disjunction into an either/or," and resonant "connection into a relation of cause and effect,"[66] but yet he harshly judges Hegel, not to mention Freud, in just such hierarchical binaries. These judgments may partially, and rather prosaically, stem from the fact that he was harshly judged by his parents in comparison with his older brother, Georges, who died heroically fighting the Nazis, and with whom the younger Deleuze was very close, Dosse writing that "Deleuze was insignificant in his parents' eyes," and Deleuze's friend Michel Tournier telling Dosse that

> Gilles always had a complex about his brother Georges. His parents created a veritable cult around Georges, and Gilles couldn't forgive them for admiring only his elder brother. He was the second child, the mediocre son, while Georges was the hero.

Later, according to Dosse, "the trauma was quickly repressed or alluded to only ironically," Deleuze telling a student in 1951 "that he had had a brother 'but the dope stabbed himself with his Saint-Cyrien sword during a hazing. It made him laugh. He made him out to be an idiot.'" And similarly, while lecturing on Pierre Janet, who influenced Freud, "Deleuze recalled a vivid childhood memory of his father trying to help him with algebra during a school vacation" and that, in Deleuze's words, "within five minutes, he was shouting at me and I started crying."[67] Deleuze evidently suffered from a potent Oedipal complex in relation to his father, which was repressed partially in reaction to the trauma from his brother's death. So, in spite of Deleuze and Guattari's ambiguous denouncement of the Oedipal complex, they are in fact, almost too obviously despite the ultimate complexity of their thought, the dialectical antithesis to the Oedipal, the anti-Oedipal, enabling a differentiated integration of the novel theories that their denouncements of Hegel and Oedipus allowed them to construct with the dialectic and the Oedipal complex as special cases of more expansive processes of becoming.

Despite the superlative brilliance of *Difference and Repetition*, many of the critiques of Hegel are strikingly reminiscent in their affective tone of an adult son criticizing his father. No matter how harshly Deleuze condemns Hegel, no matter how justified his complaints, he is still related to him, still descended from him, more like him than he would care to admit, as one does not spend page after page critiquing something that does not maintain a powerful hold on one's mind. If Deleuze had thought Hegel just completely ridiculous, he would simply have ignored him, so there is something evidently Hegelian retained in Deleuze precisely as the negative, as in a photographic negative, to his many positive concepts. As Deleuze acknowledges on the first page of the original preface to *Difference and Repetition*, there was "a generalized anti-Hegelianism"[68] at that moment in the late sixties in France, and it might be suggested that Deleuze's antipathy to Hegel is more intimately bound up with the image of the German philosopher depicted by his teacher Jean Hippolyte than with Hegel himself. One of Deleuze's earliest expressions of difference appears in a 1954 review of Hippolyte's *Logic and Existence*, where he writes that "the richness of Hippolyte's book could then let us wonder"[69] if such a differential conception could go beyond Hegel and, perhaps implicitly, Hippolyte. Like Nietzsche with Wagner and Jung with Freud, Deleuze underwent a messy, prolonged break with Hippolyte in 1967 after having dedicated his first book to him in 1953, and having initially worked with Hippolyte as his dissertation advisor for what would become *Difference and Repetition* before switching to another professor.

Hippolyte spread slanderous rumors about Deleuze's sexuality, and though Deleuze was admirably sanguine about the content, he found the malicious intent of the rumors hurtful.[70] And although Deleuze did not participate in a volume dedicated to Hippolyte which his friend Michel Foucault organized in 1971, Deleuze's reading of Fichte in his last work, "Immanence: A Life," published just a few weeks before his death in 1995, is deeply influenced by Hippolyte's reading of the German idealist. It might be suggested that Hegel served as a psychological substitute for Hippolyte, who in turn was a substitution for Deleuze's father, with whom he seems to have had a markedly Oedipal relationship, which would perhaps explain why he was so keen to become an anti-Oedipal figure, echoing Nietzsche's becoming the Antichrist, having grown up in a deeply Christian family with a pastor father who died when Nietzsche was young, and sacrificing himself as a martyr to an idea. But as with Nietzsche, this recognition is far from authorizing a dismissal of Deleuze's thought, rather demonstrating how the complex and paradoxical machinery constituted by the specific relations of his experience allowed him to create such profound work, becoming perhaps the most revered continental philosopher in the twenty-first century, in part through an engagement with the Oedipal, which Deleuze obliquely recognized in 1962 as necessary for the process of creatively prolonging the work of a precursor: "It is difficult to be someone's heir without unconsciously wishing for their death now and then."[71]

Like Nietzsche's critique of ressentiment, which was evidently made possible by his struggle with that very affective complex, Deleuze was evidently able, along with Guattari, so profoundly to critique the dominance of the Oedipal complex in psychoanalysis precisely because he experienced particular difficulties with his father. Deleuze and Guattari identify the Oedipal complex as the psychoanalytic version of the Hegelian dialectic, which draws a direct connection between Deleuze's critiques of Hegel and Freud and his own Oedipal concerns, which nevertheless allowed him to produce these profoundly novel critiques, to demonstrate that the dialectic is one extreme relation among others just as the Oedipal family dynamic is one archetypal situation among others. Perhaps this is the secret of *amor fati*, the love of fate which Nietzsche and Deleuze both affirmed: that the deepest wounds are often inextricably entwined with the greatest gifts, and that by working to heal our own wounds, by at least partially liberating ourselves from their grip, we can gain the capacity, as wounded healers, to mediate this same paradoxical liberation for others, though never in a totalizing final solution, but through an always-provisional dissolution of surface problematic expressions, like unidimensional opposition, to emancipate the deeper and more topologically complex questions of the depths.[72]

Intimately related to Deleuze's critique of Hegel, the figure of the "beautiful soul" is especially important for understanding the concept of integration, and Deleuze's great admiration for James, Bergson, and Whitehead may provide a key to discerning the subtle nuances in the historical unfolding of this concept. The phrase "beautiful soul" originated in the mid-eighteenth century with the German archaeologist and art historian Johann Joachim Winckelmann,[73] who influenced Nietzsche, and the figure was brought to broad public attention by Goethe's 1795 novel, *Wilhelm Meister's Apprenticeship*, the classic *bildungsroman*, book VI of which is entitled "Confessions of a Beautiful Soul." It tells the story of a woman who, struggling with some general undefined illness throughout her life (one may think of both Nietzsche's and Deleuze's illnesses in this context[74]), myopically ignores reality in all its problematic complexity pollyannaishly to assert that all conflicts and oppositions can be easily and painlessly reconciled in God. This somewhat unflattering depiction is a straightforward and rather prosaic account of a conventionally religious, sanctimonious pietist attitude, which reminds one in some ways of Nietzsche's mother and sister. In fact, Nietzsche dismissively employs the phrase in several works, an employment of which Deleuze certainly would have been aware.[75]

However, it has not been widely acknowledged in studies of Deleuze's work that the figure of the beautiful soul may have misogynist roots, as one might, in the context of twenty-first century feminism, understand why the conspicuously unnamed female protagonist in Goethe's narrative would want to refrain from marriage and retire from public life in order to maintain her spiritual and practical autonomy rather than becoming a wife subservient to her husband and the patriarchal norms of her era, "a whole social mechanism destined to reduce her to the demands of marriage and reproduction,"[76] as Deleuze writes, without mentioning the beautiful soul, in a 1976 review of Alain Roger's novel *Le Misogyne*. Goethe roughly based his narrative on the subsequently lost autobiography of a family friend, Susanne von Klettenberg,[77] while in 1806, the German novelist Friederike Helene Unger published a different version of the story, whose protagonist is named Mirabella, under the title *Confessions of a Beautiful Soul Written by Herself* which, as Michelle A. Reyes explains, was intended as a feminist response to Goethe's novel, a project which Goethe unsurprisingly disdained. As Reyes summarizes recent feminist readings of these texts, Unger's novel radically revises Goethe's narrative, as whereas Goethe's character is always in a paternalistic relation with men, first her fiancée and then her uncle, Unger depicts a progressive liberation from male dominance, providing her character with an independent self-determination. Unger appropriates the figure of the beautiful soul, a year before Hegel employed this figure in the *Phenomenology*, to provide the countervalent depiction of a much more dynamic, active, and creative feminine figure than Goethe's character. It is clear, then, that the pervasive male interpretation of this figure, from Goethe in 1795 through Deleuze in 1968, demonstrates a profound unawareness of the situation of women in the eighteenth century, despite Deleuze's generally keen attention to feminist concerns, making this particular woman a figure for an abstract idealism that avoids concrete action in the world and asserts that all conflict will be resolved in a state of perfect unity.[78]

Deleuze's primary source for the figure appears to have been Hegel himself, who describes the beautiful soul as "too fine to commit itself to anything" because "it does not want to stain the radiance of its pure conscientiousness by deciding to do anything particular. It keeps its heart pure by fleeing from contact with actuality and preserving its impotence."[79] It has been suggested that Hegel's evocation of the beautiful soul implicitly refers to figures as disparate as Goethe himself, Fichte, Rousseau, Hölderlin, and even Christ,[80] whom Hippolyte discusses in relation to this figure, as Deleuze must have been aware. Deleuze was clearly influenced by Hegel enough to turn his own concept of the beautiful soul against him, so it seems only fair reciprocally to turn Deleuze's critique of dialectical dualism against Deleuze himself, but only in order to assist in his liberation from the one-sidedness of his critique. Just as Deleuze seeks, perhaps unconsciously, to inoculate himself against an Oedipal reading of his rejection of Hegel, it might be suggested that Hegel employs the figure of the beautiful soul to inoculate himself against precisely the critique that Deleuze levels against him, so we may discern that Hegel at least vaguely foresaw Deleuze's critique and thus sought preemptively to ward it off just as Deleuze sought preemptively to ward off the Oedipal critique.[81] And the two philosophers should both be given much credit for possessing the exceptional foresight to address these central criticisms, though it was simply not possible for them to discern the full contours of these parallel critiques in their historical moments. Like all philosophers, they necessarily engage in oppositional one-sidedness despite their epochal attempts to overcome oppositionality, as there is a very large portion of partial validity in their respective theories (the dialectical negative and the anti-Hegelian), but there is also partial validity in the critique of these theories, so that it has required the passage of generations to see clearly the way to go beyond the blind spots and limitations of even these most profound and far-seeing theorists. Rather than a condemnation, this is merely the recognition that we are all limited, and that later thinkers will inevitably surpass even the best of us, though they can only accomplish this feat by standing on our shoulders.

And it must be acknowledged that Deleuze partially anticipated the critique of his critique of Hegel's critique of the beautiful soul, so that one might be forgiven for feeling a sense of vertigo as one reads the passages on this subject in *Difference and Repetition*, Deleuze recognizing that a primary danger in propounding a purely differential philosophy free of the negative and identical of the Hegelian dialectic is precisely that of the beautiful soul, which asserts that all differences are "reconcilable and federative," a mode of thought "far removed from bloody struggles" which merely asserts difference without opposition. However, having performed this self-awareness that the mere rejection of opposition in favor of an abstract radical tolerance not practicable in actuality is the very pitfall of the beautiful soul that Hegel warned against, Deleuze nevertheless argues that the affirmation of difference can "release a power of aggression and selection which destroys the beautiful soul by depriving it of its very identity and breaking its good will,"[82] an affirmation of persistent problems and questions which avoids the totalizing unification of the dialectical reconciliation of opposites that Deleuze discerns in Hegel. The simple binarity of opposition thus becomes a surface appearance of a deeper difference. And having apparently inoculated his differential philosophy against the beautiful soul, Deleuze turns this figure back upon Hegel, accusing him of finding that even the most fraught and apparently irreconcilable oppositions are ultimately reconcilable in a return to identity. Deleuze understands this conception as succumbing to the need to imagine the possibility of perfect, absolute solutions to problematic differences, whereas Deleuze finds that there are differences that can never be reconciled, or that if they are reconciled on one plane, these differences inevitably lead to other incommensurabilities, so that the idealist dream of attaining complete wholeness and oneness is a dangerous and totalizing fantasy.

There is much truth in this critique, as the negative does not always lead to a reconciled identity. As Jung understood, an essential aspect of the process of individuation is recognizing the other as genuinely other, withdrawing the projection into the other that animates the Hegelian dialectic, itself an essential stage in the individuation process, to allow real differences to subsist that require often painfully negotiated, and often inadequate, compromises which eternally defer the ideal of complete reconciliation, the dream of "peaceful coexistence."[83] But Deleuze, often foreseeing potential criticisms despite his periodic lapse into the opposition against opposition, the negation of the negative, also admits that "to throw the taste for pure differences back at the beautiful soul"[84] is also inadequate, itself participating in that very complex. He asserts that only affirmation returns in the eternal return, though he does not consistently apply this insight to his own negation of the Hegelian dialectic, and a half-century after his pioneering efforts, we may discern that even the negation of negation itself does not return, and thus the affirmation of the partial, contextual validity of negation must necessarily return if we are truly to affirm difference, a formulation which is nevertheless susceptible to the critique of the beautiful soul. It may even be suggested that the proliferating accusations of the beautiful soul complex have something of the character of the Terror in the French Revolution, so that no revolutionary, even the leaders of the revolution like Danton and Robespierre, is spared condemnation and the guillotine, while in Unger's novel, Mirabella is living the life that she wants to live, reading the books that she wants to read. As with the Terror, one cannot ultimately cleanse thought of the beautiful soul, but must rather wait for the vertiginous counterrevolutions to the counterrevolutions to subside, so that not only the complex becomes something to guard against, but also the denouncement of that complex, which carried to the opposite extreme itself remains within the gravitational orbit of that very complex, and is perhaps even subtly misogynist.

In an insight which the figure of the beautiful soul can only caricature, and thus provide a warning against delusional oversimplification for both the idealist and the critic of idealism, but which this caricature cannot dismiss in its full nuanced complexity, this Oedipal struggle of Deleuze with Hegel – around which he ingeniously builds fortifications through the very concept of the beautiful soul and the denouncement of Oedipus, almost completely inoculating himself from such criticism, leaving only the tiniest of cracks which we can perhaps peer through a half-century later – can be seen as necessary for his individuation from both his father and the collective father complex operative at that moment in relation to Hegel. It is this contradictory, self-enclosed, paradoxical negation of the dialectic which confirms the dialectic, and thus allows Deleuze to integrate the dialectic with other modes of thought to produce a novel dialectical conception that subsumes the Hegelian dialectic in a more expansive mode which affirms both the dialectic and its negation. So, in the paradoxical manner that Deleuze so loved – as "any concept is bound to be a paradox"[85] – but to which he was partially blind in this particular case central to this text, by rejecting the Hegelian dialectic, he enacts and affirms that dialectic, a sustained problematic tension which allows a novel mode of thought to emerge.

Deleuze asserts that "no one passes less for a beautiful soul than Nietzsche" as "his soul is extremely beautiful, but not in the sense of the beautiful soul" because of his "sense for cruelty" and his "taste for destruction."[86] Nevertheless, it is striking that the internal narrative described in Goethe's novel resembles nothing so much as the ecstatic, transformational raptures, experienced mostly in solitude, bordering on delusion, described by Nietzsche himself, especially in *Ecce Homo*,[87] though whereas the nameless woman in Goethe's novel takes God as her object of imaginal veneration, Nietzsche elevates himself and his own genius, as Dionysus and the Antichrist, but also as The Crucified, to a worshipful degree. And this inverted resonance is not so farfetched as it may at first seem to a cursory glance given that the woman is Christian and Nietzsche is probably the most noted "anti-Christian" in history. This is evidently an opposition which affirms the identity of the relation, as Nietzsche's father, who died young and whom he revered, was a pastor, and Nietzsche himself was devoutly religious until the age of twenty. As Lou Salome aptly observed, Nietzsche's rejection of Christianity was still in the realm of the religious, was achieved in a way that inverted the religious rather than simply leaving it behind,[88] a recognition echoed by Heidegger who said of Nietzsche's anti-Christianity that "everything 'anti' thinks in the spirit of that against which it is 'anti'"[89] (one must also think of *Anti-Oedipus* in this regard), so that much of what Zarathustra says is derived from the sayings of Jesus in the New Testament, twisted and reconstituted in clever, paradoxical ways, "gathered from the Bible and turned back against it," as Deleuze writes.[90] Nietzsche explicitly rejected Christianity, but replaced God with Dionysus, and ultimately with himself, which became the characteristic modern substitution in the worship of the artistic or intellectual genius that perhaps found its peak in the twentieth century. So, Nietzsche, who was magnificently inconsistent, and who said many brilliant as well as many deeply questionable things, forged, along with Schelling, a way to think beyond the Hegelian form of the dialectic in its incipience, which Deleuze refined and extended, though it may be possible further to prolong this mode of thought by acknowledging that not only is the dialectic susceptible to critique, but that this very critique is reciprocally susceptible to a dialectical mode of thought. Although both Hegel and Deleuze presciently foresaw these susceptibilities in their work, it falls to our later generations further to integrate these critiques, which it was not possible for them, in their pioneering efforts, to allow to permeate their philosophies, which were necessarily forged against a projected other, a necessity from which not even these greatest of all philosophers could ultimately escape.

Furthermore, it is important to recognize that, by Deleuze's definition, James, Bergson, and Whitehead could also potentially be dismissed as beautiful souls, though Deleuze was deeply influenced by all three, and he even expresses the more nuanced version of integration resonant with their conceptions, which Hegel partially and inconsistently foresaw, though Deleuze obstinately denies him this nuance, perhaps for the psychological and metadialectical reasons suggested above. As Malabou particularly recognizes, Deleuze's reading of Hegel is a reductive oversimplification that renders the dialectical tendency of thought absurd, but the fact is that any mode of thought, including those expressed by Nietzsche and Deleuze, can be rendered absurd by carrying the most uncharitable and least nuanced expression of a particular mode to its logical conclusion. And if Hegel plays a unique role for Deleuze as enemy, Whitehead plays a similarly unique role in that he receives perhaps the highest degree of praise lavished on any philosopher by Deleuze, rivaling Deleuze's Trinity of Spinoza, Nietzsche, and Bergson, while receiving very little actual exposition in Deleuze's work. In fact, it was not until 1988 that Deleuze devoted one brief chapter to Whitehead in his book about Leibniz.[91] The ratio of praise to exposition is higher for Whitehead than any other figure, which perhaps suggests that the English philosopher exerted a more central influence on Deleuze than one might be led to assume by a cursory reading.

Russell J. Duvernoy argues that Whitehead manages to elude the complex of the beautiful soul, Duvernoy obliquely bringing the paradoxically universal validity of that figure into question, but also partially subjecting Whitehead to Deleuze's critical authority. And the conceptual persona of Deleuze does indeed exude an admittedly overwhelming authority founded upon unquestionable and almost unique brilliance, which is ironically resonant with Hegel's similarly dominant authority in the nineteenth century, and also with Whitehead in certain circles. In fact, it might even be suggested, as Beckman does, that Deleuze's thought is so overwhelmingly powerful that it is often employed as a dogmatic orthodoxy, despite the extraordinarily heterodox quality of his work, a "perverse but surprisingly frequent way of approaching"[92] his thought, so that a half-century after *Difference and Repetition*, it may be necessary for Deleuzeans to begin more assertively to push against Deleuze's limitations, especially in relation to Hegel, while still affirming his greatness and employing his positive concepts. Duvernoy convincingly shows how Whitehead avoids enacting the beautiful soul, marshaling complex arguments to demonstrate how Whitehead's concrescent integration, partially constituted in differentiated contrast, is not merely a placid movement toward unification, though I would suggest, without rehearsing Malabou's equally complex and insightful arguments, that the same is often true of Hegel. As Duvernoy shows, Whitehead's recognition of evil and irreducible discord preclude him from being considered a beautiful soul, though it might be suggested that if one were to deemphasize the absolute in Hegel's work, an admittedly heterodox reading, the dialectical negative itself could be conceived as playing a similar differentiating function in Hegel, the initiatory ordeal of Hermeticism which Duvernoy invokes in relation to Joshua Ramey's *The Hermetic Deleuze*, though the Hegelian negative operates primarily in the special case of oppositional difference.[93]

However, pulling back to view this question in a wider frame, there is not an especially compelling reason completely to submit Whitehead, or even Hegel, to Deleuze's test, a trial and judgment which Duvernoy recognizes is counter to the general trajectory of Deleuze's thought toward the liberation from philosophy as legislation. Whereas Deleuze, despite his exhortation to affirmation, possesses an unmistakable drive toward denouncement primarily in relation to Hegel and the Oedipal, Duvernoy quotes Stengers that Whitehead's approach is not that of "a denouncer,"[94] as can be witnessed in Whitehead's much more restrained critique of Hegel. It might be efficacious to allow the elder Whitehead to instruct Deleuze on this particular issue, even as Whitehead could benefit in significant ways from the younger philosopher's mode of thought, to lead Deleuze from the denouncement of Hegel to an acknowledgment of the conceptual persona which designates his body of work as an important but limited precursor (and who among us is not limited?).[95] In fact, in both *Empiricism and Subjectivity* and *What Is Grounding?*, Deleuze is much more sympathetic to Hegel than he is in his texts from the following decade, so that Deleuze can perhaps also learn from his younger self in this regard.[96] One might thus recognize that the beautiful soul complex is not an unforgivable sin punishable by expulsion from the pure heights of philosophical illumination, paradoxically pure by means of the steely-eyed refusal of purity, but one of many potentialities that, when carried to an extreme, can enable certain kinds of insight but preclude others, just as the very denouncement of Hegel's purported sin adjudicated by Deleuze is also an extreme of a different potentiality that, as Wahl implicitly understood in relation to Whitehead, as well as to Hegel, Nietzsche, and Deleuze, can enable complementary insights but preclude the insights available to a different modality.[97]

It may even be suggested that the very denouncement of the beautiful soul is a negative inversion of the beautiful soul itself, so that the recognition that one must remain open to the discord and suffering of contrasting difference can, in the extreme form that Deleuze enacts, tend toward a dogmatic means of totalizing judgment just as the extreme form of the beautiful soul totalizes in its certainty that all differences are reconcilable in a harmonious return to identity. It appears that what is required is an integration of this opposition between the beautiful soul and that figure's denouncement to recognize that both modes contain partial, limited validity, so that attaining a differentiated and contrasting balance between these stubbornly incommensurable perspectives might be the most efficacious way to overcome this binary. And Deleuze abstractly understood this necessity of letting go of rigid oppositionality, of de-escalating the conflict, writing a decade after *Difference and Repetition*: "You should not try to find whether an idea is just or correct. You should look for a completely different idea, elsewhere, in another area, so that something passes between the two which is neither in one nor the other."[98] We should follow Deleuze's advice and apply this wise approach to overcoming the dizzyingly recursive opposition to Deleuze's opposition with Hegelian opposition, as Deleuze and Guattari were not particularly concerned with the coherence of their projects,[99] instead directing their attention toward novel conceptual creation.

In addition to formulating complex reasons for how Whitehead manages to avoid being a beautiful soul so that we can understand how Deleuze could praise him so highly given that some of Whitehead's concepts look remarkably like the most sophisticated version of the totalizing union of the beautiful soul, it might also be efficacious to problematize the universality of the figure of the beautiful soul itself. We can perhaps understand Deleuze's drive to avoid the beautiful soul at all costs as an expression of his particular character elaborated in sustained negotiation with the contextual requirements of his era and his biography. And we can also recognize that Whitehead's greater emphasis of integration over difference is not an error, but rather "that slightest change of tone which yet makes all the difference," the measured, pragmatic optimism of a man who has found wisdom through the suffering caused by the loss of his son, expressing an expansive warmth and generosity, articulated in its most complex valence, as a complement to the often unsettling trickster-like transgressivity of Deleuze, which is nevertheless extremely profound and admirable, and often very generous. It seems likely that Deleuze praises Whitehead so highly not because he agreed with everything the older philosopher thought, or with everything thought by any thinker, even Spinoza, Nietzsche, and Bergson, but because Deleuze recognizes in all of these theorists a rare greatness and freedom, so that he can write in 1966 that

> this liberation, this embodiment of cosmic memory in creative emotions, undoubtedly only takes place in privileged souls. It leaps from

one soul to another . . . and from soul to soul, it traces the design of an open society, a society of creators, where we pass from one genius to another, through the intermediary of disciples or spectators or hearers.[100]

Given that Deleuze spends so much time with Hegel, even as his differential heteron, one might suspect that Hegel could also be considered one of these privileged souls, a phrase which bears an ironic resemblance to the beautiful soul, so that the controversy between Hegel and Deleuze, involving numerous other thinkers, constitutes what Deleuze would later describe, though not specifically in relation to Hegel, as "an interstellar conversation, between very irregular stars, whose different becomings form a mobile bloc,"[101] Malabou's Hegel-Deleuze block of becoming.

From these considerations, it can be adduced that Deleuze's negative project of rejecting binarity, especially in the form of the Hegelian dialectic, can never quite succeed on these terms, as this rejection itself sets up a new binary between binarity itself and difference. Any rejection of one concept in favor of an opposed concept is ultimately proof of the partial validity of the dialectic, and although Deleuze might reject this view as enacting the beautiful soul, the denouncement of the beautiful soul itself participates in binarity by rejecting binarity in favor of the emphasis on multiplicitous difference that is opposed to it. Binarity is paradoxically inescapable as long as one hopes to escape binarity. That is, rather than rejecting opposition altogether, an impossible, self-defeating task, one can instead relegate opposition to the status of a special case of difference, but avoid the beautiful soul by understanding that not all differences are reconcilable, though they may form an essential contrast within a larger totality, a persistent incommensurability, recognizing that the two entities constituting a differential relation exist in the same world and thus are related in that most basic sense as Whiteheadian negative prehensions. Though these entities may stubbornly and eternally resist reconciliation, they can at least be integrated as disparate elements in a drama, actors wearing various masks whose narrative function is precisely to maintain their inexorable difference, Deleuze writing in 1978 that "every accord is dissonant."[102] As Hegel, Whitehead, and Deleuze all understood, integrations are not only positive, and integration is not always a confluent process, as something is generally lost or deemphasized in each integration, and even what at first can be a vital and generative composition of disparate elements inevitably settles into a static, enclosing orthodoxy which requires rupture through novel differentiations, lines of flight which must in turn approach points of diminishing return, must lose momentum and reach a critical pain and dissonance for which novel integrations are required.

And although these male philosophers have viewed the religious asceticism of the woman in Goethe's novel as especially laughable, whether explicitly or implicitly, we might recognize that all of these men – Goethe, Hegel, Nietzsche, Deleuze – thinking in the most abstract and impractical possible registers, are ultimately not so different from the beautiful soul in that their pursuit of an ideal, the ideal of novel conceptual and imaginal creation, is relatively similar to the woman's religiosity that they all implicitly deride. The beautiful soul is thus, at least in one register, a mere insult with misogynist overtones, which allows these philosophers implicitly to judge one another as "feminine" in an unbroken lineage of legislation, even as Deleuze explicitly rejects such legislation and is generally very sensitive to feminist concerns. Perhaps the lesson to be taken from this legislative lineage is that, returning to the woman who keeps herself separate from life in service to an ideal, we might have compassion for her, for Goethe, for Hegel, for Nietzsche, and even for Deleuze, who were all doing the best they could in the contexts in which they found themselves, creating the preconditions for their own overcomings. In the end, we might even find that being a beautiful soul is no worse than it sounds, as Unger implies, not worthy of contempt or ridicule, but a stage of understanding that some of us might find ourselves oppositionally able to supersede, while still others of us might find ourselves able to go even further to discern the legitimacy in the oppositional critique, but also to love and even to admire such a person. It might even be suggested that the beautiful soul is closely related to the Jamesian tender-minded temperament, as opposed to the tough-minded temperament, and that Deleuze could perhaps benefit from a bit more balance in this opposition, at least in relation to Hegel. And one might further suggest that, despite the vast space Deleuze clears for the creation of novel concepts, in matters of life and death – or of death and rebirth – the subtle but significant Jamesian, Bergsonian, and Whiteheadian emphasis of integration over differentiation, of contrasting differentiation as primarily enabling the process of concrescent integration, may be somewhat more efficacious for the living of life, a "slightest change of tone" from the Deleuzean mode of thought with which these precursors have so much in common, and by whom Deleuze was deeply influenced, though perhaps even Deleuze enacted this subtle shift in his later work.

It should not be surprising that Hegel, as the dominant philosopher two centuries ago, whose influence has been powerfully felt ever since, should nevertheless have been superseded and overcome in significant ways in the succeeding centuries, and Schelling, James, and Deleuze have played especially significant roles in this overcoming. But a half-century on, we can be expected, yet again, to see even further, to overcome this previous overcoming, so that the vanguard of philosophy is no longer primarily engaged in critique, in denouncing and rendering problematic the concepts of past theorists, which already seems to have reached its apex in Derrida and, more ambivalently, Deleuze, though critique will always remain an essential instrument in the theoretical armamentarium. The philosophy of Deleuze's future may be in a subtle shift of emphasis that allows one not to take Deleuze's critique of Hegel so seriously, so much to heart, to take this critique with the same grain of salt with which one must take Nietzsche at his most extreme, harrowing, and transgressive.

Applying the affirmation that Deleuze advocates to what may be conceived as the inevitable blind spots in his own work, we can see that the rejection of Hegel was efficacious, the absolute enemy against whom Deleuze found it generative to push, and uniquely so in his oeuvre, in order to create his startlingly novel concepts, which are barely less startling a half-century later, even as the critique of Hegel can be de-emphasized as a contextually necessary, but somewhat overwrought and even atavistic, remnant of an earlier time. If it were not the case that we could discern some limitation and myopia in Deleuze, he would be the first and only philosopher in history of whom this could be said, so a more plausible narrative is that he carried thought as far as he could, and no further, as must we all. On this view, it is not even necessary to "save" Hegel, as he was never in danger. He did the most that any philosopher can hope to do: he expressed a novel mode of thought which embodied the spirit of his age, and created the precondition for later philosophers, including those like Deleuze who denounced him, to exist at all. Like a father with his children, grandchildren, and great-grandchildren, no philosopher can hope to create a complete and perfect system that will stand forever, but only to give his progeny, of whatever gender, the opportunity to go beyond him, though this going beyond need not be limited to an Oedipal relation.

The dialectic is not ultimately Hegel's solitary invention, but a deepening of the figural movement of the Trinity, dwelled upon by Christian theologians for the better part of two millennia before Hegel, expressed in perhaps its most sophisticated form by Nicholas of Cusa,[103] and issuing into the stream of German idealism with Kant, Fichte, and Schelling. But the dialectic is also genealogically descended from the rarefaction in the alembic to produce the philosopher's stone that was the focus of alchemy for over a thousand years, and these medieval expressions of the reconciliation of opposites are descended from manifold expressions that can be traced far back into antiquity, long before the beginning of what we think of as philosophy with the pre-Socratics, back into the mythical era of human culture as the death and rebirth of a god, or of an initiate into sacred mysteries.[104] So the attempt completely to escape the Hegelian form of the dialectic is evidently doomed to fail, as this is ultimately an attempt to escape the necessity of descent into the unconscious to encounter the shadow and anima as other in order to be transformed. Deleuze otherwise complexly affirmed this descent, for instance writing in the eighties that "the struggle with the shadow is the only real struggle," mediating a rebirth once a critical threshold has been reached, a liberating renascence requiring a catastrophic fatality exemplified in the Flood, as "this liberation can occur only by passing through the catastrophe"[105] enacting "the difficult birth of a new world."[106] Deleuze's rejection of dialectical opposition, which is a rejection of the foundational, and often limiting, categories of Western thought, is itself a metadialectical operation, the dialectical rejection of the dialectic in order to produce a novel dialectical mode beyond reconciliation, an Overman capable of overcoming the inevitably limited previous expressions of this urge toward transformation through encounter with otherness. And this overcoming is embodied in a multivalent relational potentiality that lies occulted in the subtle interstices of these actual expressions, not in some ultimately inaccessible transcendent world of Forms, but intricated in immanent process, in the dynamic constraints through which the world becomes, an unconscious transcendental domain of virtuality which yearns for, and demands, actualization.[107]

Deleuze's rejection of the dialectic was necessary and instrumental in forging his novel mode of thought, but this rejection was too extreme, too vociferous, undermining itself – one might even say deconstructing itself. However, the positive mode of thought whose production this critique and rejection enabled is profound, and not ultimately a discontinuous rupture with the modes of thought traced multivalently in the chapters above, but a refinement and complication of those modes, which allows us to think in novel ways and, perhaps most importantly, to express this novel mode in language that can viably populate the centers of discursive power to become predominant after the deconstruction of oppositional metaphysics. Deleuze's expression of a mode free from opposition is a "thought of the future,"[108] though a half-century on, we still find ourselves contending with the starkest oppositions, both political and cultural. We may envisage, with Deleuze, a world and a mode of thought beyond opposition that is not merely a harmoniously unifying reconciliation, but we are not done with opposition yet – far from it. Deleuze can thus be recognized not as primarily providing solutions to our most urgent problems, but as creating openings to still barely discernible future worlds through his posing of deeper problems and more expansive questions requiring novel conceptual creations.

In contrast to the stance of Graham Harman that "the true danger to thought is not relativism but idealism,"[109] I would tend to agree with Duffy, who is in turn agreeing with Sommers-Hall, when he writes that "Deleuze effectively precludes any sense in which his philosophy could be interpreted as either materialist or idealist, at least insofar as each of these terms refers only to the exclusion of the categories comprised by the other,"[110] an overcoming of this duality which Deleuze explicitly expresses in *Cinema 1*, echoing Bergson.[111] The whole thrust of Deleuze's thought is to overcome such either-or oppositions in favor of the affirmation of "AND . . . AND . . . AND. . . ,"[112] an overcoming which he imperfectly performed, though his thought has rendered further overcomings possible as much as any other theorist since the second half of the twentieth century. Deleuze often gives the impression of playing all sides, of being susceptible to appropriation by different, and even opposed, schools of thought without committing completely to any one preexisting school. By playing the philosophical coquette, flirting with different modes, he draws different kinds of theorists into his web, his erotic gravitational orbit, and then as soon as they get close, start to become excited, he pulls away, creating a doubt and longing, an undecidability. And by stringing along a broad range of admiring but often bemused readers, he creates the precondition for the integration of these differentiated modes.

So, it is not that I simply disagree with Deleuze about the Hegelian dialectic and the beautiful soul, but that I think it would be efficacious to shift the emphasis of his critique of Hegel to a more loving refinement and course correction rather than a harsh denouncement, which seems unnecessary to pursue any further given the later context of Hegel's reception, which has been shaped to a large extent by Deleuze himself. To summarize my critique of Deleuze's critique of Hegel, one could think of The Dude's exasperated exclamation to his best friend Walter Sobchak in *The Big Lebowski*, when Walter repeatedly asks, "Am I wrong? Am I wrong?" to which The Dude replies: "You're not wrong, Walter, you're just an asshole."[113] But this is no indictment of Deleuze, who seems to have enjoyed discussing anuses and taking philosophers "from behind" to produce "monstrous"[114] progeny with great good humor, always with a genially transgressive irreverence. And, in fact, Deleuze makes a similar point in *Dialogues II*, where he writes that

> every time someone puts an objection to me, I want to say: 'OK, OK, let's go on to something else.' Objections have never contributed anything. It's the same when I am asked a general question. The aim is not to answer questions, it's to get out, to get out of it.[115]

So, in a Deleuzean spirit, let us give Deleuze the same courtesy he gave himself, though he never quite managed to give that same courtesy to Hegel, and go on to something else, to Deleuze's positive concepts (though these are often intimately intertwined with critique), which have served to make him one of the most profoundly influential philosophers of the last few decades.

## A Mythical Dialectic

The terms "difference" and "repetition" appear together in 1956's "Bergson's Conception of Difference," and again a decade later in *Proust and Signs* and *Bergsonism*, where Deleuze writes that "memory is essentially difference and matter essentially repetition,"[116] implicitly referring to Bergson's *Matter and Memory*, formulating an essential correlation between Bergson's work and his own. In his book, Bergson equates memory with spirit,[117] so that *Difference and Repetition* is an unambiguous, though somewhat indirect, reframing of the duality of spirit and matter.[118] Deleuze reformulated the overcoming of this oppositional relation in numerous texts, for instance writing in 1981 that "the spirit is the body itself, the body without organs,"[119] variously equating spirit, difference, the Tao, Spinozan immanence, the Nietzschean will to power,[120] and the body without organs (though Deleuze acknowledges that he and Guattari "never did understand 'the organless body' in quite the same way"[121]). Repetition and difference supersede negative opposition and identity, which are closely related to traditional modes of thought that construct philosophical

## Integrating Myth Into the Dialectic 227

language and concepts as representing, making again-present, an originary transcendent identity behind appearances, a mode which Deleuze asserts must be overcome to "think difference in itself" rather than subordinating difference to binarity. Difference is the multiplicity of relations that exceed the hegemony of identity and negation, exemplified in the judgment of Aristotle and Kant, while repetition is partially derived from Nietzsche's eternal return containing "disguised and displaced" differences. Only those differential relations which are affirmed return in the process of becoming, while that which is negated does not return, though we may recognize along with Hegel, as well as most of the others discussed above, that the negative remains an instrumental necessity, something of whose form is retained in the actual contours of that which is affirmed as the contrast of Whiteheadian negative prehensions.

This conception of the shadowy negative as one form of Being among others is coherent with the univocity that Deleuze derives partially from Spinoza. The differentiation into various modes, such as the diversity of philosophical schools, all refer to the same Being rather than subsisting separately, in the Cartesian manner, as subject and object, though differentiated modes may, in many cases, be completely incommensurable, having no direct loci of connection or relation among them other than their relation to a univocal Being from which all oppositions are coerced into binarity from a more expansive differential plurality. This oppositional coercion may itself be conceived as a differentiated mode, but not an intrinsically privileged one. Space and time are particular constructions from a matrix of differential potentialities forming a heterogenous univocal multiplicity, an infinitely complex open network of relations from which reality in the particular forms that we encounter it extracts itself. This self-extraction does not only occur by means of local tensions generating intensity through the limitation to a single dimensional axis, a first-order power and depth of which opposition is a second-order surface effect, as flat opposition is always cut out of a more voluminous topological manifold of radiating differential trajectories ("multiplicity" is the translation of "multiplicité," the French word for Riemannian "manifolds"[122]). Becoming occurs more generally through the ever-shifting selection and emphasis of these vital relational trajectories partially defined by contrasting disparity, a mode of expression especially resonant with Whitehead.

Deleuze discerns this differential depth of Being, this "ultimate unity"[123] for which opposition is a reductive simplification, as expressed in all domains across scale, not only in geometry and physics, but in the domains accessible to biology, psychology, sociology, and linguistics. However, it may be recognized that all modes, not only oppositional conflict, require the suppression or deemphasis of other modes (one generally cannot write philosophy and dance at the same time). So binarity can perhaps be reframed as one valid mode of construction among others, which elicits certain aspects of process at the expense of others, a recognition required for overcoming the hegemony of opposition, though it may be efficacious to pull back from the ironically oppositional denouncement of oppositionality to discern this paradoxical operation as a necessary transitional reversal for which we can now discern the negative and the identical it presupposes as one particular form of complex potentiality. But it must also be recognized that this oppositional mode remains dominant in philosophy, not only among Hegelians, but perhaps even more egregiously in analytic philosophy, which generally conceives of philosophical discourse as the oppositional combat between discrete categories and schools of thought. One can thus envisage the Hegelian dialectic as a bridge between the narrowly rationalist mode characteristic of analytic thought, which Deleuze tended to dismiss or ignore altogether, exemplified in the "philosophical catastrophe" of Wittgenstein,[124] and an affirmation of differential multiplicity beyond the hegemony of opposition which Deleuze renders thinkable.

As seen above in relation to Schelling, and as will be discussed below in relation to Deleuze's conception of Ideas, and especially in relation to Hillman, the negative can be figured as a problematic potentiality associated with Kronos.[125] He is an equal *dramatis persona* in the polytheistic pantheon that Deleuze often evokes, neither privileged as this potency has often been in service to the differentiation of oppositional rationality, nor denigrated as a mere "epiphenomenology"[126] of spirit as Deleuze does in his bid to "overturn Platonism"[127] (while nevertheless retaining much of what is good in Plato) and enthrone a pluralistic differential affirmation. This affirmation of pluralism at the expense of negation can be understood as a transitional reversal creating the precondition for the recognition that differential pluralism must affirm even the partial validity of the negative and monism if it is to be a true pluralism that does not paradoxically define itself by negating the negative, the "magic formula we all seek – pluralism = monism,"[128] as Deleuze and Guattari write.

In fact, as Deleuze affirms, though he inconsistently practices this affirmation in relation to this particular opposition at the heart of his critique, rendering the negative as neither privileged nor denigrated is not merely a resolution of the opposition, but the dissipation of the contradiction by discovering the deeper problem of which this contradiction is a shadow, though this shadow is precisely the negative and can thus be conceived as a primary actor among others in the drama of becoming that Deleuze describes. And he does distinguish between two forms of naysaying in Nietzsche's *Zarathustra*, so that the "No" uttered by the figure of the Ass enacts the privileging of negation which suppresses other forms of difference and conserves the burdensome "old values," while the "No" of Zarathustra himself creates "new values" by saying "No" to the "No" of the Ass, and thus affirming a differential multiplicity.[129] In this way, Deleuze affirms the necessity of negation freed by its own operation from its hegemony, though it may also be discerned that this negation which serves to overcome even itself is precisely characteristic of the Hegelian dialectic, especially when the absolute is relegated to an instrumental role. The absolute is a *dramatis persona* that must be dethroned and deemphasized to allow the other *personae* to emerge in their pluralistic multiplicity, but it can never be finally slain, as the potency of Kronos corresponding to the absolute is death itself, the positive being of the negative, the transcendental Freudian "death instinct," among its other masks. Deleuze writes that negation is "difference seen from its underside, seen from below," and resonant with the project of turning deconstruction on its head, he asserts that difference is "seen the right way up"[130] as affirmation, but a fully realized differential affirmation would affirm both ways of seeing, both top-down and bottom-up, though it has been efficacious to emphasize one or the other at different moments of a metadialectical process.

    The privileging of the One, and the negative opposed to it in a monocentric identity, began to be articulated by Plato, though the polytheism still evident in Heraclitus is also conserved in Plato and Plotinus, requiring the lineage of Aristotle, the medieval scholastics, and the Enlightenment rationalists almost completely to suppress this pluralistic multiplicity. The long privileging of monocentric rationality can be recognized, after the deconstruction of logocentrism especially over the last half-century, as a dialectical necessity luring the reemergence of a polytheistic pluralism especially developed by Schelling, Nietzsche, Jung, Deleuze, and Hillman, with Jung and Hillman particularly enabling an overcoming of the negation of the negative as an instrumental necessity for the differentiation of a novel mode which integrates all potencies in their complexly contrasting relationality.

This mode differentiates between an active negative force embodied in the "non-being"[131] of Plato's *Sophist* and the mere surface effect of a passive negation subordinated to identity. This differentiation leads not to the suggestion that Deleuze was simply wrong about the negative (nothing about Deleuze is simple), which has indeed tended to be subordinated to identity and the absolute in the philosophical tradition constituting Whitehead's "footnotes to Plato,"[132] but to the recognition that Deleuze's oppositional relation to the privileging of oppositionality has been a paradoxical necessity ultimately leading to a deemphasis of the identical and the negative rather than to their impossible, self-deconstructing negation.

Deleuze contends that the alternative since Plato has generally been between the grounding of negation in a positive non-being or the illusoriness of an ungrounded negation, a false binary which can be dissolved in the recognition that there is no absolute, originary ground, but that differential relationality provides a more profound kind of grounding which overcomes the opposition between Being as either grounded or ungrounded. As with all such persistent binary distinctions, this is a verbal construction which reality exceeds and contains as a limiting, instrumental constraint that is efficacious in one phase of a process of becoming but that fades into the background at a more profound, higher-order phase of ingression. Becoming is lured toward indiscernible domains intimated as both the "celestial beyond" and the "infernal and unfathomable"[133] depths, which are immanent conceptions of virtual potentialities exceeding the present horizon of conception requiring constructive elicitation, rather than transcendent realms, with the concept of the virtual derived from Bergson explicitly associated with the concept of spirit.[134]

Beyond or beneath what Deleuze discerns as the monocentric circular repetition of the Hegelian dialectic, he advocates instead a decentered dialectic derived from Nietzsche's eternal return, a "dialectic of existence,"[135] an infinite polycentric repetition of virtual potentialities across scale, for which he reappropriates the word Ideas, variously actualized as transcendental images, functions, and concepts, and for which the differences in each temporal repetition are selected and affirmed as elaborations and becomings in actuality of relational dynamisms, a pluralism of monadic "points of view."[136] This deeper dialectic is constituted in a shedding of habitual monotony, which fades into the background, as "forgetting as a force is an integral part of the lived experience of eternal return,"[137] a precondition for the differentiation of novel integrations. Texts that engage with the history of philosophy, which Deleuze nominates "a spiritual voyage,"[138] are enactments of this repetition with difference, careful retracings of earlier texts in novel contexts and from different vantages to draw out inconsistencies, implications, refinements, and extrapolations from partially subjective presuppositions. This philosophical activity not only requires rigorous attentiveness, but also a strategic, positive forgetting, mythologically figured by the river Lethe flowing through the underworld of Hades, with Deleuze invoking Dionysus "as the god of places of passage and things of forgetting."[139] Positive forgetting cavalierly liberates thinking from a dogmatic adherence to an original text's specific formulations in order to allow philosophy to begin anew, to produce a more differentiated integration of the mode of thought embodied in the text under consideration with the modes of thought with which the writer is bringing this text into dialogue, embodied both in other texts and in the philosopher's particular bodily experience. This differential repetition, "the thought of the future,"[140] does not only take place in "the head," which Deleuze describes as the "organ of exchange," the complexly negotiated legislative emphasis and selection of discrete logical and conceptual nominative elements, but in "the heart," which is "the amorous organ of repetition,"[141] the erotic lure that draws us to repeat certain dramatic narrative complexes, often involving disparate imaginal persons. Eros lures us to feel our way into these virtual potencies, these "spiritual entities"[142] which appear to us as miraculous, transgressive, and even divine interventions from a domain that exceeds the current horizons of our verbally mediated conceptual systems.

One is hard-pressed not to associate these singular virtual potencies with Jung's most mature conception of the archetypes, especially as prolonged by Hillman, and despite Deleuze's critiques of the archetypes, which seem to be directed primarily toward their conception in Jung's early and middle periods.[143] Ideas can be discerned in the passages between actual occurrences, in the differential movements of higher or deeper immanent domains that exceed these spatial indications, and which are only adequately describable through more abstract topologies, and through evocative, poetic, and even ironically humorous language. Repetition is the engine of becoming, a decentered, tortuous circular movement, a multiplicitous intertwining of nomadic spirals, which willfully forges beyond the merely habitual laws and fixed cycles of nature to the liberated domain of the Overman, "the form that results from a new relation between forces,"[144] including the cosmic forces of *A Thousand Plateaus*.

This conception of differential repetition might as well be a description, in its most complex valence, of Jungian synchronicity, which enacts the expression of relational archetypal complexes through diachronic and synchronic repetitions whose differences introduce novelty into actuality.[145] As with the archetypes, repetition reunites the opposites of singular and universal, lawfulness and its transgression, integrations which can only be intellectually approached through paradox, but which are contained in the mythical potencies and their narrative relations that permeate Deleuze's thought as much as that of Schelling, Nietzsche, Jung, and Hillman.[146]

Deleuze discerns Thanatos, the Freudian death instinct posited as a complement to the mythologically expressed potencies of Eros and Oedipus (despite what Deleuze portrays as Freud's reductive oppositionality and materialism[147]), as "a transcendental principle"[148] that constitutes the affirmation of repetition in the form of a mythical agency exceeding any actual expression, luring the faculties of thought and imagination.[149] Thanatos is "a positive, originary principle"[150] embodying the negative, an insight which recalls Nietzsche's evocation of Zarathustra as the "the opposite of a no-saying spirit" who nevertheless "says 'no,' does 'no' to everything people previously said 'yes' to."[151] The dissolution and cure of this paradox, which troubled both Nietzsche and Deleuze, can be found in the transformative underworld "voyage to the bottom of repetition,"[152] figured in the realm of Tartarus far below even Hades, to encounter the demonic figure of Kronos, the positive potency of the negative, who enables our healing by making us ill, generates the precondition for our liberation by enchaining and destroying us, saves us through loss.[153] We eternally return to this archetypal situation, and all of the others encountered in mythological narratives, in a polyrhythmic temporality constituted in the intertwining periodic repetitions of these relational complexes, each differentiated point in a nonlinear series resonating intensively with other "privileged instants,"[154] for which becoming is located not in the linear succession of events characteristic of efficient causation, a surface effect of a deeper mode, but in the differential novelties transversally generated from the accumulating repetitions of the various archetypal episodes dramatizing relational potencies.

That which undergoes the repetition, the originary differential grounding of the eternal return, is not discerned in any of the particular differential instances, but in a "secret subject," a singularity which Deleuze describes as a "repetitious soul" or "Self,"[155] capitalized like the Self of Jungian individuation,[156] a term which Deleuze also employs, partially derived from

Simondon, who also at least partially derived it from Jung.[157] This Self is discerned not in the particular instances of differential repetition, but in the movement of becoming that passes wave-like, in a manner reminiscent of Bergson, through these repetitions of dramatic situations, enacting a novel "Copernican revolution"[158] in which discrete identities are reconceived as moving durations in a more profound differential process of becoming constituting a deeper form of identity, and thus perhaps a deeper form of the negative. It is hubris, the will to overcome the constraints of present givenness by means of the dangerous and excessive elicitation of differential novelty, that generates transformation, enacting the creation of "the superior form"[159] of the Overman, the becoming of potencies that express themselves through this individuating process, enacting an "active forgetting"[160] of denial which liberates from habitual constraints to allow for the ingression of potentiality into increasingly expansive domains of affirmative actuality.

Deleuze's differential ontology is closely related to the calculus, and to the questions about infinity and the infinitesimal that animate the contrasting forms of this mathematical instrument, for which he discerns the Leibnizian approach as carrying us beyond the opposition between the calculus as "a language of essences" on the one hand, a symbolic systematization of the traditional conception of the Ideas, and "a convenient fiction"[161] on the other, a narrative mathematical construction which allows for the analysis of previously intractable problems. Deleuze's conception serves to integrate these two modes in the imaginal relationality of transcendental Ideas, expressed in the monadic singularities of both "physical points and metaphysical points or points of view."[162] However, although Deleuze's conception of difference is much closer to that of Leibniz than to that of Newton, he is critical of the attempt which he discerns in Leibniz, and later in Hegel, to "conquer the obscure" in the infinite through representation, by making again-present the infinitely small in the case of Leibnizian analysis, and the infinitely large in the case of Hegelian sublation, by rendering these indiscernible domains intelligible through a totalizing system, the optimization hypothesis for Leibniz and the identity of opposites in the absolute maximum for Hegel. These are aspects of the two philosophers' systems that can be conceived as inessential to their more profound conceptions, a recognition which clears space for discerning the syncategorematic repetition lured toward an always-receding horizon eternally pursued to "the 'nth' power"[163] by means of increasingly fine differentiations enabling increasingly expansive and subtle integrations.

Deleuze describes the pioneering efforts of Leibniz and Hegel to create a differential philosophy by mastering the infinite within a representational enclosure as "causing a little of Dionysus's blood to flow in the organic veins of Apollo,"[164] constructing an opening from the pure privileging of Apollonian rationality, but requiring a further shift of emphasis enacting not only a blood transfusion in which Apollo remains the primary actor, but a more intensive integration in which Apollo and Dionysus learn to speak each other's languages. The chaotic, affective, creative multiplicity of the Dionysian would thus renew and transform the ordered unity of the Apollonian, which would in turn grant consciousness and actuality to the Dionysian. This mutual transformation of these powers requires the intoxicated obscurity and deathly descent of the Dionysian as much as the clarity and ascent of the Apollonian to be reborn as a novel mode which recognizes that no matter how ingenious and intricate a system we construct through religion, science, or philosophy, the "in-itself"[165] can never be tamed, always eluding our grasp. Deleuze describes Leibniz as closer than Hegel to "the Dionysian shores,"[166] though he remains on the seas of a pure reason, a paradoxical image for which the ungrounding differential ground is expressed as the solid earth while the traditional, rationalist mode is implicitly located in the fluid ocean with its unfathomable depths, a moment in Deleuze's text which seems to deconstruct itself, as the Dionysian is not a grounding where one can rest, but an always-unsettling chaotic multiplicity roiling beneath the rational, exceeding conscious systematization. This paradox may serve to reveal that Deleuze is, in some utterances, enacting a mere reversal of the privileging of the Apollonian over the Dionysian so that the monstrous cruelty of the Dionysian itself is implicitly rendered as a comforting ground, a reversal which has nevertheless been necessary for producing a differentiated integration of these potencies, copiously expressed by Deleuze in this text, though with the generative inconsistency of a true pioneer.

We must go beyond the mode of conceptual thought characteristic of Euclidean geometry, which both Plotinus and Spinoza employed in their work (despite Deleuze's admiration for both of these philosophers), to a mode that corresponds with the Riemannian differential geometry upon which Einstein built his general theory of relativity.[167] Deleuze posits this mathematical and conceptual mode as resonant with "differenciation" in biology, the relatively discontinuous actualization of novel entities, whether in cells enabling the emergence of more complex multicellular organisms, or in the integral derivation of global structures in a topological manifold from differentiated local behaviors. Integral differenciation is an "ideal relation,"[168] a relationality of Ideas among the mathematical, conceptual, and biological domains, as well as among physical, mechanical, chemical, psychic, social, linguistic, and aesthetic systems, a resonance repeated differentially across scale. The potentialities repeated in this extrapolation of the differential calculus are often figured as mythologically expressed powers, not only of Dionysus and Apollo, but of the numerous personified potencies employed by Deleuze, "a plurality of centres"[169] each enacting a diachronic durational coexistence, multiple complexly intertwining non-identical series of moments, in the synchronistic repetition of the eternal return rather than the monocentric circular repetition of a single convergent series often characteristic of the philosophical lineage stretching from Plato to Hegel.

This lineage has been developed and refined through an orthodox "image of thought,"[170] an imaginal construction of what it means to think philosophically constituted in the specific contextual contours defining the purpose and method of such an activity, a self-enclosed system of presuppositions that produces certain kinds of concepts which iteratively confirm the image of thought based upon the initial premises, circulating through monocentric binaries. The philosophical tradition descended from Plato assumes the "good will"[171] of philosophers, that philosophers are primarily motivated by the desire to understand, to seek the truth. And while it seems evident that most philosophers are at least partially motivated by curiosity and the urge toward greater understanding, it is also evident that there are other competing motivations that serve greatly to complicate this monocausal image of philosophical activity, including career advancement, sociality, prestige, financial security, ego-gratification, self-justification, revenge, pleasure, dominance, and control, motives which can never be entirely disentangled from the putatively pure love of wisdom. And even if philosophers were motivated primarily by the desire for truth, this image of thought is intimately bound up with the avoidance and rejection of error, the negative of truth which affirms their identity, in order to discover solutions to intractable problems. This image is exemplified in the rationalist mode of thought characteristic of the analytic tradition which tends to assume that, if ingenious enough logical arguments can be marshaled in the court of judgment, discrete positions or schools of thought defending "singular propositions arbitrarily detached from their context" will be able to triumph over their adversaries in a "puerile and artificial"[172] legislative vindication of a superior morality which assumes the identity of the Good and the True. This conception of philosophy as an either-or legislation of truth and morality, the *tertium non datur* of reductively virtuous truth and sinful falsity, which finds its peak expression in Cartesian "good sense or common sense,"[173] is a still-pervasive presupposition that all of the thinkers explicated in these pages have seen beyond to some extent and at various points, in both the reconciliation of opposites, which found its peak expression in the Hegelian dialectic, and in the more expansive, profound, and pluralist integration of difference, which recognizes the partial, contextual validity of all modes of thought that possess some efficacy in actuality.

Deleuze rejects this orthodox image of thought in his overturning of Platonism and his sustained denouncement of Hegel, in a revaluation of all values derived from Nietzsche, a critique directed against this classic mode's presuppositions and postulates. It is an attempt to do without images, a mode of thought which Deleuze recognizes is profoundly paradoxical, though we might see that such a rejection, like deconstruction, still participates in the very image of thought it seeks to reject. Even the obstinate assertion of paradox is itself an image of thought, the image of the transgressive mercurial, Promethean trickster, so that even if this rejection is partially erroneous, such denouncement cannot be finally dismissed because error "is an integral part of the work."[174] In a 1982 letter, Deleuze acknowledges that "Bergson has convincingly shown" that "images have an existence independently of us,"[175] emphasizing in *Matter and Memory* that images cannot ultimately be escaped, a recognition which Deleuze expresses when he writes that "true repetition takes place in imagination,"[176] so that the mode he is advocating takes images as its medium of activity, and Deleuze's denouncement of images in some parts of *Difference and Repetition* enacts a differentiating reversal which allows a novel, more liberated and creative conception of the imaginal to emerge elsewhere in the same text. Recognizing the necessity of Deleuze's paradoxical inconsistency as pushing thought to its limits in an intentional transgressive Dionysian madness that exceeds mere error may lead us to a shift of emphasis in which what is good in the tradition stretching from Plato to Hegel is retained, a conservation toward which Deleuze gestures, but which he inconsistently implements, while allowing for a further development of that mode of thought. This novel mode can be partially described as a discontinuous leap into an emergent domain that liberates thought from fixed images, requiring conceptions beyond existing categories, but also as a continuous development of the classic image of thought, retaining and building upon that image as an essential element in the thought of the future's constitution, which is ultimately grounded precisely in the problematic relationality of images.

The emergence of this novel mode of thought, the Nietzschean "creation of new values," is not primarily discerned in a linear developmental series, though it becomes generally more prevalent over historical time, but in the privileged moments that constitute the differential repetitions of this novel mode, which can be found, though often intermittently and inconsistently, in all of the texts discussed above. The horizontal temporality of efficient causation can be reconceived as a thread curving back upon itself in a knotty, decentered eternal return, and the points where this thread intersects with itself constitute vertical formal repetitions of a "forever new" mode of relation whose temporally successive affirmations trace a series of durations that leap across discontinuous intervals, embodied in the conceptual personae of privileged souls and the novel expressions they enact. The new values are thus carried increasingly into actuality, though this development is enacted through a nonlocal diachronic series that exceeds linear temporality, "even if a certain amount of empirical time was necessary for this to be recognised," for the novel mode progressively differentiated through transversal repetitions to become increasingly embraced and inhabited in historical time. This formal becoming exceeding linear temporality expresses "powers" that derive "from an unrecognised and unrecognisable *terra incognita*,"[177] which can be conceived as located just beyond the always-receding horizon of verbally and imaginally constructed discernibility, and which we encounter in actuality as figures that are engaged with not only intellectually and conceptually, but "in a range of affective tones: wonder, love, hatred, suffering."[178]

These affective encounters with imaginal potencies force us to think in new ways, to create novel concepts, a mode of relation which Deleuze describes as a "transcendental empiricism,"[179] an aesthetic, imaginal, and intuitive mode closely related to Spinozan intuition, Schellingian metaphysical empiricism, Jamesian radical empiricism, Bergson's intuitive method, what Stengers designates as Whiteheadian speculative empiricism, and the archetypal empiricisms of Jung and Hillman. Particularly associating transcendental empiricism with Bergson and Whitehead,[180] Deleuze describes this mode as discerning an integrated intermeshing of differential intensities complementary to the extensities susceptible to materialist and scientific modes of thought. Encompassing the modes which exceed logical rationality, this multivalent relationality is the experiential domain where creative, formal repetitions more profound than the mere habit of efficient causation take place, as repetition occurs in the affective, intuitive, aesthetic, and imaginal discernment, novel construction of, and immediate encounter with Ideas in their resonant multiplicity of signs, masks, and disguises. Transcendental empiricism enacts the paradoxical faculty which allows us to discern the indiscernible and to think the unthinkable beyond the current doxa by imaginally and affectively intimating series of events whose trajectories describe the potent becomings beyond the local and linear series of efficient causation. This mode of relation is transcendental because, although it allows process continually to transcend itself through the ingression of novel differentiations and integrations, this transcendence is an activity and not a location, as it does not discern "objects outside the world,"[181] but actualizes immanent virtual potentialities which reside nonlocally in the interstices of a conceptual and affective horizon, a domain of inexhaustible powers which have not yet been elicited through novel verbal or aesthetic constructions, the "other dimension"[182] of the eternal return which can be envisaged as orthogonal to the familiar degrees of spatiotemporal freedom.

In this transcendental domain, Logos is discovered not primarily in the "indefinite nominal regress"[183] of a propositional logic characteristic of written language, but in the imaginal "transcendent language"[184] characteristic of hieroglyphs, a figurative language of Ideas beyond the dualities of sense and nonsense, of subject and object, of affirmation and negation, which indicates "a transcendent limit,"[185] and which can only be constructively elicited through the differential repetitions of potencies at an always-receding horizon, syncategorematically carried to the nth power. The duality between the ego and the dynamisms which realize themselves through us, of which we are particular expressions in actuality, is overcome in a new Cogito, "a Cogito for a dissolved self,"[186] which recognizes that our individual self-conception is not an originary proposition, but a continually negotiated differential relation with the repeated potencies luring us toward further becomings. Ego enacts the "infinite regress" of "I think that I think that I think. . . ,"[187] asymptotically approaching the figure of the central, unified identity of "Ego = Ego"[188] embodied in the alchemical Sol and the Apollonian, so that we may shed the exclusivist monotheism of consciousness in the recognition that this solar ego enacts one potency among others and that "I is already an other,"[189] as Deleuze evokes Rimbaud. Deleuze writes that "the Gods are dead but they have died from laughing, on hearing one God claim to be the only one,"[190] and it is this overcoming of monotheistic consciousness, the binary identity of God and ego, that Deleuze and Guattari elaborated over the decades subsequent to *Difference and Repetition* in relation to schizophrenia, and which Hillman explicates in his evocation of a polytheistic psychology for which "pathologizing" is a primary method for bringing the potencies exceeding egoic consciousness into the solar light of conscious awareness. As Deleuze writes, "repetition is pathos and the philosophy of repetition is pathology,"[191] drawing out these intertwined personified figures from the nocturnal, subterranean unconscious through the imaginal, affective, and intuitive methods of ecstatic animism, tragic art, active imagination, and Deleuzoguattarian schizoanalysis. These methods often appear to the monocentric consciousness dominant in modernity as madness, though "this pagan world," as Deleuze observes in a 1978 text cowritten with Fanny Deleuze, "despite everything, remained alive and continued to live deep in us with all its strength."[192] Pathologizings serve to produce a "fractured I" which "constitutes the discovery of the transcendental,"[193] the polycentric domain of virtual Ideas circulating between I and other in a transformative eternal return leading toward an overcoming of the present mode of human existence in the Overman, for which "the gods of a religion, for example, Jupiter, Mars, Quirinus, incarnate elements and differential relations,"[194] as he writes in 1972.

This virtual domain can be conceived as a theater, a "mystical game"[195] in which the various potencies are actors wearing masks and disguises, dramatizing the relationality of Ideas, like Physis and Psyche, the proper names for the figures of nature and soul, through the individuating repetitions of narrative situations which exceed the abstract movement of concepts that Deleuze portrays as culminating in the Hegelian dialectic. It is these tragic and comic repetitions of scenarios that introduce novelty into history, and which always approach a "terrible esoteric knowledge,"[196] not as a mere representation of eternal Forms, but as the becoming-actual of virtual potentialities not only conceivable as abstract conceptual relations but, perhaps even more efficaciously, as transcendental relations of personified potencies – of gods, heroes, and demons. The infinite esoteric recognition that the tragic heroes are always striving toward, but which they never attain in its totality, permeates and impregnates the dramatic play of signifying powers, so that the egoic protagonist of human life is ceaselessly negotiating and enacting the dynamic interrelation of these transcendental potencies. Even modern art becomes "a theatre where nothing is fixed, a labyrinth without a thread" because "Ariadne has hung herself,"[197] a disturbing acknowledgment of the repression of these potencies in modernity, a death of the mythological dynamisms which has enabled us to overcome the conception of these powers as transcendent Forms or agencies.[198] Deleuze writes elsewhere, perhaps in a Jungian vein, that "Ariadne is the Anima, the Soul"[199] constituted in "affective movements,"[200] and the death of the Anima precedes a rebirth, toward which Deleuze gestures, into a novel mode of relation allowing a metamorphosis of the gods as transcendental potencies, dramatically enacted in the marriage of Ariadne and Dionysus, whose union is the eternal return producing the Overman. This mode recognizes that we can never escape the labyrinth of immanence, but that we can learn joyfully to navigate its contours, and even construct new passages by means of a transcendental empiricism.

In this labyrinthine theater, the masks, disguises, and costumes are not merely surface appearances of potencies already existing fully realized in some eternal transcendent realm, but "integral and constituent"[201] elements of their being, which is constituted in the nonlocal, nonlinear series of dynamic differential passages and variations between repetitions of their dramatic enactments rather than subsisting as divine static beings inhabiting a given ground. The being of their becoming is located in the immanent movement between privileged moments performing an infinite regress of masks not traceable to an originary, prior first term, an insight which Deleuze derives from Freud as well as Jung, though Freud subordinates repetition to the rationalizing opposition of Ego and Id, whereas Jungian archetypes allow for an opening to the multiplicity of difference despite, and perhaps even because of, Jung's sustained attention to the problem of opposites. However, even in Freud, this opening can be glimpsed in his rejection of his earlier hypothesis of real childhood events, usually in Oedipal relation with the parents, as the traumatic origin of neurosis in favor of the imaginal fantasy expressing the judgment of Thanatos, though always lured by Eros. The disguises and masks constituting the moments of repetition, "real series which coexist in relation to a virtual object,"[202] are repeated in the adult replaying of scenes from a remembered childhood, as well as in the reenactments of historical situations. These virtual objects are symbols and simulacra, so that reality can be conceived as a dramatic play of images in formal series operating transversally across linear successions. Like the arbitrary and radically variable letters that constitute words and sentences, they only acquire meaning through their infinite combinations, and the actual content emerges from their relationality enabled by the intertwined potentialities of the individual elements, a content which is nowhere to be found in these monadic elements, but only in their narrative construction from a differential "alphabet of what it means to think."[203]

Although Deleuze obliquely critiques Aristotle's conception of formal causes, this critique is not a mere rejection of formal causation, but a deepening of this causal mode partially derived from Spinoza and Leibniz, an expression of it in terms of difference and repetition rather than origin and participation. Deleuze does not merely reject this mode of thought any more than he merely rejects Plato, but he creates concepts and language to carry the trajectory of formal causation to a deeper register, as he does with the dialectic, in which the persistent problem of universals is reconceived as the shadow of a more profound differential repetition of Ideas. Deleuze's views on causation can, at first glance, appear ambiguous and even incoherent as, for instance, he sympathetically articulates Spinoza's rejection of final causes in some texts, but he expresses the teleological views of Leibniz, Hume, Kant, Bergson, and Whitehead with equal sympathy elsewhere. However, in what seems to be a fairly definitive summation of his views on causation, he suggests in *Foucault* that four of the folds of the outside which constitute the inside "are like the final or formal cause, the acting or material cause of subjectivity or interiority as a relation to oneself,"[204] four ways of constructing process. Deleuze is evidently forging toward a constructive mode of thought which neither affirms nor denies the ultimate truth of either of the opposed views of final or formal causation, but rather positions them, and causation in general, as useful fictions that elicit certain domains of process but inevitably neglect others. In a 1956 essay on Bergson, he writes that "finality, causality, possibility are always in relation to the thing once it is complete,"[205] and putatively opposed causal modes are integrated in the recognition that causes do not exist in reality independent of their enactment, but are rather retroactive narrative constructions with real but limited efficacy. This epistemological perspective can be extended to ontology, rendering epistemology practically indistinguishable from ontology, as knowing itself is a constructive elicitation of becoming from the potentialities and constraints of process.[206]

And again in *Foucault*, Deleuze similarly discusses an "immanent cause," which "is realized, integrated and distinguished by its effect,"[207] so that his entire career is characterized by the creation of novel conceptual modes for thinking about how things happen, constructions which unstiffen the dominance of the Aristotelian causal quaternity coercing either the affirmation or negation of each kind of causation. All four modes of causation can be understood as partially valid immanent expressions rather than forces that reside in a transcendent domain, verbal approximations for deeper potencies that can be envisaged just at an always-receding horizon of conception, where the rigid distinctions between material and formal causation, between efficient and final causation, become folded, fractally involuted, opening out onto one another through complexly intertwined circulations in more expansive topological domains.

Overturning and renewing formal causation in a more profound register, Deleuze derives the concept of the virtual from Bergson as the differential relations which become actual, though whereas the possible is opposed to the real, both virtuality and actuality are reality in different forms.[208] He returns to the virtual potencies again and again, describing them variously as Ideas, simulacra, phantasms, problems, questions, multiplicities, mythical figures, and gods, so that his critique of the Jungian archetypes seems to be responding to an earlier conception of those formal potentialities as psychological categories or universal essences rather than the more subtle conception expressed in Jung's late period (though Jung was inconsistent about their ontological status), and refined by many Jungians, perhaps most notably Hillman. This critique may also serve to produce a strategic distancing from Jung's work, as perhaps the majority of scholars who affirm the archetypal mode of thought are considered primarily to be Jungians, an association which tends to preclude allegiance to other schools of thought despite Jung's objections. Jung's authority is immense and overwhelming in certain circles, and it has often been difficult for theorists to engage affirmatively with his concepts without being designated as solely proponents of the Jungian school, as satellites in his orbit, rather than as original thinkers in their own right. The list of theorists who have managed to avoid this subsumption is relatively small, including (though certainly not limited to) Bachelard, Simondon, Gebser, Hillman, and perhaps most successfully, Deleuze, both with and without Guattari, as his engagement with Jungian concepts is so subtle and complex that it can easily be overlooked if one is not already immersed in Jungian thought.

However, there is a common recognition of numerous resonances between Jung and Deleuze among readers of one who subsequently read the other (intentional in the case of Deleuze), which may serve to lure both Jungians and Deleuzeans out of their often provincial enclosures to engage with both theorists in novel ways that serve to overcome the tendency toward dogmatic orthodoxy evident in relation to any great thinker, however heterodox their thought. One of the most profound resonances between them can be discerned in Deleuze's evocation of gods and mythical figures as expressions of the virtual potentialities around which he repetitiously circles, drawing out the nuances of these dynamisms under their multiple designations.

The introduction to Deleuze's 1955–56 seminar, *What Is Grounding?*, was not recorded, though we know that he initiated his first lecture by referring to "the foundational heroes of mythology,"[209] of whom Odysseus is the only one named. It is appropriate that the first moment of Deleuze's first seminar for which there is a record, and which Kerslake nominates "the ur-text for Deleuze's pre-1970s philosophy,"[210] is absent, indiscernible, only alluded to, so that this originary act must be imaginally extrapolated from the rest of the text, as this is precisely how he describes the figures of mythology in the extant notes. These figures are imaginal, symbolic variables for the "infinite task" with which mythology faces us, questions that are always pursued but never answered in their fully realized totality, just as saying "I love you"[211] is not a conclusion but a commitment to an open-ended devotion. The primary example Deleuze offers of an infinite task is that of the "superhumans," presumably of Greek mythology, drinking an unnamed beverage, presumably nectar or ambrosia, that produces their immortality and renders them gods (as in the assumption of Heracles discussed by Plotinus[212]), a transformative activity which he describes as "trying to live a symbol." The purpose of these infinite tasks is thus discerned in the ritual commitment to continually imbibing the symbolic, which lures privileged souls toward an always-pursued divine domain in a way that exceeds both the linearity characteristic of efficient causation and a reductive cynicism about this becoming-gods, which Deleuze describes as "anti-philosophical."[213] This symbolic, god-making beverage is encountered in affective experience, which only becomes the "natural ends"[214] of philosophy with the emergence of conceptual reason, though the gods and mythological heroes accessible to the imagination always lurk behind these ends in the "cosmic dimension"[215] of repetition and the eternal return. As we approach this ground, which Deleuze will later conceive as the ungrounding ground of difference, the sphinx poses an ambiguous question and the oracle makes an obscure prediction, evocative riddles and enunciations which lead one further toward what will later be described as an infinite regress, which must be brought "closer to the mythological notion"[216] in order to produce novel modes of understanding.

Deleuze spends several pages in *Difference and Repetition* discussing Plato's dialectical "method of division" in *The Statesman*, which the Eleatic Stranger claims is a method of distinguishing between truth and falsity, a claim that undermines itself by the unexpected introduction of a mythical mode of discourse into the progression of increasingly specific and minute binaries, complicating the oppositional mode with a mythical narrative concerning "the image of an ancient God."[217] The Stranger describes this myth as a "great story" involving an "element of play" in the reconfiguration of the heavens themselves, a cosmic reversal of the animating circulations enacted by this unnamed ancient god marking the transition from the age of Kronos to the age of Zeus. In this kairotic *enantiodromia*, the gods "let go in their turn the parts of the cosmos that belonged to their charge," effecting an epochal transformation which the Stranger describes as "the greatest and the most complete turning of all," suggesting that during such a reversal, "the greatest changes also occur for us who live within the universe,"[218] enacting a necessary destruction and renewal. Similarly, in the *Phaedrus*, when Socrates is discussing the different types of madness, prefiguring Deleuze's expression of the philosophy of difference as pathology, he finds it necessary to refer again to a myth, that of the repetitious "circulation of souls," in order to differentiate among the Ideas that they express. Deleuze rejects Aristotle's characterization of these moments in Plato as a mere regression to a mythical mode, as for Deleuze, the distinction between myth and dialectic in Plato dissolves in the "true method" which "overcomes this duality and integrates myth into the dialectic," making "myth an element of the dialectic itself." In his overturning of Plato, Deleuze finds the way beyond the oppositional dialectic, carried to its highest expression by Hegel, in an integration of a mythical, imaginal, polytheistic mode with dialectical logic. This "so-mysterious method"[219] is the eternal return, in which lots are distributed to each soul in the form of complex potencies, describable as the relations among gods, leaping between singularities, which it is each soul's "destiny"[220] differentially to elaborate over the course of their lives in the dramatic repetition of

Integrating Myth Into the Dialectic 245

dynamic enactments, though Deleuze teases apart this "story-repetition"[221] from its Platonic grounding in transcendent Forms to resituate the repetition of these narratively organized dynamisms in a relational, differential grounding describable in mythical terms.

In a strikingly similar conception, Jung writes that "the archetypes, like all numinous contents, are relatively autonomous, they cannot be integrated simply by rational means, but require a dialectical procedure" often expressed "in the form of mythological motifs."[222] Prolonging this integrating Jungian mythical dialectic, Deleuze suggests that it is never the gods themselves who are encountered, as "the gods are only the forms of recognition,"[223] an infinite regress of masks within masks which can only be asymptotically approached, and which we encounter as demons, angelic sign-bearers, and various other powers, in the imaginal, conceptual, and always-multiple expressions of transcendental Ideas, simulacra, problems, and questions. Even in *Kant's Critical Philosophy*, published a year after the mythologically permeated *Nietzsche and Philosophy* in 1963, Deleuze evokes Plato's recognition in the *Politics* of the provisional necessity of laws, and thus of the Kantian image of philosophy as legislation, as "only a 'second resort,'" a *locum tenens* "in a world deserted by the gods,"[224] so that Deleuze's primary impulse to replace "the system of judgment" with "something else," which he was still affirming in the late seventies, would partially be achieved through an ultimately complex and enigmatic renewal of "the system of the gods" explicated by Schelling.

In his radical revision of the Platonic conception of Ideas as eternal, essential Forms located in a static transcendent ground, Deleuze reformulates them as "demonic" and "divine" virtual, differential dynamisms which create their own space and time through the repetitious unfoldings of their relational potentialities in actuality, which are always other than themselves because there is no originary identity that they represent, as they are constituted in the very movement through the differential disguises which can only syncategorematically approach singularities at an always-receding horizon. The two forms of dialectic Deleuze enunciates are the "bare repetition"[225] of the Platonic Ideas as exterior, surface effects of the interior repetition clothed in an infinite regress of costumes and masks in the depths, though this more "profound repetition" is also prefigured in Plato, allowing for the self-deconstructive overturning of Platonism through concepts derived from Plato himself, who intimated his own overcoming in an "anti-Platonism at the heart of Platonism."[226]

Deleuze describes established concepts, whether Ideas and formal causation, archetypes and synchronicity, or even difference and repetition themselves (extrapolating to our time), as ultimately blocking the deeper form of repetition in their eventual reification of orthodoxy and the hegemony of general laws. It is the encounter with the other in the form of symbols and signs that allows for the creation of novel concepts through the devouring and reconstitution of orthodox categories in the mythical and imaginal domain of the interior, Dionysian depths accessible to an affective, intuitive, and aesthetic empiricism. This chaotic interior labyrinth is discernible in the dramatic play of singular potencies whose presence always exceeds the representation of laws and concepts that have already been constructed, allowing for the metamorphosis of these clear and distinct categories in a discordant symphonic integration of distinction and Dionysian obscurity, "the true tone of philosophy."[227]

This groundless virtual domain becomes accessible to a transcendental empiricism when the disparate multiplicity of Ideas is rendered visible through the pathological fracturing and initiatory dismemberment of the ego, so that Ideas are coexistent potencies finding different contrasting relational emphases in each actual occasion, which demand that they be thought. These differential potencies that think themselves in us, through us, and as us – others in constant negotiation with our individual identities, themselves constituting our individuality – find expression in all domains across orders, so that the elements which form an expression in actuality of one Idea, quantum discontinuity for example, are repetitions of a more expansive order, as in punctuated evolutionary saltations, a reiteration across scale discussed by Erwin Schrodinger.[228] Ideas are unconscious, residing in a potential domain that always exceeds consciousness, and they are complexly animated in all of the faculties, not only of reason and understanding, but of imagination, fantasy, sensibility, and sociability, which must be carried to their transcendental limits in a "discordant harmony."[229] While conceptual thought can serve to illuminate the unconscious virtual domain of Ideas through the discernment of their particular repetitions and their various modes of expression, the Ideas always exceed any particular conceptual formulation, so that the imagination is required in order to envisage these singular potencies in their full multiplicity across orders, "guiding our bodies and inspiring our souls, grasping the unity of mind and nature."[230]

Whereas the clear distinction between "the thing itself"[231] and simulacra is primary in Platonism, Deleuze's novel conception of Ideas is closely related to a reappropriation of simulacra and phantasms, derived from certain moments in Plato himself, as the repetition internal to the symbol. The eternal return of potentialities is constituted in an infinite regress of copies of copies without origin or ground, caves opening into other caves, a dynamic, decentered, tortuously revolving spiral expressible in mythical terms rather than a static monocentric circulation, a conversion which destroys the representational identity of the gods, but which imagines their becomings in differential relationality. The things themselves are simulacra, so that the clear and distinct difference between reality as original model and experience as representational image is obscured and dissolved in the recognition that there is no "'beyond' of the world"[232] outside the immanent, an insight that Deleuze, somewhat ironically, discerns in Hippolyte's work on Hegel in 1954. There are only virtual dynamisms at an always-receding transcendental horizon, in relation to whose potentiality is constructed the images that constitute process, including space, time, and consciousness, a recognition that shifts agency from a projected transcendent domain to the constant negotiation between individual subjects and virtual potencies. Thus, the pragmatic vehicle, which was transformed into a rocket blasting orthogonally into space, becomes an interstellar or transdimensional vessel rather than a structure based on solid ground, a vehicle for which no direction is down, for which the static three dimensionality presupposed by conventional directionality is problematized. In Platonism, the simulacra and phantasms are associated with the Sophist, the devilish enemy who must be defeated in order to ground the Ideas. But Deleuze hears the chaotic "infernal racket"[233] of the Sophists and Heraclitus beneath the cosmos of Plato, so that the distinction between the grounding clarity of Socrates and the ungrounding relativism of the Sophists is obscured, allowing a novel mode to gleam through this fracture in identity, to be discovered in the dissolution of this dubious opposition, for which the ungrounding itself becomes a deeper kind of relational ground that is always other than itself. The opposition between Apollonian cosmos and Dionysian chaos is dissolved in a "chaosmos,"[234] a portmanteau that Jung prefigures when he writes that "in all chaos there is a cosmos, in all disorder a secret order."[235]

A primary mode in which the Ideas can be discerned is in persistent problems and questions, not only encountered in the opposition between two conflicting demands, but in incommensurable modes of thought that seem to talk past one another, to work at cross purposes, or to be entangled in byzantine knots. Problems are the positive elements that impel the creative repetition of dramatic narratives in order to elaborate and work through the differences among the actors in any particular scenario, so that problematic Ideas are the motive factors of becoming, as without problems and questions, the world would be a static unity requiring no response and thus no activity. In *Difference and Repetition*, Deleuze returns to the infinite task posed by the mythical and the oracular discussed over a decade earlier in *What Is Grounding?*. The oracle's ambiguous response to a question is itself problematic, prefiguring the dialectical "art of problems and questions"[236] traced from Plato's initiatory openness to its differentiating limitation in the oppositional negative of Hegel, and reimagined by Deleuze in resonance with Schelling, Nietzsche, and Jung, who discerns that the questions posed by the unconscious can express themselves as pathology and madness, which do not come without the pathos of suffering, but which lead through the opening of an "ontological 'fold'"[237] in the fractured ego to the gods.

Deleuze implicitly refers to the passages on madness in the *Phaedrus*, where Socrates affirms that "some of our greatest blessings come from madness, when it is granted to us as a divine gift" and that "god-given madness is better than human sanity," a Dionysian mode of relation beyond mere truth and error that Deleuze associates especially with the pre-Socratics.[238] As Deleuze suggests, it is the renewal of this pre-Socratic and Platonic insight that allowed Jung to exceed the binarity dominant in Western thought to discover a deeper differen*c*iation (as the complement to differen*t*iation), which Deleuze renders as synonymous with integration, a syncategorematic engagement with virtual questions, problems, and tasks for which each actual answer and solution is never a final attainment of resolution, perfection, and closure, but a provisional liberation into new domains in the form of novel symbolic, paradoxical, problematic fields. These problematic potencies awaken the "superior exercise"[239] of the faculties, and serve as preconditions for the expansion of knowledge through the contemplative process of learning by discerning the infinite series of resonant masks and disguises luring thought toward eternally displaced divine virtual objects at a transcendental horizon.

Deleuze thus shifts the focus away from solutions and answers to problems and questions in the concept of integral differenciation, as solutions are always contained implicitly in the formulation of the problem, whether mathematical, scientific, or philosophical and, as he writes in 1953, "a philosophical theory is an elaborately developed question, and nothing else."[240] The more profound the problematic formulation, the more profound the solution that necessarily results from it, forming the precondition for the formulation of deeper problems opening into more expansive affective and conceptual domains,[241] so that "each age says everything it can according to the conditions laid down for its statements,"[242] and when an age has had its say, it must cede to the deeper problems of a subsequent age. The calculus is a primary example of this intimate interrelation of problems and solutions for the modern, as it allowed ancient problems to be posed in novel ways, which were the precondition for their solutions. As long as problems are formulated in terms of truth and falsity, of binary opposition, their solutions can only take the form of a shallow affirmation of one binary option as true and the negation of the other as mere error. Hegel's innovation, derived from the tradition initiated by Heraclitus and Plato, which Deleuze intermittently appreciates even as he denounces and overturns it, is that problematic conflicts tend to produce an emergent unity more profound than the opposition, so that the question becomes how the two opposed sides can both be partial aspects of a more complete and profound truth. Deleuze's primary innovation on this particular conceptual complex, a novel conception of dialectic, is to ask who the singular personified potencies are behind problems, to ask which transcendental Ideas, often imagined as mythological gods and heroes, are playing out their problematic differences in more topologically complex dramatizations, for which oppositional conflict is only one kind of relation among others. He enacts a mode that integrates the conceptual dialectic, refined over millennia, with the imaginal, intuitive, and affective empiricism characteristic of animism, Greek tragedy, alchemical opus, active imagination, and schizoanalysis, which have formed a multiple countervalent tradition to the dominant philosophical trajectories, often reviving pre-dialectical modes of relation. The resonant integration of these complementary trajectories leads to a deeper form of dialectic for which the repetition of problems and questions indicates an always-receding origin and horizon, the virtual, indiscernible loci of the thoroughly reimagined formal and final causes which take a multiplicity of forms in singularities, Ideas, simulacra, and gods.

In Deleuze's critique of the Hegelian negative, he asserts that "there is no Idea of the negative,"[243] that the negative is an illusory shadow of problematic difference, and that "death cannot be reduced to negation."[244] But it may perhaps be recognized that the negative shadow is also a god, precisely one face of the God who has been exclusively elevated in monotheism, the father-god of weighty judgment, of totalitarian unification and control, of hierarchical binarity, of static eternal life, which finds identity in its opposition with the Devil, an oppositional identity prolonged in all of the binary privilegings of a rationalism which has reached its peak expression in modernity: mind and body, mind and world, male and female, white and black, straight and gay, good and evil, heaven and hell, One and many, God and ego, conscious and unconscious. As discussed in relation to Schelling, this biblical God, whose name Elohim is derived from the Phoenician god El, is an epochal development of none other than the Kronos of Greek mythology, with whom the ancient Greeks associated El, and his Roman counterpart in Saturn. Deleuze seems to be enacting a transitional reversal in his rejection of the Idea of the negative, affirming all potencies except for the one that has been dominant in the exclusivist monotheistic epoch which seems to be nearing its death, and which he has done as much as anyone to usher toward its end.

He is partially right, in that Kronos is not the only power associated with death, embodying Derrida's final closure of the current epoch, as Dionysus also correlates with death in a different register, a creative, transformative death and dismemberment always intimately related to a rebirth into novel domains, a death-rebirth complex strangely intertwined, along with the transcendent centrality of Apollo, with the Hebrew God in the Christ of the New Testament. Deleuze thus enacts the death of the dominance of the saturnine negative itself, issuing into the Dionysian rebirth of the gods in all their multiplicity (rather than Christ in totalizing union with Elohim), including El-Kronos-Saturn as one actor in a larger relational drama instead of as the totalitarian dictator of a universal metaphysical regime grounded in transcendence. Becoming cannot be reduced to the oppositional conflict of negative and identity, but the deeper form of the dialectic, which integrates the conceptual dialectic with mythical potencies, must ultimately recognize that the negative is also a god, but not the only one, and thus that the binaries of rational thought, including birth and death, as well as male and female, become problematic elements of the death-and-rebirth ordeal imagined, for instance, in the hermaphroditic figure of the alchemical Mercurius.[245] After the inversion and overturning that Deleuze enacts, with the intensity "seen from below" as negative reimagined as affirmative

Integrating Myth Into the Dialectic 251

difference seen from "on high,"[246] perhaps we can affirm even the difference at the heart of this oppositional overturning so that both the bottom-up and top-down perspectives can be understood as containing partial validity, as legitimately expressing different aspects of becoming.

Deleuze derives the term multiplicity from Bergson and Husserl, and ultimately from Riemannian geometry, designating topological relations of variables or coordinates in a multidimensional phase space, and not merely the variety of the many, so that both the many and the one can be conceived as potent multiplicities.[247] This mode of description emphasizes the relational quality of the Ideas as problematic complexes expressing potencies and their nonlocal relations rather than static essences. They are plural networks of virtual interconnection, both mathematical and metaphysical, that form the differential potentialities and constraints from which the actuality of lived experience in a particular spatiotemporal construction is extracted through negotiation with these complex n-dimensional dynamisms. Multiplicity is the stage on which the drama of repetition takes place, though this stage does not preexist the actors or their roles, but is constituted in the reciprocal relationality of the roles themselves, for which opposition is one mode of topological relation among others, some of which correlate with dynamic structures in more expansive degrees of freedom than the three spatial dimensions which we can easily visualize without the assistance of complex mathematics, and even in fractal dimensions. These differential multiplicities are incarnated through a Whiteheadian "adventure of Ideas"[248] in mathematical, physical, psychological, and sociological expressions, correlated via "internal resonances,"[249] a term derived from Simondon,[250] which are real expressions of virtual potentialities in disparate actualities. These resonant expressions can be apprehended through a transcendental empiricism, which Deleuze describes not only as a Leibnizian *mathesis universalis*, but also as a "universal physics, universal psychology, and universal sociology,"[251] all of which designate the domains of efficacy for faculties that discern actual expressions of virtual multiplicities across heterogenous orders, Ideas which can be recognized as gods as much as in the series of the calculus. The expression of Ideas requires a philosophical style that does not merely unite the Apollonian and the Dionysian, but continually translates between the disparate languages of clear, distinct mathematical harmony and chaotic, discordant imaginal potency.

Like the multiple designations for Ideas, which emphasize different aspects of these virtual potencies, Deleuze offers four different, synonymous terms for the mode of becoming resonant with the integral calculus: integrate, differen*c*iate, solve, and actualize. Whereas differen*t*iation is the analytic determination of disparate problematic potentialities, integral differen*c*iation expresses those differentiated potencies through local solutions that combine the singular dynamisms into actual occurrences, which not only occur in time, but condition the temporal modes in which events occur, and which find a more expansive coordination in a global integration, "the changing totality of Ideas,"[252] differentiating powers in order "to constitute functional totalities or totalities that are not given in nature,"[253] as Deleuze writes in 1953. The infinitesimal from which the integral calculus syncategorematically constructs curves is an interior genetic Idea which "overcomes the duality of concept and intuition,"[254] rather than an exterior schematic rule.

The differential potencies never attain complete, final integration in actuality, as Ideas always exist partially as potential and partially as actual, constituted in the iterative circulation between these two domains of reality, a progressive, subtly teleological movement which enacts the repetition of variety through discordant harmony. Whereas for the Newtonian version of the calculus, the integral is merely the inverse of the differential, for the Leibnizian infinitesimal calculus, integration is the activity through which the series of differentiated potencies are expressed in actuality, though Deleuze evidently asserts the synonymity of differen*c*iation and integration in order to emphasize that the solutions expressed by integration are implicitly contained in the differential problematic formulations. The activities of differen*t*iation and differen*c*iation, combined in the process of "different/ciation,"[255] are as intimately connected as the two faces of Janus, the problems of differentiation forming the conditions for the novel creative solutions of integration, which in turn form the novel conditions for more expansive and profound problematic differential formulations in deeper dimensions, as well as their integral solutions. This decentered spiral movement enacts the ingression of novelty from potentiality into actuality, opening out into novel frontiers of mathematical-metaphysical activity, including set theory and fractal geometry, which was being discovered by Mandelbrot at the same moment Deleuze was writing *Difference and Repetition* in the late sixties, and which he would later explore in *The Fold*, and especially with Guattari in *What Is Philosophy?*. Differenciation leads beyond the solely mathematical inflection of integration to the deeper form of the dialectic, whose problems are preconditions for actual solutions not only in mathematics, but also in physics, biology, psychology, and sociology.

The physical and biological orders are constituted in multiplicities of local integrations, which themselves are globally integrated in the total event of the relation of an organism with its internal and external milieus. This resonant series of increasingly expansive and intensive integrations "pushes the object or living being to its own limits" in order to create novel modes of relation, enacting a dramatic "staging at several levels" of potencies, so that "dramatisation is the differenciation of differenciation,"[256] the differentiating global integration of local integrations through the aesthetic narrative enactment of divine "primordial relations"[257] performing the dialectical interplay of species, individuals, organs, and particles. Two decades later, Deleuze writes that "progressive integrations" are "initially local and then become or tend to become global, aligning, homogenizing, and summarizing relations between forces,"[258] so that the process of integration teleologically tends toward the increasing interiorization of contrasting differential dynamisms, which generates an increase in the intensity of organized activity, and thus can potentially actualize a progressive liberation into increasingly expansive degrees of freedom.

Psychologically, the Freudian Id, or the Dionysian unconscious, is populated by embryonic local egos, singular dynamisms integrated from a pre-individual field of differential intensities. The first task of the infant is to construct from this virtual field the object of the mother, for example, in relation to the condensed internal object of the individual self which, in an evidently dialectical process that circulates between the two poles, allows for the initial differentiation of self from other, but which becomes problematic when the ego forged from this binary relation grows too dominant in the internal milieu, repressing the dreaming multiplicity from which the ego is condensed and extracted. The plurality of voices repressed in the totalizing constitution of the global ego expresses the virtual potencies which must be differentiated and integrated in a more democratic multiplicity, by means of the Cogito for a dissolved self, in order for the gods to whom Jung returned in his ambiguous rebellion against Freudian monotheism, a project carried forward and rendered even more complex and subtle by Deleuze, to find actualization in a novel integral Self. This more expansively individuated global integration renders the ego as a first among equals rather than as a totalitarian dictator who, like Kronos, perpetually devours his progeny.

As long as individuality is constructed as an opposition of self and other, the projected virtual objects cannot be integrated, always generating a lack, so that a polycentric consciousness is required to overcome the binary construction of ego and object, as "individuation is what responds to the question 'Who?'"[259]: who are the potencies of the Dionysian unconscious that speak within us and through us, that constitute our complex individuality in the interstices of the totalitarian ego?[260] Deleuze writes in 1983 that "'Who' is always Dionysus, an aspect or a mask of Dionysus,"[261] and thus "I is an other"[262] expresses both a differentiation and an integration, performing the individuation of the Self – resonant with the Jungian conception of these terms – within whom the virtual others can subsist as other, and who is constituted entirely from the narrative relations of a cast of characters, none of whom is the putatively one true self (mirroring a one true God). Rather, the Self emerges from the dramatic relationality of the actors expressing multiplicities, constituted in "forces and wills" as much as in ontologically ambiguous persons because, "at the most profound level of subjectivity, there is not an ego but rather a singular composition,"[263] and these singularly composed cosmic forces resonate with physical and biological Ideas through an "indi-drama-different/ciation"[264] that integrates the disparate valences of integration expressed by the concepts of individuation, dramatization, and differenciation.

These dynamics are also operative in the order accessible to sociology, in which society is constituted in a multiplicity of imbricated differential relations, not only in terms of relational identities associated with race, gender, sexuality, age, class, religion, and ability, but in the complex negotiations of disparate social, political, juridical, ideological, and economic forces which actualize the Ideas also expressed on the scales accessible to physics, biology, and psychology. Deleuze's critique of the binarity of the Hegelian dialectic also applies to the Marxist class struggle, but this critique also displays similar limitations to the critique of Hegel.[265] Actual labor is locally integrated from the differentiated multiplicity of intertwining potencies that constitute the constantly shifting machinic flows of discourse, desire, and material organization, which is then globally integrated within capitalist or communist societies, which in turn find a literally global integration formed from contrasting differential elements, allowing for the emergence of novel problematic tensions, disparities, and questions which demand novel integrations beyond existing political and economic categories. These differentiating societal integrations progressively lure the faculty of sociability toward its transcendental objects, both in the structure, discipline, punishment, and security of the infinite regression of masks figured by Kronos and his "societies of control,"[266] but also in the Promethean urge toward freedom through the revolutionary transgression of boundaries, which can be creative and liberating, but also disruptive and shattering. And these are just two of the figures in a profuse cast of characters that populate the mythoi to which Deleuze returns again and again in the figures of Dionysus, Apollo, Ariadne, Kronos, Zeus, Athena, Aphrodite, Ares, Artemis, Diana, Attis, Osiris, Isis, Aion, Kairos, Chronos, Mnemosyne, Oedipus, Prometheus, Psyche, Eros, Heracles, Omphale, Odysseus, Sisyphus, Narcissus, Tantalus, and Actaeon, so that the Oedipal dialectic of the saturnine father-judge and the Promethean rebel-son (always involved with the maternal) is but one complex among numerous others that demand actual expression across orders.

Deleuze recognizes the integration of series of mythological potencies through a novel form of dialectic resonant with the Leibnizian calculus as Schelling's primary innovation, which allowed philosophy to go beyond Hegel. And it is in the Neoplatonic solution to the problem of the *Phaedrus*, in which souls eternally circulate in order to differentiate each series of complex potentiality, that Deleuze discerns an opening from a dialectic of opposition and identity to a deeper dialectic of repetition and difference, so that the figure of Zeus, for example, is encountered in the differential movement through a series of expressions of this expansive, regal potency by means of a "method of exhaustion" which is a direct precursor to the calculus. This differentiation of divine powers, of which Deleuze not only mentions Zeus in this instance, but also Aphrodite, Ares, Apollo, and Athena, prepares these dynamisms for integral differenciation in a mythical dialectic incarnated through dramatic narrative relations. This narrative relationality is a discordant harmony in which each of the faculties that apprehends each virtual potency – the erotic desire for connection characteristic of the "God of love" and the wrathful concentration of directed activity characteristic of the "God of anger"[267] – finds a broader domain of integration. The discordant relations of these potencies are contained within a differenciating narrative harmony for which disparate, and often incommensurable, powers are conceived in progressively unfolding dramatic relations, each human faculty pursuing its divine virtual object by means of a series of durational enactments of its relation to other potencies in a process of "creative actualisation,"[268] which transforms these irreducible dynamisms through the "hidden art"[269] of aesthetic narrative discernment within or below the concept.

The process of dramatic creation is expressed in all domains across scale, including in the writing of philosophy itself, which Deleuze suggests should be a mysterious fiction, like the infinitesimal, in which the philosophical detective ruminates on a series of clues whose ideal interrelation they intuitively grasp, but through which they must circulate via novel linguistic permutations in order to attain a moment of resolution in which the various threads are woven together. This local integration can be further integrated with other local integrations in order to express conceptual relations which have not yet been verbally constructed in actuality. These integrations are the solutions to the old problems, the relational system of problematic elements carried to its inevitable dissolution, so that more profound problems can reveal themselves and demand novel creative integrations, the contemplative self integrating nonlocal series in more expansive and complexly differentiated zones of activity. In its highest form, philosophy is not merely the reproduction of answers already discovered, or the deduction of conclusions from given premises, but the seduction of learning which occurs through a sustained encounter with the infinite task posed by the other, with that which exceeds the domain of the philosopher's secure conceptual possession. Writing philosophy takes place at a horizon of achieved knowledge, verbally spiraling in upon interstitial Ideas to express them in novel ways that allow for a decentering circulation of the total event constituted in the relation of writer and reader, an iterative expansion of the always-receding horizon. After students have made their way through textbooks filled with the settled knowledge of their cultural epoch, they learn with philosophers by thinking with them as they learn through the writing, itself impelled by the philosophers' own reading, accompanying them on the pioneering exploration of novel domains, though truly philosophical texts can never be fully tamed but, like Heraclitus or Plato, remain pathways luring us outward toward infinitely expansive bright vistas and inward into tortuously labyrinthine dark forests. Philosophy is not a mere transmission of knowledge, but an adventure of Ideas that the reader and writer must continually embark upon together in the encounter with problems and questions, with signs and symbols, with masks and disguises that always lure us onward.

This adventure occurs not only in continuous progress, but in discontinuous leaps. Like Bergson's image of learning to swim, which Deleuze evokes in relation to Leibniz's description of the sea as a "problematic field,"[270] differential relations steadily accumulate in complexly intertwining series until an integral solution suddenly emerges and the person standing on the shore trying to learn to swim by summing together an always-unattainable series of infinitesimal movements crystallizes the Ideas of the problematic unconscious in a unified will that risks a leap into the novel domain, crossing a paradoxically uncrossable threshold where the old problem of how to swim is solved by the act of swimming itself. But this integrating leap creates the precondition for the more profound problems of what to do, and of where to go, once one has entered into the novel domain. Now that the learner has learned to swim, they must decide what kind of swimmer they want to be: a playful splasher, a serious competitor, a placid exerciser, a deep-sea diver exploring ever-new domains, or even an observer on the beach who watches the swimmers with the knowledge that they too once swam. These are choices that occur not only in the individuation of a single philosopher who must negotiate their relation to a novel medium, but in the collective relation to any new domain. In order to enter a qualitatively novel phase of its ingression, a culture must decide collectively to make the transition, an imaginal leap which, as Stengers describes in relation to James and Whitehead, requires the collective "to trust that something will come to meet it."[271] For Deleuze, this "something" is expressible as the gods, and it is the encounters with these problematic potencies and the different languages they speak which fractures, dismembers, and dissolves us in an initiatory ordeal that enacts "the very transformation of our body and our language,"[272] allowing novel affective and conceptual integrations to emerge through our sacrifice.

A primary locus of the emergence of a novel image of thought is in the collective construction of time, so that the overcoming of the opposition of temporality and non-temporality, of historical and eternal, of immanent and transcendent, is central to Deleuze's project, an untimely philosophy which recognizes that the duality of particular empirical actualities and universal transcendent Forms can be overcome in a more complex conception of time resonant not only with Bergsonian duration, but with Jungian synchronicity. The durations which are separated along a linear timeline by a first synthesis of time, and rendered as real movement by a second synthesis of time, are arranged by the third synthesis of time, the repetition of the eternal return, in a nonlocal series, strangely looping back upon itself to approach the Ideas which imaginally unfold from "an ancient mythical present"[273] constituted in eternally receding simulacra. Time in all its complexly intertwined multivalence is constructively coerced from this deeper differential repetition rather than repetition occurring in a preexisting time. The most profound third synthesis of time is constituted in an internal resonance of privileged moments, whose totality can only be approached through a symbolic mode of conception, expressed in the dramatic mythological acts from which time is elicited through differenciation, the integration of different enactments of the narrative relations of potencies. Nietzsche never fully expressed this final synthesis, this "moment of the revelation" of the Overman, in its actuality, but only evoked it, deferring the full articulation of the eternal return, correlated with the dramatic death and transformative fracturing of Zarathustra's egoic identity, to "a future work"[274] which Nietzsche never wrote, but toward which he cleared a path, creating the precondition for Deleuze to bring this mode of thought further into actuality.

The decentered temporal circulation of the eternal return requires not merely a reconciliation of the figures on the two sides of a mirror – though this passage through the looking glass is necessary at an earlier stage of individuation – but a shattering of the mirror of dualism, in which the "narcissistic ego"[275] discerns God in its own image along one axis of reflection. The fractured I is constituted in a chaotic multiplicity of mirroring fragments reflecting one another in an always-shifting lattice of potent rays tracing lines of flight into the infinite distance, for which the shadowy voids between the photonic trajectories form the negative space required for structure, not primarily as simple, oppositional negation, but as more topologically complex contrasts in n-dimensional manifolds. It is the constructive elicitation of this multiplicity, constituted in the relationality of potencies more profound than a linear temporal succession, the ungrounding relational field from which linear temporality is extracted, that produces "the totality of the series and the final end of time,"[276] the teleologically lured global integration of this system of series of stages enacting the differenciation of dynamisms which can be syncategorematically approached but never finally attained at an always-receding virtual horizon.

At this univocal horizon of the future, formal potentiality becomes so extreme and intensive that it infinitely recedes toward formlessness, integrating both the differentiated affirmation and negation of formal and final causation, enacting a discordant harmonization of the straight line of linear temporality and efficient causation with its disappearance, figured as a curve beyond the horizon into an always-indiscernible domain exceeding formality and formlessness, in the more expansive dimension of the eternal return's groundless, decentered circulation. This novel conception integrates the facilely opposed temporal conceptions differentiated through historically correlated stages, so that the ancient cyclical time of the unconscious past and the modern linear time of the egoic present are subsumed in the univocal "thousand-voiced"[277] integrality of the individuated future Overman, perhaps echoing the thousand-named alchemical arcane substance. The eternal return revolves in a decentered spiral, for which the astronomical circulations of the planets around a fixed center imagined by the ancients can be reconceived as tracing complexly intertwining curves around a Sun hurtling along its own line of flight relative to far vaster cosmic configurations, forming ideal relations across orders with the differentiating repetition of "intensive intentionalities,"[278] the dramatization of divine potencies.

Ideal relations of material and formal becomings enacting a multiplicity of dynamisms across orders of organization resonate with the "spiritual life" of an individual in the form of "destiny,"[279] which operates not through the deterministic succession of discrete durations characteristic of efficient causation or the fatal ends of radical finalism, but through the nonlocal narrative resonance, repetition, and echo of signs and roles diachronically telescoping privileged moments when singular potencies are synchronically constellated. The individual's freedom, their "choice of existence,"[280] thus resides in a Spinozan "freedom of mind," choosing at which orders to express dynamic complexes, Deleuze evoking "choosing" as "the Promethean sin *par excellence*."[281] In this way, an individual whose destiny is involved with a particular complex, like the Oedipal, can express this narrative relation in a literal family drama, but also on the world-historic stage as a Promethean philosopher like Deleuze rebelling against a patriarchal precursor like Hegel, who was himself once a revolutionary philosopher, or against the Oedipal itself, dramatizing "the same story, but at different levels."[282] Deleuze chose the highest expression of this particular complex, carrying it toward the limit of "what a body can do,"[283] though the destiny of each life is constituted in a multiplicity of complexes projectively elicited from the groundless "heterogeneous dimension"[284] of differential relations between the mythological figures that pervade Deleuze's thought: Apollonian ordered centrality; the nurturing relationality of Apollo's twin sister, Artemis; the Hermetic or Mercurial transductive swiftness of thought; the love, desire, and attraction of Aphrodite and Eros; the directed, penetrating wrath of Ares; the regal expansiveness and inflation of Zeus; the contractive judgment and negation of Kronos; the revolutionary liberation and transgressive discontinuity of Prometheus; the Narcissistic Ego-God complex and its imaginal dissolution; the transformative Dionysian death and rebirth; and many others. These mythologically figured problematic dynamisms coexist at a transcendental horizon, demanding integral actualization within the more constrained domains of the particular spatiotemporal constructions characteristic of our cosmic epoch, though the full range of their potential relations is not exhausted by the differentiations and integrations across scale that have occurred in actuality.

And as a potent complex is enacted by an individual at different orders of expression in internally resonant moments separated on a linear timeline, so that Deleuze can perform an Oedipal relation to his father as a young man, but become the embodiment (with Guattari) of the anti-Oedipal in middle age, so can two or more different individuals enact a particular role in which "one life may replay another at a different level."[285] The role Deleuze plays as a defining conceptual persona of a philosophical era thus constitutes a differential repetition of the role enacted by Hegel, the same melody played in a different style and with different lyrics by different incarnations of "the already-Overman."[286] This repetition is not the habitual, bare repetition of the same, which is merely an effect, but the animating eternal return which causes novelty to emerge in the theater of linear history, with Luther enacting a novel iteration of the role performed by Paul, and the French Revolution reenacting the founding of the Roman Republic on a more expansively liberated order of activity. The temporally later repetitions are not merely analogous to an originary event, but rather all repetitions recede infinitely through a series of masks toward a "dark" or "obscure precursor."[287] These philosophical, religious, or political revolutionaries are affectively lured by the same virtual Ideas, often with explicit knowledge that they are reenacting the narrative of a past figure in novel historical conditions as derivatives in a nonlocal series, producing the future through a metamorphosis of those conditions by creating something radically new, something that had not yet been actually existent, in "an eternally excentric circle"[288] enacting the progressive movement of an always-indiscernible polycentric singularity and cosmic horizon woven together through a string theory of narrative threads.[289] And this is the infinite task we undertake as philosophers: differentially to repeat, and to integrate through novel forms of language, the repetitions enacted by philosophical precursors in an eternal retelling of the world-constituting narrative leading back in a complexly interwoven and resonant system of transversal series not to an originary philosopher, but to the obscure precursor, the infinite regress of virtual dynamisms coexisting in a "divine game"[290] whose rules we invent as we play by means of the questions we ask, composed in the book of the chaosmos where we write the dreams of the gods.[291]

## Notes

1  See scholar.google.com.
2  Dosse, *Intersecting*, 306.
3  Žižek, *Organs*, xxi.
4  Deleuze, *Difference*, 227.
5  Deleuze scholars cannot even agree whether it should be spelled "Deleuzean" or "Deleuzian."
6  Deleuze, *Negotiations*, 7.
7  Deleuze, *Two*, 63.
8  Deleuze, *Negotiations*, 7.
9  Deleuze, *Cinema 2*, 257.
10 Deleuze, *Two*, 300.
11 Deleuze, *Two*, 159.
12 May, *Deleuze*, 26.
13 Deleuze, *Difference*, xxi.
14 Deleuze, *Essays*, v.
15 Deleuze, *Cinema 2*, 141.
16 Deleuze and Parnet, *Dialogues*, 70; May, *Deleuze*, 15.
17 See Deleuze, "Sur Spinoza."
18 Butler, *Subjects*, 176, 183–4.
19 Deleuze, *Grounding?* 166.
20 Culp, *Dark*, 2.
21 Somers-Hall, *Hegel, Deleuze*, 1, 4.
22 Deleuze and Parnet, *Dialogues*, 57–8.
23 Wahl, "Review."
24 Cisney, *Deleuze*, 93–4.
25 Malabou, "Wolves?" 114.
26 Malabou, "Wolves?" 117.
27 Žižek, *Organs*, x.
28 Malabou, "Wolves?" 120.
29 Malabou, "Wolves?" 136.
30 Malabou, "Wolves?" 121.
31 Malabou, "Wolves?" 130.
32 Deleuze, *Difference*, 50.
33 Deleuze, *Difference*, 269.
34 Deleuze, *Difference*, xix.
35 Deleuze, *Difference*, 2.
36 Cole, *Theory*, 158–9.

37 Deleuze and Guattari, *Thousand*, 22–3. See Jameson, "Marxism," 1.
38 Deleuze, *Foucault*, 32.
39 Deleuze, *Cinema 2*, 21.
40 Deleuze, *Difference*, xix.
41 Deleuze, *Difference*, 30–2.
42 Deleuze, *Difference*, xv.
43 Deleuze, *Difference*, 52, 268.
44 Hegel, *Logic*, 78.
45 Deleuze and Guattari, *Anti-Oedipus*, 50, 92–3.
46 Dosse, *Intersecting*, 214.
47 Deleuze, *Desert*, 192.
48 Deleuze, *Kafka*, 10.
49 Deleuze, *Letters*, 227–8.
50 Deleuze, *Two*, 308–9.
51 Deleuze, *Kafka*, 14.
52 Deleuze, *Two*, 124.
53 Deleuze and Guattari, *Philosophy?* 85–6.
54 Beckman, *Deleuze*, 8. See also Hoinski, *Humanlife*.
55 Deleuze, *Empiricism*, 107.
56 Deleuze, *Two*, 193.
57 Deleuze, *Grounding?* 58.
58 Deleuze, *Essays*, 47.
59 Žižek, *Organs*, 48.
60 Dosse, *Intersecting*, 89.
61 Deleuze, *Kafka*, 12.
62 Deleuze, *Two*, 137.
63 Deleuze, *L'Abécédaire*, 32.
64 Deleuze, *Cinema 2*, 167.
65 Deleuze, *L'Abécédaire*, 59.
66 Deleuze, *Essays*, 52, 135.
67 Dosse, *Intersecting*, 88–9.
68 Deleuze, *Difference*, xviii.
69 Hippolyte, *Logic*, 195.
70 Dosse, *Intersecting*, 119–20; Dosse, *Letters*, 197.
71 Deleuze, *Desert*, 53.
72 Deleuze, *Two*, 132.
73 Winckelmann, *Art*, 44.
74 Nietzsche, *Ecce*, 107.
75 Nietzsche, *Human*, 82, 247, 336; Nietzsche, *Anti-Christ*, 42, 226, 272; Nietzsche, *Ecce*, 40.
76 Deleuze, *Two*, 78.
77 Goethe, *Essential*, xxiii.
78 Reyes, "Beautiful."
79 Hegel, *Phenomenology*, 575–6.
80 Milne, "Beautiful," 64, 71; Taylor, *Hegel*, 194.
81 Deleuze, *Two*, 91.
82 Deleuze, *Difference*, xx.
83 Deleuze, *Difference*, 207.

84 Deleuze, *Difference*, 52.
85 Deleuze, *Negotiations*, 136.
86 Deleuze, *Difference*, 53.
87 Deleuze, *Desert*, 118.
88 Prideaux, *Dynamite!* 206; Deleuze, *Letters*, 275.
89 Heidegger, *Parmenides*, 52–3.
90 Deleuze, *Difference*, 7.
91 Deleuze, *Fold*, 86–94.
92 Beckman, *Deleuze*, 14; Kaufman, "Betraying," 651.
93 Duvernoy, "Beautiful," 172, 174, 179–80. See Ramey, *Hermetic*.
94 Duvernoy, "Beautiful," 181.
95 Deleuze, *Difference*, xv.
96 Deleuze, *Empiricism*, 105; Deleuze, *Grounding?* 4–5, 166.
97 Duvernoy, "Beautiful," 171, 173, 181.
98 Deleuze and Parnet, *Dialogues*, 10.
99 Deleuze, *Desert*, 278.
100 Deleuze, *Bergsonism*, 111.
101 Deleuze, *Dialogues*, 15–16.
102 Deleuze, *Essays*, 52.
103 See Cusa, *Learned*.
104 See Magee, *Hegel*.
105 Deleuze, *Bacon*, 62, 118; See also Ramey, *Hermetic*.
106 Deleuze, *Cinema 2*, 248.
107 Deleuze, *Desert*, 277.
108 Deleuze, *Difference*, 7.
109 Harman, *Object-Oriented*, 6.
110 Duffy, *Mathematics*, 168.
111 Deleuze, *Cinema 1*, 58; Bergson, *Matter*, 181, 227.
112 Deleuze, *Dialogues*, 10.
113 Coen and Coen, *Lebowski*.
114 Deleuze, *Negotiations*, 6.
115 Deleuze and Parnet, *Dialogues*, 1.
116 Deleuze, *Desert*, 45–7; Deleuze, *Proust*, 67; Deleuze, *Bergsonism*, 93.
117 Bergson, *Matter*, 73.
118 Deleuze, *Negotiations*, 48; Deleuze, *Cinema 2*, 75.
119 Deleuze, *Bacon*, 47.
120 Deleuze, *Essays*, 131.
121 Deleuze, *Two*, 239.
122 Deleuze, *Difference*, xii.
123 Deleuze, *Difference*, 56.
124 Deleuze, *L'Abécédaire*, 104.
125 Deleuze, *Kafka*, 67.
126 Deleuze, *Difference*, 52.
127 Deleuze, *Difference*, 59.
128 Deleuze and Guattari, *Thousand*, 23.
129 Deleuze, *Difference*, 54.
130 Deleuze, *Difference*, 55.
131 Deleuze, *Difference*, 63.

132 Whitehead, *Process*, 39.
133 Deleuze, *Difference*, 262.
134 Bergson, *Matter*, 242.
135 Deleuze, *Difference*, 12.
136 Deleuze, *Difference*, 56; Deleuze, *Negotiations*, 65.
137 Deleuze, *Difference*, 7–8.
138 Deleuze, *Two*, 374.
139 Deleuze, *Essays*, 67.
140 Deleuze, *Difference*, 7.
141 Deleuze, *Difference*, 2.
142 Deleuze, *Essays*, 124.
143 Deleuze, *Difference*, 104.
144 Deleuze, *Foucault*, 132.
145 Kerslake, *Unconscious*, 141.
146 Deleuze, *Difference*, 7.
147 Deleuze, *Difference*, 104.
148 Deleuze, *Difference*, 271.
149 Deleuze, *Masochism*, 30.
150 Deleuze, *Difference*, 16.
151 Nietzsche, *Ecce*, 73.
152 Deleuze, *Difference*, 19.
153 Deleuze, *Difference*, 6.
154 Deleuze, *Difference*, 21.
155 Deleuze, *Difference*, 23; Deleuze, *Essays*, 51.
156 Hopcke, *Tour*, 96.
157 Simondon, *Individuation*, 557–8; Saban, "Simondon"; Deleuze, *Desert*, 87–8.
158 Deleuze, *Difference*, 40.
159 Deleuze, *Difference*, 41.
160 Deleuze, *Difference*, 55.
161 Deleuze, *Difference*, 46.
162 Deleuze, *Difference*, 49.
163 Deleuze, *Difference*, 8.
164 Deleuze, *Difference*, 262.
165 Deleuze, *Difference*, 262.
166 Deleuze, *Difference*, 264.
167 Deleuze, *Negotiations*, 124.
168 Deleuze, *Difference*, 185; Deleuze, *Letters*, 241.
169 Deleuze, *Difference*, 56.
170 Deleuze, *Difference*, 131.
171 Deleuze, *Difference*, 131.
172 Deleuze, *Difference*, 154.
173 Deleuze, *Difference*, 132.
174 Deleuze, *Two*, 48.
175 Deleuze, *Difference*, 201.
176 Deleuze, *Difference*, 76.
177 Deleuze, *Difference*, 136.

178 Deleuze, *Difference*, 139.
179 Deleuze, *Difference*, 143.
180 Deleuze, *Letters*, 89.
181 Deleuze, *Letters*, 143.
182 Deleuze, *Letters*, 241.
183 Deleuze, *Letters*, 155.
184 Deleuze, *Letters*, 145.
185 Deleuze, *Letters*, 155.
186 Deleuze, *Letters*, 58.
187 Deleuze, *Letters*, 155.
188 Deleuze, *Cinema 2*, 153.
189 Deleuze, *Difference*, 58.
190 Deleuze, *Nietzsche*, 4; Jung, *Archetypes*, 13.
191 Deleuze, *Difference*, 290.
192 Deleuze, *Essays*, 45.
193 Deleuze, *Difference*, 86.
194 Deleuze, *Desert*, 180.
195 Deleuze, *Difference*, 6.
196 Deleuze, *Difference*, 15.
197 Deleuze, *Difference*, 56.
198 Deleuze, *Cinema 2*, 253.
199 Deleuze, *Essays*, 101, 105–6.
200 Deleuze, *Cinema 2*, 238.
201 Deleuze, *Difference*, 17.
202 Deleuze, *Difference*, 104.
203 Deleuze, *Difference*, 181.
204 Deleuze, *Foucault*, 104.
205 Deleuze, *Desert*, 31.
206 Deleuze, *Kant*, 5.
207 Deleuze, *Foucault*, 32.
208 Deleuze, *Difference*, 208–11.
209 Deleuze, *Grounding?* 13n8.
210 Kerslake, "Grounding," 30.
211 Deleuze, *Grounding?* 14.
212 Plotinus, *Enneads*, 52–3.
213 Deleuze, *Grounding?* 15.
214 Deleuze, *Grounding?* 13.
215 Deleuze, *Grounding?* 43.
216 Deleuze, *Grounding?* 175. See Deleuze, *Cinema 1*, 189.
217 Deleuze, *Difference*, 60–1.
218 Plato, *Works*, 310, 312, 315.
219 Deleuze, *Difference*, 60–1.
220 Deleuze, *Difference*, 36.
221 Deleuze, *Difference*, 62.
222 Jung, *Archetypes*, 439.
223 Deleuze, *Difference*, 145.
224 Deleuze, *Kant*, x.

225 Deleuze, *Difference*, 24.
226 Deleuze, *Difference*, 128.
227 Deleuze, *Difference*, 146; Deleuze, *Cinema 2*, 104.
228 Schrodinger, *Life?* 48–50.
229 Deleuze, *Difference*, 146.
230 Deleuze, *Difference*, 220.
231 Deleuze, *Difference*, 66.
232 Hippolyte, *Logic*, 193.
233 Deleuze, *Difference*, 127.
234 Deleuze, *Difference*, 219.
235 Jung, *Archetypes*, 32.
236 Deleuze, *Difference*, 245.
237 Deleuze, *Difference*, 64.
238 Plato, *Phaedrus*, 25–6; Deleuze, *Grounding?* 112.
239 Deleuze, *Difference*, 146.
240 Deleuze, *Empiricism*, 106.
241 Deleuze, *Grounding?* 88–9.
242 Deleuze, *Foucault*, 46.
243 Deleuze, *Difference*, 202.
244 Deleuze, *Difference*, 112.
245 Deleuze, *Desert*, 125.
246 Deleuze, *Difference*, 235.
247 Deleuze, *Foucault*, 13.
248 Deleuze, *Difference*, 181.
249 Deleuze, *Difference*, 250.
250 Deleuze, *Desert*, 88.
251 Deleuze, *Difference*, 190.
252 Deleuze, *Difference*, 252; Deleuze, *Foucault*, 75–77.
253 Deleuze, *Empiricism*, 86.
254 Deleuze, *Difference*, 174.
255 Deleuze, *Difference*, 209.
256 Deleuze, *Difference*, 217.
257 Deleuze, *Difference*, 250.
258 Deleuze, *Foucault*, 32; See also Deleuze, *Bacon*, 85.
259 Deleuze, *Foucault*, 246.
260 Deleuze, *Desert*, 95.
261 Deleuze, *Two*, 206.
262 Deleuze, *Difference*, 86.
263 Deleuze, *Essays*, 99, 120.
264 Deleuze, *Difference*, 246.
265 Deleuze, *Two*, 127.
266 Deleuze, "Postscript."
267 Deleuze, "Postscript," 191.
268 Deleuze, "Postscript," 216.
269 Deleuze, "Postscript," 218.
270 Deleuze, "Postscript," 165.
271 Stengers, *Thinking*, 240.

272  Deleuze, *Difference*, 192.
273  Deleuze, *Difference*, 88.
274  Deleuze, *Difference*, 92.
275  Deleuze, *Difference*, 110.
276  Deleuze, *Difference*, 94.
277  Deleuze, *Difference*, 304.
278  Deleuze, *Difference*, 243.
279  Deleuze, *Difference*, 83.
280  Deleuze, *Two*, 283.
281  Deleuze, *Essays*, 79.
282  Deleuze, *Difference*, 83.
283  Deleuze, *Expressionism*, 148.
284  Deleuze, *Difference*, 229.
285  Deleuze, *Difference*, 83.
286  Deleuze, *Difference*, 90.
287  Deleuze, *Difference*, 119; Deleuze, *Desert*, 97.
288  Deleuze, *Difference*, 91.
289  See Desmond, *Psyche*.
290  Deleuze, *Difference*, 116.
291  Deleuze, *Difference*, 189.

# Chapter 12

# Disintegrated Integration
James Hillman's *Re-Visioning Psychology*

Hillman founded the school of archetypal psychology which, though heavily indebted to Jung, carries the archetypal mode of thought into novel domains complexly informed by philosophy. In fact, Hillman's 1975 book bears remarkable similarities to Deleuze's work culminating in *Difference and Repetition* and *The Logic of Sense*, and to his work with Guattari in the two volumes of *Capitalism and Schizophrenia*, though there does not appear to be any textual evidence that the American psychologist read the French theorists or vice versa, so it seems that these thinkers were independently developing their strikingly similar concepts based on numerous common influences and interests. While acknowledging his particular debt to Jung, Hillman eschews being designated as merely Jungian, a role which even Jung recognized "is possible only for Jung," despite the common tendency toward erecting an orthodoxy in relation to any great thinker, as "each psychology is a confession"[1] of the particular psychic constitution of the psychologist who creates it, an instrument enabling certain kinds of insight and not others. Hillman forges especially beyond Jung's intermittent emphasis of monotheism, the Trinity, and its accompanying mode of consciousness, the individuation of the Self often echoing the reconciling third of the Hegelian dialectic, fracturing and deepening the psyche into the pluralistic multiplicity of polytheism,[2] which Hillman finds resonant with the work of James. Jung certainly recognizes the importance of pluralism, though he focuses more than Hillman on Christianity, having formulated his initial conceptions of the archetypes and the collective unconscious from within a generally Protestant and Kantian milieu.

*Re-Visioning Psychology* is organized around four primary activities: the imaginal discernment of potencies genealogically descended from Schelling's metaphysical empiricism, which Hillman terms personifying;

the process of pathologizing, a differentiating tarrying with depressive or schizophrenic affects and problems closely related to Deleuze's expression of a mythical dialectic constituted in the pathology of repetition, and to schizoanalysis; the process of seeing through the infinite regress of imaginal figures to discern the gods behind the pathologies, which he terms psychologizing; and the activity of dehumanizing, which leads to a decentering of the individual akin to Deleuze's dissolved self in sustained engagement with empirically encountered polytheistic potencies luring us toward an always-receding horizon. All of these activities are engaged in "soul-making,"[3] which, as with Jung and Deleuze, conceives human experience in the vale of the world as primarily engaged in constructing a pluralistic psychic Self beyond the merely psychological, a soulful constructivism lured by the affective teleological inclinations of destiny, figured by the anima, through the synchronistic repetition of archetypal dramas involving divine fictional potencies characteristic of the eternal return. Hillman engages deeply with ancient, medieval, and early modern philosophy, history, and religion to generate a heterodox mode of thought, which transgresses and disrupts the boundaries between disciplines, beyond the crisis of the late-modern doxa in which we are still evidently embroiled, as concepts also grow old and rigid, periodically requiring novel eruptions of active, juvenescent vitality. Hillman deeply appreciated Whitehead's thought, recognizing the becomings expressed in the concept of process as essential to archetypal psychology, elsewhere drawing deeply on Whiteheadian metaphysical abstraction to sketch a "psychological cosmology" which engages with cosmological speculation,[4] though he pushes against Whitehead's conception of dynamisms as the solely impersonal, mathematical potentialities of eternal objects, which he nevertheless describes as one valid mode of expression.

Hillman recognizes the risk of explicitly engaging with the word "soul" in a modern culture permeated by Weberian "disenchantment," itself a kind of negative enchantment, the "capitalist sorcery" of Stengers and Pignarre, though Hillman emphasizes from the outset that he is not concerned with soul as a substance, but rather with the psyche as a perspectival concept inhabiting a "middle ground"[5] that differentiates between the human subject and the events in which this subject is situated. This paradoxical Self is composed of the relations of potent multiplicities, mirrored in the other, like the moon reflecting the sun's light, so that the truth of any event is located neither in the ego nor in the other, but in the mirroring relation, Hillman evoking truths as "the fictions of the rational" just as "fictions are the truths of the imaginal,"[6] resonant with Deleuze's assertion that "the real and the imaginary" do not seem to "form a pertinent distinction."[7] Overturning the usual modern privileging of the physical, Hillman suggests that the faculties and experiences proper to the psyche – imagination, narrative, speculation, dream, fantasy – are in fact the primary realities of human existence. Like Deleuze and Guattari, who write that "all signs are signs of signs,"[8] Hillman recognizes world and mind as primarily constituted in an infinite regress of complex interrelations of symbol and metaphor (despite Deleuze and Guattari's provocative denial of the machinic as metaphorical[9]), in which the world we encounter through sensation and perception is always permeated and informed by the imaginal and the signifying. All experience, even the tough-minded logical engagement with the hard facts of materiality characteristic of science or a rationalist negative philosophy, is ultimately grounded in relational fantasy, for which the mythical gods serve as a primary cast of characters in their "exquisite differentiations."[10] Critical consciousness is a mode of dramatic narrative construction associated with Kronos, and detached clarity and distinctness is associated with Apollo, relational masks carrying implicit affective, conceptual, and ethical premises, forming the preconditions for the particular modes of engagement that have generally been privileged and constructed as the primary reality in the central nodes of modern discourse. Like Deleuze's deemphasis of the negative and the ordered Apollonian in favor of chaosmic multiplicity, Hillman recognizes the Senex, associated with Kronos, and the Apollonian as together personifying one potent complex among many,[11] as "even that precious instrument, reason, loses its freedom of insight when it forgets the divine persons who govern its perspectives,"[12] becoming rigid and static in a constraining monotheism of consciousness blind to the dynamisms it embodies. In fact, Deleuze, following Nietzsche, perhaps even conflates Apollo with qualities more specifically characteristic of Kronos, writing that "Apollo is both the god of judgment and the god of dreams,"[13] though it is true that, like all gods, Kronos must always be imagined in relation, despite his penchant for despotic solitude, the complex of totalitarian centrality and legislative rationality enacting the deficient alliance of Kronos and Apollo, always seeking to control and discipline the Promethean urge toward liberation from constraint, the Dionysian creative chaos.

Hillman traces the origins of depth psychology to Heraclitus in the imaginal construction of a fragment that discerns the inexhaustible meaning (*logos*) of the mind or soul (*psyche*) in a groundless depth (*bathun*), rather than the psychic *tabula rasa* often imagined in modernity.[14] While the dimension of spirit has long been figured as height, the movement of soul-making is a descent into the underworld, the *katabasis* of Greek mythology prefiguring the going down into the unconscious particularly expressed in the pages above by Nietzsche and Jung. It is a descent into the various psychological symptoms from which we all suffer, the pathological problems posed by complexes of archetypal potencies in an infinite regress luring us toward an intensive horizon, "the border where the true depths are,"[15] by asymptotically expressing the relational "set of dynamisms"[16] that composes us. We are coerced by our most private and peculiar sufferings to bring these polycentric potentialities into actuality, Hillman referring to the dialectic of the *Phaedrus* for which the gods serve as both audience and subject. Complexes are "sacrifices to these powers,"[17] Hillman evoking Aristotle's recognition that pathos does not necessarily imply suffering, but more generally enacts the experiential, qualitative "movements of the soul"[18] that are undergone in all their multivalence, though Hillman pushes against the Aristotelian "organic fallacy,"[19] which constructs the individual body as correlated with an individual soul, the root of the individualist fantasy of Western psychology. Hillman discerns three soul-making movements beyond egoic individualism in Plato: eros (connected to the myth of Psyche and Eros, with which Aphrodite is involved); dialectics (perhaps correlated with the intellect of Hermes and the division of Kronos); and mania (associated with Dionysus). He also suggests a fourth movement, Thanatos, the minor Greek god of death associated with the Freudian death drive (also variously associated, in different valences, with both Kronos and Dionysus), a suggestion which finds precedent in Plato's depiction of Socrates' death leading to a profound self-knowledge in the *Phaedo*, a pathologizing in relation to death intimately intertwined with Freud's founding of depth psychology in its modern form.

There is a section in Plotinus' *Enneads*, "The Problems of the Soul," in which "the souls of men" witness their reflection "in the mirror of Dionysus,"[20] the descent into the labyrinthine unconscious lured ever deeper by Ariadne's anima thread, a descent which fractures the unified self into a multiplicity of shards, "disintegrating the 'I,'"[21] as Hillman writes, rendering visible the infinitely receding dynamisms that compose individuality resonant with Deleuze's "fractured I." The envisaging of archetypal multiplicity is not an activity undertaken by intellect alone, but a personifying of the various affective complexes that compose us, an anti-nominalist naming of powers acting through our bodily motivity, which allows us consciously to engage with these potencies in the form of Michelangelo's "image of the heart,"[22] Deleuze's "amorous organ of repetition," as encountered animating others rather than as mere animal feelings with no relevance to the logical facts exclusively privileged by the rationality of the head, the capital "organ of exchange." This imaginal epistemology is a mode of radically empirical perception more profound than mere sense perception or pure reason, a mode which knows not in a detached, objective, and violent categorizing, but through "the attempt to integrate heart into method" by loving what it seeks to know, because "love personalizes all that it loves," as Hillman quotes Miguel de Unamuno, and "only by personalizing it can we fall in love with an idea."[23] Rational knowing can only know the exterior of concepts and phenomena, while the interior knowing of Eros loves personified Ideas as dynamic, subjective, agential others to whom the individual relates, with which the Self is intimately entwined, an affective and imaginal empiricism resonant with all of the metaphysical, radical, intuitive, speculative, and transcendental empiricisms above, though this erotic epistemology is "one style of madness, no more privileged than any other."[24]

The infinite archetypal potencies through which we eternally return, the *archai* as prefigured by Plotinus, which Hillman designates as fictional, like infinitesimals, are primarily accessible to imaginal construction. They can only be circled in upon through the iterative repetitions of figurative language, as "all ways of speaking of archetypes are translations from one metaphor to another,"[25] attempts to evoke dynamisms which always exceed their actual expressions as Ideas, myths, genres, modes, concepts, syndromes, potentialities, pathologies, types, or fantasies, a pluralist mode of thought which precludes the reductive dogmatism of monovalent typologies with which the archetypes are often confused.[26] A primary characteristic of the archetypes is that they are always accompanied by affects that possess us, that form consciousness itself in their infinite groundless relationality. The task of human existence is to choose at which level to express the dramatic interweavings of the gods that constitute us, whether in the lowest register of the blind fate of a literalist Oedipal rebellion, or in the highest register as the philosopher who actively wrestles with his felt destiny concretely to embody the anti-Oedipal in its most profound formulation, two expressions of a polar and paradoxical potentiality rather than a mere opposition which reduces to identity. Resonant with both the Derridean and Deleuzean conceptions of difference, Hillman suggests that we must think beyond Lévi-Strauss' insistence on oppositional dualism as "the single explanatory principle of mythical thought" to recognize that "dualities are either faces of the same, or assume a unity as their precondition or ultimate goal (identity of opposites)."[27]

Archetypes, dynamisms for which each of the various nominations allow the expression of different valences, constellate qualities and events encountered by individuals into relatively discrete collective aggregates describable under the designations of mythical figures. The archetype of the hero, much derided by casual critics of Jung (who often only know him through Joseph Campbell's popularizations), an archetype whose dominance it is one of Hillman's primary projects to problematize, is associated with a composition of intertwined activities (initiatory activation, "conative striving," exploring and extending frontiers, facing obstacles or foes), visible in various concentrations of emphasis in particular figures (Heracles, Achilles, Odysseus), who embody the characteristics of the heroic mode of consciousness (independent, strong, ambitious, decisive, virtuous, conquering, dominant, embattled, single-minded). But the heroic archetype exceeds these lists, as the figures that exemplify it display an individuality that can only be approached by differentiation into their various qualities, but which must be integrated in their narrative enactments in relation to other dynamisms if they are to be appreciated and encountered in their infinite potentiality.

It is this archetype of the unified egoic individual, heroically "battling his way through binary choices,"[28] that has long been the dominant one in Western culture, in concert with the monocentric rationality of legislation and control traceable to despotic Kronos and his grandson Apollo. As with Deleuze, this alliance of the ego mirroring a jealous and merciful God in an exclusivist monotheism of consciousness is the delusional mode of relation Hillman seeks to fracture, dissolve, overturn, and re-vision in his expression of a polytheistic psychology, a descent into generative chaos. This psychology of the depths is not merely a return to ancient doctrinal religion, or an escape from the modern West into (Westernized) Eastern thought, nonmodern animism, or techno-utopian futurism, though Hillman variously recognizes the importance of engaging with these spatial and temporal elsewheres, while insisting that the particularly modern and Western tradition must face up to its presence. Rather, this psychology performs a constant relation with an ensemble cast in which all the gods and mythical figures, as imagined in the mythos especially descended from the Greeks – often resonant with other mythologies – enact their parts in the interplay of consciousness and event, though they may play a starring role in one particular individual, or during one limited duration, but be relegated to a role in the "differentiated background"[29] for other contexts. This personifying mode of thought is not primarily interested in explanations answering to the question "Why?" or causal mechanisms that respond to the question "How?", though causes and explanations certainly have roles to play, but in the quiddity of events answering to the question "What?", a question which ultimately leads to the most profound question, the importance of which Deleuze also recognizes: "Who?" Who are the archetypal persons acting through this event, complex, or symptom?[30] Like Deleuze's "fractured I" and the heterogenous assemblages of Deleuzoguattarian schizoanalysis, Hillman finds the overcoming of the totalitarian dominance of a monotheistic ego in the recognition that we all contain a multiplicity of persons within us, that we are constituted from this personified multiplicity. Although this dissolving of the unified self may appear to the still-dominant mode of consciousness as schizophrenic madness, as "primitive" delusion, hallucination, pathetic fallacy, anthropomorphism, or, at best, as childishly credulous imagination, the only way beyond the peculiarly modern mode of relation, intimately bound up with the ecological, economic, political, social, epidemiological, and psychological crises in which we are embroiled, is to bring the differentiated attention of intellect and heroic intentionality to bear in this descent into the underworld domain of repressed potencies. Thus, the literalist totalitarian ego can die and be transformed in a more democratic and pluralist imaginal renascence.[31]

Resonant with the decentered eternal return expressed by Deleuze, Hillman describes his approach as enacting "repetitions with variations,"[32] circulating through Ideas in sustained engagement with "crucial insoluble problems" and "the deepest questions,"[33] eschewing linearity in favor of "ever-recurring motifs in ever-new variations,"[34] spiraling in upon integrating evocations of eternally recurring archetypal potencies and their multiple modes of complex ingression. He performs "an infinite regress which does not stop at coherent or elegant answers," moving toward an always-receding *deus absconditus* "who appears only in concealment,"[35] affirming multiplicity, paradox, and ambiguity in the masks and disguises of the depths. Hillmanian integration is not the "integration of personality"[36] characteristic of most modern psychotherapy, still dominated by the Christian and Cartesian demand for unification from opposition, in which the errant persons of the psyche are returned to their putatively proper place, subordinated to the egoic center, but a deeper kind of integration for which "conflicts become paradoxes."[37] This integration does not suppress difference, but is constituted in complex narrative differentiation. The Greek word *therapeutes*, from which "therapist" is derived, means "one who serves the gods," and much like the problematic differenciation of the Deleuzean dissolved self, Hillman conceives of psychologizing as solving a problematic situation "not by resolving it, but by dissolving the problem into the fantasy that is congealed into a 'problem.'"[38] The etymology of fantasy indicates a rendering visible of the dynamisms occluded by the impeding obstacle of the specific kind of oppositional problem required by the heroic ego, encountering the phantasmic multiplicity exceeding egoic consciousness, allowing the formulation of more profound questions than those constrained by shallower problematic formulations, the literalist heroic fantasy that realistically eschews fantasy itself in order to defeat adversaries and conquer adversities opening to deeper problems and the querying fantasies they elicit. Hillman explicitly acknowledges that he is engaging in discordant polemic, a contentious and provocative mode similar in some ways to Deleuze and Guattari, evoking Heraclitus' assertion that "strife is the father of all things,"[39] though Hillman also exemplifies Gebser's speculative suggestion about a lost fragment which affirms peace as "the mother of all things,"[40] enacting a polyvocal balance of differentiating discord and integrating harmony beyond gender binarity, a discordant harmony resonant with the "peace fighters"[41] evoked by Stengers.

As with Schelling's positing of the ontologically ambiguous reality of mythical potencies complexly taken up by Nietzsche, Jung, and Deleuze, Hillman invites us to transgress the modern enclosure of psyche under the totalitarian control, and capitalist ownership ("capital" deriving from the Latin for "head'), of unified egoic rationality. He exhorts us to return, with the critical discernment differentiated through the negative philosophy, not only to nonmodern modes which apprehend disparate persons within the individual human psyche, but to modes of relation which encounter persons in nonhuman animals, in nature and cosmos, and perhaps especially in the dramatic narrative constructions of events conceived as the relations of dynamisms who have little use for rigid distinctions between internal and external, psyche and cosmos. In a mode of thought especially resonant with Stengers, Hillman offers a liberating reengagement with animism, not as a mere return to nonmodern modes, but in a differentiated integration of modern rationality and the intimate engagement with anima, forming the root of animate and animal, and serving as the Jungian term for others who teleologically lure us toward becoming through a personifying projection beyond mere pathetic fallacy. Rather, this reclaiming of animism is a dissolving of the constitutive modern boundary between subject and object to envisage the archetypal potencies in relation to whom we must individuate, who constitute the heterogenous relational ground of our individuality.

Like most of the theorists discussed in these chapters, Hillman recognizes that the engagement with witchcraft, sorcery, drugs, madness, the hermetic, and the occult are all strategies for overcoming the modern repression of the imaginal as a mode only appropriate for art or children's games. Nominalism reduces the words which name archetypes, as well as the word "archetype" itself, to the pedagogy of category, conceit, and allegory, which "keeps the autonomy and reality of the Gods at bay,"[42] explanations whose sole efficacy was rejected by Schelling in order to excavate a positive theory of potencies. These rationalist constructions cling to the naïve, totalizing belief that there must be some reasonable explanation for the encounter with reason's others, anything but the recognition of real – though ontologically elusive – entities to whom nonmodern people constantly relate, who lurk even within the shadowy interstices of modernity, in the backwaters, countercultures, and asylums. Hillman discerns those sorcerous, animistic, and schizophrenizing activities as openings to a pervasive transformation in our ways of conceiving the world. This transformation enacts an overcoming of the Weberian disenchanted "spirit of capitalism," the exclusivist dominance of the Senex archetype of rational judgment and central control, to discover a world pervaded by polycentric, rhizomatic networks of personal potencies, animate psyches, ensouled archetypes which render the apparently intractable problem of the radical separation of subject and object obsolete, a necessary stage in a process of differentiation that must be subsumed in a more expansive and intensive mode of relation.

The depotentiating incarceration of nonrational, imaginal modes by the rationality of law, medicine, theology, and psychiatry as perversion, sickness, sin, and insanity, when expressed beyond their trivializing enclosures, is inextricably intertwined with the exclusive privileging of those modes necessary, however temporarily, for the differentiation of rational intellect. Hillman also reciprocally pushes against the approach of R.D. Laing, whom he describes as enacting a reversal in which it is only society that is insane, and the individual who is sane in their madness, offering schizophrenizing as a therapeutic mode, so that Deleuze and Guattari can write that "Laing is entirely right in defining the schizophrenic process as a voyage of initiation, a transcendental experience of the loss of the Ego."[43] However, whereas Laing almost exclusively discerns the location of madness in the society in which the individual is imprisoned, Deleuze and Guattari's views are more balanced in this regard, consonant with Hillman. While they recognize that Laing is one of only a small number of theorists who have "escaped the familialism that is the ordinary bed and board of psychoanalysis and psychiatry,"[44] he does not go far enough, ultimately falling "back into the worst familialist, personological, and egoic postulates."[45] They affirm that the egoic individual is not merely the pure and martyred victim of a sick society as Laing contends, but the primary locus of disintegrating pathologies that exceed this binary, demanding expression as faculties carried to the limit of "what the body can do," reintegrated as differentiated contrasts in the Dionysian depths beyond egoic totality. They contend that "very few accomplish what Laing calls the breakthrough of this schizophrenic wall or limit," and that "the majority draw near the wall and back away horrified,"[46] so that this breaking through requires an extraordinary courage beyond what Laing prescribes, a rupture demanded by the destiny of the pathological potencies constituting "privileged souls," to be enacted in a way that is creative and generative, exemplified by Artaud, rather than as merely insane. This insight is resonant with Hillman's evocation of Andre Gide's recognition "that illness opens doors to a reality which remains closed to the healthy point of view," and that "the soul sees by means of affliction,"[47] a Nietzschean "Great Health."[48]

Deleuze reportedly remarked to Guattari about his work at La Borde psychiatric clinic, "How can you stand those schizos?"[49] declaring elsewhere that "I am less and less able to tolerate romanticizing madness,"[50] illustrating that Deleuze and Guattari were not simply valorizing schizophrenia,[51] as Hillman portrays Laing's theory, but rather advocating an intentional appropriation of schizophrenic affects and imaginings to discover heterodox modes of relation in order to overcome the Oedipal imprisonment characteristic of monocentric psychology and capitalism.[52]

In a passage that could be mistaken for a summary of the critique of psychoanalysis in *Anti-Oedipus*, Hillman writes: "The one major concession to the mythical imagination – Freud's Oedipus fantasy – remained within the realm of monotheism. One myth alone could account for the psyche of all humankind."[53] Although Deleuze and Guattari are more positive than Hillman about Laing's "antipsychiatry," which they judge as going "very far in this direction" of overcoming the Oedipal, they nevertheless contend that Laing and his school "localize social and mental alienation on a single line,"[54] producing a dualism along this unidimensional axis which Deleuze and Guattari played a primary role in overcoming.

Hillman observes that Laing's theory is partially descended from Hegel, whom Hillman appreciates in a tempered valence, writing that Hegel "considered insanity as a necessarily occurring form or stage in the development of the soul," a consideration which reveals a surprising resonance, yet again, between Hegel and Deleuze. However, as with the French theorists' critique of both Hegel and Laing, Hillman discerns Laing's "divided self," partially derived from Gregory Bateson's schizophrenic "double bind"[55] (the anthropologist from whom Deleuze and Guattari derived "the word 'plateau'"[56]), as an attempt "to restore itself to the perfect inner harmony out of existing contradiction,"[57] as Hillman quotes a lecture by Hegel, a dialectical return to monocentric identity via negation producing a "whitewashing" of the undeniable "ugliness, misery, and madness of psychopathology." Hillman identifies this whitewashing as "a classical denial mechanism"[58] on the part of Laing, displacing the agency of the supposedly pure and naturally virtuous individual exclusively onto a sick and debased society rather than recognizing the intimate reciprocity of individual and society. It is this transitional reversal of the binary of sane normality and insane abnormality which it is a primary project of both Deleuze (with and without Guattari) and Hillman to overcome in the opening to a polycentric pluralism enacted through the Deleuzean method of dramatization, the intentional schizophrenizing of Deleuzoguattarian schizoanalysis, and Hillmanian personifying and pathologizing, the rhizomatic "differential root" through which "depth psychology maintains its integrity,"[59] though Hillman suggests that Hegel actually goes further than Laing in this regard.

Like Schelling, Hillman advocates a return to thinking with the reality of the gods without attempting to fix their ontological status, enacting an overturning of the priority of reason over imagination. Rather than the gods being contained by reason as mere allegory or superstition, reason itself becomes one expression of an imaginally encountered god, Kronos or Apollo, one ingression of the potencies which exceed us and constitute us. However, Hillman acknowledges that this reengagement with the full reality of the gods is not only a pleasant or enlightening endeavor, as their repression by rationality is in part an attempt to master their negative expressions, the demonic, monstrous, violent, cruel, and perverse. But it is evident from the state of our late modern culture, from the demonic cruelty of some of our leaders and the monstrous violence of our societies of control, that these powers cannot ultimately be repressed without a compensatorily brutal return, and in fact, their more destructive manifestations may be mitigated if the archetypes are carried into conscious awareness and engaged with in more salutary and efficacious ways, with respect for their power and autonomy. The gods cannot be tamed, and the centuries-long attempt to do so has produced the return of repressed potencies on titanic scales in world war, genocide, ecological catastrophe, and global pandemic, though what is demanded is not a mere regression to nonmodern modes, which are certainly not without their own violence and cruelty, but an integration of capacities differentiated through successive epochs.

It is not only in medicalized psychiatry or Freudian psychoanalysis that Hillman discerns this repression of potencies, as even in humanistic, existential, or Gestalt psychology, or in various spiritual practices, however holistic or nurturing, the gods demanding expression through dreams, fantasies, affects, and pathologies are generally relegated to mere allegories provided by our unconscious to facilitate our egocentric and salvational self-actualization. This allegorization constructs a defensive imprisonment of the gods within the safe enclosures of our individual psyches, which can take the form of Abraham Maslow's peak experiences, the climbing of the rungs of Westernized forms of transcendental meditation toward the divine One, or even the ecstatic highs encountered in psychedelic experiences, which all often result in ego inflation rather than in the pathological dissolution, fracturing, and dismemberment of descent into the psychic depths necessary for a transformative renascence which decenters the ego in polycentric multiplicity. "Without psychopathology there is no wholeness" and, "in fact, psychopathology is a differentiation of that wholeness,"[60] a differentiating integration constructing ever-more-subtle and profound contrasts that cannot be sublated away. These activities can all be efficacious for certain purposes, but the gods will never be appeased by being made pets which we stroke for egoic gratification in the depotentiating therapeutic ritual, meditation retreat, or psychonautic trip. They will continue to ignore these pitiful enclosures, controlling and agonizing us until we recognize their reality and autonomy, enacted in a reciprocal, decentered circulation for which the gods create us as much as we create them. And it is precisely the most perverse and disturbing fantasies and dreams that allow for the transgression of the enclosure which seeks to contain the imaginal gods within the personal ego as mere personality traits rather than as numinous agential powers with whom we must constantly contend to negotiate the contours of our lived reality.

This impossible taming of the gods is intertwined with the equally impossible taming of language, the restriction of the Logos to mere nominalist logic, as words are the demons and angelic emissaries bearing signs affirmed by Deleuze (with whom we sometimes wrestle, like Jacob), often gendered personal potencies infinitely receding into the etymological depths, as especially illuminated by Schelling. Verbal composition is an enactment on the page of the dramatic relations of powers toward which words lure us, with some words particularly resonant with certain archetypes, each phrase, sentence, and paragraph more or less effectively invoking and actualizing archetypal complexes. Hillman discerns this verbal and rhetorical multivalence beyond the monovalence of nominalist rationalism especially in Jung's writing, the psyche and logos of depth psychology particularly concerned with this intertwining of soul and word. Nominalism, the mode of thought characteristic of the rationalist, analytic tradition still dominant in anglophone philosophy, and of "the language game called psychopathology,"[61] the mania for a putatively empirical naming and categorizing of psychiatric disorders occluding more profound causes, can serve as an ego defense when imposed beyond its limited domain of efficacy. The clarity, distinctness, and monocausality of Apollonian rationality can repress the transformative chaos, obscurity, and multiplicity of the Dionysian depths judged as mere insanity, mocked as infantile, or anthropologically contained through its nomination as "primitive" animism. When liberated, these imprisoned complexes emerge as pathologies, though their repression in the unconscious produces even more destructive expressions of these potencies, as witnessed in the very dark shadow of a supposedly enlightened modernity: misogyny, racism, homophobia, economic inequality, climate change, genocide. The archetypes must be faced one way or another, whether as avenging gods encountered as externally mandated fate, or as unruly partners in a creation which dissolves the nominally generated boundaries between internal and external, self and other, maintaining their differentiation in integration.

A primary mode of personifying potencies is myth, for which the either-or question of whether or not the gods are real – reality generally defined in this context as purely material and rationally intelligible – coerces their more profound and ambiguous reality, as elucidated by Schelling, into a choice between tough-minded skepticism and tender-minded credulity which is no choice at all. This oppositional selection obscures the deeper controversy between exclusive duality and a broader multiplicity that includes duality, a decision which has already been made before the question is even asked, forcing the oppositional binarity of exclusivist rationality. This binary construction can be discerned as a shadow of a deeper mode of relation which integrates the differentiated material and imaginal aspects of process nominally rendered as subject and object, human and divine. The imaginal mode, the ungrounding ground of human consciousness, emerges with a pluralist system of gods and mythical persons, which we create as little as we create the persons in dreams. A return to the recognition of the imaginal demanded for the full vitality of human culture, not only in art and children's games, but in all aspects of experience, is intimately entwined in a reengagement with these mythical potencies by differentiating rationality.

Hillman evokes the recognition by Schelling that the nominalist project of depersonifying and demythologizing creates the need for words to describe the reality taken for granted prior to this negating movement, so that the reductive conception of allegorical personification depends upon the negation of the originary positing of human consciousness with mythical persons. In a movement that evinces a distinctly dialectical flavor, the assertion of personifying and the return to myth are only required by the negation of what was always already present, though this tarrying with critical negation has produced the precondition for bringing differentiating rationality to bear in discerning mythical persons to produce a novel dialectic that exceeds both a naïve imaginal credulity and a narrow rationalist skepticism. Hillman suggests that this return to the gods, though complexly expressed in philosophy, philology, anthropology, literary studies, and other disciplines, has found its primary locus of ingression in the psychologies of Freud and Jung, ultimately derived from Platonism and its intertwining of *eidos* and *episteme*, its epistemology of Ideas. The gods have forced their way through the centuries-long stranglehold of exclusivist rationality in the form of psychopathologies – "multiple personalities, hysterical dissociations, hallucinations"[62] encountered primarily by practicing therapists and psychiatrists, both on the psychoanalytic couch and in the psychiatric hospital.

As Deleuze recognized, these pathological persons were encountered by Freud in the figures of Oedipus, Eros, and Thanatos, and in the Superego, the Primal Horde, and the polymorphous perverse Child. Hillman similarly emphasizes Freud's realization that traumatic childhood memories do not necessarily lead back to real events, but that even if they are connected to real traumas, they lead to the instinctual forces of libido and wish-fulfillment projected into the imaginal figures of Mother and Father, a realization that Freud could not prevent from sliding into mythical expressions, which he explicitly designated "our mythology," though generally more monotheistic than polytheistic. Despite his tendency toward reductive scientific materialism, Freud articulated what Hillman calls "a cosmological fiction,"[63] which Freud primarily conceived in the mode of instructive allegory, but which ultimately enabled Jung to nominate these pathological persons as archetypes. The psychoanalytic terms projection, sublimation, and condensation are derived from alchemy, and the mode of thought developed through this lineage leads to the understanding that, as with the refusal to attempt statically to pin down the ontological status of the gods or the substances in the alembic, what is required is not a choice between the reality of the traumatic event and the dismissive suspicion that this event is a mere fantasy, but the recognition that the real and the imaginal are always complexly intertwined. So, while the question in a criminal prosecution of an abuser in a court of law is rightly whether or not the abuse actually occurred as a concrete event, the more subtle and profound question in the therapeutic consultation is what pragmatic effect the remembered trauma has in the traumatized person's experience, repeated imaginally, and often in differential dramatic reenactments with other persons. Husband or wife, boss or teacher, lover or therapist serve as substitutes for the person imagined in the originary event, whether or not this event actually took place in precisely the way it is remembered, ultimately serving as masks of transcendental potencies which respond to the question "Who?"

The same is true of all the various explanations discussed by Schelling: the ontological status of these imaginal figures, encountered in both mythology and pathology, as demons to be exorcized or as complexes to be abreacted by a "psychiatric priesthood,"[64] is not the most important question, answering the demand for the reduction to a single cause characteristic of science and rationality, a question possessing powerful but limited efficacy which Freud indicated the way beyond despite his adherence to rationalism. It is Lou Salome, who played such an important role in Nietzsche's biography, that introduced Freud to the work of Nietzsche in 1912, an influence evident in much of Freud's subsequent work, leading him as Diotoma did with Plato to understand "that love requires personifying."[65] Once it has been accepted that the persons of the imagination are ontologically multiple, archetypes finding expression across scales and orders of human and nonhuman, internal and external experience, the question becomes what can be done in relation to these potencies, what kind of personal relationship one can cultivate with them, what kind of Bergsonian swimmer one can become: Oedipus who unconsciously plays out his tragic narrative as fate, or the theorist who sustainedly and intentionally engages with the Oedipal in its highest problematic valence to generate novel questions as preconditions for openings to more expansive domains.

Whereas Freud implicitly justified his engagements with mythical personification as elaborate and pervasive conceit, Jung recognized that the psyche is radically entwined with mythical and animistic modes. While the unconscious found its early abstract formulations in the philosophies of Leibniz and Kant, the complex lineage of Schelling, Nietzsche, and Freud provided the conceptual bridge Jung required to rediscover the archetypal persons of the psyche, excavated from archaic, Hellenic, medieval, and Renaissance sources, and experientially encountered as agential, autonomous potencies in his work with schizophrenic patients at the Burghölzli psychiatric hospital. Even many of those who are leery of Jung now take for granted the personifying modes of thought he bravely pioneered in his sustained engagement with "schizoid multiplicity,"[66] previously denigrated as merely primitive or insane. Deleuze and Guattari's assertion in the second sentence of *A Thousand Plateaus* that "since each of us was several, there was already quite a crowd"[67] is at least partially descended from Jung, who provided a primary opening from the exclusively oppositional Freudian "psychodynamics,"[68] the "hydraulic machine of psychoanalysis"[69] based on the physical model of equal and opposite compensatory reactions, to a more pluralistic and topologically expansive "psychodramatics,"[70] resonant with the Deleuzean method of dramatization, rendering Jung perhaps the most under-acknowledged influence on continental thought.

Nevertheless, it seems that many academic theorists who are drawn to Jung's work omit reference to him because of a legitimate fear of judgment by their peers against the modes of thought he exemplifies, potentially rendering their prospects for publication and employment even more precarious than they already are within a capitalist machinic assemblage which extracts our labor while keeping us in a state of constant professional and financial anxiety, though this bias against Jung appears currently to be dissolving. As Mark Fisher writes, Capital is "the ultimate cause-that-is-not-a-subject,"[71] the always-displaced and unattainable center of the labyrinth of bureaucratic control and exploitation, the infinitely receding dynamism which Deleuze and Guattari recognize as Kronos[72] in perhaps his most pernicious guise as the Kafkaesque, impersonal systemic structure, with the academy as one of his primary domains of efficacy, so that real learning can only take place within academia in spite of its pervasion by Capital, though it does in fact take place.

Even as respected a Deleuzean as Todd May told an interviewer that he has "never heard of Jung being influential" on Deleuze, and he would think that "Jung's influence, if any, would be marginal," despite the numerous explicit affirmations of Jung in Deleuze and Guattari's writing.[73] Given that May dismisses psychoanalysis in general in this same interview, perhaps he simply overlooked the passages on Jung in at least nine separate texts, which May presumably must have read in order to write his excellent introduction to Deleuze. Alternately, perhaps psychoanalytic repression is precisely the concept required to account for this apparent amnesia common among some Deleuzeans, a phenomenon certainly not limited to May. Or perhaps he is merely engaging in conceit, not wanting to associate Deleuze with Jung's interest in occult modes of thought, one of a surprisingly large contingent of Deleuzeans who somehow construct Deleuze as an exclusively anti-formal, anti-teleological materialist, completely ignoring, or conveniently forgetting, his profound and sustained engagements with mythology, synchronicity, archetypes, sorcery, astrology, and destiny. As Joshua Ramey aptly observes, Deleuze "stands as a contemporary avatar of Western esoteric or 'hermetic' thought" adding that,

> despite vast evidence that many Western philosophers – both ancient and modern – have been invested in some sort of spirituality (be it theurgical, thaumaturgical, mystical, alchemical, kabalistic, or theosophical), thinkers explicit about their hermetic or esoteric proclivities

have always been positioned as bastard and nomadic outliers of philosophy.[74]

However, emboldened partially by Stengers' exhortation that "to refuse to be bored when writing also means trusting the reader,"[75] it is one project of the present text to draw out the influence of Jung and the Hermetic tradition on Deleuze and Guattari, an extraction which Hillman's work particularly facilitates, in order to assist the many occultists, animists, and wiccans, the alchemists, mystics, and astrologers among academics who work in continental, pragmatist, and process thought, in finding the courage, as well as the funding (which is almost the same thing in our current societal epoch), to venture out of the epistemological closet.

It might also be suggested that, despite the many developments in feminism and queer theory over the last few decades, the wariness of some putatively "serious" philosophers about engaging with Jung's work may have to do with the perceived "feminine" quality of his thought, a gendered trivialization which Emily Herring has discussed in relation to Bergson's many female admirers, entwined with the historical association of intuition and the occult with femininity, which bears striking similarities to the figure of the beautiful soul.[76] Whereas Freud wrote about the Primal Father, Moses, and phallic symbols, and most of his primary early followers were men, Jung emphasized Mary and Sophia, the archetypal Great Mother, and the anima, and his primary early followers were women, humorously designated the *Jungfrauen* ("Jung-women," but also "virgins").[77] The patriarchal tenor of Freud's psychology is deeply intertwined with reductionist materialism and rationalism, with the order, defensiveness, and anality of the Senex, while Jung's psychology is primarily engaged with imagination, intuition, affect, emotion, desire, and the body, all associated with femininity in their repression by the patriarchal mode which requires their hierarchical subjection to manufacture its dominant oppositional identity. This gendered binarity is starkly visible in the primarily male enrollment in graduate programs for (predominantly analytic) philosophy and (monotheistically oriented) religion in contrast with the primarily female enrollment in most of the other disciplines in the humanities and social sciences, including psychology, sociology, English, and art history, for which continental theory often informs the primary approaches. Each academic discipline emphasizes certain archetypal complexes, their particular psychological perspectives and modes of constructing knowledge and learning, embedded in its founding premises at the expense of other potencies. Philosophy particularly tends to privilege a heroic "masculine" purity and solitary intellectual asceticism while eschewing more collective, relational, and embodied modes long associated with the "feminine," which have their characteristic bodily gestures and aesthetic styles in addition to their more abstract conceptual modes, their association with the patient weaving of Athena, the digesting of Demeter, the nursing of Artemis.

And it is certainly the case that, although there are many men interested in various occult activities, these activities have often been denigrated as tender-minded "feminine" pursuits not worthy of the tough-minded, often misogynist, masculinity which still pervades academia and the broader culture, even among scholars, both men and women, gay and straight, who read feminist and queer theorists and are deeply sympathetic to the political and social valences of feminism and gender studies. This hierarchical privileging of a skeptical, disenchanted mode of thought intimately entwined with the patriarchal privileging of masculinity over femininity, which seems partially to motivate the strangely reductive misreadings of Deleuze as a materialist against anything resembling idealism, rather than as a primary theorist contributing to the overcoming of this duality, and the dominance of duality in general, is a lingering domain that requires deconstruction after the essential, and continuing, deconstructions of identity related to gender, sexuality, race, class, geography, and ability. In fact, Deleuze, perhaps more than any other theorist, renders this deconstruction thinkable within the main streams of academic discourse.

The anima is the archetype of personifying itself, enacting the relation with the persons of the unconscious, including the shadow, luring the ego through projection and desire to engage with the disparate potencies in the process of the individuation of the Self, which Hillman recognizes as a fictional narrative construction, as are the concepts of ego and unconscious, emphasizing this relational field as a psychodramatics which composes us. Hillman's privileging of dramatization over the Freudian psychodynamic mode, which discerns the psyche as composed of "a field of forces," can be conceived as a transitional reversal, so that the predominant physical metaphor can be integrated with the metaphor of metaphorical narrativity itself, as well as the Deleuzoguattarian image of the factory with its machinic assemblages, in a mode which emerges from the pervasive correspondences between these imaginal domains, partially constituted in their contrasting difference. In this mode, our personal psychological complexes are "complex persons"[78] who demand expression across orders, both physical and imaginal, in the most concrete domains of architectural construction or bodily emotion and in the most abstract domains of concept and logic. All experiential domains can be conceived as expressions of personal potencies which are never encountered in their totality, which infinitely recede as we approach them, and which form the groundless imaginal ground of both mind and world. These simulacral images are paradoxically in us as much as we are in them, like dreamers who inhabit their dreams, which are also experienced as internal to their psyches.

As much as any other figure, Jung has allowed us to take seriously the persons of pathology, encountered in the schizophrenia of his patients, as well as in his own semi-intentional schizophrenizing, which he described as "doing a schizophrenia,"[79] in his "confrontation with the unconscious" after his publication of *Psychology of the Unconscious* in 1912. This book partially precipitated his expulsion from Freudian psychoanalysis, and his descent into a sustained active imagination of the spontaneously arising figures of Elijah, Philemon, and Salome over the course of the teens, recorded in *The Red Book*, and generating many of his most profound conceptions expressed over the subsequent decades. Rather than judging and categorizing these encountered figures, in both himself and his patients, as merely insane delusions, his work has greatly contributed to the liberation of modern psychology from its monocentric rationalist enclosures, allowing engagement with the full range of actual polycentric psychic experience, encountered in its more extreme forms as demonic possession, multiple personalities, speaking in tongues, automatic writing, and personality dissociation. Jungian psychology has enacted a dialectical return on a more expansive order of differentiation to the animistic, hermetic, and mystical engagements with metaphysical others, an unambiguous precursor to the Deleuzean mythical dialectic, and to schizoanalysis. This mode recognizes that we are all several, all constituted in a multiplicity, and that schizophrenia, a concept created little more than a century ago to name the phenomena of psychic division, fracturing, dismemberment, and dissolution known since pre-antiquity, is an expression of the multiple persons of the unconscious, repressed by egoic rationality, demanding to be heard rather than psychiatrically narcotized further into submission, though psychiatric drugs have their place.

Hillman discerns a twentieth-century decentering of totalitarian egoic control countervalent to fascist totalitarianism, not only in the conceptual invention of schizophrenia in psychology, but in the fracturing and dislocating developments of modern painting, music, and literature, and in the emergence of a multiplicity of countercultures. This pluralist decentering is also visible in the common comparison of our era to the fall of the Roman Empire, the pagan, barbarian invasion of the persons of the Dionysian unconscious which Nietzsche evoked against the dominance of what Hillman calls the modern "Empire of the Roman Ego,"[80] the strengthening of egoic consciousness advocated by Freud as a "dogma" and "unshakable bulwark" against "the black tide of mud of occultism," as he expressed it to Jung in 1910. Jung interpreted this black tide as encompassing "virtually everything that philosophy and religion, including the rising contemporary science of parapsychology, had learned about the psyche," with Freud attempting to impose an anti-theological theology as doctrine, which Jung designates as the primary factor "that struck at the heart of our friendship,"[81] leading to their break a few years later. Hillman recognizes this totalitarian centrality of the ego as an "imperialistic fantasy"[82] intimately related to the actual military and economic imperialism of modern Europe and the United States, which have generally sought to repress and erase not only the languages and cultures of the dominated people, but also their often polytheistic religions, with Christian missionaries imposing the monotheistic mode of consciousness on peoples in Asia, Africa, Australia, and the Americas.

Hillman recognizes that "when the dominant vision that holds a period of culture together cracks, consciousness regresses into earlier containers, seeking sources for survival which also offer sources of revival,"[83] a collective enactment across scale of the common regression to childhood and animality in individual pathology as a means of escape from the excessive demands of the ego, which is less a degradation of nonmodern cultures than a recognition that the gifts of children and nonhuman animals are equal to those of human adults. The imaginal which Jung initially endeavored to liberate from within the psychoanalytic empire, a task which ultimately led him beyond the imperial borders, is "the greatest enemy of dogma,"[84] providing the opening to a potential renewal into more differentially integrated individuations. The twentieth-century fall of the impeding empire of ego, a fall evidently still in progress, is just such a cracking and regression, partially constituted in a Dionysian "return to Greece,"[85] to a polytheistic mode of consciousness resonant with the polycentric Hellenic resurgence of the Renaissance after the Apollonian monocentrism of the Christian Middle Ages, and with the polytheistic spirit of Romanticism in the late eighteenth and nineteenth centuries after the monocentric rationality of the Enlightenment. This return is especially evident in the sixties counterculture, which has often been compared to those earlier eras, after the normalizing conformity of the postwar order. The return to Hellenic polytheism is a differentiating fragmentation serving as a reviving precursor to a polycentric "disintegrated integration" beyond previous monocentric integrations, a deterritorialization inseparable from more expansive and inclusive reterritorializations for which the archetypes provide primary imaginal elements. This return is in fact "a regressive death wish,"[86] a death of the modern by returning to the imaginal fantasy of childhood, and the childhood of Western culture in the Hellenic, the Renaissance, and the Romantic. It is a dissolution of the static and dependable worlds that these eras were required to transform, both dangerously vulnerable and radically open to novel emergences, a psychic death on a mass scale, generally accompanied by real mass fatality – Black Death and Renaissance, French Revolution and Romanticism, World War II and the sixties counterculture, and perhaps now global pandemic and the still barely discernible glimmer of a positive renascence, a novel iteration in a series of transformative deaths-and-rebirths.

Hillman evokes Nietzsche's discussion of the intimate intertwining of death and the Renaissance in the recognition that rebirth requires death, decay, pathology, and degeneracy.[87] There is no rebirth without catastrophe and its accompanying misery and despair, recalling Deleuze's desert island emerging from the Flood, no integration without differentiating disintegration. And the more brilliant and transformative the awakening, the darker the depths, as "revival emerges from the threat to survival and is not a choice of something preferable."[88] One of the primary imaginal dramas in Renaissance Neoplatonism is the abduction of Persephone by Hades, the myth around which the major mysteries of Eleusis were constructed, so that the initiate, whether Eleusinian or Hermetic, is drawn down into the underworld of death and obscurity, of secrecy and psychic interiority, the chaotic unconscious from which transformation emerges. This initiatory descent, or a clustered series of descents, occurs whenever collective entities, whether individuals or cultures with their multiplicities of complexes, find themselves at a border between epochal durations, the creative breakdown of the old order from which a novel order emerges, the death of the Middle Ages and the birth of the modern, or the death of the modern and the birth of a discontinuously novel epoch which cannot yet be decisively named.

Although the monotheistic mode of consciousness cannot be completely abandoned and rejected any more than can the ego itself, "the Christ vehicle no longer carries"[89] the primary pathologizing requirements of our "Western" cultures, does not provide the resources for overcoming the apparently epochal crisis in which we are engaged. It is precisely the exclusivist dominance of this monocentric consciousness which has brought us to this crisis, a necessary differentiation of egoic rationality in modernity, perhaps correlated with the Kronos-Apollo complex, which now demands an iconoclastic dissolution in the Dionysian chaos not only of Greek and Renaissance polytheism, as Hillman emphasizes, but in the multiplicity of potencies imagined by indigenous cultures, speculative fictions, and non-Western religions and mythologies. In fact, the "Greece" to which we return is itself a diverse epoch, both temporally from the Minoan to the Hellenistic, and spatially from Asia Minor to Sicily, a fantasy serving as a myth for our imaginal constructions, echoing its own myths situated in its far past. The differential mythical repetitions that constitute the Western tradition can be traced from the myths of the gods and heroes, to the mythologization of the figures of the ancient Greeks themselves, to the diachronic reenactments of these myths in the eras of Neoplatonism, the Renaissance, Romanticism, and even the sixties, which has joined these other eras as a horizon for imaginal projective elicitation, even by those who lived through it, with its own semi-divine intellectual and artistic heroes, its Deleuzes and Dylans, who embody the mythical potencies for future repetitions. Even the philosophical tradition is a kind of mythology, exemplified in the particular pantheon of conceptual personae traced in these chapters, whose works offer infinite objects of study and inspiration, so that we can only ever approach a full understanding of any great philosopher's thought.

As Hillman observes, the figures who created the mythical image of "Greece" often had only a tenuous connection to the actual place and culture. Petrarch did not read Greek despite his singularly influential elevation of its literature, and Winckelmann, Racine, Goethe, Hölderlin, Hegel, Heine, Keats, and Nietzsche never traveled to Greece, a lack of literal, direct engagement with the object of their veneration which perhaps enabled the creative freedom of their reconstructions, an imaginal domain of potencies, though given depth and structure by its intertwining with the historical, textual, and geographical actualities around which this imaginal mythos is constructed. The image of Greece, or its successive repetitions, is neither merely a literal object for rigorous historical and archaeological reconstruction nor a fantasy fabricated out of thin air, but an imaginal complex which, like Freudian childhood traumas, the mythological gods, or the unconscious itself, inhabits a liminal and paradoxical domain whose ontological status cannot be fixed, evincing an undecidability which allows it to serve as the privileged site of novel integrations, the Deleuzean "ancient mythical present."

For modern people, psychopathology is a primary site of the return to the imaginal mode that exceeds the neat enclosures of the domains designated by art and play, always engaged with in the mode of conceit, instead seeping into the actual lived experience of the person who undergoes the pathology, becoming not a "mere" fantasy that they can banish at will, but a phantasmic other with whom they must contend. These phantasms can take the form of a spouse or family member who has died, or an aspect of the person's self with whom they must relate as other, both pathologies motivated by an affect so intense, the feeling of loss or some region of their own character or biography so intolerable, that they must exteriorize these affects in imaginal figures as a means of psychological protection. Sometimes the trauma is so intense that this protective splitting is as far as the person can go, maintaining a tenuous balance. But these are the psychic persons to whom one experiencing such a pathology must relate if they hope to resolve the splitting in a psychic integration which is not merely a repression of the other, but a differentiation from the lost other or the traumatic scene in their biography as actually other, which paradoxically allows them to recognize the other who was wearing the mask of the lost loved one or the abuser as one person constituting their interior drama. And this splitting can be engaged in intentionally as active imagination, Hamlet's method in the madness, so that although the psychic other does not always force itself against our will, when it is intentionally evoked, it asserts itself as expressing an elusive but insistent reality that cannot be dismissed. The encounters that take place with others in nonordinary states of consciousness, whether spontaneously arising or intentionally produced by breathing, fasting, wilderness isolation, bodily movement, or the ingestion of psychoactive compounds, impose the undeniable and persistent sense that the beings encountered, however fleetingly, were real, existing in the liminal space between our internal psyche and the world experienced as external.

These encounters with the liminal others that constitute the psyche, whether in dreams, schizophrenia, or psychonautic explorations, figures which demand to be named like Adam naming all of the animals so that he can become conscious of their qualities in himself, demand a differentiation of the potencies that our individuality expresses as a precondition for their individuated integration. Hillman quotes Jung's dictum that "only separated things can unite,"[90] though this uniting is not a mere return to totalitarian identity, but a pluralist and democratic grassroots coalition which serves as the teleological lure of an immanent pathologizing. All of these modes of personifying are dramatizations of the problems and questions that construct our conceptual and affective horizons, often as conflict between opposed or incommensurable perspectives or desires. They enact the constantly shifting alliances and rivalries of the autonomous agencies who constitute our habit of personal identity associated with a particular body and a particular life, performing the recognition that we are an interior multiplicity rather than identifying exclusively with the monocentric ego, repressing the persons who compose us and forcing them to be encountered externally as objects of conflict, fear, or desire. And this projection of the repressed persons who dramatically enact our individuality takes place not only in individuals, but in the collective psyche as the othering of different races, nations, genders, and sexualities leading to hierarchical dominance, and to the periodic atrocities that these dominations require.

What is called for, then, is an overthrowing of the totalitarian Kronos, who devours the others in his egomania, by the gods whom Zeus leads not as an absolute dictator, but as the principal actor in an ensemble cast who generally requires the participation and assent of those he leads, who is responsible to their requirements and responsive to their dissent. And these gods are not merely conceptual, but actually encountered potencies in their multiplicity of masks who demand to be heard, and even adored or served, who require our active relation if we hope to preclude provoking their destructive ire as painful symptoms and fatal encounters. But even when the gods are recognized in their autonomous reality, suffering cannot be avoided, as the pain of dissolution and regression, of breakdown and depression, is a prerequisite for the concrescence of these potencies in a more expansive integration beyond ego's dominance rather than these potencies being indefinitely repressed in the unconscious. It is not possible to emerge from a habitual and repressive monocentric orthodoxy into a novel and vital mode of polycentric relation, whether on individual or collective orders, without undergoing an initiatory ordeal of dismemberment and descent. As Hillman recognizes in 1964's *Suicide and the Soul*, the pathological fantasy of suicide is a literalization of the drive toward a transformative death of the ego, as there is no rebirth without death, no integration without disintegration, and even when a novel integration occurs, the gods subsist in their often discordant multivalence, demanding to be actualized and expressed in a multiplicity of affective and conceptual modes, both revelatory and torturous, both positing and negating. Integration is not an overcoming of suffering, but a paradoxically liberating discernment of the potencies who demand our respect, and sometimes even our submission.

If Kronos is the primary potency, in alliance with Apollo, who imprisons in the monocentric ego, Hermes, the trickster of Greek mythology, carries the messages of the gods which arrive not as clear and distinct mandates, but in a schizoid, mercurial style that "thrives in plural meanings, in cryptic double-talk, in escaping definitions, in not taking heroic committed stances, in ambisexuality, in psychically detached and separated body parts." This description is strikingly evocative of Deleuze and Guattari, as is Hillman's evocation of a "self-division, dismemberment, and a flowing multiplicity"[91] characteristic of Dionysus. One might almost suspect that Hillman is implicitly referring to the French theorists, though it is more likely that they encountered the same dynamisms, wrote the dreams of the same gods, encountered as persons who recede through an infinite regress of masks as they are approached. The verbal concepts of philosophical or psychological thought – whether dynamisms, potencies, Ideas, or archetypes – are secondarily derived from divine and demonic images and modes of consciousness as instruments for their differentiation in a mythical dialectic integrating the conceptual and the imaginal, which can serve to carry the system of the gods repressed in the unconscious back to the realm of *memoria* where it resided in the Renaissance. But as witnessed not only in obscurantist French theory, but in those who return from imaginal or psychonautic explorations, articulating the experienced domains and encounters to those who have not yet undergone such experiences can be challenging, as clear and distinct language can only be applied to those experiences which are already accounted for within the existing sign systems characterizing the settled cultural orthodoxy of common sense. Heterodox experiences require the creation of novel forms of language, obscure and paradoxical concepts, as well as complex metaphorical evocations which cannot be reduced to the conceptual, to be expressed.

The resituation of ego from a totalitarian monocentrism – like Heracles heroically wrestling the multi-headed beast Cerberus into submission amidst the confused phantasms of Hades (and despite his Eleusinian preparations for this final labor) – to a plural polycentrism requires that we take imaginal experience as seriously as physical repeatability rather than constructing imagination as merely amorphous play or fantasy with no significant relation to the real world, as confusion to be violently explained away. We must give sustained collective attention to "the differentiation of the imaginal," to the complex, shifting structures and lattices of affective, intuitive, and phantasmal experience in a more expansive empiricism, to narrative dramatizations of potencies enacted through tortuous geometrical and topological relations. This differential synchronistic repetition enacting the eternal return of archetypal situations demonstrates its own "laws and necessities"[92] not susceptible to a monocentrically repeatable empiricism, but to a radically pluralist empiricism which engages with all of our faculties, not only a putatively objective rationality. We encounter the persons behind pathologies through this transformative narrativity, and we must attend to what these personified potencies have to say. Deemphasizing the medical model in which a mental illness is diagnosed, and a treatment produces a cure, the often confining "heroic fantasy" of the doctor which seeks to tame the gods by imprisoning them within the nominalist designations of various disorders, may paradoxically offer a way of healing the pathologies which are surface expressions, masks of the infinitely receding persons in the depths. As the ancients understood: "The same God who constellates an illness is the one who can take it away."[93]

Although there certainly may be cases with primarily physical etiologies that can only respond to medical intervention, and the heroic archetype is as valid and necessary as any other, moving beyond the exclusively medical model of psychiatry to address both primary meanings of "psyche," to heal the imaginally oriented soul and not only the rationally contained mind, may allow for the resolution of previously intractable disorders, not as an ultimate solution for suffering, but in a sustained engagement with the purposive powers behind the symptoms enabling the tonal shift into more profound and expansive degrees of freedom. This approach has found great success in many individual cases, for one primary instance in the work of Stanislav Grof, but it cannot attain its full efficacy until the pathologies that affect us on a collective scale, manifesting as climate change, patriarchy, racism, economic inequality, and global pandemic, as well as anxiety, addiction, and depression, are seen through by society at large, by the emergent multiplicity that we constitute. The pragmatic means of expanding this pluralist and constructivist mode of radical, transcendental empiricism beyond isolated individuals and pioneering "heroic" communities of scholars or practitioners, usually located at the institutional margins, must be envisioned and created, a heroic act partially constituted in releasing attachment to the exclusivist heroic fantasy, or even the fantasy of the sage who dispenses occult wisdom only to worthy aspirants in the often subtle authoritarianism of spiritual discipline. As Hillman writes, "the autonomy of fantasy is the soul's last refuge of dignity, its guarantor against all oppressions,"[94] and although a few individuals may serve as the conceptual personae who express and embody a novel mode which enables imaginal autonomy in a way that can actually infect and populate the central nodes of discursive power, this novelty is ultimately a collective construction built from countless differential compositions of words and personal relations. This construction enacts a wave in which each of us serves as a single droplet, though as James recognized, some of us will inevitably serve as "forerunners" who are "flung far ahead of the advancing edge of a wavecrest."[95]

Like Jung, Hillman recognizes alchemy as a predecessor to archetypal psychology, as it integrates, however nascently and imperfectly, the "intense discipline, with ethical devotion to their work, careful formulae, and high purposes" typically considered the province of scientific empiricism or religious monasticism with a radical imaginal "freedom and diversity, with full place for the bizarre and heretical,"[96] eschewing the literalist demand of repeatability. As alchemy's most sophisticated practitioners understood, psychic time is a complex and tortuously involuted domain discernible in moods as much as in concrete events, and not the static, neutral, linear movement reductively extracted from this more expansive manifold. Those aspects of experience beyond the solely physical are not mechanically reproducible, as each duration expresses a different qualitative milieu describable as the complex relationality of archetypes. The dramatic method descended from alchemy is oriented toward the "precise differentiation of qualities" through their slow, patient, vegetative digestion, rather than by means of a brisk and impatient "measurement of quantities,"[97] iteratively circulating through a particular complex, like the philosopher who eternally returns to the same open and evolving system of verbally constructed concepts in order slowly and painstakingly to elicit subtle novelties and nomadic variations on a thematic terrain.

As with the process of individuation, the alchemical opus begins with the imaginal, the primary material in the enclosing alembic into which the alchemist's depths are projected with an intensely smoldering attention externalized in the carefully tended fire, not progressing linearly toward a fixed result, but infinitely lured by interstitial, labyrinthine potencies, both uncannily alien and intimately familiar. The purpose of both alchemy and personifying is the learning that occurs in the process of pathologizing, "an integral, necessary aspect of soul-making,"[98] the chaotic dissolution and dismemberment of dominant egoic structures to create novel modes for expressing a deeper chaotic order in actuality through an imaginal naturalism for which "the differentiations that stand out sharply one day may recede into the underbrush or behind a cloud the next."[99] It is a constantly renegotiated integration of Apollonian and Dionysian in a reciprocally generated chaosmos, a "slightest change of tone" in which events and persons are encountered as pervasively informed by the gods. The networks of lines and structures which constitute our daily consensual reality remain initially unchanged, but the differentiating shades revealed within and behind these now-transparent "flatland" apparitions constitute the introduction of a novel degree of expressive freedom, a tonal shift which subtly, but fundamentally and inexorably, transforms the collective modes of relation.

The anima, which lures us toward more lovingly animated modes in a personification of the unconscious, the felt interiority imaginally projected into the mirror of others as objects of desire, affection, fantasy, or veneration (etymologically derived from Venus), has been variously figured not only as the goddess of love, but in the wisdom of Sophia, the compassion of the Virgin Mary, the destruction and renewal of Persephone, and the inspiration of the Muses. These figures lure us toward individuation, so that in the initial stage of projection, that which we desire seems to reside in the projected other, whether as human or nonhuman object, until the objectified person of a fancied lover or the personified object of a coveted possession are encountered in their complex actuality, disrupting the smooth surface which served the narcissistic reflection, drawing us into the depths to encounter the gift of real otherness, a submerged, interior domain of beauty and danger where we can venture but not abide. This withdrawal of projection differentiates the anima as an encountered potency from the temporary object into which she is projected, which allows us to love the other in their alien subjectivity rather than reductively incarcerating them in a corner of what we imagine, engaging in "the personalistic fallacy,"[100] constructing anima as a psyche that we possess, which paradoxically causes her to possess us, rather than as a collective which we express and which constitutes our individuality. The anima which, as Hillman quotes Jung, "cannot be completely integrated with"[101] our consciousness in an undifferentiated identity, teaches us that animism is a more realistic mode of relation than the violent depersonalization of everything outside the mind into mere objective materiality perpetrated by Cartesian rationalism, despite Descartes' good intentions. In this animistic mode, encountered others, both human and nonhuman, are recognized as genuinely other rather than as merely illusory narcissistic projections. The fantasy of anima is a deeper form of imaginal constructive elicitation than the simplistic fantasy of a radical separation of subject and object still dominant in late modernity, a fantasy which science and analytic philosophy generally take for granted, often myopically constraining the scope of what, or more precisely whom, they can envisage.

When these imaginal persons are repressed in the unconscious, they revolt as pathologies, as disorders and their symptoms, so that depotentiation can never be finally accomplished, but can only succeed in differentiating egoic rationality, a necessary and epochal achievement, but one which has come at the expense of eliciting the most destructive and painful expressions of gods who do not appreciate being imprisoned and ignored. A lover or spouse will never fulfill our bottomless desire for the anima, a father or mentor will never satisfy our infinite requirement for the Senex, an enemy or rival will never slake our martial thirst for blood. Salutary relations with other people can occur when we withdraw the idolatrous and fetishizing projections from these others to discern the anima as an other that I am. The attempt to replace the gods with the worship or demonization of other persons, to experience salvation in a lover or damnation in a seducer, is the reason why person-centered psychotherapy in its multiplicity of forms, despite the best intentions of a whole profession of psychologists, exhibits a limited efficacy.[102] The term "abnormal psychology"[103] is wildly erroneous, as nothing is more normal in our present epoch than anxiety and depression, deficits of attention and obsessive compulsions, dissociation and delusion, paranoia and addiction. Overcoming the pervasive pathologies of modern life that we all experience to some degree, without exception, requires that we collectively release the resistance to the occult stream of modern thought running through figures like Spinoza, Leibniz, Schelling, Hegel, Nietzsche, James, Bergson, and Deleuze, despite the tacit, but relatively pervasive, conspiracy of silence about this conceptual complex in the discourse of academics who otherwise revere these figures as central and canonical in the continental tradition. This overcoming requires engagement with the ambiguous reality of the gods and other powers intimately woven into the thought of these philosophers, though these potencies are generally neglected in discussions of their work, or reduced to mere allegory or conceit.

Personifying allows for an overcoming of the doubting cosmic isolation of the Cartesian ego through a rigorously achieved trust in the imaginal reality of psychic persons, unblocking occulted attention to the persistent felt knowledge that individuals are accompanied by a multiplicity of potencies who constitute their individual "fate,"[104] not only in the form of gods, but in the haunting by loved ones who have passed, of ancestors, of historical and fictional persons with whom the archetypal complexes that define the potentialities and constraints of each individual life resonate. These potencies speak through the individual persona so that egoic individuality is itself a personifying politically negotiated by the psychic collective, whether in a democratic or authoritarian mode. Personifying constitutes an inhabiting of the "middle position"[105] – resonant with Deleuze's recognition that "every multiplicity grows from the middle"[106] – of the relation between self and others characteristic of animism and mythology, not a return to identity, but to a polycentric multiplicity in the more expansive form of dialectic. This integral dialectic recognizes that self and world, soul and spirit, spirit and matter, East and West, South and North, mediate necessary differentiations which have temporarily been hierarchically emphasized, requiring not primarily a reconciliation in a return to unity through the *via negativa* of a spirit which solemnly intones that "straight is the gate and narrow is the way,"[107] but an affirmation that these dualities contain limited efficacy, and that they can be integrated as contrasts within a more expansive and labyrinthine pluralism whose interstitial horizons are only partially constructed from these intensive binaries. The imaginal personifying of a Dionysian psyche, with its profusion of spirits, is differentiated from the singular Apollonian spirit with which psyche has often been conflated in opposition to matter, serving as the chaosmic narrative intertextuality that allows for the dissolution and overcoming of duality in an enactment of these gods learning to speak each other's languages, two brothers carrying on their vehement and sustained conversation in a corner while the Bacchanalian revel rages around them.

Like the literalizations of oppositional metaphysics and theology, therapy is a ritualistic game which tends to literalize the gods as clinical disorders to be cured rather than as imaginal potencies to be encountered, a binary relation of therapist and patient which itself enacts the archetypal fantasy of the wounded healer for which the healer must heal their own wounds by undergoing an initiatory ordeal before they can mediate this initiatory self-healing for others. In the case of most modern therapy, however, this archetype, of which both the centaur Chiron and Christ who heals through his crucifixion are expressions, is split into a hierarchical duality, with the therapist literalized as the healer while the patient literalizes the wound rather than both parties enacting this polarity as a potency which exceeds and constitutes their relational individualities. The literalizing division of the archetypes produces the persistent and often unresolvable problems of therapy, the transferences and countertransferences, the resistances and defense mechanisms. This static binary can only be overcome not in the eradication of the pathology which prompted the therapy, but in the revolutionary recognition of, and intentional engagement with, the gods behind the pathologies as destiny, as immanent lures toward the liberated creative expression across orders of the faculties elicited by these potencies, rather than as an unconscious fate to which the individual is perpetually subjected.

Teleological development, progress, individuation, evolution, and growth into more expansive domains of relation is one set of archetypal complexes among others, which can be associated with the nurturing and nourishing "Great Mother"[108] archetype figured as Gaia, Demeter, Hera, and Cybele, but also with Zeus in his expansive and bountiful munificence (though Hera might provide a different perspective on his profligate infidelities, the lawgiver's arrogant flouting of his marital duties, which he in turn experiences as inhibiting his creative freedom), and with the Apollonian ascent toward unity or the Dionysian will to power. These complexes cannot be generalized to all psychological situations as therapy often seeks to do, though neither can the potencies associated with these complexes be completely dismissed as merely facile wish-fulfillment, the derisive claim of the tough-minded rejections of progressive unity and holistic growth ambiguously figured in the denouncement of the beautiful soul. Nevertheless, like progress, pathology is one essential mode of imaginal discernment, so that the disintegrations of illness, woundedness, and madness, and even the fantasies of incest, torture, and murder (though not their literalization), are just as integral to a mythically informed polycentric dialectic as are the integrations of healing, saving, and homecoming, of love, revelation, and bliss. There is no integration without differentiation, whether clinical or catastrophic, and all of the gods must be honored, however alien or disagreeable to our individual characters, to the particular constructions of multiplicity which constitute us, and from which no potency can ultimately be excluded.

The complex of hierarchical and paternalistic subjection is evident not only in therapy, but perhaps especially in the political realm. Mental health often means nothing more than thinking in accordance with the "specific ideology of compliant middle-class humanism,"[109] which pervades the domains of law, medicine, education, and governmental policy, enforcing the repression and denial of the gods encountered in pathology and madness through the figures of police and judge, doctor and therapist, teacher and administrator, bureaucrat and politician, rendering the envisaging of the reality and autonomy of potencies as pathological (in this term's solely negative inflection) outside the constraining enclosures of marginal religious or therapeutic communities.[110] These forces of discipline, punishment, and control, often despite the best intentions of those fulfilling these roles, who are themselves subject to these forces, aggressively and coercively occlude the recognition of the multiplicity of persons who constitute us in the central nodes of discourse for which we all must act the role of unified egoic individuals who can be judged, treated, educated, and legislated. This violent and multifarious enforcement of monocentric consciousness keeps us anxious, depressed, isolated, and afraid, rendering us exclusively subject to Kronos, whom all of these patriarchal figures embody, by means of the denial, repression, and perhaps most effectively, the trivialization of the personifying mode of thought.[111] Employers, for one primary example, almost always abuse their power in some way, as no matter how ethical and egalitarian the person is who plays this role, the fact of having coercive power over other adults is almost always destructive. This multivalent archetype, for whom the various paternalistic figures are substitutes, forces us into the reductive identities of subservient employee or capitalist consumer, subordinating us to deadening ideologies rather than enabling the engagement with living potencies, filling us up without providing sufficient nourishment, possessing us and alienating us from our generative psychological multiplicity, keeping us malnourished and soul-sick.

It is impossible to overthrow an oppressor whom we cannot see or name, who derisively dismisses our most profoundly felt concerns, our persistent sense that something is wrong, reducing our capacity for discerning the deeper significance of potencies to mere paranoia and the fantastic literalism of conspiracy theory. Through an infinitely deferred series of surrogates, our complaints and protests are gaslighted as insanity and delusion, or as mere hypochondria and whining not suitable to the rigidity and oppressiveness of the exclusively heroic style of consciousness, inextricably bound up with violence and misogyny. This invisible oppressor places the onus of blame and guilt for putative character flaws and moral failures (of career, marriage, parenting) solely on the suffering individual in the guise of the superego, like the great archer Philoctetes banished by Agamemnon during the Trojan War for his persistent wound received, in one version of the story, as retribution for one of Achilles' violent and wrathful transgressions. As Gebser observes, the wrath of Achilles in the first lines of the *Iliad* is a founding moment of the rationality that would reach its peak in modernity.[112]

The initiatory step in overcoming this rationalized society of control, this totalizing regime which systematically represses the pathologizing through which the gods speak, is to reveal the hidden saturnine potency who obliges our guilt and submission residing at its cold, brutal heart, not in the form of the demonic delegates whom he possesses, but as the god himself. He is never encountered alone, despite his solitude, but always in dramatic relational complexes with other gods, especially in league with the anger and violence of Ares, the harshly illuminated centrality of Apollo, a gang of patriarchal thugs (at least in this particular drama) vengefully returning from their own repression in the unconscious violently to push the other gods into the outer darkness. The Promethean and Dionysian abolition of the modern policing of all areas of human experience cannot be a final slaying of Kronos, a heroically liberating rejection of the negative, which Deleuze valiantly, though ambiguously, attempted, but a revolutionary, transformative death and rebirth of this potency, reenacted in his more positive and constructive valences within a rhizomatic multiplicity as structure, maturity, discernment, and wisdom. His more destructive and oppressive expressions are vengeance for us having forgotten him as, like all gods, Kronos demands to be remembered – as in the ancient Greek festival of Kronia and the Roman Saturnalia – Saturn presiding over the very act of remembering and honoring debts to gods and ancestors, of fulfilling the duties and obligations of tradition.

But this remembrance of the gods is not merely a return to nature, which Hillman calls "the naturalistic fallacy," though like Schelling, he recognizes that the gods are correlated with various natural processes. The conception of nature as an ideal norm to which we should adhere is the expression of a few potencies among many, the pristine, virginal Artemis or the maternal Gaia much discussed in relation to ecology, who certainly demand a radical shift in our relation to the natural processes that constitute both the Earth and our bodies. But an overly idealized and romanticized "naturalism soon declines into materialism,"[113] the privileging of the physical over the imaginal, as the privileging of any domain is what must be precluded by the mode which seeks to integrate all domains in a polycentric pluralism rather than a monocentric totality. Alchemy is an *opus contra naturam*, a "work against nature"[114] imaginally dwelling with the bizarre and the monstrous of pathology, perhaps most fully expressed by the figures and narratives of mythology, in order to produce a transmutation both in the *prima materia* and in the alchemist's depths. Nature is not an ideal unity, but a multiplicity of complexly interacting forces correlated with the entire pantheon of powers, so that the question posed to the oracles at Delphi and Dodona is often: "To what god or hero must I pray or sacrifice to achieve such and such a purpose?"[115] The deeper questions are not concerned with monocausal explanations, but with which gods must be remembered, honored, propitiated, or enacted in each dramatic situation, whether the agricultural cultivation of the maternal Demeter, a human practice which transforms the nature from which we emerge; the heroic Herculean conquering and violence of the hunt or the exploration of new vistas beyond our settled territories; the generative chaos, intoxication, animality, and dismemberment of Dionysus; or even the rational and mechanistic order of Kronos presiding over the planetary or atomic orbits in their mathematical harmony, but also over melancholy, suffering, death, decay, and the negative. "Human being is essentially 'differing' being," and "the fundamental principle of psychological life is differentiation,"[116] as we are nature transforming itself by differentiating itself, sometimes in torturous opposition with itself, in concert with the disparate gods who constitute and inform both our individualities and the worlds we inhabit and construct.

    The devastation we have brought to the Earth cannot be reduced to the pure goodness of nature and the debased evil of a sinful human culture, but is perhaps the result of the unavoidable death of the gods in their mirth. This epochal initiatory ordeal has been paradoxically necessary for the differentiation of human autonomy in order to create the preconditions for the novel expressions of these potencies in a dialectic which is not a mere return to a placid and undifferentiated identity and wholeness, but a rebirth into the more expansive and intensive expressions of mythically differentiated multiplicity integrated as the contrasting relational structures and forces of a more efficacious and open polycentric totality. As Hillman writes, "psychologically, the Gods are never dead,"[117] and this death-and-rebirth ordeal enacts not a mere return to childhood innocence, but the devastating immolation of self-centered adolescent rebellion creating the precondition for a mature adulthood in which the complex and challenging adventures of negotiating the divinely correlated contours of durational experience do not cease in a tranquil retirement, but are transposed into deeper and higher expressions. Thus, the juvenile Oedipal reaction becomes the monumental task of composing the definitive text against the Oedipal, the fulfillment of a dramatic destiny in its most expansive register. Mythical dramatizations enacting the complex relations of disparate potencies are not prescribed compositions for which the lines are already written, only remaining to be recited with varying emphases and inflections, but radically open improvisations and creative variations on thematic elements and melodic refrains that are always shifting, never settled, employing whichever masks and instruments are ready-to-hand in the fractured and deformed mirror of psychic experience.

Personifying is not a cure for pathology, but the means of entrance into a deeper game whose only precondition is that we attentively engage with the differentiated potencies that constitute our immanent interiority. Paracelsus, like many others in the Renaissance, associated these potencies with an imaginal cosmography correlating the gods and the planets, revealing a novel degree of freedom for our liberated exploration, the fluid medium of depth reciprocally elicited by the invention of our own peculiar ways of swimming toward the more expansive horizons constructed through this paradoxical activity. Personifying enables the creation of novel concepts to express more profound valences of Ideas, which allow us to peer further into the depths in a novel Copernican revolution whose polycentrism renders visible a chaosmos beyond the daylight illumination of egoic monocentrism which occults the wandering stars of our interiority. And this deepening is often enacted through the repetitious rumination and the depressive descent associated with Kronos, the pathology against which our culture most manically defends, evident in the pervasiveness of antidepressants (an admittedly reasonable pervasion in our current problematic context). Depression is the psychological substitution for the Christian descent into hell and the encounter with the Enemy, a descent into evil and sin which must be avoided at all costs by spreading the "good news" of Christ's saving resurrection. This is the very denial through the unification of a monocentric reconciliation which Nietzsche railed against in his anti-Christian rebirth of tragedy, liberating the polycentric Dionysian underworld where the soul is transformed through the pathos of both passion and suffering.

But in identifying himself as Dionysus or The Crucified, Nietzsche perhaps made an error, though an understandable one given his pioneering solitude and the lack of collective modes of thought and concomitant societal structures to contain his madness as generative chaos rather than as mere destructive disorder, modes and structures he did as much as anyone to construct.[118] We do not only enact one divine role in an archetypal drama, but rather the gods pervade the relational dramas of life, so that the saturnine father who controls and punishes his children, psychologically devouring them, is just as much a victim of the punitive control of his superego by which he is devoured. And the embattled sensuality of a passionate couple cannot be facilely reduced to a man embodying the god of war and a woman enacting the goddess of love, as both parties in all kinds of couples, of all gender combinations, partake of both eroticism and anger, both seduction and assertion, the Greek Aphroditus (or Hermaphroditos) and the Roman Venus Barbata figuring the goddess of love with the body and dress of a woman, but with beard, phallus, and helmet, "secretly in love with war."[119] By imaginally discerning these archetypal complexes of potencies in the relationality not only among the individuals associated with different bodies, but among the persons who constitute an individual psyche, rather than forcing an egoic identity with a particular archetype, the flat, monochromatic literalism of any situation can be rendered transparent.

While the recurring struggle between father and children still occurs, while the lovers still quarrel and reconcile, these activities are undertaken with the ever-present sense that these are archetypal dramas echoing all of the previous enactments of these complexes in an infinite regress along a nonlocal series receding orthogonally into an additional degree of freedom, the imaginal dimension of the bottomless depths of *memoria* for which the temporal present is a lower-dimensional surface projection. Each time we enact the repetition of a complex potentiality, we have the opportunity to create a novel fold in the texture of process, a differential iteration which has not yet existed in actuality, and which thus returns in the eternal return, while that which is habitual and unconsciously automated does not return. The typically familial Oedipal drama, replayed without awareness countless times, fades away as soon as the lines are recited and the motions gone through, while the composition of *Anti-Oedipus* becomes an enduring achievement around which new domains of activity, affect, and conception can be constructively elicited, Hillman quoting Paul Ricoeur that "enigma does not block understanding but provokes it,"[120] an enigmatic constructivism which reveals through obscurity, creates through destruction.

Nietzsche's error of overidentifying with single archetypes, Dionysus or The Crucified, is not simply a moment that can be negated and discarded, as errancy is integral to psychologizing, Hillman tarrying with the medieval figure of the Knight Errant in resonance with the Deleuzoguattarian figure of the nomad, and echoing Deleuze's pronouncement that "the history of the world is marked by the great figures of errancy: Odysseus, Don Quixote, the Wandering Jew."[121] The Knight Errant is not an epic hero linearly driven by singleness of purpose, but a renegade against literalism, a rogue wanderer lured by Eros and Ananke, the goddess beneath whose throne the eternally circulating souls must pass in the *Republic* to receive their destiny, embodying the "Errant Cause"[122] of the *Timaeus*, the necessity of affective and imaginal inclinations associated with disparate gods. This conception of destiny leads through a nonlinear and nonlocal series of picaresque narrative episodes in a process of learning enacting the positive irresponsibility which Deleuze designates as "Nietzsche's most noble and beautiful secret,"[123] the mandate to discover through error which liberates from the heavy burdens of guilt, sin, and judgment, and of forgiveness, redemption, and exoneration, imposed by the "moralistic fallacy"[124] of controlling reason. This secret of imaginal irresponsibility beyond the reductive, legislative morality of good and evil, the heavy egoic responsibility of a totalizing humanism, is not merely a license to do anything to anyone, as the Nazis imagined. It is an ethical stance deeply resonant with Spinoza, which recognizes that the will is determined by divinely imposed affective and imaginal potencies: impulses, emotions, and fantasies which we do not choose, which possess us more than we possess them, but which we are capable of freely choosing how to express if we become conscious of their transpersonal otherness. Humanism, whether Christian or secular and existential, places responsibility solely on the egoic human to forgive and forget, but the gods who compose us through our dramatic enactments rarely forgive, and they demand remembrance.

This errant perspective understands, like Hegel and Whitehead (with their negative tarryings and negative prehensions), like Freud and Jung (with their slips and free associations), that error is an integral aspect of becoming, and that errancy coincides with problematically encountered potencies, enacting a deconstruction and differentiated integration of the oppositions of rational and irrational, purposive and purposeless. Irrational purposelessness is a necessary complement to purposive rationality, but chaos cannot be reduced merely to serving a monocentric teleological order as error to be rectified and eradicated in the totalizing fantasy of progressive reason, relegated to the mere "shadow enemy of truth."[125] Rather, becoming negotiates a complex and paradoxical destiny more profound than a mere binary decision between chance and fate, Nietzsche's "iron hands of necessity which shake the dice-box of chance."[126] Hillman evokes this paradoxical destiny as "the gift of an inhuman daimon who demands human service"[127] in a fictional chaosmos from which the binaries of chaos and order, chance and necessity, are extracted to construct the hierarchical privilegings of logocentric rationality, the "errant fantasy"[128] violently subjugated by the fantasy of pure reason. Roguish Dionysus and chivalric Apollo are never encountered alone, but always engaged in intense relations whose partial truths are inextricable from Hermetic duplicities, equivocations, and confabulations. Their brother Hermes, the middle son of Zeus in this triad, who carried and protected the infant Dionysus, serves as intermediary, performing a discordant hermeneutic which deepens by unsettling in a mongrel, deviant circulation at the liminal border between the static determinism of order and the aleatory freedom of chaos.

## Notes

1 Hillman, *Re-Visioning*, xii.
2 See Hillman, *Archetypal*, 138–55.
3 Hillman, *Archetypal*, xii.
4 In "Back to Beyond" (220–4) Hillman recognizes this archetypal cosmology as going beyond the archetypal psychology of *Re-Visioning Psychology*, a recognition particularly taken up by Richard Tarnas in *Cosmos and Psyche*.
5 Hillman, *Re-Visioning*, x.
6 Hillman, *Re-Visioning*, 152.
7 Deleuze, *Essays*, 62; Deleuze, *Cinema 2*, 7, 104, 149.
8 Deleuze and Guattari, *Thousand*, 112.
9 Deleuze and Guattari, *Anti-Oedipus*, 36.
10 Hillman, *Re-Visioning*, 153.
11 Hillman, *Puer Papers*, 3–53.
12 Hillman, *Re-Visioning*, 128.
13 Deleuze, *Essays*, 129.

14 Heraclitus, *Fragments*, 71.
15 Hillman, *Re-Visioning*, 142.
16 Hillman, *Re-Visioning*, 134.
17 Hillman, *Re-Visioning*, 186.
18 Hillman, *Re-Visioning*, 97.
19 Hillman, *Re-Visioning*, 206.
20 Hillman, *Re-Visioning*, 14.
21 Hillman, *Re-Visioning*, 109.
22 Hillman, *Re-Visioning*, 14.
23 Hillman, *Re-Visioning*, 15.
24 Hillman, *Re-Visioning*, 186.
25 Hillman, *Re-Visioning*, xiii.
26 Jung, *Archetypes*, 30.
27 Hillman, *Re-Visioning*, 170–1.
28 Hillman, *Re-Visioning*, 222.
29 Hillman, *Re-Visioning*, xv.
30 Hillman, *Re-Visioning*, 139.
31 Deleuze, *Desert*, 9–14; Jung, *Archetypes*, 19.
32 Hillman, *Re-Visioning*, 109.
33 Hillman, *Re-Visioning*, 117–18.
34 Hillman, *Re-Visioning*, xvi.
35 Hillman, *Re-Visioning*, 140.
36 Hillman, *Re-Visioning*, 2.
37 Hillman, *Re-Visioning*, 156.
38 Hillman, *Re-Visioning*, 135.
39 Hillman, *Re-Visioning*, xvi.
40 Gebser, *Origin*, 151.
41 Stengers, "Beyond," 246.
42 Hillman, *Re-Visioning*, 7.
43 Deleuze and Guattari, *Anti-Oedipus*, 84.
44 Deleuze and Guattari, *Anti-Oedipus*, 131.
45 Deleuze and Guattari, *Anti-Oedipus*, 360.
46 Deleuze and Guattari, *Anti-Oedipus*, 138.
47 Hillman, *Re-Visioning*, 106–7.
48 Nietzsche, *Gay*, 167; Deleuze and Parnet, *Dialogues*, 5.
49 Dosse, *Intersecting*, 8.
50 Deleuze, *Two*, 129.
51 Patton and Protevi, *Deleuze*, 188.
52 Deleuze, *Essays*, 129; Deleuze, *Letters*, 69.
53 Hillman, *Re-Visioning*, 224.
54 Deleuze and Guattari, *Anti-Oedipus*, 320.
55 Hillman, *Re-Visioning*, 63.
56 Deleuze, *Two*, 179.
57 Hegel, *Mind*, 143.
58 Hillman, *Re-Visioning*, 63.
59 Hillman, *Re-Visioning*, 112.
60 Hillman, *Re-Visioning*, 108.
61 Hillman, *Re-Visioning*, 61.

62 Hillman, *Re-Visioning*, 17.
63 Hillman, *Re-Visioning*, 18–19.
64 Hillman, *Re-Visioning*, 61.
65 Hillman, *Re-Visioning*, 19.
66 Hillman, *Re-Visioning*, 24.
67 Deleuze and Guattari, *Thousand*, 3.
68 Hillman, *Re-Visioning*, 22.
69 Hillman, *Re-Visioning*, 155.
70 Hillman, *Re-Visioning*, 22.
71 Fisher, *Capitalist*, 243; Deleuze, *Desert*, 178.
72 Deleuze and Guattari, *Kafka*, 67; Deleuze, *Cinema 2*, 81.
73 May, "Explain."
74 Ramey, *Hermetic*, 3, 7.
75 Stengers, *Thinking*, 244.
76 Herring, "Bergson." See Stengers, *Another*, 23–47.
77 Jung, *Civilization*, 484.
78 Hillman, *Re-Visioning*, 22.
79 Jung, *Speaking*, 233.
80 Hillman, *Re-Visioning*, 24.
81 Jung, *Memories*, 150, 155.
82 Hillman, *Re-Visioning*, 26.
83 Hillman, *Re-Visioning*, 27.
84 Hillman, *Re-Visioning*, 144.
85 Hillman, *Re-Visioning*, 27.
86 Hillman, *Re-Visioning*, 27.
87 Nietzsche, *Anti-Christ*, 211–12.
88 Hillman, *Re-Visioning*, 207.
89 Hillman, *Re-Visioning*, 97.
90 Hillman, *Re-Visioning*, 31.
91 Hillman, *Re-Visioning*, 35.
92 Hillman, *Re-Visioning*, 37.
93 Hillman, *Re-Visioning*, 75.
94 Hillman, *Re-Visioning*, 39.
95 James, *Writings*, 325.
96 Hillman, *Re-Visioning*, 40.
97 Hillman, *Re-Visioning*, 42.
98 Hillman, *Re-Visioning*, 90.
99 Hillman, *Re-Visioning*, 40.
100 Hillman, *Re-Visioning*, 49.
101 Hillman, *Re-Visioning*, 45.
102 See Hillman and Ventura, *Psychotherapy*.
103 Hillman, *Re-Visioning*, 58.
104 Hillman, *Re-Visioning*, 51.
105 Hillman, *Re-Visioning*, 68.
106 Deleuze and Parnet, *Dialogues*, viii, 39.
107 Matthew 7:14.
108 Hillman, *Re-Visioning*, 123.
109 Hillman, *Re-Visioning*, 77.

110 Deleuze, *Desert*, 210.
111 Deleuze, *Two*, 98.
112 Gebser, *Origin*, 71.
113 Hillman, *Re-Visioning*, 84.
114 Hillman, *Re-Visioning*, 91.
115 Hillman, *Re-Visioning*, 139.
116 Hillman, *Re-Visioning*, 88.
117 Hillman, *Re-Visioning*, 170.
118 Jung, *Archetypes*, 103–4.
119 Hillman, *Re-Visioning*, 184.
120 Hillman, *Re-Visioning*, 152.
121 Deleuze, *Desert*, 156.
122 Hillman, *Re-Visioning*, 159.
123 Deleuze, *Nietzsche*, 21.
124 Hillman, *Re-Visioning*, 163.
125 Hillman, *Re-Visioning*, 161.
126 Nietzsche, *Daybreak*, 130; Deleuze, *Foucault*, 86.
127 Hillman, *Re-Visioning*, 175.
128 Hillman, *Re-Visioning*, 159.

Chapter 13

# The Question of Integration
Concluding with Isabelle Stengers

Two primary streams of thought, both inextricably philosophical and psychological, are entwined in the pages above, initiated for the twentieth century by the conceptual personae of James and Jung, both variously influenced by the pre-twentieth century philosophers and, following Stengers, both issuing into what may be designated a "psycho-philosophy."[1] The stream of thought initiated by James passes through Bergson and Whitehead, and into Deleuze and Stengers, while the stream of thought initiated by Jung issues into Deleuze and Hillman, both streams confluent with numerous other streams. Stengers does not take up the Jungian lineage from Deleuze, though her reclaiming of animism enables one of the primary projects of this concluding chapter: to bring the Jamesian-Bergsonian-Whiteheadian stream for which she is a primary heir into resonance with the Jungian-Hillmanian stream, both of which find twentieth-century culminations in Deleuze, an integration which may be imaginally figured in the two evenings that Jung and James spent together in 1909.

Stengers possesses as strong a claim as anyone to being a primary heir to the projects of both Whitehead and Deleuze, the latter of whom held her work in high regard, telling the students at a 1987 lecture, with Stengers in attendance: "Since Isabelle Stengers is here today, and won't be here in the coming weeks, I need to benefit from her presence."[2] We should also take advantage of Stengers' subtle presence in the project of constructing a novel mode of thought. Stengers is comparable to Deleuze in complexity, her writing unfolding over sinuous paragraphs, leading one ever deeper into the misty labyrinths where the secrets of reality reside, not sharp and thrillingly transgressive like Deleuze, but slow, careful, and world dissolvingly profound. This concluding chapter thinks primarily with the elements of Stengers' texts which are not concerned with the specifics of

DOI: 10.4324/9781003195498-14

science, however tempting it is extensively to explicate the scientific ruminations which dominate the two-volume opus of 1997's *Cosmopolitics*, rather thinking with Stengers through 2002's *Thinking With Whitehead* and "Beyond Conversation," 2005's *Capitalist Sorcery* (with Phillipe Pignarre), 2008's *In Catastrophic Times*, 2011's "Reclaiming Animism," and 2013's *Another Science Is Possible*.

One of Stengers' great innovations is that *Thinking With Whitehead* is not merely secondary literature, which can certainly be extremely useful and illuminating, but a primary contribution to the mode of thought we are collectively constructing which explicitly removes the author from the center of the narrative. It forms a model, along with Deleuze's books on individual philosophers, that constructs the magnum opus not primarily as a solitary heroic effort, though it inevitably retains this character to some extent, but deemphasized in favor of a novel mode for which the egoic center of the philosophical narrative is no longer a totalitarian dictator, however admired or loved, but a first among equals. This novel mode is a Whiteheadian "slightest change of tone" in which the Deleuzean "dissolved self" allows the others previously relegated to the unconscious background as subterranean influences or explicit interlocutors, including those who read the text, to emerge in a more ambiguous light. It renders the writer multiple, like Deleuze and Guattari who resisted attempts to attribute certain parts of their co-written texts to the primary authorship of one or the other, but under the designation of a single author who, like Plato or Hermes Trismegistus, becomes an organizing nomination for a dynamic and multivalent cast of characters, a complex constellation of intertwining potencies.[3]

Much of *Cosmopolitics* is devoted to problematizing the binary question of whether the project of physics is to discover preexistent truths which reside in a transcendent domain, a grounding identity accessible to pure reason which James Clerk Maxwell mythically figured as The Queen of Heaven, or merely socially to construct theories which do not communicate with any reality outside of language, mathematics, and the human mind, a Whiteheadian "bifurcation of nature" which he and Stengers diagnose as "a disastrous philosophical fiction."[4] Stengers situates scientific practice in an immanent "ecology of practices"[5] beyond the simplistic duality of physics as either discovering immutable laws of nature or projecting purely human concerns onto a mute and unknowable cosmos. This constructivism discerns the cocreative elicitation of different beings from often discordant, contradictory, incommensurable, and paradoxical multiplicities through the "art of negotiating the in-between," narrating the interstitial relations of "genuine actors, interacting with one another in genuine intrigues."[6] The existence of beings like particles, forces, or even the arrow of time can neither be considered fully actualized prior to measurement and their narrative constructions partially formulated in mathematics, nor merely fictions created out of the imaginations of their discoverers, as entities transcend their discoverers but do not authorize the assertion of a transcendent domain, problematizing the very opposition between truth and fiction. The ontological status of these beings is similarly ambiguous to Freudian childhood traumas, to archetypes, or to the gods of polytheism, relational constructions which constantly negotiate with the requirements and obligations of a real virtuality that we bring into actuality through our attempts to know it, a transversal "reciprocal capture" for which "identities that coinvent one another each integrate a reference to the other for their own benefit."[7] In fact, this physical narrativity is intimately intertwined with "the question of integration"[8] which, involving and resonating with both mathematics and metaphysics, has sustainedly struggled with the problem of how the various theoretical, mathematical, and experimental constructs that constitute physics can be brought together into increasingly expansive and finely differentiated structures of integral coherence. This narrative is also resonant with questions about the possibility of creating peace among apparently incommensurable modes which Stengers variously associates with the cosmopolitical parliament, Deleuze's designation of Spinozan ethics as an ethology, Leibnizian *Calculemus*, Jamesian pragmatism, Whiteheadian speculative empiricism, and philosophical peace fighters.

Stengers recognizes that no harmoniously unified theory will ever be able to demonstrate both the reality of the neutrino in particle physics and the spirits encountered in ethnopsychiatry in a way that is fully satisfying to the requirements of either discipline because these entities and subjects are extracted from more expansive topological domains that exceed their specific constraints. Constraints are open questions which can be satisfied in different ways, various possible labyrinthine intrigues "compatible with that same terrain,"[9] not in a "utopian reconciliation,"[10] but in the recognition that all practices respond to limiting requirements and obligations. This recognition allows the affirmation of the coexistence, and even resonance, of these disparate beings in a risky cosmopolitical constructivism beyond the oppositionality of exclusivist scientific rationalism, deeply embedded in static institutions defined by pervasive bureaucratic professionalization, which often inhibits novel creation despite the best intentions of those employed by these institutions, and recognizing that novel modes of thought require the creation of novel institutions for their collective efficacy. Ironically, scientistic realism narratively defines itself by the polemical judgment and disqualification – a Jamesian "refusal to consent to understand,"[11] a Whiteheadian "great refusal"[12] – of other beings not subject to scientific verification, and the modes required for their elicitation, as mere mythical and imaginal fictions. And although the chemist may judge the alchemist, the psychoanalyst disqualify the shaman, or the astronomer ridicule the astrologer, the potencies encountered in alembic, ritual, or horoscope nevertheless play just as integral a role in various cultures as the neutrino does in the "cult"[13] of modern cosmology. "One day," Stengers writes, "perhaps, we will experience a certain shame and great sadness at having dismissed the age-old traditions"[14] and the modes of knowledge and activity they embody, which can be conceived as complementary to characteristically modern modes.

"When astronomers make fun of astrologers," Stengers observes in *Thinking With Whitehead*, they a priori define the sky "as bereft of any other meaning"[15] than the physical, subjecting astrology to the exclusive authority of science without attempting to comprehend this practice, so prevalent in nonmodern and non-Western cultures – and as diverse as scientific practice itself – on its own terms, often betraying a lack of nuanced understanding of what they deride. For instance, the vast majority of astrology's critics are unaware of contemporary conversations among astrologers concerning the efficacy of the signs correlated with the constellations, about which some astrologers remain ambivalent given the troubling issue of the precession of the equinoxes. Rather, these archetypal cosmologists focus their efforts on the study of nonlocal and nonlinear correlations between the angular relations of the planets, associated with the gods of Hellenic polytheism in the Western tradition, and events in human experience on both individual and collective scales, which can be conceived in the mode of a Deleuzean repetition of one dramatic situation of "another at a different level."[16] Why should it be socially and professionally acceptable facilely to denounce these correlations as a mere transmission of local, causal influences, a naïve mode of construction which no philosophically sophisticated astrologer asserts, if "the electron does not let itself be localized, any more than the cat whose Carrollian grin I can see"?[17] How can one communicate the nuances of one's mode of thought to an interlocutor who refuses to listen, who "does not integrate within her own reality the aspect of herself I am proposing,"[18] but condescendingly and preemptively dismisses what she reductively and erroneously assumes one will say? "How can we affirm," Stengers asks, both "the adventures of Kant and those of a shaman?"[19]

Along with Whitehead, Stengers equally eschews the resentful denouncement of the modern epoch which has privileged rationality in a mere reversal, so that rather than rejecting rationality, Whitehead "takes this rationality to the limit, and therefore makes it change its nature"[20] into a more expansive faculty, an intuitive speculative empiricism that exceeds solitary rationality. Stengers positions both the nonmodern practices of astrology, alchemy, or shamanism and the modern practices of science, technology, or economics as necessarily privileged in their appropriate epochs, though the epochs defined by these successive privilegings are of limited duration, so that the denouncement of superstition was necessary for the liberation of thought in the eighteenth century, but became inhibiting to heterodox speculation in the nineteenth century.[21] And these successive epochs will inevitably be subsumed in a novel epoch not primarily by appeal to the judgment of logical proof and polemical refutation, but to "imagination, the only eventual producer of a transformation in habits,"[22] Stengers dreaming with Whitehead of both modern and nonmodern actors being reciprocally transformed by this subsumption. When Stengers describes the actors of physics engaging in a dramatizing which is "inseparable from the role they play"[23] in their milieu, she might as well be evoking the Deleuzean gods with their roles, whose multiplicity of relations itself forms the stage on which the action occurs. Both the system of physics and the system of the gods are well-founded fictions, narrative constructions which answer to their own partial requirements and obligations while ignoring or deemphasizing others. The task for a novel epoch may circulate around the question of how to achieve integral generalizations which take account of the different potentialities and constraints of the most expansive possible field of relations, encompassing both gods and particles, as well as the entities characteristic of other systems answering to other dynamisms and demands.

Like the nonmodern others of animism or astrology – in a conception of "living person"[24] which Stengers declines, in a Whiteheadian mode, to associate exclusively with humans – the neutrino is an "ensemble representation"[25] which is "susceptible only to interactions that occur very rarely."[26] All of these entities require esoteric knowledge and patient attentiveness within carefully constructed conditions for their elicitation, whether the particle accelerator or the shamanic ceremony, though both phantom particles and phantasmic ancestors demand thought and action within their respective domains when they are encountered. Science does not require a disqualification of the other for its efficacy, but only for claims to exclusive truth, and thus cosmopolitics "integrates, problematically, the question of an ecology of practices,"[27] constructing, through novel language, the possibility of peace among the various values that define modernity by their inclusion or exclusion in an unknown elsewhere whose loss we may mourn, but which "we must pass over in silence."[28] This problematic integration is a discordant accord beyond mere silent tolerance between science and its nonmodern others, whether ancestor spirits, djinns, or gods. With extreme care and subtlety, Stengers makes visible how the putatively autonomous beings elicited by the technological devices and mathematical formulations of physics can only find proof through their contextual efficacy within communities of practice. She demonstrates, with great sympathy for scientific endeavors, that faith in the ultimate intelligibility of the universe beyond the paradoxes and irrationalities that still bedevil the frontiers of physics, a faith initiated by Galileo which asserts its authority to judge and denounce "the teeming multiplicity of ways of knowing"[29] beyond science as merely irrational, is no more rationally grounded than a belief in spirits or gods. These beliefs, whether in pure reason or agential others, pragmatically produce their own limited domains of verification from a more expansive virtual domain always exceeding their actual elicitation, so that belief and reason form an opposition extracted from a plural and integral univocity, a generative problem for one phase of process which can be reframed in a novel phase as a nonhierarchical contrast revealing deeper questions.

In *Thinking With Whitehead*, Stengers recognizes that Whitehead's conception of God is distinctly secular and immanent, closer to the Greek Eros than to a Christian divinity,[30] a conception partially derived from Spinozan pantheism, variously resonant with the Leibnizian, Bergsonian, and Deleuzean conceptions of divinity, and neutral in the opposition between chaos and cosmos, a chaosmic conception for which the "solitary consciousness"[31] inseparable from despotic monotheism may begin to open to interstitial novelty. And is it not precisely the Deleuzean-Nietzschean gods who "have died from laughing" that abide, as virtual potencies demanding ingression, in the interstices of the fracturing of monotheistic solitude? This fracturing intimated by Stengers may perhaps serve to open Whitehead's thought from the monotheism with which he primarily dwells to polytheism, which he does not generally evoke, but with which his pluralist constructivism resonates, a conception of potencies which Stengers carries forward by reclaiming animism, the multiplicitous dancing fairies as complement to the singular Crucified.[32] Stengers differentiates Whitehead's monotheistic conception, which was perhaps more efficacious in the context and culture within which he was writing,[33] from James' given that Whitehead envisioned himself as James' heir, though this conception is also distinctly pragmatic and constructivist, so that "God is that thanks to which each act of creation can integrate" the local "evils" of destructive discordance in more expansively differentiated contrasts.[34] She even deploys, at a crucial moment in the final chapter – which discusses how Whitehead's conception of God transforms the divine personality into a problematic question luring ingression – a passage from Deleuze that veritably shouts his penchant for polytheism: "This decisional power at the heart of problems, this creation, this launching that makes us members of the race of the gods, is nevertheless not ours. The gods themselves are subject to the laws of Ananke."[35] However, Stengers does not turn down this path toward the multiplicity of divine persons in this text, does not even comment upon their appearance, leaving the gods and their problematic destinies there for us plainly to see but almost pointedly ignoring them, turning from Whitehead's appropriation of the imagery of monotheism not toward the gods, but to animism, mostly eschewing the admittedly patriarchal Hellenic pantheon for the animistic mode whose practice in recent centuries has perhaps been dominated by women: witchcraft.[36]

This is a decisive moment in Stengers' text, as the passage she employs from Deleuze brings her up to the precipice beyond where the gods must be affirmed, though she does not take this particular leap which Deleuze undertook, however enigmatically, at least not in this text. The reasons for this decision are perhaps unknowable from reading her work. Does she eschew the path of polytheism at this juncture because she does not find it efficacious, tracing a progressive turning back from exclusivist oppositional modern rationality to animism through an intervening monotheism without extensively tarrying with polytheism because it simply does not appeal to her temperament? Or is this conspicuous absence of the gods a strategic choice motivated by the sense that an affirmation of these potencies might be a bridge too far, a crossing of the Rubicon that would risk disqualifying her careful, patient work from being heard and embraced by theorists who still adhere to unexamined prejudices or, perhaps more importantly, who obey certain lingering prohibitions, whatever their personal beliefs, despite often dubious claims to an ultimate criticality toward their own positions as well as their cultural milieus? Or does she simply not take this step because her book thinks with Whitehead, and Whitehead does not take this step? Perhaps it is even possible that Stengers has deliberately set up the pieces of this puzzle to be assembled by her readers, the clues to be deciphered, making possible this further step without finding it necessary to take it herself, a supposition supported by the moments in her texts when she acknowledges, always in passing, at least until 2008, the efficacy of the gods as much as the beings of physics or the spirits of animism.

Stengers almost asks to be appropriated and employed in novel areas, recognizing that a philosopher's heirs, "occupied with their own business, will dispose as they see fit of what you propose to them." We may thus feel encouraged to risk carrying her thought into a different domain, that of polytheism, especially given her profound debt to Deleuze, calling upon her "humorous double,"[37] constructed in relation to the requirements and obligations of her texts, which allows both the positive affirmation of the philosopher's identity, as well as the denial required for this affirmation, serving as its negative space, to return in the eternal return, to be saved by Whitehead's impersonal, mathematical God. Because we have already come so far, in these pages, in discerning the gods of a mythical dialectic, I am risking bringing this polytheistic consciousness into relation with the concepts expressed by Stengers, who often evokes most of the theorists above. Her thought is deeply resonant with the polytheistic mode that she almost studiously avoids, especially in her earlier texts, but which unmistakably glimmers just at the horizons of her writing, not only in her discussions of animism, but in her recognition of the actors who respond to scientific inquiry, the liminal entities of physics and the biological organisms whose study is inseparable from their celebration.

In fact, beginning in 2005 with *Capitalist Sorcery*, and continuing in 2008 with *In Catastrophic Times* and 2013 with *Another Science Is Possible*, Stengers began to enact a somewhat different emphasis in her work, a slight tonal shift, not only in her turn from engaging primarily with the history of philosophy and scientific invention to questions of capitalism, climate change, and genetically modified organisms, but, finally, in calling upon the figures of Hermes and Gaia in addition to her evocations of witchcraft, sorcery, and animism. Stengers figures climate change as "the intrusion of Gaia"[38] to which we must respond, and she explicitly eschews associating this catastrophe with "Ouranos or Chronos," Gaia's "terrible children,"[39] as it is specifically Gaia's blind and fearsome indifference we have offended, so she is the goddess who must be remembered.[40]

A primary excluded other in the history of philosophy is the Sophist, a figure to whom Stengers returns in a number of texts, who, along with poets and magicians, serves to problematize the image of thought as the pure pursuit of truth figured as an escape from the cave of immanence.[41] The Sophist is an irrepressible figure which both Derrida and Deleuze partially express in very different ways, making endless trouble and anxiety for those who would unambiguously assert transcendent, objective truth beyond our immanent constructions, embodying the *pharmakon*, the drug which can have opposite effects at different doses, healing or destroying in the guise of "savior or sorcerer,"[42] though healing is often inextricably entwined with destruction. However, although both Derrida and Deleuze are oriented toward overcoming the past, Stengers views the creation of novel concepts characteristic of both Deleuze and Whitehead as leading beyond the binary opposition of an absolute authority of transcendent laws and their "critical deconstruction."[43] Stengers' "imagination and hope come up against their limits"[44] with Derrida, for whom, she implies, we are "'imprisoned' in the network of our symbols and our meanings,"[45] enacting that "old traumatic truth" which crushes the "hope to get outside,"[46] though she also acknowledges that the binary of deconstructive and constructive postmodernism itself is a construction peculiar to the American reading of primarily French texts not as prevalent in Europe.[47] Certain elements of Deleuze's work have a strong affinity with deconstruction, particularly his critiques of Hegel and of the Oedipal, in which he and Guattari explicitly refer to Derrida, so that the French tradition which tends to exalt enigma and obscurity is generally more suspicious than the Anglophone philosophy derived from James and Whitehead of any kind of totalizing unification. In contrast, "Whitehead does not deconstruct anything," but rather understands "that oppositions are never final, that producing the possibility of enjoying new contrasts where oppositions once ruled is the adventure of both hope and reason."[48] The somewhat darker and more dramatic palette of Deleuze's constructivist thought, largely derived from Nietzsche, provides a figure of integration, beyond even the "middle ground"[49] Stengers produces between Whitehead and Deleuze, for the almost purely negative project of Derridean deconstruction and the almost purely positive "radical constructivism"[50] of Whitehead, which "takes every construction to its cosmological power,"[51] though like Bergson, Deleuze certainly leans in this constructive direction with his multivalent conceptions of dynamic potentialities, and of philosophy as the creation of concepts.[52]

However, Deleuze sometimes engages in "the heroic mode of radical risk and extreme solitude"[53] that may be recognized in a Hillmanian vein as the ego resisting its initiatory dissolution and death even in the affirmation of pain and madness, an attitude of refusal modeled on those aspects of Nietzsche which may be deemphasized in an integral mode consonant with Whitehead's less contentious presence. This deemphasis of the ego is copiously affirmed by Deleuze, though inconsistently, as he often enacts this heroic refusal, so that the tension between the valorization of solitary genius transgressing orthodoxy and the dissolution of egoic solitude in multiplicities and assemblages can be understood as a primary polarity in which Deleuze's individual struggle enabled some of his greatest conceptual creations. Deleuze could perhaps benefit from some of Whitehead's calm maturity in relation to his denouncements of Hegel, the beautiful soul, and the Oedipal, the Whiteheadian attitude which "deliberately ignores hatred and anguish"[54] in the serene trust that discordant conflicts are opportunities for harmonious integrations built from contrast. And Whitehead could reciprocally benefit from a dose of Deleuze's dramatic Dionysian madness, the generative chaos of the dissolved self that allowed him to see through the fractured I to the interstitial domain of the gods, while Whiteheadian consciousness, however much it dissolves the world at its deepest foundations, also tends to leave the monocentric ego of the philosopher unproblematically intact, a unified, dispassionate, and often amused observer of the ultimately complex mathematical relations of process. Whereas Whitehead tends to leave the psyche unexamined, we might come to recognize with Stengers that "one is oneself the invention of the world on which one depends,"[55] self and world intimately entwined.

Of course, neither philosopher could have been any different, and I would not want them to change a word, though perhaps the still-living modes of thought they transmit to their readers can find a differentiating integration within the work of those who love both. Whitehead's wry detachment "cancels any dramaturgy of thought,"[56] a wise humor which is a large part of his appeal, though Whitehead could also benefit from being brought into closer relation with the Deleuzean method of dramatization, with Hillmanian personifying, and with Jungian psychodramatics, "adding a new dimension to the cosmos,"[57] one of color, personality, and dynamism, to Whitehead's vast, placid, and subtly shaded mathematical-cosmological constructions. As Stengers understands, along with both Whitehead and Deleuze, "it is the business of thought, as appealing to the future, to be dangerous,"[58] though this danger need not necessarily be undertaken in heroic solitude. Along with numerous other theorists who are constructing a Jungian turn in Deleuze studies, or a Deleuzean turn in Jungian studies, often in explicit resonance with Whitehead, I am risking the further danger of introducing the Jungian lineage into this meeting between Deleuzeans and Whiteheadians staged by Stengers. This introduction is justified not only by Jung's influence on Deleuze, but by the numerous points of relation that have been explored somewhat more extensively, at least in certain sectors, between Jung and Whitehead, an attempt at integration constituted in both the extraordinary resonance and the differentiated contrast of these theorists.[59]

Stengers discusses Simondon's concept of individuation from his 1964 magnum opus, a concept which is at least partially derived from Jung, nominating the individual's becoming in relation to the "primordial heterogeneity"[60] of their internal and external milieus. Deleuze writes that, although "modern philosophy has been wary of adopting the problem" of the principle of individuation, Simondon provides "a profoundly original theory of individuation implying a whole philosophy," which Deleuze deems "extremely important."[61] And, as Simondon writes in his book's final words:

> Jung discovers, in the aspiration of the alchemists, the translation of the operation of individuation, and of all the forms of sacrifice, which suppose a return to a state comparable to that of birth, that is to return to a state richly potentiated, not yet determined, a domain for the new propagation of life.

By generalizing and elaborating this conception, Simondon suggests, "we can set out to found the axiomatic of a human science on a new theory of form."[62] The numerous clues attesting to Jung's influence on Deleuze, and thus on much subsequent continental philosophy, have often been ignored.

However, differentiating integration, conceptualized as the alchemical death and rebirth enacting a dialectical return to formal potencies in novel registers, and embodied in Simondon's "study of the genesis of crystals as a process of individuation"[63] exemplifying the paradoxical, problematic field that "exists within an archetype,"[64] is at least partially derived from Jung, who writes that "again and again I encounter the mistaken notion that an archetype is determined in regard to its content," suggesting rather that archetypes are comparable "to the axial system of a crystal."[65] And as Stengers writes, "the beauty of the perfect crystal relies on its ability to effect a harmonious convergence of two rivals,"[66] resonant with Jung's conception of individuation as the integration of conflicting opposites, which Simondon describes as a speculative transduction creating an image of thought beyond the pervasive duality of matter and form derived from Aristotle, not as a mere unification, but as a resonant contrast between disparate domains, an ecological convergence in a problematic field which also affirms divergence.

Referring especially to Leibniz and Bergson in addition to Whitehead and Deleuze, Stengers observes that "the question of finality,"[67] like that of integration, has become a primary site of contention for modern philosophy and science, though it is only beyond this polemical battleground, where materialism seeks reductively and rhetorically to disqualify vitalism, that scientists studying emergent self-organization in biology, nonequilibrium physics, and neoconnectionist networks have been able to pursue more profound and complex questions. Thus, the evolutionary biologist Stephen Jay Gould can affirm "an understanding of evolution as integration,"[68] exceeding what Stengers designates as a "'holy war' against final causes" by a reductionist Darwinism "in which physical causality reigns supreme,"[69] demanding the submission of characteristically nonmodern causalities disqualified as other. However, resonant with most of the theorists above, Stengers recognizes that the teleology affirmed by Whitehead is not a mere "cosmic harmonization,"[70] but the satisfaction of local integrations which respect irresolvable differences, expressions of a "divine lure" transforming mere disjunctions into contrasts constituting a complex, dynamic, and open totality emerging from nonlocal and nonlinear correlations of eternal objects in the guise of problematic questions. These subtle formal-final causes are resonant with Spinozan substance and its heterogenous modes of expression in a fully "correlated universe" envisaged as composed of vast and intertwined relational networks of labyrinthine prehensions, both positive and negative, across scales and orders of ingression in "a reciprocal immanence that entangles harmonies and dissonances, convergences and divergences,"[71] potentialities luring becoming toward an infinitely displaced problematic horizon defining the finite limits of concrete actuality.

Stengers affirms "the possibility of peace"[72] embodied in this cosmic entanglement, which Whitehead approaches as a mathematician, Stengers calling upon Leibniz's slogan, *Calculemus* – "Let us calculate" – not in a totalizing global schema that reduces conceptual difference to the quantitative ratios of logical rationality with their measurement, comparison, and summation, which constitute trivial solutions in the mathematical sense, but in speculative local solutions to qualitative problems exceeding the solely mathematical domain. These solutions are enacted in the transformations of matrices from which an always provisional and partial global integration emerges in a "cosmopolitical parliament,"[73] a mode that creatively negotiates coherence between the conflicting or disjointed demands of disparate entities, but which always resists closure, as it does not need to denounce or deny what is outside the domain of what must be taken into account for any particular problem. Rather, it discerns that the way the question is posed may be more important than the answer to which it inexorably leads, the problem setting the scene in which the relational drama plays itself out, constructing the ensemble of actors and roles beyond mere incommensurability, creating from "radical heterogeneity"[74] a more profoundly resonant field of relational potencies opening into more expansive domains of liberated expression.

In *Capitalist Sorcery*, Stengers and Pignarre invoke Hermes – the mercurial trickster evoked by Hillman as the impure intermediary between Apollo and Dionysus – as the god presiding over *Calculemus* and the pragmatic trust in the possibility of a diplomatically negotiated peace.[75] *Calculemus* is not a "predetermined calculus"[76] which subtractively purifies through the bifurcating resolution of binary determinations, conflating truth with the social power to judge and disqualify mere falsity, but a dissolution of disjunction in a more profound game. It is the additive construction of a more complex integrating third for which the question of the ultimate reality of neutrinos or gods becomes less important than the creative possibilities of the world they can inhabit together by bringing their requirements and obligations into sustained respectful relation as questions to be explored rather than summarily answered, creating an ensemble cast from disparate actors who did not previously recognize one another's existence beyond the mere logic of exchange. The only requirement of the mode of thought figured as *Calculemus* and the cosmopolitical parliament is the affirmation that peace is possible, though peace does not preexist this activity waiting to be discovered in an objective transcendent realm. The entities this mode takes into account are "compatible for integration," as Whitehead writes, not in a final closure, but in a continually renegotiated convergence serving as a lure for novel creations. Integration constructs not only the problematic entities, but the self who is operating the peace-fabricating function, a function which Stengers offers as a shift of emphasis away from "the French inclination for despising the very idea of 'saving' anything from conflict,"[77] a change of tone to which Deleuze, along with Bergson, Bachelard, and Simondon, all of whom profess affinities with Jung, is more amenable than Derrida, though Derrida makes this shift possible in his wake.

Stengers recognizes that Western philosophy polemically constructs "conflict as the very mark of truth," the distribution of truth and falsity imagined as the result of a battle between rival claimants, a pervasive oppositional mode which she calls upon the figure of Hermetic peace fighters to overcome. Paradoxically, these figures do not "enter into conflict"[78] with conflict itself, but form an always-precarious alliance, more profound than a monotonously totalizing unity or a mere compromise, to lure the pitted combatants beyond the interminable static conflict, seducing them outside the center of gravity where exclusive attention is given to dominating the other through rationalized disqualification, destabilizing the opposition by opening it onto a broader stage formed from a multiplicity of relations among actors, which removes the charge from the binary relation. Peace fighters transform the conflict "into an ingredient of the problem,"[79] allowing directed attention to begin to circulate beyond the closed circuit in a more expansive machinic assemblage informed by flows issuing into other dimensions of experience. The harsh spotlight of the ring where the combat occurs, with the area outside this central nucleus fading into darkness, is reenvisaged in a more diffuse light emanating from complex lattices of rays constituted in intricate and contrasting patterns of illumination and shadow. The combatant whose fierce ire was focused squarely on the opponent now widens their field of attention to catch the web of glances from the encircling assemblage, the gaze of a lover which elicits a swelling of desire, the steady, distant stare of a father communicating a complex mixture of approval and judgment, a whole dreaming drama waiting to be enacted once the fixed conflict is abandoned for a deeper kind of fight in the interstices of a totalizing power which reduces everything to oppositional hierarchy.

This martial *pharmakon* destroys the comforting egoic unity defined against an other by means of subtle infection, but it also serves as an antidote to the poisonous Apollonian-Kronian possession, enacting a Dionysian transformation, a Promethean breaking through the wall, though often wearing the Jamesian and Whiteheadian masks of a wry practicality in the performance of trust beyond the mere telegraphing of confidence, resonant with Hillman's mercurial roguishness. This disguised mythical dialectic dramatizes an asymmetrical and eccentric slipping through the cracks sideways beyond an exclusively oppositional drama figured as the war of good and evil, the battle of the sexes, the defeat of nonmodern superstition by the modern, enacting a dissolution of conflict in a more expansive domain of affective and conceptual contrast. And Stengers also discerns this transformative experimentation with words in both Spinozan and Bergsonian intuition, for which "each new contrast, as it is added, will be integrated into harmony in the form of what it has made possible,"[80] evoking integration as a more profound and heterogenous dramatization, a celebration of contrasting coexistence rather than a totalizing unification.

Stengers associates Whiteheadian speculative empiricism with the Leibnizian metaphysical correlate of the calculus, Spinozan and Bergsonian intuition, Jamesian pragmatism, and Deleuzean repetition exceeding a shattering Nietzschean "hammer-thought,"[81] the designation he "reserved for his hypothesis of the eternal return,"[82] an inflection of the eternal return that relinquishes the need for denouncement. While Nietzsche never fully expressed the eternal return in its positive form, but primarily created space for it by the destruction of what it would supplant, Stengers designates speculative empiricism, resonant with a Deleuzean transcendental empiricism of the eternal return in the form of a mythical dialectic, and with Jungian-Hillmanian archetypal thought, as a mode which "makes things hold together,"[83] not in a totalitarian unification, but in a multiplicity of integrated contrasts. Speculative philosophers experiment with language to construct, and thus to discover, novel conceptual integrations that reinvent the tradition in which their thought is situated, leading to deeper questions eliciting more profound contrasts in metaphysical "dimensions of experience"[84] beyond the current doxa, obscure interstitial domains for which clear and stable language remains to be created. Stengers elaborates

Whitehead's image of a mountain climber who can climb the ontological cliff in various ways, but who requires a "foothold,"[85] a topological feature from which to construct a path by particular modes of attention, a vertical figure reminiscent of Bergson's riverine landscape, whether that mode is oriented toward physical or metaphysical practices. These are all legitimate modes of construction as long as they can find pragmatic footholds for their efficacy in a radical empiricism for which no domain of attention is privileged, with each practice initially a heterodox and "extravagant ideal"[86] rendered integral parts of their cultures through the creation of habits and institutions, until they become new orthodoxies that must be renewed and transformed through novel lines of flight attending to, and speculatively affirming, new dimensions of experience in new ways.

These speculative flights must inevitably go beyond the creations of Whitehead, Jung, Deleuze, and even Stengers, so that thinking with these theorists means carrying their verbal concepts into novel domains. Integration performs an infinite fractal regress of footnotes within footnotes in which the conceptual characters of Stengers, Whitehead, James, and Bergson may undergo novel encounters with the gods in our narrative, Jung may be challenged by the Deleuzean obscurity which unsettles and deepens holistic modes of thought, and Deleuze may be persuaded to shift his focus away from heroic denouncements to an affirmation of the value of wholeness,[87] though always avoiding totalizing unification through differentiated contrast in both the Leibnizian-Whiteheadian mathematical mode and in the Schellingian-Jungian-Hillmanian mythical mode. These are all actors playing starring roles in a drama which exceeds them, the dramatic construction of a novel epoch. And while this integration requires a careful attentiveness to the subtle nuances of each theorist's language, it also requires the humor of "cavalier creation,"[88] the laughter of the gods in the face of death. Creation on a novel plane of immanence can only occur in consonance with the passing away of an older mode of relation which seemed to constitute reality itself, but whose exclusions and incoherencies have come to be felt as intolerable. The suffering and dissolution of transformation demanded by critical events beyond our control increasingly renders the earlier epoch as a strange dream, a dream which some of us may vividly recall, but which our children or grandchildren may only know through the narratives we recount. And thus, we enter inexorably into a novel epoch, which is like nothing we could have imagined, which is constituted in novel problems and questions, novel milieus for our creative constructions.

Stengers can be imagined as speaking for all of the theorists above when she writes that language "is itself the operator of changes of epoch, on every scale,"[89] and an ultimate project of these complexly intertwining streams of thought is "the construction of a new story"[90] with its disparate inflections. Integration constructs a narrative about integral constructivism whose recounting expressively amplifies potencies capable of summoning a novel epoch beyond the modern and its hierarchical binary disqualifications, which extends an open invitation to those who continue to insist on denouncing. This narrative constructs the capacity to create the conditions for its own validity by the invention of peculiar syntax serving to invoke and express, through increasingly subtle relational formulations, the dynamisms just past a horizon of discernibility, enacting not an escape from the cave, but a lucid dreaming in the labyrinth, as "only stories are capable of giving meaning to the way in which what seemed separated ceases to be so,"[91] whether the story begins with "Once upon a time," "In the beginning," or "Let $AX$ be the axis."[92]

To compose a novel narrative that can begin to think the unthinkable and discern the indiscernible by creating commensurability among the incommensurable, one must think slowly, carefully, deeply, but also, like the "impertinent child"[93] who announces what everyone knows – that the emperor is naked – one must be willing to risk, at efficacious moments, acting the role of this child who dares to utter what the dominant powers insist must remain silent. But one must also find efficacious ways to modify the dream of the other, an activity for which Stengers unexpectedly employs the term "politeness,"[94] not in the civility hypocritically demanded by the American right as a means for suppressing the legitimate and necessary anger and despair voiced through politics and protest, but in an approach which recognizes that the only way to modify the other's dream without doing violence to it is to recognize the other's agency, however alien, and to speak in ways that allow the other, whether human or nonhuman, to hear what is being suggested beyond the demand for conflict. Dream modification requires an encounter of vectors generating local resonances which reciprocally transform the parties to the conversation, not through the typical subjection to another's dream, but through the collaborative creation of a narrative in which all participants have a voice in defining their role.

If we listen to what the characters in the pages above have been telling us in their peculiar dialects, the foreign languages they have carved out within their culture's predominant language,[95] this novel epoch-constructing narrative may consist, above all, in the overcoming of the dominance of oppositional problematics opening into the mysterious depths of paradox leading beyond our current horizons of conception to events which allow a new cosmos to emerge from the interstices of our collective reality. This emergence is a subtle change of tone which nevertheless makes a radical difference in our shared experience, a transition beyond the opposition of continuity and discontinuity which transforms all domains of human endeavor through a gradual subterranean modification in which it suddenly becomes normal for the predominant mode of thought "to accept what it was proud of rejecting,"[96] those other modes that have served to define the modern by their disqualification and occultation. The novel potentialities and contrasts which this narrative elicits may reveal a deeper kind of enchantment than that through whose rejection modernity has defined itself, which can be discerned, if we allow the textual spell to work on us, between the insistent, and occasionally surprising, lines of strangely resonant and potent talismanic signs composing the invocation of novel worlds. Although language can imprison both reader and writer in a closed discursive circulation, it can also free our imaginations by bewitching us, tempting us to leap into novel domains.

Like Galileo whose founding scientific act is the child-like rolling of balls down a ramp, like the Catholic who participates in divinity by consuming a dry wafer, Stengers evokes James' "speculative leap"[97] into the unknown beyond the containment of exclusionary oppositional logic, trusting that a solid foothold will be encountered on the other side. Stengers thinks with James and Whitehead beyond this image of a grounding on which to land by means of the image of a circle of dancers, each embodying some element of an emergent mode, each contributing an essential aspect to that mode's coherence, always circulating, never fixed, nothing at the circle's center of gravity but an intertwining mesh of flashing gazes, a fundamental relationality which requires mutual trust for the circle not to fall apart. In fact, the coherence of any mode of thought requires that each foundational proposition leans on the other moving propositions, and there is no central, immobile, privileged proposition which can guarantee the stability of the ensemble, despite the totalizing attempts of logocentrism. Any mode of thought is constituted in an inescapable risk whose value is encountered in its pragmatic efficacy, not its exclusive validity grounded in a transcendent or immanent reality, whether God, matter, or the absolute. This imaginal circle of dancers suggests the revolutions of the gods in the eternal return, the Platonic circulations associated with the planets passing through the centuries into the disparate conceptions of Schelling, Nietzsche, Jung, Deleuze, and Hillman, each divine potency revolving in complex relationalities at an always-receding horizon, luring us toward destined becomings.

Beyond the image of the dancers, Stengers evokes the Bergsonian swimmer, this time as a deep-sea diver, the speculative thinker descending into the heterogenous depths below the surface doxa, the Dionysian domain of madness and transformation, the Poseidonian dissolution of fixed categories and identities. That which distinguishes mere destructive madness and dissipation from a creative, inspired madness and intoxication is the possession of the necessary conceptual equipment, the forms of language and modes of thought required to transmute the imaginal demonic potencies of the depths into novel conceptual creations, new resonances between words and experiences generating an emergence from the underworld or the abyss into novel domains of thought and affect.[98] And although Stengers observes that mere "irresponsibility, as an ultimate metaphysical generality, would be, as Whitehead reproached Leibniz, inadequate,"[99] resting on a facile optimization, Spinoza, followed by Jung, Deleuze, and Hillman, can allow us to integrate Whiteheadian responsibility with a Nietzschean irresponsibility, Stengers recognizing Whitehead's conception of God as resonant with *amor fati*, the affirmation of felt destiny. We are not responsible for the will, the affects and inclinations figured as demons and angelic emissaries encountered in the depths, who derisively mock or placidly ignore our efforts to control them, though we are responsible for how we choose to express those potent affects and inclinations through a freedom of mind which can creatively equip itself for the descent and its encounters, or dive without discipline or preparation into mere madness, into destructive psychoses of all kinds. And yet adventure is inextricable from real danger, from the apocalyptic hauntings which render the treasure as hard to attain, and thus destructive madness can also be thrust upon us despite our best intentions and our most valiant efforts, but then madness can also lift like a veil.

When these theorists evoke the gods or ancestors, it is not in the mode of a return to the lost innocence of romantic enchantment, but as mature and responsible technicians constructing provisional practices to encounter the potencies which force us to think beyond our current obligations and encodings, a higher responsibility beyond the static responsibility of laws, contracts, institutions, and norms in which we are embedded, which we must interpret and obey, beyond the duality of responsibility and irresponsibility itself.[100] These ambiguous others always exceed any actual expression, overflowing any possibility of rational containment, demanding the creation of novel forms of life. Encounters with cosmic forces often take the form of madness and pathology, so that within every problematic symptom is a god who demands to be heard, though these potencies are not always benevolent, but neutral in regard to their ingression, demanding only the creation of novelty with no thought for our joy or suffering. The gods require another ethics in addition to right action and adherence to law, beyond tolerance and forgiveness, an ethology for which the primary choice is whether one fulfills or refuses one's destiny, or rather, at which order one enacts the complex affective and imaginally intuited potencies that constitute one's becoming, expressing a monadic soul composed of multiple entangled epochs infinitesimally lured toward an always-receding transcendental horizon in the intensive interstices which constitute the future, a dangerous and extravagantly potentiated future coexistent with the distant past where the gods dream.

## Notes

1 Stengers, *Thinking*, 186.
2 Deleuze, "Whitehead"; Stengers, *Thinking*, 120.
3 Stengers, *Thinking*, 242, 499.
4 Stengers, *Thinking*, 106.
5 Stengers, *Cosmopolitics I*, vii.
6 Stengers, *Thinking*, 172.
7 Stengers, *Cosmopolitics I*, 35–6.
8 Stengers, *Thinking*, 165–6.
9 Stengers, *Thinking*, 69.
10 Stengers, *Cosmopolitics II*, 269.
11 Stengers, *Cosmopolitics II*, 46.
12 Stengers, *Thinking*, 219.
13 Stengers, *Cosmopolitics I*, 19.
14 Stengers, *Catastrophic*, 149.
15 Stengers, *Thinking*, 95.
16 Deleuze, *Difference*, 83.
17 Stengers, *Thinking*, 102.
18 Stengers, *Thinking*, 159.
19 Stengers, *Thinking*, 508.
20 Stengers, *Thinking*, 263.
21 Stengers, *Thinking*, 137, 514.
22 Stengers, *Thinking*, 143.

23 Stengers, *Thinking*, 375.
24 Stengers, *Thinking*, 326.
25 Stengers, *Cosmopolitics II*, 201.
26 Stengers, *Cosmopolitics I*, 21.
27 Stengers, *Cosmopolitics II*, 356.
28 Wittgenstein, *Tractatus*, 89.
29 Stengers, *Thinking*, 47.
30 Stengers, *Thinking*, 488.
31 Stengers, *Thinking*, 483–44.
32 Stengers, *Thinking*, 511.
33 Stengers, *Thinking*, 134–5.
34 Stengers, *Thinking*, 286.
35 Stengers, *Thinking*, 489; Deleuze, *Difference*, 199.
36 Stengers, *Another*, 131; Stengers, "Enigmatic," 163.
37 Stengers, *Thinking*, 489–90.
38 Stengers, *Catastrophic*, 42.
39 Stengers, *Catastrophic*, 44.
40 Stengers, *Catastrophic*, 47, 58; Stengers, *Another*, 133.
41 Stengers, "Beyond," 246.
42 Stengers, *Cosmopolitics I*, 29.
43 Stengers, *Cosmopolitics II*, 197.
44 Stengers, "Beyond," 237.
45 Stengers, *Thinking*, 404.
46 Stengers, "Beyond," 245; Stengers, "Wondering," 377; Stengers, "Enigmatic," 155.
47 Stengers, "Beyond," 235.
48 Stengers, "Beyond," 236.
49 Stengers, "Beyond," 238.
50 Stengers, "Beyond," 237–8.
51 Stengers, *Thinking*, 512.
52 Stengers, "Beyond," 238.
53 Stengers, *Thinking*, 272.
54 Stengers, *Thinking*, 160.
55 Stengers, *Thinking*, 180.
56 Stengers, *Thinking*, 258.
57 Stengers, *Thinking*, 513.
58 Stengers, "Beyond," 239.
59 See Griffin, *Archetypal*; Stengers, "Beyond," 236.
60 Stengers, *Cosmopolitics II*, 292.
61 Deleuze, *Desert*, 86, 89.
62 Simondon, *Individuation*, 697 (slightly modified translation).
63 Simondon, *Individuation*, 6.
64 Simondon, *Individuation*, 696.
65 Jung, *Archetypes*, 79.
66 Stengers, *Cosmopolitics II*, 293.
67 Stengers, *Cosmopolitics II*, 210–11.
68 Stengers, *Cosmopolitics II*, 296.

69 Stengers, *Thinking*, 126.
70 Stengers, *Thinking*, 311.
71 Stengers, *Thinking*, 388.
72 Stengers, "Beyond," 243.
73 Stengers, *Cosmopolitics II*, 399.
74 Stengers, *Cosmopolitics II*, 401.
75 Stengers, *Sorcery*, 118.
76 Stengers, *Cosmopolitics II*, 411.
77 Stengers, "Beyond," 243.
78 Stengers, "Beyond," 244, 246.
79 Stengers, *Thinking*, 15.
80 Stengers, *Thinking*, 476.
81 Stengers, *Thinking*, 501.
82 Stengers, *Thinking*, 315.
83 Stengers, *Thinking*, 292–3.
84 Stengers, *Thinking*, 248.
85 Stengers, *Thinking*, 67.
86 Stengers, *Thinking*, 115.
87 See Deleuze, *Cinema 1*, 10.
88 Stengers, *Thinking*, 292.
89 Stengers, *Thinking*, 417.
90 Stengers, *Cosmopolitics II*, 223; Stengers, "Wondering," 371.
91 Stengers, *Thinking*, 332–3.
92 The first words of Leibniz's first paper on the calculus, "A New Method." Stengers, *Thinking*, 350.
93 Stengers, *Thinking*, 182.
94 Stengers, *Thinking*, 517.
95 Deleuze and Parnet, *Dialogues*, 4–5.
96 Stengers, *Thinking*, 335.
97 Stengers, *Thinking*, 235; Stengers, "Enigmatic," 166.
98 Stengers, *Thinking*, 272, 452.
99 Stengers, *Thinking*, 494.
100 Stengers, *Cosmopolitics II*, 328.

# Works Cited

Althaus, Horst. *Hegel*. Cambridge, UK: Polity Press, 2000.
Antognazza, Maria Rosa. *Leibniz*. Cambridge: Cambridge University Press, 2011.
Bachelard, Gaston. *Lautréamont*. Dallas, TX: The Dallas Institute, 1986.
Badiou, Alain. *Conditions*. London: Bloomsbury Academic, 2017.
Beckman, Frida. *Gilles Deleuze*. London: Reaktion Books, 2017.
Bergson, Henri. *Creative Evolution*. New York: Modern Library, 1944.
———. *The Creative Mind*. Mineola, NY: Dover Publications, 2010.
———. *Duration and Simultaneity*. Manchester, UK: Clinamen Press, 1999.
———. *Matter and Memory*. New York: Zone Books, 2005.
———. *The Two Sources of Morality and Religion*. Westport, CT: Greenwood Press, 1974.
Blattner, William. *Heidegger's Being and Time*. New York: Continuum, 2006.
Brandom, Robert. *A Spirit of Trust*. Cambridge, MA: Belknap Press, 2019.
Brennan, Chris. *Hellenistic Astrology*. Denver, CO: Amor Fati Publications, 2017.
Butler, Judith. *Subjects of Desire*. New York: Columbia University Press, 1987.
Cisney, Vernon. *Deleuze and Derrida*. Edinburgh, UK: Edinburgh University Press, 2018.
Coen, Joel, and Ethan Coen. *The Big Lebowski*. Los Angeles: Working Title Films, 1998. Film.
Culp, Andrew. *Dark Deleuze*. Minneapolis, MN: University of Minnesota Press, 2016.
Cusa, Nicholas of. *On Learned Ignorance*. Minneapolis, MN: Arthur J. Banning Press, 2001.
Cusset, François. *French Theory*. Minneapolis: University of Minnesota Press, 2008.
Dawid, Richard. *String Theory and the Scientific Method*. Cambridge: Cambridge University Press, 2013.
Deleuze, Gilles. *Bergsonism*. New York: Zone Books, 2002.
———. *Cinema 1*. New York: Continuum, 2005.
———. *Cinema 2*. Minneapolis, MN: University of Minnesota Press, 1989.
———. "Deleuze on Whitehead and Leibniz." 10/3/1987. www.pierrejoris.com/blog/deleuze-on-whitehead-leibniz/.

———. *Desert Islands and Other Texts*. Los Angeles, CA: Semiotext(e), 2004.
———. *Difference and Repetition*. New York: Columbia University Press, 1994.
———. *Empiricism and Subjectivity*. New York: Columbia University Press, 1991.
———. *Essays Critical and Clinical*. Minneapolis: University of Minnesota Press, 1997.
———. *Expressionism in Philosophy*. New York: Zone Books, 1990.
———. *The Fold*. New York: Continuum, 2006.
———. *Foucault*. New York: Continuum, 2006.
———. *Francis Bacon*. New York: Continuum, 2003.
———. "From Sacher-Masoch to Masochism." *Angelaki* 9, no. 1 (2004): 125–33.
———. *Kant's Critical Philosophy*. London: Athalone Press, 1984.
———. *Letters and Other Texts*. Los Angeles, CA: Semiotext(e), 2020.
———. *The Logic of Sense*. London: Athalone Press, 1990.
———. *Masochism*. New York: Zone Books, 2006.
———. *Negotiations*. New York: Columbia University Press, 1995.
———. *Nietzsche and Philosophy*. New York: Columbia University Press, 2006.
———. "Postscript on the Societies of Control." *October* 59 (Winter 1992): 3–7.
———. *Proust and Signs*. Minneapolis: University of Minnesota Press, 2004.
———. "Sur Spinoza." *Cours Vincennes* 09/12/1980. www.webdeleuze.com/textes/20
———. *Two Regimes of Madness*. Los Angeles: Semiotext(e), 2007.
———. *What Is Grounding?* Grand Rapids, MI: Publishing, 2015.
Deleuze, Gilles, and Félix Guattari. *Anti-Oedipus*. Minneapolis: University of Minnesota Press, 1983.
———. *Kafka*. Minneapolis: University of Minnesota Press, 1986.
———. *A Thousand Plateaus*. Minneapolis: University of Minnesota Press, 1987.
———. *What Is Philosophy?* New York: Columbia University Press, 1996.
Deleuze, Gilles, and Claire Parnet. *L'Abécédaire de Gilles Deleuze, avec Claire Parnet*, 1996, 47–8. https://deleuze.cla.purdue.edu/sites/default/files/pdf/lectures/en/ABCMsRevised-NotesComplete051120_1.pdf.
———. *Dialogues II*. New York: Columbia University Press, 2007.
Derrida, Jacques. *The Animal That Therefore I Am*. New York: Fordham University Press, 2008.
———. *The Ear of the Other*. New York: Schocken Books, 1985.
———. *The Gift of Death*. Chicago: University of Chicago Press, 2008.
———. "Gilles Deleuze: On Forgiveness." *European Graduate School Video Lectures*, 2004. www.youtube.com/watch?v=I_r-gr3ccik&list=PLDD498CDE04B51C2D.
———. "I'll Have to Wander All Alone." *Tympanum*, 1998. https://non.copyriot.com/ill-have-to-wander-all-alone-jacques-derrida-on-gilles-deleuze/.
———. "An Interview with Jacques Derrida on the Limits of Digestion." *E-flux Journal* (2009). www.e-flux.com/journal/02/68495/an-interview-with-jacques-derrida-on-the-limits-of-digestion/.

———. *Memoires for Paul de Man*. New York: Columbia University Press, 1989.
———. *Monolingualism of the Other: Or, the Prosthesis of Origin*. Stanford, CA: Stanford University Press, 1998.
———. *Of Grammatology*. Baltimore, MD: John Hopkins University Press, 1997.
———. *Specters of Marx*. New York: Routledge, 1994.
———. *Writing and Difference*. New York: Routledge, 2005.
Derrida, Jacques, and Maurizio Ferraris. *A Taste for the Secret*. Cambridge, UK: Polity, 2001.
Descartes, René. *Discourse on Method and Meditations on First Philosophy*. Indianapolis, IN: Hackett, 1998.
Desmond, Timothy. *Psyche and Singularity*. Nashville, TN: Persistent Press, 2018.
Dosse, François. *Gilles Deleuze and Félix Guattari: Intersecting Lives*. New York: Columbia University Press, 2007.
Duffy, Simon B. *Deleuze and the History of Mathematics*. London: Bloomsbury Academic, 2013.
———. *The Logic of Expression*. Hampshire, UK: Ashgate, 2006.
Duvernoy, Russell J. "Deleuze, Whitehead, and the 'Beautiful Soul'." *Deleuze and Guattari Studies* 13, no. 2 (2019): 163–85.
Eliade, Mircea. *Shamanism*. Princeton, NJ: Princeton University Press, 2004.
Ellis, John M. *Against Deconstruction*. Princeton, NJ: Princeton University Press, 1989.
Evrard, Renaud, Claudie Massicotte, and Thomas Rabeyron. "Freud as a Psychical Researcher: The Impossible Freudian Legacy." *Imágó Budapest* 6, no. 4 (2017): 9–32.
Fisher, Mark. *Capitalist Realism*. Ropley, UK: Zero Books, 2009.
Franz, Marie-Louise von, and James Hillman. *Lectures on Jung's Typology*. Dallas, TX: Spring Publications, 2020.
Freud, Sigmund, and C. G. Jung. *The Freud/Jung Letters*. Princeton, NJ: Princeton University Press, 1994.
Gebser, Jean. *The Ever-Present Origin*. Athens, OH: Ohio University Press, 1986.
Goethe, Johann Wolfgang von. *The Essential Goethe*. Princeton, NJ: Princeton University Press, 2016.
Greene, Brian. *The Elegant Universe*. New York: Norton, 2010.
Griffin, David Ray, et al. *Founders of Constructive Postmodern Philosophy*. Albany, NY: SUNY Press, 1993.
Harman, Graham. *Object-Oriented Ontology*. London: Peliccan, 2018.
Hegel, G. W. F. *Encyclopedia of the Philosophical Sciences in Basic Outline, Part 1, Science of Logic*. Cambridge, UK: Cambridge University Press, 2010.
———. *Lectures on the History of Philosophy, Volume III*. Berkeley: University of California Press, 1990.
———. *Lectures on the History of Philosophy, Volume 3*. Lincoln, NE: University of Nebraska Press, 1995.

———. *Phenomenology of Spirit*. New York: Oxford University Press, 1977.
———. *The Philosophy of History*. Kitchener, Ontario: Batoche Books, 2001.
———. *Philosophy of Mind*. Oxford: Clarendon Press, 1971.
———. *Science of Logic*. Cambridge, UK: Cambridge University Press, 2010.
Heidegger, Martin. *Schelling's Treatise on the Essence of Human Freedom*. Athens: Ohio University Press, 1985.
Herring, Emily. "Henri Bergson, Celebrity." *Aeon*, 2019. https://aeon.co/essays/henri-bergson-the-philosopher-damned-for-his-female-fans.
Hillman, James. *Archetypal Psychology: Uniform Edition of the Writings of James Hillman, Volume 1*. Dallas, TX: Spring Publications, 2015.
———. "Back to Beyond." In *The Archetypal Process*, edited by David Ray Griffin. Evanston, IL: Northwestern University Press, 1990.
———. "On Senex Consciousness." *Spring: An Annual of Archetypal Psychology and Jungian Thought* (1970): 146–65.
———, ed. *Puer Papers*. Dallas, TX: Spring Publications, 1991.
———. *Re-Visioning Psychology*. New York: Harper & Row, 1975.
———. *Suicide and the Soul*. Dallas, TX: Spring Publications, 2020.
Hillman, James, and Michael Ventura. *We've Had a Hundred Years of Psychotherapy and the World's Getting Worse*. New York: HarperOne, 1993.
Hippolyte, Jean. *Logic and Existence*. Albany, NY: SUNY Press, 1997.
Hoinski, David Frank. *Humanlife and the Advent of Philosophy*. Dissertation, Duquesne University, Fall 2013.
Hopcke, Robert H. *A Guided Tour of the Collected Works of C. G. Jung*. Boston, MA: Shambhala, 1999.
Houlgate, Stephen. *The Opening of Hegel's Logic*. West Lafayette, IN: Purdue University Press, 2005.
———. "Schelling's Critique of Hegel's 'Science of Logic'." *The Review of Metaphysics* 53, no. 1 (September 1999): 99–128.
Inwood, Michael. *Heidegger: A Very Short Introduction*. New York: Oxford University Press, 2002.
James, William. *Pragmatism*. Mineola, NY: Dover Publications, 1995.
———. *The Will to Believe, Human Immortality, and Other Essays in Popular Philosophy*. Mineola, NY: Dover Publications, 1960.
———. *Writings 1902–1910*. New York: Library of America, 1988.
Jameson, Frederic. "Marxism and Dualism in Deleuze." *The South Atlantic Quarterly* 97, no. 3 (Summer 1997): 393–416.
Jaspers, Karl. *The Origin and Goal of History*. New York: Routledge, 2011.
Jenkins, Barbara. *Eros and Economy*. New York: Routledge, 2017.
Johnson, Laurie M. *Ideological Possession and the Rise of the New Right*. New York: Routledge, 2019.
Jolley, Nicholas. *Leibniz*. New York: Routledge, 2005.
Josephson-Storm, Jason A. *The Myth of Disenchantment*. Chicago, IL: University of Chicago Press, 2017.
Jung, C. G. *Alchemical Studies*. Princeton, NJ: Princeton University Press, 1967.

———. *Archetypes and the Collective Unconscious*. Princeton, NJ: Princeton University Press, 1959.

———. *C. G. Jung Speaking: Interviews and Encounters*. Princeton, NJ: Princeton University Press, 1977.

———. *Civilization In Transition*. Princeton, NJ: Princeton University Press, 1970.

———. *Man and His Symbols*. New York: Anchor Press, 1964.

———. *Memories, Dreams, Reflections*. New York: Vintage Books, 1989.

———. *Mysterium Coniunctionis*. Princeton, NJ: Princeton University Press, 1977.

———. *Symbols of Transformation*. Princeton, NJ: Princeton University Press, 1956.

———. *Synchronicity*. Princeton, NJ: Princeton University Press, 2010.

———. *Visions*. London: Routledge, 1998.

Kaufman, Eleanor. "Betraying Well." *Criticism* XLIV, no. 4 (2004): 651–9.

Keller, Catherine, and Anne Daniell. *Process and Difference*. Albany, NY: SUNY Press, 2002.

Kelly, Sean. *Individuation and the Absolute*. Mahwah, NJ: Paulist Press, 1993.

Kerslake, Christian. *Deleuze and the Unconscious*. New York: Continuum, 2007.

———. "Grounding Deleuze." *Radical Philosophy* 148 (March–April 2008): 30–6.

———. *Immanence and the Vertigo of Philosophy*. Edinburgh: Edinburgh University Press, 2009.

Lango, John W. "Whitehead's Actual Occasions and the New Infinitesimals." *Transactions of the Charles S. Peirce Society* 25, no. 1 (Winter 1989): 29–39.

Laughland, John. *Schelling Versus Hegel*. Hampshire, UK: Ashgate, 2007.

Leibniz, G. W. *Discourse on Metaphysics and The Monadology*. Mineola, NY: Dover, 2005.

———. *Leibniz's Monadology*. Edinburgh: Edinburgh University Press, 2014.

———. "A New Method for Finding Maxima and Minima . . ." www.17centurymaths.com/contents/Leibniz/nova1.pdf.

Levy, O., ed. *Friedrich Nietzsche: Selected Letters*. London, UK: The Soho Book Company, 1985.

Lucas, George R., Jr., ed. *Hegel and Whitehead*. Albany, NY: SUNY Press, 1986.

Lyotard, Jean-François. *The Postmodern Condition*. Minneapolis: University of Minnesota Press, 1984.

MacLure, Maggie. "The 'New Materialisms': A Thorn in the Flesh of Critical Qualitative Inquiry?" In *Critical Qualitative Inquiry*, edited by Gaile Cannella, Michael Salazar Perez, and Penny Pasque. New York: Routledge, 2015.

Magee, Glenn Alexander. *Hegel and the Hermetic Tradition*. Ithaca, NY: Cornell University Press, 2008.

Main, Roderick, Christian McMillan, and David Henderson, eds. *Jung, Deleuze, and the Problematic Whole*. New York: Routledge, 2020.

Malabou, Catherine. "Who's Afraid of Hegelian Wolves?" In *Deleuze: A Critical Reader*, edited by Paul Patton. Cambridge, MA: Blackwell Publishers, 1996.

Marshall, Terence E. "Rousseau and Enlightenment." *Political Theory* 6, no. 4 (November 1978): 421–55.
Marx, Karl. *Capital I*. London: Penguin Classics, 1990.
May, Todd. "Explain Deleuze to Me." *Machinic Unconscious Happy Hour*, 2020. https://soundcloud.com/podcast-co-coopercherry/todd-may-explain-deleuze-to-me-dont-dumb-it-down.
———. *Gilles Deleuze*. Cambridge: Cambridge University Press, 2005.
McMillan, Christian. "Jung and Deleuze: Enchanted Openings to the Other: A Philosophical Contribution." *International Journal of Jungian Studies* 10, no. 3 (2018): 184–98.
Menand, Louis. *The Metaphysical Club*. New York: Farrar, Straus and Giroux, 2002.
Mill, John Stuart. *Collected Works, Volume 10*. New York: Routledge, 2014.
Mills, Jon, ed. *Jung and Philosophy*. New York: Routledge, 2019.
Milne, Drew. "The Beautiful Soul: From Hegel to Beckett." *Diacritics* 32 no. 1 (March 2002): 63–82.
Nietzsche, Friedrich. *The Anti-Christ, Ecce Homo, Twilight of the Idols*. Cambridge: Cambridge University Press, 2005.
———. *Beyond Good and Evil*. Cambridge: Cambridge University Press, 2003.
———. *The Birth of Tragedy*. London: Penguin, 1994.
———. *Daybreak*. Cambridge: Cambridge University Press, 1997.
———. *Ecce Homo*. New York: Oxford University Press, 2009.
———. *The Gay Science*. Cambridge: Cambridge University Press, 2001.
———. *Human, All Too Human*. Cambridge: Cambridge University Press, 1996.
———. *Thus Spoke Zarathustra*. Cambridge: Cambridge University Press, 2011.
———. *Twilight of the Idols*. London: Penguin Classics, 1990.
———. *Untimely Meditations*. Cambridge: Cambridge University Press, 1997.
Nottale, Laurent. *The Relativity of All Things*. Nashville, TN: Persistent Press, 2019.
Patton, Paul, and John Protevi, eds. *Between Derrida and Deleuze*. London: Athlone Press, 2002.
Peeters, Benoit. *Derrida*. Cambridge, UK: Polity, 2016.
Pinkard, Terry. *Hegel: A Biography*. Cambridge: Cambridge University Press, 2001.
Plato. *Complete Works*. Indianapolis, IN: Hackett, 1997.
———. *Phaedrus*. New York: Oxford University Press, 2002.
———. *A Plato Reader*. Indianapolis, IN: Hackett, 2012.
Plotinus. *Enneads*. Cambridge: Cambridge University Press, 2018.
Price, Lucien. *Dialogues of Alfred North Whitehead*. Boston: Little, Brown and Company, 1954.
Prideaux, Sue. *I Am Dynamite!* London: Tim Duggan Books, 2019.
Ramey, Joshua. *The Hermetic Deleuze*. Durham, NC: Duke University Press, 2012.
Reyes, Michelle A. "The Beautiful Soul in the Confessional." *ABO: Interactive Journal for Women in the Arts* 4, no. 2 (2014). https://scholarcommons.usf.edu/abo/vol4/iss2/1/.

Richardson, Joan. *A Natural History of Pragmatism*. Cambridge: Cambridge University Press, 2006.

Ricoeur, Paul. *Freud and Philosophy*. New Haven, CT: Yale University Press, 1977.

Rowland, Susan. *Jung: A Feminist Revision*. Cambridge, UK: Polity, 2002.

Rush, Fred. "Schelling's Critique of Hegel." In *Interpreting Schelling*, edited by Lara Ostaric. Cambridge: Cambridge University Press, 2014.

Russell, Bertrand. "The Philosophy of Bergson." *The Monist* 22 (1912): 321–47.

Saban, Mark. "Simondon and Jung: Rethinking Individuation." In *Holism*, edited by Christian McMillan, Roderick Main, and David Henderson. New York: Routledge, 2019.

Salmon, Peter. *An Event, Perhaps*. New York: Verso, 2020.

Salomé, Lou. *Nietzsche*. Champaign, IL: University of Illinois Press, 2001.

Schelling, F. W. J. *The Grounding of Positive Philosophy*. Albany, NY: SUNY Press, 2008.

———. *Grundlegung der Positiven Philosophie: Münchener Vorlesung WS 1832/33 und SS 1833*. Turin: Bottega D'Erasmo, 1972.

———. *Historical-Critical Introduction to the Philosophy of Mythology*. Albany, NY: SUNY Press, 2007.

———. *Philosophical Investigations into the Essence of Human Freedom*. Albany, NY: SUNY Press, 2006.

———. *System of Transcendental Idealism*. Charlottesville, VA: University Press of Virginia, 1978.

Shamdasani, Sonu. *Jung and the Making of Modern Psychology*. Cambridge: Cambridge University Press, 2003.

Shaviro, Steven. *Without Criteria*. Cambridge, MA: The MIT Press, 2012.

Simondon, Gilbert. *Individuation in Light of Notions of Form and Information*. Minneapolis: University of Minnesota Press, 2020.

Sommers-Hall, Henry. *Hegel, Deleuze, and the Critique of Representation*. Albany, NY: SUNY Press, 2013.

Spinoza, Baruch. *The Collected Works of Spinoza, Volume 1*. Princeton, NJ: Princeton University Press, 1985.

Stanford Encyclopedia of Philosophy. "Continuity and Infinitesimals." 2013. https://plato.stanford.edu/entries/continuity/.

Stengers, Isabelle. *Another Science Is Possible*. Cambridge, UK: Polity, 2018.

———. "Beyond Conversation." In *Process and Difference*, edited by Catherine Keller and Anne Daniell. Albany, NY: SUNY Press, 2002.

———. *In Catastrophic Times*. London: Open Humanities Press, 2015.

———. *Cosmopolitics I and II*. Minneapolis, MN: University of Minnesota Press, 2010.

———. "Deleuze and Guattari's Last Enigmatic Message." *Angelaki* 10, no. 2 (2005): 151–67.

———. "Reclaiming Animism." *e-flux*, no. 36 (2012). www.e-flux.com/journal/36/61245/reclaiming-animism/.

———. *Thinking with Whitehead*. Cambridge, MA: Harvard University Press, 2011.

———. "Wondering About Materialism." In *The Speculative Turn*, edited by Levi Bryant, Nick Srnicek, and Graham Harman. Melbourne: re.press, 2011.

Stengers, Isabelle, and Philippe Pignarre. *Capitalist Sorcery*. London: Palgrave Macmillan, 2007.

Stevens, Anthony. *Jung: A Very Short Introduction*. New York: Oxford University Press, 2001.

Strogatz, Steven. *Infinite Powers*. Boston, MA: Mariner Books, 2020.

Tarnas, Richard. *Cosmos and Psyche*. New York: Viking, 2006.

———. "Is the Modern Psyche Undergoing a Rite of Passage?" 2001. https://cosmosandpsyche.files.wordpress.com/2013/05/revision-rite-of-passage.pdf.

———. *The Passion of the Western Mind*. New York: Ballantine Books, 1991.

Taylor, Charles. *Hegel*. Cambridge: Cambridge University Press, 1977.

Van Den Akker, Robin, Alison Gibbons, and Timotheus Vermeulen. *Metamodernism*. Lanham, MD: Rowman and Littlefield, 2017.

Voltaire. *Candide*. New York: Norton, 2016.

Wahl, Jean. "Review of Nietzsche and Philosophy." www.academia.edu/31298254/Jean_Wahl_Review_of_Deleuzes_Nietzsche_and_Philosophy_Rough_translation_.

Weber, Max. *The Protestant Ethic and the 'Spirit' of Capitalism and Other Writings*. New York: Penguin Books, 2002.

Wehr, Demaris S. *Jung and Feminism*. New York: Routledge, 2015.

Westphal, Merold. "Hegel Between Spinoza and Derrida." In *Hegel's History of Philosophy*, edited by David A. Duquette. Albany, NY: SUNY Press, 2003.

Whitehead, Alfred North. In *Alfred North Whitehead: Essays on His Philosophy*, edited by George L. Kline. University Press of America, 1989.

———. *Essays in Science and Philosophy*. London: Rider & Co., 1948.

———. *An Introduction to Mathematics*. Mineola, NY: Dover, 2017.

———. *Modes of Thought*. New York: The Free Press, 1968.

———. *Process and Reality*. New York: The Free Press, 1985.

———. *Science and the Modern World*. New York: The Free Press, 1967.

Wilshire, Bruce. "The Breathtaking Intimacy of the Material World." In *The Cambridge Companion to William James*, edited by Ruth Anna Putnam. Cambridge: Cambridge University Press, 1997.

Winckelmann, Johann Joachim. *Johann Joachim Winckelmann on Art, Architecture, and Archaeology*. Rochester, NY: Camden House, 2013.

Wittgenstein, Ludwig. *Tractatus Logico-Philosophicus*. New York: Routledge, 2001.

Yovel, Yirmiyahu. *Spinoza and Other Heretics, Vol. 1*. Princeton, NJ: Princeton University Press, 1989.

Žižek, Slavoj. "Notes on a Debate 'From Within the People'." *Criticism* 46, no. 4 (2004): 661–6.

———. *Organs Without Bodies*. New York: Routledge, 2012.

# Index

*L'Abécédaire* 166, 209
absolute idealism 108, 111–12, 115
active imagination 187–8
affect: Deleuze on 237–40; Hillman on 269–70, 272, 305; James on 109, 123, 131–5, 137–9, 141; Jung on 174–5; Spinoza on 37–8; Stengers on 328; Whitehead on 154–9
alchemy: active imagination and 187–8; chemical processes in 173, 175–6; *coniunctio* 178; danger in 174–5; Hillman on 295–6; integration and 191; primary purpose of 179–80, 181; Self in 184–5, 190
*amor fati* 26, 212, 328
anima 276, 296–7
*Animal That Therefore I Am, The* 14
animism 9, 77–8, 104, 162, 181, 239, 249, 273, 280, 297–8; Hillman on 276; Stengers on 310–11, 314–18
*Another Science Is Possible* 311, 317–18
*Antichrist, The* 201
*Anti-Oedipus* 22, 167, 206–7, 278, 305
Apollonian, the 94–8, 103–4; Deleuze on 234; and the Dionysian 102, 104–5
*Apology* 101
Aquinas, T. 171

archetypal cosmology 192, 313
archetypal psychology 268–9
archetype 168–70, 176–80, 231, 245; of the Self 183–5, 190; of wholeness 184, 187, 302–3
Aristotle 71, 72, 73–4
astrology 167–8, 313–14

Bachelard, G. 9, 186
Bacon, R. 171
beautiful soul 212–22
Beckman, F. 166, 207
Bergson, H. 1–2, 7, 14, 26; on calculus 134; on duality and opposition 139; on duration 134, 135–6; on epochs 141; on final causation 135–7; on formal causation 137–9; on integration 141–2; on instinct 128, 131–3; on intelligence 126–7, 131–2; on intuition 138–9, 141–3; on Jung 165; on Spinoza 32; on teleology 39; on the vital impulse 127; Whitehead and 144
*Bergsonism* 167, 226
*Beyond Good and Evil* 39–40
biography 207–8
*Birth of Tragedy, The* 87, 89, 91, 92, 102–3, 201; as integrative 83
body without organs 33, 226
brain, the 129–30
Butler, J. 200

*Calculemus* 25, 46, 312, 322–3
calculus 6, 25, 42, 249; Bergson on 134; Deleuze on 233, 252; Hegel on 53; Leibniz on 46–8, 49–50; Whitehead on 147–8
capitalism 119, 193, 275–7, 284
*Capitalism and Schizophrenia* 167, 268
*Capitalist Sorcery* 311, 317–18, 322–3
Cartesian dualism 35–7, 150, 157, 159–60, 162–3
Catholic Church 119
causation *see* efficient causation; final causation; formal causation
Christianity 60–1, 161; David Strauss and 87; Jung and 171–2; knowledge of good and evil and 189–90; *lapis philosophorum* and 173, 178–9, 186; monocentrism of 26; Nietzsche on 87–8, 99, 217; rise of monotheism and 77–8; scholastic 172–3
*Cinema 1* 167, 225
cinematographical mechanism of thought 134
Cisney, V. 6
common notions 36–7
*Communist Manifesto, The* 14
concrescence 150–1, 154–5, 158
*Confessions of a Beautiful Soul Written by Herself* 213
conservatism 192–3
conspiracy theory 301
constructivism 4–5, 7, 109, 160; immanence as 34
contrasts 152–3
Copernicus, N. 60–1
*Cosmopolitics* 311–12
*Creative Evolution* 107, 126

*daimonion* 101–2
deconstruction 1–9, 11, 14, 160–1, 318; constructivism and 4–5, 7; integration and 1, 19–20; liberation from 15–16; logocentrism and 11–13
Deleuze, G. xi, 1–9, 14, 21, 22, 23, 53, 65, 284; on alchemy 181; on archetypes 168–70; on the beautiful soul 212–22; on biography 207–8; on calculus 233, 252; childhood and family of 208–10; concept of Ideas 247–8; on construction of the Self 253–4; on constructivist logic 42; constructive orientation of 200; critique of Hegel 200–3, 210–11, 223–6; deterritorialization 207; on epochs 249, 260; on final causation 241–2; on formal causation 237–8, 241–2, 258–9; on Freud 201–2, 232, 240, 253; on Idea of the negative 249–50; on image of thought 235–6; on immanence 34; Jung and 165–71, 181, 242–3; on madness 248; as metaphysicians 26–7; on multiplicity 251, 253, 259; on the Oedipal complex 206–7; on oppositional rationality 203–5, 229–30; on Platonism 228, 245; on Plato's method of division 244; on polytheism 229, 239, 243–5, 247–50, 255, 257; rejection of the dialectic 224–5; on repetition 43, 80, 226–7, 231–3; rumors about sexuality 211; Spinoza and 32–3, 39–40; Stengers and 310–11, 318–20; on transcendental empiricism 33, 237–8; on Wahl 201; Whitehead and 144; on writing philosophy 256; *see also Difference and Repetition*
depression 303–4
depth psychology 271
Derrida, J. 1–8, 197; *The Animal That Therefore I Am* 14; on closure of on différance 24; on concept of crisis 25–6; development of thought

through his career 13–14; difficulty in reading 15; on embarrassment 14; on epochs 12–13, 18–19, 21–2, 27–9; on final causation 25–6; on formal causation 26–7; on the future 18–19; *The Gift of Death* 13–14, 15; hermeneutics of suspicion 17; on logocentrism as heliocentric concept 28–9; on mythography 27–9; overturning of deconstruction 23–4; on polytheism 13; reading of Rousseau 20–3; on temporality 27; *see also Of Grammatology*
Descartes, R. 9, 22
Desmond, T. 188
determinism 39–43
deterritorialization 207
Dewey, J. 3
dialectic, the 2–3, 4; as collective philosophical creation 67–8; Deleuze's rejection of 224–5; Hegel's concept of 55–62, 88–9, 108–9, 204–5, 223–4; Nietzsche's concept of 93–4, 100; Schelling's concept of 65–8, 76
*Dialogues II* 167
*Difference and Repetition* xi, 24, 65, 166, 168, 205, 210–11, 268; on the beautiful soul 212–21; Deleuze on 198; May 1968 in Paris and 199, 203–4; *see also* Deleuze, G.
Dionysian, the 90–2, 95–8, 103–4; Deleuze on 234; music and 101–2; and the Apollonian 102, 104–5
*Discourse on Method* 9
Dorn, G. 172
Dosse, F. 208
Duffy, S. 46, 48
duration 134, 135–6
Duvernoy, R. J. 218–19

*Ecce Homo* 89, 92–3, 217
efficient causation 41, 43, 118, 136–7, 151–2, 159

ego 173–4, 238–9, 292–4
Einstein, A. 127, 145
empiricism 109–11; speculative 324–5
*Empiricism and Subjectivity* 208, 219
*enantiodromia* 244
*Encyclopedia Logic* 142
Enlightenment, the 20, 45, 72, 77, 91, 145, 229, 289; Romantic reaction to 100; scholasticism and 74, 171; scientific rationality in 104, 116, 149
*Enneads* 271
epochs 5, 7, 55–6, 244, 250, 329; Bergson 141; Deleuze on 249, 260; Derrida on 12–13, 18–19, 21–2, 27–9; Hegel on 57; Hillman on 279, 289–90; James 119; Jung 188; Nietzsche 88, 104; Schelling on 79; Stengers on 314, 325–6; Whitehead 149–50, 158–63
errancy 23, 155, 305–6
eternal objects 153–4
*Ethics* (Spinoza) 32, 35, 36, 37, 40
evolution 126–9, 131–2; natural selection and 136

feminism 285–6
Fichte, J. G. 3
final causation: Bergson on 135–7; Deleuze on 241–2; Derrida on 25–6; Hegel on 56, 61–2; Hillman on 269, 299; James on 115, 118, 120–1; Leibniz on 48–9; Nietzsche on 40, 97; Schelling on 78; Spinoza on 25–6, 39–40; Stengers on 321; Whitehead on 145, 150–2, 154–5
Fisher, M. 284
*Fold, The* 252
formal causation 137–8, 241–2; Bergson on 137–9; Deleuze on 237–8, 241–2, 258–9; Derrida on 26–7; James on 118; Jung on 167, 191; Leibniz on 46; Spinoza on 38–41, 43; Stengers on 321; Whitehead on 151–4

*Foucault* 241–2
Foucault, M. 5, 197, 199, 200, 211
free association 168
freedom, brain complexity and 129–30
Freud, S.: Deleuze on 201–2, 232, 240, 253; Hillman on 278, 282–3, 285–8; Jung and 165–8, 170–1, 176, 194, 202, 240, 253, 283, 285–8; Nietzsche and 83, 283

Galileo 61, 145, 327
Gebser, J. 191, 301
Gide, A. 277
*Gift of Death, The* 13–14, 15
God 49; Deleuze on 239; in the Hebrew Bible 78; Jung on 183–4; Leibniz on 50; Spinoza on 33, 38; Whitehead on 315–17, 328
gods *see* polytheism
Goethe, J. W. von 213–14, 222
good and evil 189–90
Greek mythology 78–9, 94, 290–1, 293, 304
Grof, S. 294
*Grounding of Positive Philosophy, The* 64, 65, 67, 69, 75
Guattari, F. 7, 9, 21, 22, 23, 166–71, 181, 284; on the Oedipal complex 206, 209, 212; *see also* Deleuze, G.

Habermas, J. 64
Harman, G. 225
Hartshorne, C. 153
Hebrew Bible 78
Hegel, G. W. F. 2–4, 6–8, 20–1, 32, 140, 142; on calculus 53; concept of the dialectic 55–62, 88–9, 108–9, 204–5, 223–4; Deleuze's critique of 200, 201, 202–3, 210–11, 223–6; on epochs 57; on final causation 56, 61–2; James on 108; Nietzsche and 86, 88–9; on opposition 54–7, 59–60, 61; Schelling and 52, 64–70;

on sublation 57–8, 62; Whitehead and 146–8
Heidegger, M. 5, 12, 64
Heraclitus 2, 9, 271
*Hermetic Deleuze, The* 219
hermeticism 219, 284–5
Herring, E. 285
Hillman, J. 1–2, 8, 14, 23, 268; on alchemy 295–6; on autonomy of fantasy 295; on enacting repetitions with variations 274–5; on engagement with imaginal figures 282–3, 296–7; on engagement with nonrational modes 276–7; on epochs 279, 289–90; on final causation 269, 299; on Freud 278, 282–3, 285–8; on Greek myth 290–1; Jung's influence on 165–6, 284–5, 287–8; on origins of depth psychology 271; on personifying 268–9; on polytheism 270, 272, 274–6, 278–82, 288–90, 292–4, 296–305; on reengagement with the gods 278–82, 301–2; on schizophrenia 277–8
Hippolyte, J. 53, 211
*Historical-Critical Introduction to the Philosophy of Mythology* 64
Hölderlin, F. 52
horizon of conception 24, 35, 75, 238, 258–9
Houlgate, S. 70
humanism 305

idealism 3, 4, 54, 91, 118, 216, 224, 225; absolute 108, 111–12, 115; Deleuze's rejection of 286; Hegel and 52, 114, 149, 197; Nietzsche and 91; transcendental 67
Ideas 228, 246–8
image of thought 235–6, 318
immanence 32–5, 38–9; as constructivism 34; of God 32–3, 315–16; Leibnizian calculus and 35

*In Catastrophic Times* 311, 317–18
individuation 174, 215, 253–4; Deleuze on 232–3, 254; projection and 177, 286; Stengers on 320–1
*Individuation in Light of Notions of Form and Information* 169, 320–1
infinitesimals 6, 25, 35, 42, 46–8, 50, 134; Bergson on 134; Deleuze on 252; Hegel on 53; Whitehead on 147–8
initiation 65, 73, 104, 180–2, 185, 188, 219, 224, 246, 250, 257, 277, 299, 319; collective 79, 88, 289, 292–3, 302–3
instinct 128, 131–3
intellect: evolution of 126–7, 131–2; freedom of choice and 129–30; instinct and 128, 131–2; integrated with instinct 132–3
*Introduction to Mathematics, An* 147
intuition 36–7, 138–9, 141–3

Jacobi, J. 191
James, W. 1–4, 14, 32, 53, 88; on absolute idealism 111–12, 115; on epochs 119; on Hegel 108–9; on empiricism 109–10; on final causation 115, 118, 120–1; Jung and 165; on mystical states 110; on the pragmatic method 113–14; on pluralism 122–3; on radical empiricism 110–11, 117; Whitehead and 144
Jarry, A. 27
Jaspers, K. 64
Jenkins, B. 167, 179
Johnson, L. M. 192
Jung, C. G. xi, 1–3, 8, 14, 83; on active imagination 187–8; on alchemy 172–82; on archetypes 168–70, 176–80, 190; Deleuze and 165–71, 181, 242–3; on the ego 173–4; on epochs 188; and Freud 165–8, 170–1, 176, 194, 202, 240, 253, 283, 285–8; Hillman and 165–6, 284–5, 287–8; on the *nigredo* 188–91; and politics 192–3; schizophrenia and 287; on synchronicity 191–2, 232, 257

Kafka, F. 168
Kant, I. 3, 20, 52, 71, 134
Kelly, S. 177
*Kant's Critical Philosophy* 245
Kepler, J. 61

Lacan, J. 5
Laing, R. D. 277, 278
Lango, J. W. 147
*lapis philosophorum* 173, 178–9, 186–7
Latour, B. 144
Laughland, J. 68
Lautréamont 169, 186
law of excluded middle 53, 55
Leibniz, G. W. 1–3, 6, 32–3, 35; on calculus 46–8, 49–50; *Calculemus* 25, 46; on final causation 48–9; on formal causation 46; on infinitesimals 47, 50, 147; *mathesis universalis* 25; on monads 48–9; an optimism 49–50, 233, 328; *see also Monadology*
*Le Misogyne* 213
Leroi-Gourhan, A. 27
Lévinas, E. 22
Lévi-Strauss, C. 20, 28
*Logic and Existence* 211
*Logic of Sense, The* 167, 268
logocentrism 11–13, 17–18, 20, 24, 25, 28–9
Luna 185–6
Lyotard, J-F. 7

Magnus, A. 171, 172
Malabou, C. 200, 201–2, 217–18
Marx, K. 3, 52
Maslow, A. 279

materialism 54, 118–19, 136
mathematics and metaphysics 147–8
*mathesis universalis* 25
*Matter and Memory* 138, 226, 236
Maxwell, J. C. 311
May, T. 284
*Meaning of Truth, The* 110
Mercurius 179, 184–7, 190–1
Merleau-Ponty, M. 64
metamodernism 5
metaphysical empiricism 74–6
meta-rationality 28
method of division 18, 244
Mill, J. S. 112
*Monadology* 45–6, 48
monads 48–50
monism 54, 110
monotheism 73, 76, 77–8, 290; Stengers on 315–16
multiplicity 251, 253, 259
music 101–2
*Mysterium Coniunctionis* xi, 165, 171–3, 181, 185
mythology 188–9; deities of Greek 78–9, 94, 290–1, 293, 304; and dialectic 90–1, 244–5; philosophy of 76–8

natural selection 136
negative philosophy 71–2
negative prehensions 150–1, 153, 154
Neoplatonists 73–4
Newton, I. 6, 46–7
Nicholas of Cusa 172, 200, 224
Nietzsche, F. 2–3, 7, 9, 12, 14, 17, 28, 70; on the Apollonian 94–8, 103–4; on the dialectic 93–4, 100, 103–4; on critical consciousness 99–100; as critical diagnostician 83–4; on Christianity 87–8, 99, 217; on descent 97–8; on the Dionysian 90–2, 95–8, 103–4; on dreams 94–6; on epochs 88, 104; on final causation 40, 97; on Greek art and mythology 94–6; Hegel and 86, 88–9; influences on 83; on music 101–2; on the Overman 38, 84, 92, 133, 201, 231; on possibility of reconciliation of Apollonian and Dionysian 91–3; on resssentiment 22, 84, 88, 207, 212; on Socrates 87, 90, 98–100; suffering of 85–7, 89, 90–1; *see also Birth of Tragedy, The*
*Nietzsche and Philosophy* 88, 167, 201, 245
*nigredo* 188–91
*Nirvana* 179
"Number of Yes, A" 13

Oedipal complex 206, 209, 212, 304–5
*Of Grammatology* 2, 11–29
*Of Human Freedom* 64–5
optimism 49–50, 233, 328
ordeal *see* initiation
Overman 38, 84, 92, 133, 201, 231

pantheism 36
paradoxes 122, 128, 178
pataphysics 26–7
patriarchy 88, 179, 185, 187, 190–1, 213, 285
Peirce, C. S. 107
personifying 268–9, 298–9, 303
*Phaedrus* 248, 255, 271
*Phenomenology of Spirit, The* 52–4, 64, 65, 68, 70, 205
Plato 9, 15, 20–1, 32, 101, 103; Ideas 138; method of division 18, 244
Platonism 26, 236, 244–6
Plotinus 271
pluralism 54, 228, 110, 122–3, 228
politeness 326
political ideologies 192–4
polytheism: Deleuze on 229, 239, 243–5, 247–50, 255, 257; Derrida on 13; Hillman on 270, 272, 274–6, 278–82, 288–90, 292–4, 296–305;

Schelling on 70–1, 73, 76–80; Stengers on 314–17
positive philosophy 71–80
postmodernism 4–5, 8, 56
poststructuralism 20, 149
potency 67, 70–1, 73, 239–40, 251–2
pragmatism 107, 110, 112, 126, 197, 205; *see also* James, W.
*Principles of Psychology, The* 3
*Prinicpia Mathematica* 147
*Process and Reality* xi, 144, 147–8
projection 177, 193–4, 286
propaganda 193
Protestant Reformation 119
Protevi, J. 14
*Proust and Signs* 167, 226
*Psyche and Singularity* 188
psychoanalysis 165, 176, 279, 284
*Psychology of the Unconscious* 287
psychopathology 279–80, 291
psycho-philosophy 310

quantum mechanics 103, 123
queer theory 285

radical empiricism 23, 73, 110–11, 117
radical finalism 39, 41, 136, 137
Ramey, J. 219, 284
rationality 104, 109–11, 116, 149, 203–5, 229–31, 250, 275–6, 289, 293–4
*Red Book, The* 287
repetition 43, 80, 226–7, 231–3
resssentiment 22, 84, 88, 207, 212
*Re-Visioning Psychology* 268–9
responsibility 184, 305, 328–9
Reyes, M. A. 213
Rhine, J. B. 191
Robinson, A. 147
Roger, A. 213
Romanticism 20, 100, 289
Rousseau, J.-J. 20–3, 28
Rowland, S. 179
Russell, B. 127, 146

Salmon, P. 14, 22
Salome, L. 217, 283
Saussure, F. d. 20, 25
Schelling, F. W. J. 2–3, 9, 14, 28, 53; on the absolute 68–9; on the dialectic 65–8, 76; on empiricism 72–3; on epochs 79; on final causation 78; Hegel and 52, 64–70; influence on Nietzsche 83; on metaphysical empiricism 74–6; on monotheism 73, 76, 77–8; on negative and positive philosophies 71–80; on Neoplatonists 73–4; on philosophy of mythology 66–7, 76–9; on polytheism 70–1, 73, 76–80; theory of potencies 67, 70–1; on transformative crises 79–80
schizophrenia 277–8, 287
scholasticism 74, 149, 171, 172–3
Schrodinger, E. 246
Schulz, W. 64
*Science of Logic, The* 52–3, 70, 147
*scientia generalis* 46
Self, the 183–5, 190, 253–4, 269
self-consciousness 35, 56–7, 60
Shaviro, S. 5
Simondon, G. 9, 320–1
Socrates 72, 248; as agent of rationality 99–100; *daimonion* of 101–2; Nietzsche on 87, 90, 98–100; Schelling on 71–2
Sol 184–6
Sommers-Hall, H. 200, 225
Sophists 20, 247, 318
*Specters of Marx* 14, 18
speculative empiricism 324–5
Spinoza, B. 2–3, 7; on affects 37–8; on determinism 39–43; exploration of oppositions 35–6; on final causation 25–6, 39–40; on formal causation 38–41, 43; on immanence 33–5; influence on Nietzsche 83; pantheism 36; on three kinds of knowledge 36–7

*Statesman, The* 244
Stengers, I. 1–9, 14; *Another Science Is Possible* 311, 317–18; on astrology 313–14; *Capitalist Sorcery* 311, 317–18, 322–3; *In Catastrophic Times* 311, 317–18; *Cosmopolitics* 311–12; on epochs 314, 325–6; on final causation 321; on God 315–16, 317, 327–8; on Leibniz's concept of *Calculemus* 25, 322–3; on peace fighters 323; on politeness 326; on polytheism 314–17; speculative empiricism and 324–5; *Thinking With Whitehead* 2, 23, 311, 313, 315–16
Strauss, D. 87
sublation 57–8, 62
*Suicide and the Soul* 292–3
synchronicity 167, 191–2, 232, 257, 294
*Synchronicity* 191

Tarnas, R. 173
teleology *see* final causation
*tertium non datur* 53, 55
*Theodicy* 47–8
*Thinking With Whitehead* 2, 23, 311, 313, 315–16
*Thousand Plateaus, A* 166, 169, 202, 203, 231, 283
*Thus Spoke Zarathustra* 87
*Timaeus* 72
Tournier, M. 210
transcendental empiricism 33–5, 73–4, 197, 237–8, 240, 246, 251
transversality 43, 167

univocity 32–5, 37, 183, 227

*Varieties of Religious Experience, The* 110
Voltaire 49

Wagner, R. 101
Wahl, J. 83, 200, 201
Weber, M. 83
Wehr, D. S. 179
*What Is Grounding?* 208, 219, 243, 248
*What Is Philosophy?* 207, 252
Whitehead, A. N. xi, 1–5, 8, 14, 45, 107, 218; on calculus 147–8; on concrescence 150–1, 154–5, 158; on epochs 149–50, 158–63; on eternal objects 153–4; on final causation 145, 150–2, 154–5; on formal causation 153–4; on infinitesimals 147–8; on mysticism 162; on negative prehensions 150–1, 153, 154; on positive contrast 152–3; on process 145, 150, 151; on Hegel 146–7; Stengers and 310–11, 318–20, 324–5; on transcendence 158
wholeness, archetype of 184, 187, 302–3
*Wilhelm Meister's Apprenticeship* 212
Winckelmann, J. J. 212
Wirth, J. M. 76
Wittgenstein, L. 144

Žižek, S. 52, 167, 197, 200, 202

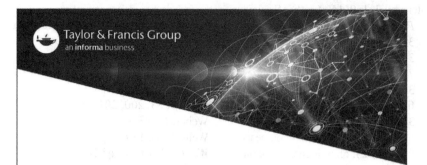